Everyday Aesthetics

Everyday aesthetic experiences and concerns ~~~~ a large part of our aesthetic life. However, because of their prevalence and mundane nature, we tend not to pay much attention to them, let alone examine their significance. Western aesthetic theories of the past few centuries also neglect everyday aesthetics because of their almost exclusive emphasis on art. In a ground-breaking new study, Yuriko Saito provides a detailed investigation into our everyday aesthetic experiences, and reveals how our everyday aesthetic tastes and judgments can exert a powerful influence on the state of the world and our quality of life.

By analysing a wide range of examples from our aesthetic interactions with nature, the environment, everyday objects, and Japanese culture, Saito illustrates the complex nature of seemingly simple and innocuous aesthetic responses. She discusses the inadequacy of art-centered aesthetics, the aesthetic appreciation of the distinctive characters of objects or phenomena, responses to various manifestations of transience, and the aesthetic expression of moral values; and she examines the moral, political, existential, and environmental implications of these and other issues.

Yuriko Saito is Professor of Philosophy at the Rhode Island School of Design.

Everyday Aesthetics

Yuriko Saito

OXFORD

UNIVERSITY PRESS

OXFORD

UNIVERSITY PRESS

Great Clarendon Street, Oxford OX2 6DP

Oxford University Press is a department of the University of Oxford.
It furthers the University's objective of excellence in research, scholarship,
and education by publishing worldwide in

Oxford New York

Auckland Cape Town Dar es Salaam Hong Kong Karachi
Kuala Lumpur Madrid Melbourne Mexico City Nairobi
New Delhi Shanghai Taipei Toronto
With offices in
Argentina Austria Brazil Chile Czech Republic France Greece
Guatemala Hungary Italy Japan South Korea Poland Portugal
Singapore Switzerland Thailand Turkey Ukraine Vietnam

Oxford is a registered trade mark of Oxford University Press
in the UK and in certain other countries

Published in the United States
by Oxford University Press Inc., New York

ISBN 978-0-19-957567-1

Printed in the United Kingdom by
the MPG Books Group Ltd

Acknowledgments

This book represents a culmination of both my teaching at the Rhode Island School of Design (RISD) and my own research, thinking, and writing for more than two decades. The numerous students I had the privilege of teaching helped me shape my thinking on everyday aesthetics. Not only their contributions in class through comments, examples, or sometimes criticisms, but also their studio works that many of them shared with me provided a constant food for thought. I made acknowledgements throughout this book for the specific comments and examples I gained from some of them, but I am indebted to so many more students for their more general contribution.

I am grateful to RISD for its support of this project by granting me a release time through the school-wide Professional Development Grant and Liberal Arts Division's Humanities Fund. Thanks to these two sources of funding, I was able to devote one whole semester to writing. Over the years I have also been blessed with friends and colleagues here at RISD who helped nurture my work and lend both professional and moral support throughout the process in so many different ways. Simply mentioning them will not do justice to the many intangible gifts they have given me. I will be thanking them individually, but I also want to give public acknowledgement here. Scott Cook, Lindsay French, Elizabeth Grossman, the late Ken Hunnibell, Gerry Immonen, Don Keefer, Marilyn Rueschemeyer, and David Warner have all been great cheerleaders, giving me unfailing support all these years. Many of them also provided me with invaluable references and articles for which I am grateful.

I am also greatly indebted to my professional colleagues, many of whom are true mentors, who have guided my professional work with their knowledge, wisdom, and experience, not to mention generosity. I thank Don Crawford, who patiently guided me through the trial and trepidation of my doctoral dissertation on the aesthetic appreciation of nature in the B(efore) C(omputer) era. Arnold Berleant's interest and support for my work has been immeasurable. Not only studying his own works but also working with him closely on *Contemporary Aesthetics* have provided me with such enlightening and rewarding experiences, and they all had an impact on my own thinking. I am also grateful for the many years of support given by Allen Carlson who, with his writings on nature aesthetics and environmental aesthetics, set a high standard for these fields, to which I always tried to aspire. Working with Steve Rabson for many years on a number of Japan-related publications, both his and mine, has been extremely beneficial and productive. Over the years Barbara Sandrisser raised my awareness of Japanese aesthetics even more with her work on this subject and numerous newspaper articles that she sent me for my reference. Although I was raised in Japan, I credit Barbara for helping me become more sensitive and appreciative of my cultural heritage. David Hanson has also been a source of inspiration, with his unfailing commitment to addressing environmental issues through his photographic works. If Barbara, along with my RISD colleague Gerry Immonen, has been my personal librarian for Japanese materials, David has been the same for environmental issues.

My greatest academic appreciation goes to the two reviewers who read and commented on the earlier draft of this book: Carolyn Korsmeyer and Larry Shiner. They went far beyond what is expected of manuscript reviewers by not only providing me with numerous helpful comments and examples but also correcting my writing which is still reflective of mistakes typical of a non-native writer. Their suggestions were invaluable and I thank them for making the revising process an educationally beneficial experience. I tried to respond to and incorporate their comments and suggestions in this final version. I only hope I did justice and honor to their reviews.

Peter Momtchiloff, the Philosophy Editor of Oxford University Press, has been most patient and supportive throughout the writing process. I thank him for initiating and facilitating this project. I also thank Jack Sinden for his meticulous and timely copy-editing.

Last but not least, my greatest appreciation goes to my family: Gerry, Sarah, and Adam. For the past few years I have been preoccupied with this writing project, at times neglecting what needs to be taken care of on the home front. I thank them for their patience and good cheer. My husband, Gerry, constantly reminded me of the importance of saying "no" to various requests and invitations until the manuscript was completed. Part of the motivation for writing this book with a heavy emphasis on Japanese aesthetics is to put in writing the cultural heritage that I tried to impart to my children, Sarah and Adam. It is my hope that, with the help of what I put down here, all those years of "lecturing" to them about moral values and many summers spent in Japan with their grandparents will leave a lasting mark on them as life values. The more I delve into Japanese aesthetics and cultural values, the more I realize how much my parents taught me through their everyday acts (including how to stuff a garbage bag that I refer to in Chapter V). If I succeeded in shedding some light on the moral dimension of Japanese aesthetic sensibility, that is a tribute to the treasures that they have handed down to me.

Contents—Summary

Contents

Introduction

Often defined as the philosophy of art, aesthetics, at least in its modern Western formulation, is predominated by examinations of art. My first foray into the aesthetics of something other than art was my doctoral dissertation that dealt with the aesthetic appreciation of nature. That was in the 1980s. While it was a relatively unexplored field then, environmental aesthetics, nature aesthetics in particular, has been gaining a wider recognition and it is now an established sub-discipline within aesthetics. The same can be said of a discourse on popular arts, such as TV, popular music, video game, and cartoon. These subject matters certainly share many issues in common with fine arts, such as aesthetic experience, aesthetic properties, expressive qualities, objectivity of aesthetic judgments, to name only a few. At the same time, there are issues that are distinct in each. For example, the definition of art occupies an important aspect of our discussion of art, which is not (at least straightforwardly) applicable or relevant to nature. On the other hand, literal threat to one's physical well-being posed by certain natural phenomena, such as hurricane and earthquake, is normally inapplicable to fine arts and popular arts. Factors such as commercial success and popular appeal may not be irrelevant to fine arts, but they are certainly an important issue regarding popular arts.

However, even with the expanded scope of aesthetics that includes nature, environment, and popular arts, I always felt that it is not broad enough to capture every aspect of our aesthetic life. This feeling emerged out of my interactions with students at the Rhode Island School of Design, where I have been teaching for more than twenty-five years. Many of my students are design students, pursuing careers in industrial design, graphic design, furniture design, apparel design, architecture, interior architecture, and landscape architecture. They design objects that we use every day, ranging from kitchen utensils, furniture, clothing, toys, and computer graphics to houses, office space, and waterfront development. Working with students and sometimes going to their final presentations given in front of studio teachers and professional designers as their critics, I have gained insight into what is involved in designing seemingly simple, innocuous objects or environments. I have also developed a deep respect for what designers have to deal with, which includes not only the technical aspect of design itself but also other factors such as environmental ramifications, observance of various regulations regarding safety and accessibility, consideration of cultural factors depending upon the expected users, not to mention cost and, last but not least, *aesthetics*. I am repeatedly awe-struck by the responsibility, but also an opportunity and power, designers have for improving people's lives and the state of the world through the artifacts they help create.

After realizing the way in which designers affect or sometimes determine the quality of people's lives through their works, I began to think more carefully about the works' sensuous qualities like size, shape, color, texture, sound, sometimes smell, and the arrangement of parts. After all, it is these sensuous qualities with which we interact on daily basis that, along with natural elements, make up the world in which we live. Most of the time our interactions with those everyday artifacts and environments are taken for granted and experienced mostly for their functional values. Furthermore, except under a very unusual circumstance or with a special effort, we do not take special note of our everyday experience with those objects. As a result, it appears as if there is nothing aesthetically significant in our experience of everyday objects. One of the aims of this book is to show that nothing is further from the truth. Whether we are aware or not, there are many aesthetic issues involved in our dealings with everyday things, some of which have serious ramifications: moral, social, political, or environmental. One could characterize everyday aesthetic issues as being hidden in plain sight. Because I gained a glimpse into the complicated thought process that goes into designing even a simple object, I thought I would try to dig into the opposite side, that is the user's and receiver's side, in experiencing an object so designed.

My subsequent exploration into everyday aesthetics can be likened to a treasure hunt. At every turn of my research and investigation, I found a gem lying around, ready to be polished and brought to life. I feel I only scratched a surface by concentrating my discussion on only a few of them. My hope is that this book opens a door for further explorations of numerous issues in everyday aesthetics.

While the subject matters and issues relevant to everyday aesthetics are boundless, the subsequent discussion is dominated by environmental aesthetics and Japanese aesthetics. It is partly because my previous works focused on these two areas. But more importantly, environmental aesthetics as an established field today provides a foundation distinct from fine-arts-based aesthetics. Furthermore, environment, whether natural or built, surrounds us all the time, and, as such, it can never be dissociated from the everyday life. Japanese aesthetics, which happens to reflect my own cultural upbringing, also cannot be separated from the everyday. While there are distinct art media in the Japanese aesthetic tradition, including those familiar to the West, such as painting, sculpture, literature, music, and theater, as well as more unique ones like flower arrangement and tea ceremony, I find that there is a prevailing aesthetic sensibility that permeates everyday objects and activities such as cooking, packaging, and seasonal celebration. I regard those everyday objects and phenomena to embody Japanese aesthetic sensibility most eloquently, which in turn sharpens people's aesthetic sensibility and nurtures aesthetic appreciation of the mundane. Indeed, I find that the Japanese aesthetic tradition provides a rich array of ingredients for everyday aesthetics and I hope that the examples I cite illustrate this dimension of Japanese aesthetics effectively.

While I draw heavily from environmental aesthetics and Japanese aesthetics, this book is not about either of them specifically. They provide examples and possibilities, but the scope of everyday aesthetics is much wider. Another way of putting it is that I am placing both environmental aesthetics and Japanese aesthetics under the big umbrella of everyday aesthetics. Although theoretically everything comprises environment, not only including built structures and nature but also artifacts and individual natural objects and creatures, environmental aesthetics is generally concerned only with the former. I also do not want to put a spotlight on Japanese aesthetics, as it is certainly not my intention to imply that one has to adopt a non-Western approach and attitude in order to explore everyday aesthetics. While opening oneself to a different cultural tradition is always beneficial, everyday aesthetics does not need to be exoticized to justify its importance and claim its full impact.

One may characterize my approach as feminist. My focus is the often-neglected aspect of our aesthetic life, just as feminist philosophy takes up aspects of our lives that have traditionally been ignored in a serious academic discourse due to their ordinary and mundane nature, such as domestic chores and mothering activities, generally relegated to the female domain. At times I do make specific connections to feminist issues in my discussion, such as the aesthetic expressions of (feminine) moral virtues of caring and considerate attitude toward others (Chapter V) and the neglect of qualities such as "clean" and "dirty" in the aesthetic discourse partly due to their association with feminine chores (Chapter IV). While I do not object to characterizing my discussion as feminist-oriented, I am reluctant to put any specific label to my project for fear that it may give an impression that my orientation is specifically informed by a clearly defined and well-established viewpoint. I consider my discussion to be a rather open-ended exploration without any prior commitment to an agenda. My only agenda is to unearth the very familiar and commonly shared dimensions of our lives that have been neglected in theoretical aesthetics and to appreciate their significance, aesthetic or otherwise. As such, I hesitate to define what follows as a work in environmental aesthetics, Japanese aesthetics, or feminist aesthetics.

Because of its close and sometimes exclusive association with art, the aesthetic experience is often described as disinterested and contemplative. Such a contemplative experience does happen in an everyday setting, such as regarding a beautiful sunset, radiant smile on a child's face, or a comical episode witnessed on a street. However, unlike the quintessential spectator-like experience of art, everyday aesthetics is diverse and dynamic, as more often than not it leads to some specific actions: cleaning, purchasing, repairing, discarding, and so on. I would suppose that our typical experience of art may lead to a specific action, such as checking out a book about the artist, purchasing his recording, or joining a political group. However, these actions are premised upon first experiencing art as a spectator, which then moves us to act in a certain way. In contrast, actions prompted by everyday aesthetic judgments we make are often unreflected. Sometimes they are almost like knee-jerk reactions; at the very least we usually do not have a spectator-like experience which then leads us toward a certain action. This action-oriented, rather than contemplation-oriented, dimension of everyday aesthetics tends to move it outside the aesthetic radar calibrated to capture contemplative experiences; hence, the neglect of everyday aesthetics. However, as I hope to show in the subsequent discussion, there is a surprising degree of complexity involved in what otherwise may appear to be an almost automatic response on our part, sometimes with serious practical ramifications. Philosophy is often characterized as the art of wondering at the obvious. I am trying to apply this spirit of philosophical investigation to our aesthetic life by excavating and examining what may appear to be obvious and taken for granted.

The first chapter starts with the observation that, even with the recent inclusion of non-art objects and phenomena, such as nature, popular arts, food, games, sports, and the like, today's aesthetic discourse is still under the influence of art-centered aesthetics. I shall argue that it is problematic to examine the diverse aesthetic phenomena by applying a uniform standard derived from art-centered aesthetics, even with the expanded scope of art that includes newer forms of art as well as non-Western art. First, such an attempt tends to characterize non-art objects and phenomena aesthetically inferior to art. Secondly, issues that may be relevant and important in everyday aesthetics may not be relevant or applicable to art; hence, art-centered aesthetics is inadequate in accounting for some crucial aspects of everyday aesthetics. Thirdly, art-centered aesthetics, with its emphasis on contemplative, spectator-like experience, misses a large part of everyday aesthetic experience that results in various actions. In short, the first chapter argues for the necessity of everyday aesthetics to complement art-centered aesthetics.

The second chapter also argues for the necessity of everyday aesthetics, this time for pragmatic reasons. While appearing innocuous and inconsequential, everyday aesthetic judgments and preferences we make on daily basis do have surprisingly serious implications. By taking environmental consequences of our everyday aesthetic choices and attitudes as an example, I illustrate how important it is for the aesthetic discourse to attend to those judgments. With these first two chapters, therefore, I try to establish the need to explore everyday aesthetics for both aesthetic and pragmatic reasons. That is, everyday aesthetics makes the aesthetic discourse more truthful to the diverse dimensions of our aesthetic life and enriches its content. Furthermore, everyday aesthetics helps us fully appreciate the aesthetic concerns to influence, sometimes determine, the quality of life and the state of the world in the most literal sense.

The following three chapters are devoted to exploring some specific aspects of everyday aesthetic experience that should be familiar to many. With each subject matter, I first engage in an aesthetic analysis, followed by its pragmatic implications. By pursuing those consequences, I am trying to establish what I call "the power of the aesthetic" to affect various aspects of our lives and the state of the society and the world. That is, what at first may appear to be trivial, negligible, and inconsequential aesthetic responses that we make on daily basis do often lead to serious moral, social, political, and environmental consequences.

Chapter III examines the often-felt, but rarely articulated or analyzed, appreciation of distinctive character or ambience of an object or a phenomenon. Substantiated by many examples from both the eighteenth-century British aesthetics and Japanese aesthetics, I discuss what is involved in appreciating an object exhibiting its distinctive characteristics. I then go on to discuss the moral dimension of this kind of appreciation by exploring how the attitude underlying this aesthetic appreciation helps nurture a humble and respectful stance toward the object of appreciation by accepting and celebrating its own attributes. It encourages us to meet the object on its own terms and appreciate what it has to offer, even if some of its attributes at first may not be appreciable for various reasons. At the same time, I argue that this move toward deriving a positive aesthetic experience from all kinds of different objects must be tempered by other moral considerations.

Chapter IV pursues another set of familiar experiences that have to do with the qualities such as clean, organized, messy, old, dilapidated, and the like. These qualities are dependent upon the universal law of existence: transience. Nothing stays the same, despite our efforts to keep objects permanent and in their mint condition, and this inevitable change results in the qualities that I discuss in this chapter. Again there are abundant historical examples regarding these aesthetic qualities both in the eighteenth-century British aesthetics and Japanese aesthetics. However, the experience here is not limited to historical examples; all of us are familiar with cleaning a room, straightening out the desktop, removing a stain from a shirt, mowing the lawn to make it look neat and tidy, or throwing away a threadbare couch. At the same time, we are also familiar with prizing the aged look of an antique table, musty smell and brittle feel of an old book, and the faded color of an ancient painting. These different reactions to the aged appearance of objects betray surprisingly complex beliefs and attitudes on our part.

In addition to analyzing the aesthetics, I also pursue some implications of this complex response toward the mark of transience and aging. First, whether wise or unwise, right or wrong, the appearance of ourselves and our possessions often leads to others' judgment not only on our aesthetic taste but also on our moral character. Secondly, our reaction to the aging process that any material objects go through is intricately intertwined with an existential outlook and attitude. On the one end of the spectrum is a desire to exert total control over what actually is not controllable, translating into an unforgiving, yet ultimately futile, battle against clutter, mess, dirt, and signs of aging. On the other end of the spectrum is resignation, acceptance, and ultimately a celebration of succumbing to the inevitable, leading to an acceptance of whatever *is*, including the impermanence of everything. I interpret our sometimes ambivalent and contradictory reactions to the sign of aging as an existential struggle to determine to what extent we should relinquish human control over nature's working, in this case specifically the process of change. This latter stance works as an effective antidote to the Western Enlightenment and modern scientific project of exerting human control over nature, sometimes with force, which has recently come under scrutiny as its harmful effects on the environment began to be recognized. However, just as I argue that there is a moral constraint on appreciating things exhibiting their distinctive characteristics and ambience, I also argue in this chapter that the value of relinquishing control and submitting oneself to *what is* must be carefully qualified. In particular, if this aesthetics refers to accepting the status quo of a social condition, such as a political agenda or a social system, this attitude can have a disastrous consequence. I illustrate this point by citing the strategy used by the Japanese military before World War II that effectively appropriated the traditional aesthetic appreciation of the beauty of fallen cherry blossoms.

The final chapter of this book considers what I call "moral-aesthetic judgments" regarding everyday artifacts and built environment. They are judgments of moral virtues, such as care, considerateness, sensitivity, and respect, or lack thereof, made on artifacts and built environments on the basis of their perceptual features resulting from design. Although inseparable from the functional value, moral-aesthetic judgments go beyond it by appraising the way in which the care and respect for the materials, users, and dwellers are embodied, expressed, or reflected in the choice of materials and their arrangements. I point out that the Japanese aesthetic sensibility is often inseparable from these moral values and provide a number of examples. However, instead of simply providing what to many readers may appear as exotic examples from an unfamiliar cultural tradition, my aim is to make a case that the cultivation of these moral virtues needs to be practiced not only through actions but also through creation and appreciation of sensitively and respectfully designed objects. Any good society, in addition to ensuring justice, freedom, equality, and welfare, I argue, must nurture these moral virtues through creation of humane environments and artifacts made with care in order to provide a good life to its citizens.

The upshot of my exploration is that attention to everyday aesthetics is necessary not only for giving a more faithful account of our rich aesthetic life with diverse dimensions but also for raising consciousness for the profound consequences our everyday aesthetic attitudes and responses invoke. The aesthetic in our life is neither dispensable luxury nor inconsequential triviality. In particular with everyday aesthetics, there is a direct and literal connection to everyday life. We will only lose by continuing to ignore the aesthetic dimension of our everyday life. At the same time, we can only gain by acknowledging its existence and exploring its significance.

I

Neglect of Everyday Aesthetics

Our aesthetic life is rich and multifaceted. Its objects range from conventional forms of Western art, such as paintings, music, literature, dance, and theater, to newer art forms, such as happenings, performance, earth art, chance music, installation, and interactive art, not to mention art from non-Western traditions. Aesthetic objects also include nature and environment, popular entertainment provided by television, pop music, movies, sports, and games, as well as daily activities such as eating, walking, and dressing up. Sometimes our aesthetic interests and concerns generate memorable aesthetic experiences, while other times they simply lead to further thoughts, judgments, or actions, without inspiring special moments that stand out from the flow of our daily affairs.

This multifaceted nature of our aesthetic life poses a challenge for defining its distinguishing characteristics. Accordingly, various attempts have been made. Some hold that "the aesthetic" refers to certain qualities, such as gracefulness and forcefulness, which are constituted by, but not reducible to, a set of sensory qualities. Others contend that "the aesthetic" designates a special kind of experience. Yet others claim that it is a specific kind of attitude that renders an experience aesthetic. The notion of "the aesthetic" that I will be using throughout this book encompasses what these existing theories indicate, but much more. In the realm of "the aesthetic," I am including any reactions we form toward the sensuous and/or design qualities of any object, phenomenon, or activity.[1] This means, first of all,

---

[1] By invoking both the sensuous and design features, I am agreeing with Noël Carroll's "deflationary account" of aesthetic experience, in which "design appreciation and quality detection are each disjunctively sufficient conditions for aesthetic experience." It is because "one could apprehend the aesthetic qualities of a work without scrutinizing its form, or examine the structure of the work without detecting its aesthetic qualities." "Four Concepts of Aesthetic Experience" in *Beyond Aesthetics: Philosophical Essays* (Cambridge: Cambridge University Press, 2001), p. 60. Another reason I specify both is to be able to account for the typical experience of literature, which usually does not involve the

my notion of "the aesthetic" is decidedly not honorific, in contrast to its common usage as well as what many attempts to define the aesthetic imply. As some recent writers point out, our aesthetic life includes not only pleasant, but also unpleasant experiences characterized as depressing, disgusting, or dreary. In my view, the aesthetic further includes reactions toward qualities such as dingy, nondescript, or plain-looking, which may or may not be accompanied by emotionally tinged quality like disgust. My negative, though mild, reaction to a dingy-looking wall, no matter how trivial and unsophisticated, I believe is an *aesthetic* reaction.

This example suggests another way in which my view on the aesthetic expands on the existing theories. I include in the realm of the aesthetic those experiences that stand out from the flow of everyday experiences, aesthetic experience *par excellence* according to traditional aesthetic experience theories. These experiences perhaps constitute the core of our aesthetic life. However, I hold that an aesthetic reaction can also be a seemingly insignificant, and sometimes almost automatic, response we form in our everyday life. It can be our response to everyday phenomena, such as mess and dirt. Furthermore, while aesthetic attitude theories emphasize the contemplative stance toward an object, I am including those aesthetic reactions that do not presuppose or lead to such spectator-like experiences but rather prompt us toward actions, such as cleaning, discarding, purchasing, and so on. Such is typically the way in which aesthetics functions in everyday life, as Arthur Danto points out, when "selecting garments or choosing sexual partners or picking a dog out of a litter or an apple out of a display of apples."[2]

My proposal to expand and diversify the domain of the aesthetic is analogous to Noël Carroll's attempt to encompass different features of

appreciation of the sensuous, such as the visual image of the printed pages or the sound of the sentences (of course excepting many examples of poetry, visual poetry, and literary works written in Japanese). "Design" may not be a typical term used to describe features of literature, but I am using it to include things like character development, plot organization, and the like.

By emphasizing the sensuous and design as the focus of the aesthetic, I am not denying the aesthetic relevance of the conceptual. On the contrary, as my subsequent discussion will illustrate, even the seemingly simple reaction, such as our response to the "unsightly" stain or "dirty" spot on our shirt, upon closer examination, turns out to be dependent upon further conceptual and contextual considerations, though rarely do we recognize, let alone articulate, such cognitive factors. Hence, in my view, although I am identifying the aesthetic with our responses to the sensuous and design, I am not committed to the formalist aesthetics that excludes the cognitive from the realm of the aesthetic.

[2] Arthur Danto, *The Abuse of Beauty: Aesthetics and the Concept of Art* (Chicago: Open Court, 2003), p. 7.

experiences that are illuminated by different theories of aesthetic experience of art, thereby providing "a disjunctive set of sufficient conditions for categorizing aesthetic experiences of artworks."[3] Specifically, according to him,

a specimen of experience is aesthetic if it involves the apprehension/comprehension by an informed subject ... of the formal structures, aesthetic and/or expressive properties of the object, and/or the emergence of those features from the base properties of the work and/or of the manner in which those features interact with each other and/or address the cognitive, perceptual, emotive, and/or imaginative power of the subject.

What I am proposing is to adopt a similar strategy to define the realm of the aesthetic by including not only such aesthetic experiences of art, however broadly defined, but also those responses that propel us toward everyday decision and actions, without any accompanying contemplative appreciation.

Now, among these diverse dimensions of our aesthetic life, there seems to exist an implicit hierarchy that pervades today's academic discourse on aesthetics. Despite the recent inclusion of nature, popular culture, and other aspects of our daily life, the core subject matter of philosophical aesthetics seems to remain Western fine arts. Other objects are almost always discussed in terms of their affinity (or lack thereof) to such art. Even when the discussion focuses on the content, rather than the object, of our experience, the primary interest is an aesthetic experience as something special that stands out from ordinary experience in general. As a result, other dimensions of our aesthetic life that we engage in almost daily, in forming preferences, judgments, design strategies, or courses of action, become neglected.

I find this hierarchical treatment of the diverse aspects of our aesthetic life both problematic and unfortunate for several reasons. First, the theoretically neglected area of our aesthetic life, that is, our aesthetic engagement with the world beyond art, often unaccompanied by a special aesthetic experience, offers a treasure trove of materials for investigation, not provided by art and special aesthetic experiences. Secondly, when we broaden our

---

[3] Noël Carroll, "Aesthetic Experience: A Question of Content," included in *Contemporary Debates in Aesthetics and the Philosophy of Art*, ed. Matthew Kieran (Malden: Blackwell Publishing, 2006), p. 89. The next passage is also from p. 89.

perspective by adopting a multi-cultural, global viewpoint, we realize that what has been regarded as mainstream aesthetics based upon art and its experience turns out to be specific to, and circumscribed by, the practice primarily of the last two centuries in the West. However, aesthetic concerns and interests, with or without institutionalized art, seem universal. Furthermore, even within a society like ours with an established institutional artworld, as Victor Papanek points out, "it is possible to avoid theatre and ballet, never to visit museums or galleries, to spurn poetry and literature and to switch off radio concerts. Buildings, settlements and the daily tools of living however, form a web of visual impressions that are *inescapable*."[4] Finally, contrary to popular perception that "the aesthetic" deals with something either highly specialized and isolated from our daily concerns, namely art, or else something trivial and frivolous, not essential to our lives, such as beautification and decoration,[5] those neglected dimensions of our aesthetic life do have serious practical ramifications. They often affect and sometimes determine our worldview, actions, the character of a society, the physical environment, and quite literally the course of history.[6] By liberating the aesthetic discourse from the confines of a specific kind of object or experience and illuminating how deeply entrenched and prevalent aesthetic considerations are in our mundane everyday existence, I hope to restore aesthetics to its proper place in our everyday life and to reclaim its status in shaping us and the world.

As a first step of this exploration, in this chapter I will review two major directions of modern Western aesthetics: art-centered aesthetics and aesthetic experience-oriented aesthetics. I shall argue how both directions unduly compromise the rich diversity of our aesthetic life and how this problem not only impoverishes the content of aesthetic discourse but also fails to account adequately for the important ways in which the aesthetic profoundly affects the quality of life and the state of the world.

---

[4] Victor Papanek, *The Green Imperative: Natural Design for the Real World* (New York: Thames & Hudson, 1995), p. 174.

[5] The term "aesthetic" is often used in commercial enterprise dealing with our physical appearance, such as The American Society for Aesthetic Plastic Surgery, Aesthetic Dental Care, and Aesthetic Rejuvenation Center (taken from my phone book). Larry Shiner, one of the reviewers of the earlier draft, pointed out that in France what we call "beautician" is called "esthétician."

[6] I give some specific examples to illustrate this point throughout the rest of the book.

1. Art-centered aesthetics

i. Art as the model for aesthetic object

I believe it is safe to assume that no aestheticians will dispute the claim that there is no theoretical limit to what can become the object of an aesthetic experience.[7] Except for some things that are extremely dangerous, evil, or physically over-taxing (such as a deafening sound), the catholicity of possible aesthetic objects is generally accepted. Even with respect to those exceptions, either a case can be made for their possibly sublime appeal, or, if they cannot or should not be appreciated aesthetically, the reason cited is usually not aesthetic, but psychological, moral, or physical.

However, it is also commonly observed that in the actual practice of aesthetics, art is almost always regarded as the quintessential model for an aesthetic object. In discussing how the notion of disinterestedness was formulated by the eighteenth-century British aestheticians as a way of defining aesthetic experience in general, Jerome Stolnitz observes that "this catholicity in the denotation of 'aesthetic object' ... has gone strangely unremarked."[8] Similarly, Thomas Leddy points out that "although many aestheticians insist that aesthetic qualities are not limited to the arts, even *those* thinkers generally take the arts as the primary focus of their discussion."[9]

These observations are confirmed most notably by the content of standard textbooks used for teaching aesthetics. Many are anthologies with

---

[7] This point has been stressed by a number of writers, starting with Jerome Stolnitz, whose view represents the so-called aesthetic attitude theory. He holds that "anything at all, whether sensed or perceived, whether it is the product of imagination or conceptual thought, can become the object of aesthetic attention." *Aesthetics and the Philosophy of Art Criticism*, originally published in 1960, included in *Introductory Readings in Aesthetics*, ed. John Hospers (New York: The Free Press, 1969), p. 27. The same point is made by Paul Ziff who contends that "anything that can be viewed is a fit object for aesthetic attention," including "a gator basking on a mound of dried dung." "Anything Viewed," originally published in 1984, included in *Oxford Readers: Aesthetics*, eds. Susan L. Feagin and Patrick Maynard (Oxford: Oxford University Press, 1997), pp. 29 and 23. He reiterates the point by saying: "one can view things in the world aesthetically without being concerned with or inhibited by their lack of status as artefacts."(p. 24). More recently, a number of writers make a point of including nature, popular culture, and life itself as aesthetic objects.

[8] Jerome Stolnitz, "On the Origins of 'Aesthetic Disinterestedness'," originally published in *The Journal of Aesthetics and Art Criticism* (Winter 1961), included in *Aesthetics: A Critical Anthology*, eds. George Dickie and R. J. Sclafani (New York: St. Martin's Press, 1977), p. 624.

[9] Thomas Leddy, "Everyday Surface Aesthetic Qualities: 'Neat,' 'Messy,' 'Clean,' 'Dirty,'" *The Journal of Aesthetics and Art Criticism* 53:3 (1995), p. 259.

obligatory sections on the definition of art, the artist's intention, expression in art, the function of art criticism, interpretation of art, objectivity of aesthetic judgment, as well as issues specific to individual art media. An underlying assumption seems to be that art, however it is defined, provides the model for aesthetic objects, and the aesthetic status of things outside the artistic realm is determined by the degree of their affinity to art. The only topic that takes the discussion beyond art is the notion of aesthetic experience/attitude, but even its treatment, as I will discuss later, implicitly takes our experience of art as the model for aesthetic experience.[10]

This narrowing of the range of aesthetic objects is not unique to philosophical aesthetics, as pointed out by an anthropologist who complains that "progress in the anthropological study of visual aesthetics has been hampered by an undue concentration on art and art objects."[11] In a less academic, yet still educational, setting, our primary and secondary education relegates aesthetic education to specific classes, notably art, music, and to some extent literature. These courses usually adhere to an established practice, by appreciating and analyzing works of art and/or creating objects with those established works of art as their model and guide. For this reason, Paul Duncum makes "a case for an art education of everyday aesthetic experiences," because he believes, and I agree, that "ordinary, everyday aesthetic experiences are more significant than experiences of high art in forming and informing one's identity and view of the world beyond personal experience."[12] This is particularly true for young children, as "for the great majority of children, the many sites of everyday aesthetic experiences outside the world sanctioned by art institutions are likely ... to be even more powerful in forming and informing minds."

I shall call this mainstream tendency of aesthetics "art-centered aesthetics," for it takes art and its appreciation as the core of our aesthetic life. The "art" and its experience that is essential to what I call art-centered

---

[10] In this regard, *Aesthetics in Perspective*, ed. Kathleen M. Higgins (Fort Worth: Harcourt Brace & Company, 1996) is noteworthy for its substantial sections on "Beyond Traditional Models," "Popular Culture and Everyday Life," and "Aesthetics around the World."

[11] Jeremy Coote, "'Marvels of Everyday Vision': The Anthropology of Aesthetics and the Cattle-Keeping Nilotes," included in *Anthropology, Art and Aesthetics*, eds. Jeremy Coote and Anthony Shelton (Oxford: Clarendon Press, 1992), p. 245.

[12] Paul Duncum, "A Case for an Art Education of Everyday Aesthetic Experiences," *Studies in Art Education* 40:4 (Summer 1999), p. 296. The following passage is also from the same page. As much as I agree with his view, I believe he does not go far enough in his promotion of everyday aesthetic sites. I will take up this point later in this chapter (2. iii).

aesthetics is primarily paradigmatic Western art, such as a Rembrandt painting, a Beethoven symphony, or a Shakespearean sonnet, the typical examples of art enumerated by those who are versed in Western art history. Furthermore, most discussions regarding the definition of art even today take those paradigmatic Western art objects as a starting point to determine how far and in what way the familiar notion of art should be stretched. Of course today's artworld and aesthetic theories have an expanded scope, including newer forms of art, such as James Turrell's *Roden Crater*, Vito Acconci's performance pieces, and Mierle Laderman Ukeles's installation pieces, as well as non-Western art, such as Tibetan monks' sand paintings and Navajo woven baskets. However, rarely are they cited as paradigm examples of art; instead, they are often treated as posing a challenge or an alternative to mainstream paradigmatic art. Later in this chapter (Section iii), I shall explore how this expanded scope of art affects my discussion of art-centered aesthetics; however, my initial examination of art-centered aesthetics will focus on paradigmatic Western art.

What is noteworthy about art-centered aesthetics is that its discussion focuses exclusively on how art objects and their experiences *differ* from other objects and experiences. At the same time, any discussion regarding the aesthetic dimension of non-art objects is almost always conducted by examining to what extent they are *similar* to art. As a result, the aesthetics of non-art objects is typically discussed in terms of whether or not they can be considered art. I believe that this art-centered approach misconstrues the nature of our aesthetic lives, as well as unduly limits its scope.

For example, citing the composition of parts as a characteristic of art, one discussion of food considers whether ordering of various tastes and smells is possible, concluding that "surely there are *some* serial orderings which people have long since noted concerning gustatory and olfactory qualities."[13] Another debate regarding food revolves around whether its temporality, lack of representational content, and inability to "move" us disqualify it from art-hood.[14] Or another inquiry regarding chess as

[13] Marienne L. Quinet, "Food as Art: The Problem of Function," *The British Journal of Aesthetics* 21:2 (Spring 1981), p. 167.

[14] Glenn Kuehn develops this debate in his response to Elizabeth Telfer's argument against the art-hood of food. See his "How Can Food Be Art?," included in *The Aesthetics of Everyday Life*, eds. Andrew Light and Jonathan M. Smith (New York: Columbia University Press, 2005). Carolyn Korsmeyer also examines this debate in ch. 4 of her *Making Sense of Taste: Food and Philosophy* (Ithaca: Cornell University Press, 1999).

an art form argues that this game satisfies several requirements of art because the players create "something with the intention of rewarding aesthetic contemplation" with " 'artistic riches' which are imperishable (... recorded in permanent form, using standard chess notation)." In addition, "originality" is highly prized.[15] As for sports, a pioneering work debates whether "any sport can justifiably be regarded as an art form" and concludes in the negative because the sports' ultimate end, unlike art, is "not to produce performances for aesthetic pleasure." Furthermore, sports cannot "consider ... issues of social concern," such as "contemporary moral, social, political and emotional issues."[16] In contrast, other commentators argue for the art-hood of sports by citing its playfulness and dramatic narrative structure, though improvised like jazz, culminating in a climax or ending with closure, as well as the virtue of graceful, effortless, or economical body movements featured in some.[17] Finally, when arguing for the art-hood of sports, Wolfgang Welsch characterizes its symbolic status and being an end in itself as "distant from ordinary life" and "separate from the everyday world" like art, and claims that "by neglecting the *artlike* character ... we ... fail to understand why it is so fascinating for a large public."[18]

In general, however, non-art objects, not specifically or primarily created for generating aesthetic experience, do not provide coherent design, dramatic tension, or intense expressiveness to the same degree that many works of art do. Consequently, even when they are considered to be art or like art, they are treated as a kind of "wannabe" art or second-rate art, which falls short of those qualities expected in art. Calling this tendency

---

[15] P. N. Humble, "Chess as an Art Form," *The British Journal of Aesthetics* 33:1 (January 1993), pp. 61, 60–61, and 61.

[16] David Best, "The Aesthetic in Sport," originally published in 1978, included in *Philosophic Inquiry in Sport*, ed. William J. Morgan and Klaus V. Meier (Champaign: Human Kinetics Publishers, 1988), pp. 487, 488, and 488. Best is credited for distinguishing art from aesthetics and arguing for the presence of aesthetic qualities in sports while denying their art-hood. He calls attention to "the distinction which is almost universally overlooked or oversimplified, and therefore misconceived, between the aesthetic and the artistic" (p. 487).

[17] For example, see "Sport—The Body Electric" by Joseph H. Kupfer, originally published in 1983, included in Morgan and Meier, Joseph H. Kupfer, "Waiting for DiMaggio: Sport as Drama," Drew Hyland, " 'When Power Becomes Gracious': The Affinity of Sport and Art," and Ted Cohen, "Sports and Art: Beginning Questions," all included in *Rethinking College Athletics*, eds. Judith Andre and David James (Philadelphia: Temple University Press, 1991).

[18] Wolfgang Welsch, "Sport Viewed Aesthetically, and Even as Art?," included in Light and Smith, pp. 142 and 149, emphasis added.

"art chauvinism" when applied to the aesthetics of environment, Yrjö Sepänmaa points out its "danger of putting the environment in second place."[19] Carolyn Korsmeyer also makes a similar point regarding food: "the addition of taste and food to the domain of established aesthetic theory presents problems: both inevitably come off distinctly second rate, trailing the distance senses and fine art."[20] Even those who argue for the art-hood of non-art objects and phenomena, accordingly, often admit that they do not have the same degree of those qualities that make other objects bona fide art. Welsch, for example, concedes that "sport best fills in for the *everyday longings* of art. But it cannot substitute for Schönberg, Pollock, or Godard."[21]

The problem of establishing a mono-framework for aesthetic discourse is not limited to this implied hierarchy. Perhaps more importantly, it impoverishes the scope of investigation by neglecting those features shared by many non-art objects and practices, which tend to disqualify them from being art-like. Such non-art features include absence of definite and identifiable object-hood and authorship, our literal engagement, transience and impermanence of the object, and the primacy of practical values of the object. Typically, either the art-hood of non-art objects is rejected for embodying too many disqualifying features, or their art-hood is established by an argument that, contrary to the first impression, they actually do satisfy requirements for art-hood. In the former case, somehow we are led to believe that rejection from the art-hood renders them aesthetically inferior or impoverished, depriving us of the opportunity for an aesthetic treasure hunt. In the latter case, on the other hand, Sepänmaa warns us that "the environment is easily forced into a foreign mode of observation by raising the similarities to art to a more exalted position than the environment's own system would grant them."[22] In a similar vein, commenting on the art-hood of food, Korsmeyer also cautions that "the concept of art, dominated as it is today by the idea of *fine* art, is a poor category to capture the nature of foods and their consumption. While one earns a bit of stature for food by

[19] Yrjö Sepänmaa, "The Utilization of Environmental Aesthetics," included in *Real World Design: The Foundation and Practice of Environmental Aesthetics*, ed. Yrjö Sepänmaa (Helsinki: University of Helsinki, 1995), p. 8, and "The Two Aesthetic Cultures: The Great Analogy of an Art and the Environment," included in *Environment and the Arts: Perspectives on Environmental Aesthetics*, ed. Arnold Berleant (Hants: Ashgate, 2002), p. 42.

[20] Korsmeyer, p. 66.   [21] Welsch, p. 150, emphasis added.

[22] Sepänmaa, "Two Aesthetic Cultures," p. 42.

advancing it as an art form, the endeavor is apt to divert attention from the interesting ways in which the aesthetic importance of foods diverges from parallel values in art."[23] Either way, these disqualifying characteristics are never explored for their possible aesthetic significance. However, the fact that these features count against something being an art object does not mean that they are aesthetically uninteresting, insignificant, or irrelevant. It is quite the contrary. In the next section, I shall take those salient features of paradigmatic art and illustrate how focusing on them will lead us to overlook other aspects of our aesthetic life, which are equally as interesting and important as those characteristics of art.

ii. Characteristics of paradigmatic art

a. *Frame* One feature of paradigmatic art is that its ingredients are more or less determined, primarily according to conventional expectations and the artist's control of the material. Painting is confined to the visual elements of one side of the canvas within the frame viewed from a certain distance while standing straight.[24] Its smell of fresh paint, its relationship to the surrounding wallpaper, the back of the canvas, and its upside down view, no matter how intriguing, are to be intentionally bracketed. Our experience of a symphony consists of the sounds conforming to the score created by the musicians on the stage. The outside traffic noise, the cough of the audience, the feel of air-conditioned breeze blowing on our face, and the texture of the seat, are again consciously ignored, though they are part of our experience contemporaneous with the symphonic sound.[25] Despite various controversies regarding what is and is not a part of a work of art, in general, an art object presents itself to us more or less with a determinate boundary. Sometimes the frame is supplied literally as in the frame of a painting, but, more importantly, it is derived from our conceptual understanding such as the conventional agreement concerning

---

[23] Korsmeyer, p. 141.

[24] For the purpose of the present discussion, I am going to generalize and discount possible counter-examples, many of which are both intriguing and important. To give one example, Paul Ziff considers the possibility of not being able to ignore the surrounding wall, if we are "viewing a yellow version of Josef Albers' *Homage to the Square* displayed in a yellow frame on a yellow stuccoed wall," in "Anything Viewed," p. 27.

[25] John Cage broke away from this convention governing Western classical music by declaring all "noise" is part of his music, illustrated by *4' 33"*. The revolutionary character of his stance and his music underscores the deeply entrenched assumption of what qualifies as musical sounds. I thank Larry Shiner for pointing out Cage's example.

the medium, the artist's intention, the cultural and historical context, and the like.

In contrast, the absence of an equivalent conventional agreement on medium or evidence of the artist's intention renders a non-art object "frameless," making us a creator of it as aesthetic object. As Ronald Hepburn points out, the aesthetic price we pay for the frameless character of non-art objects, such as the lack of a unified design, can be compensated by exercising our imagination and creativity in constituting the aesthetic object as we see fit.[26] For example, the appreciation of a baseball game may include the noisy cheers of the fans, the hot sun beating down our neck, and the smell of hot dogs, in addition to the quasi-artistic elements such as the players' body movements, the thrill of a tight competition, and the drama of the record-breaking home run. Or, New York City's "sense of place" cannot be separated from the smell of burnt pretzels and chestnuts, the feel of vibration and steam coming from below, the chaotic honking of the cabs, though we *can* choose to ignore all of these and concentrate specifically and exclusively on its architecture. In appreciating the smell and taste of green tea, I may incorporate the visual and tactile sensation of the tea bowl, as well as the sound of slurping. In constructing the object of our aesthetic experience in these cases, we do select and specifically attend to certain ingredients in our perceptual field, just as we do when we appreciate art as art. However, in our operations regarding art, the primary criteria for selection are for the most part determined by various factors other than our personal preference, taste, and inclination,[27] while an equivalent conventional or institutional agreement does not exist with respect to non-art. As a result, we are free to rely on our own imagination, judgment, and aesthetic taste as the guide.

---

[26] "[W]here there is no frame, and where nature is our aesthetic object, a sound or visible intrusion from beyond the original boundaries of our attention can challenge us to integrate it in our overall experience, to modify that experience so as to make room for it. This of course, *need* not occur; we may shut it out by effort of will, if it seems quite unassimilable. At any rate, our creativity is challenged, set a task; and when things go well with us, we experience a sudden expansion of imagination that can be memorable in its own right." Ronald Hepburn, "Contemporary Aesthetics and the Neglect of Natural Beauty," included in *"Wonder" and Other Essays: Eight Studies in Aesthetics and Neighboring Fields* (Edinburgh: The University Press at Edinburgh, 1984), p. 14.

[27] I am not denying that we do rely on our sensibility, judgment, in constructing the proper object for art appreciation (such as whether to include the title of a painting or the painter's signature as an integral part of the object), but it is constrained by other considerations such as extra-sensory information and conventional agreement.

b. Engagement with the aesthetic object   Because of the absence of conventional or institutional agreements concerning how to experience non-art objects and activities, we are also free to engage ourselves literally in the aesthetic experience in any way we see fit. This is in contrast to the prescribed mode of experiencing paradigmatic art. We sit still and quiet during a classical music concert or theater performance, and we look at a painting or sculpture without touching, smelling, moving, or holding it. We are distanced from the object, both literally and metaphorically. Indeed, most of the conventional agreements and institutional settings for experiencing art facilitate such distancing and disengagement from the object, determining *the* proper stance that would induce the optimal experience.

This spectator mode, while most appropriate and rewarding with respect to paradigmatic art, may not provide the most satisfying experience of non-art. We *can* appreciate the aesthetic value of a chair, an apple, a landscape, and rain as if they were a sculptural piece, a landscape painting, or a music piece, by becoming a pure spectator/listener. However, more often than not, we experience a chair not only by inspecting its shape and color, but also by touching its fabric, sitting in it, leaning against it, and moving it, to get the feel for its texture, comfort, and stability.[28] Our typical experience of an apple starts by beholding its perfect round shape and delicate colors ranging from red to green and holding it in our hand to feel its substantial weight and smooth skin. Then we proceed to engage all of our senses and enjoy the crunching sound when we first bite into it, the contrast between the firmness of its contents and the sweet juice flowing from it, and, of course, its smell and taste.[29] A landscape can be looked at from an upside-down position, as recommended for one of Japan's three

---

[28] We experience a sense of frustration at a museum exhibition of utilitarian objects, where "don't touch" command dominates. Although, as Virginia Postrel points out, art museums are increasingly exhibiting designed objects, such as sneakers, salad bowls, chairs, etc., such exhibits still do not achieve the collapse of the separation between art and everyday life. The primary reason is that as they are items in museum exhibits, we are prevented from experiencing them in our everyday usage by using or wearing them. (See p. 15 of her *The Substance of Style: How the Rise of Aesthetic Value is Remaking Commerce, Culture, and Consciousness* (New York: HarperCollins Publishers, 2003)) From the perspective of the aesthetic attitude theory, however, it will be questioned whether those considerations regarding their functionality are aesthetically relevant. I will argue below that they are.

[29] I think the experience of eating is one of the most multifaceted experiences we have, *and* ALL of us have them on daily basis. I will address this multi-sensory aspect of eating in Chapter III (2.i) and its moral implications in Chapter V.

scenic places consisting of a sandbar in a bay, or more typically today as a moving panorama from a car window.[30] As for rain, we sometimes experience raindrops falling on our heads as we skip and jump over puddles while "singin' in the rain," feeling our pants and shoes getting wet, as well as savoring the taste of raindrops (hoping that they are not acidic!). Or some other times we may experience rain by sitting under the hanging roof of a Zen temple, looking out on its attached rock garden, attending to the way in which the surface of each rock glistens with wetness and noting the elegant movement of raindrops as they dance downward along the linked chain hanging from the gutter. Yet another way of experiencing a rainstorm is to perch oneself on the treetop in the middle of a forest, as John Muir did in the Sierra Woods.[31] Is one way more "appropriate" or "correct" than others in experiencing rain?

In all these examples, there is no institutional or conventional agreement determining the mode of our experience. The only guide, if we may even call it that, may be in terms of what is aesthetically more rewarding. For example, experiencing a chair or an apple as a piece of sculpture without ever touching and handling it is likely to be less interesting and satisfying than more normal ways of experiencing them.

c. Privileging higher senses   The examples of the last two sections indicate another notable feature of Western paradigmatic art: its exclusive reliance on senses of sight and sound. In the Western aesthetic tradition, (successful) art has been variously described as organic unity, a temporal sequence with a beginning, middle, and end, purposiveness without a purpose, significant form, or intensity, complexity, and unity.[32] These definitions of aesthetic achievement all presuppose some kind of composition with

---

[30] One of the historically designated three scenic places of Japan, Ama-no-Hashidate (Bridge over Heaven) has an associated legend which created this bizarre manner of viewing it. According to the legend, a famed ninth-century poetess, Ono no Komachi, answered the call of nature while viewing this landscape from a hill above and is said to have marveled at the splendid upside down view which looked as if the bridge is over the sky. This episode and the resultant "scenic view" concerning this landscape are explored by Ashihara Yoshinobu in *Zoku Machinami no Bigaku* (*Aesthetics of Townscape II*) (Tokyo: Iwanami Shoten, 1995), pp. 65–74. Following the Japanese custom, I put the last name first for Japanese names, unless the work is in or translated into English.

[31] John Muir recounts his experience of wind storm atop a tree in "A Wind-Storm in the Forests" in *The Mountains of California*, first published in 1894, included in *The American Landscape: A Critical Anthology of Prose and Poetry*, ed. John Conron (New York: Oxford University Press, 1973), pp. 264–70.

[32] The first two definitions are from Aristotle, the third from Kant, the fourth from Clive Bell, and the last from Monroe Beardsley. I thank Carolyn Korsmeyer for reminding me of Beardsley's view.

parts/ingredients arranged and organized in a certain way. Sight and sound have traditionally been regarded as "higher" senses for their affinity to the conceptual and the intellectual. Visual images and sounds can be arranged according to some rational scheme; hence, they are amenable to objective, sometimes even mathematical, analysis. In contrast, the so-called "lower senses," smell, taste, and touch, as well as kinesthetic sensations are considered to be too visceral, animalistic, and crude to allow intellectual description, conceptual analysis, and rational organization. Monroe Beardsley, for example, compares the senses of smell and taste with sight and sound by citing the formers' lack of enough "order… to construct objects with balance, climax, development, or pattern."[33] This is the reason, he claims, why we do not have "taste-symphonies and smell-sonatas."

It is clear that once we set paradigmatic art of sight and sound as the model for an aesthetic object, we neglect a large portion of the aesthetic dimension of our daily affairs. In addition to this cost to aesthetic theories, what is often not noticed is the fact that denying aesthetic membership to lower senses and bodily sensations has morally problematic consequences. I will explore this less obvious point in Chapter V.

d. The authorial identity   Part of the reason why we abide by the framed character of an art object and the conventionally agreed manner of experiencing it is because we suppose that an art object is made by an artist as art. Because of this attribution of an artist/author, a number of specific considerations govern our experience. Because the object came into being at a particular time, with primarily one person responsible for its birth, we cannot but pursue when, where, under what circumstances, and with what sort of intention the object was created. Of course, many non-art objects elicit the same kind of response from us. We look at an ancient monument and try to figure out its meaning, historical context, religious symbolism, and so on. Or, I may be quite fascinated by the romantic writing, both visually and content-wise, of my grandfather's letters to my grandmother on his way to study in Europe, and try to imagine the extent of his loneliness on the boat and affection towards his wife.

---

[33] Monroe C. Beardsley, *Aesthetics: Problems in the Philosophy of Criticism* (Indianapolis: Hackett Publishing Company, 1981), p. 99 for both this and the next passage.

However, it is also characteristic of many everyday objects and practices that they lack any particular authorship, making our quest for authorial intention and the circumstances surrounding the creation irrelevant. For example, despite some specific designs created by specific people at a specific time, the current townscape with which I live is a cumulative effect of numerous works and activities over the years, indeed centuries, by both humans and nature. Some of the human contributions may be intentional, such as a town-wide landscaping plan and various restrictions posed by the zoning ordinance, but other aspects of the townscape occurred quite by happenstance, such as the weather-beaten appearance of some buildings, the color pattern created by individual houses' painted walls, the traffic volume which doubled during the past decade, and abandoned stone walls found in the woods. There is no specific point at which this townscape was born; nor is there a specific author or a group of authors whose intention may shed light on its current appearance. This does not mean, however, that the townscape is without aesthetic interest. On the contrary, we often derive a rewarding aesthetic experience deciphering from its sensuous surface a number of things, such as the geological and meteorological conditions, the historical development of the town, its social, economic, and political climate, sometimes even its racial politics, as well as the general ethos of the community. While information pertaining to the town is certainly relevant and helpful, our experience here is not bound by what a particular individual intended the object to function as, be, or mean.

e. Permissibility of modification   Our acknowledgement that a work of art was made by an artist leads to another difference between our experience of art and non-art. With respect to non-art, we literally engage ourselves by handling, changing, modifying, or working on many of them. Of course, moral and legal restrictions prevent me from trimming tree branches in my neighbor's yard, spray-painting saints' names on the church wall, or planting exotic flowers in the middle of a national park, no matter how aesthetically motivated these actions may be. However, within these parameters, often guided by aesthetic concerns and interests, we engage with objects around us by cleaning, organizing, mending, rearranging, relocating, and eating on a daily basis.

Now, such modifications are not generally accepted with art objects (except for restoration, although it is accompanied by various restrictions), even if they are deemed aesthetically desirable. We refrain from eliminating several bars at the end of Beethoven's later symphonies, erasing some pencil marks from a painting, or adding another chapter to a novel.[34] We normally respect the integrity of a work of art and give it precedence over possible aesthetic improvement. And this respect often seems to override the legality of the case because we seem to (or at least wish to) restrict even what the legitimate creator or owner of a work of art can do with his/her creation or property. For example, the whole world was horrified to learn that a Japanese company president, the rightful owner of van Gogh's *Irises*, wished to be cremated with this painting upon his death. Or, more recently, the publishing director of The Modern Library was dismayed to find that Joyce Carol Oates revised her *A Garden of Earthly Delights* extensively for its new hardcover edition.[35]

f. Stable identity   Another contrast between art and non-art is the presumed/preferred permanence and stability of the former in contrast to the transience of the latter. Perhaps reflecting the Western metaphysical priority given to permanent and static entities, we regard, and try to keep, art permanent and unchanging. Of course, art objects embodied in physical materials are subject to the same process of change as anything else. A painting gets dirty, its colors fade, and its surface cracks. However, our typical reaction to this natural process of aging, when it concerns art objects, is to try to arrest its progress with cleaning, restoration, preservation, and by providing a temperature-, moisture-, and light-controlled environment.

As for those art objects not embodied in physical materials, such as music, literature, and performance, their interpretation and execution vary greatly from time to time, translation to translation, or performer to performer, creating various debates about what constitutes the authentic performance or the interpretation faithful to the artist's intention. However, despite these variations and questions concerning what constitutes the identity of these art works, we assume that we can identify Beethoven's Fifth Symphony or Dostoevsky's *Crime and Punishment*.

---

[34]   It is often remarked by music critics that Beethoven's later symphonies suffer from the overly long coda, attributed to his need to repeat the sound as if to compensate for his worsening deafness.

[35]   Hillel Italie, "When Authors Rewrite Themselves, It Sparks Debate," *Providence Journal*, 31 July 2003.

Furthermore, art objects are generally atemporal in the sense that the particular temporal context in which they are experienced is normally irrelevant to its qualities and values. The sealed environment of a museum, concert hall, or theater, the typical setting for presenting paradigmatic art, ensures this atemporal nature by obliterating the temporal context of our experience as much as possible. So, it does not matter whether I view Cezanne's *Mt. Sainte-Victoire* in the middle of the summer or winter, during a rainstorm or under a sunny sky, or midday or at night, whereas it makes a *big* difference if I am viewing the actual Mt. Sainte-Victoire.[36]

When we experience non-art objects, we do identify objects in many ways: the corner store, the oak tree in my front yard, my black dress, Old Faithful, my office at school, and so on. However, they are subject to vicissitudes and are always experienced in a certain temporal context which changes the nature of our experience. The time of the day and the year, as well as weather conditions, affect the appearance of my oak tree. The basic structure of my office may stay the same (unless I or the school remodel it), but its content changes constantly—sometimes neatly organized and cleaned while at other times completely messy and disorganized, or I may move the furniture around. As Kevin Melchionne points out in his discussion of domestic aesthetics, "unlike paradigmatic art forms like painting or poetry, interiors do not just sit around after their completion unaltered for the centuries. They are lived in, worked in, and worked on and so they are also transformed, if only by being worn upon daily."[37] Thus, just as the absence of conventional/institutional agreement in the case of non-art allows free range for constituting the object and the manner for facilitating aesthetic experience, the temporal character of our experience outside art also affords numerous possibilities of differing experiences, even regarding the same "object."

g. Aesthetic value and other values Another aspect in which art objects differ from everyday objects and activities is this: fine art objects are created and appreciated primarily for their aesthetic significance, even if they serve ˎ

---

[36] Notable exceptions are outdoor sculpture, particularly those which make use of the outdoor environment with all its changing conditions, such as wind and light, and Japanese Noh theater in its original performing environment—outdoors—which prompted instructions to the actors that they be sensitive to the season and time of performance.

[37] Kevin Melchionne, "Living in Glass Houses: Domesticity, Interior Decoration, and Environmental Aesthetics," *The Journal of Aesthetics and Art Criticism* 56:2 (Spring 1998), p. 199.

other purposes, such as religious or political. Some literary works and visual art objects affect us and move us profoundly and motivate us to engage in a political activity, change our worldview, or enhance our religious devotion. Some music pieces help promote nationalistic fervor. Furthermore, some of these art objects are specifically intended to have these effects on us. However, rarely do works of fine art affect us most directly on a daily basis, serving our physical needs, changing our environment, and prompting immediate actions.

When it comes to non-art objects, except for pure spectator sports and other forms of entertainment and amusement, most of our everyday objects and activities are created, used, or performed first and foremost for non-aesthetic purposes. We clean our kitchen and bathroom for hygiene, cook and eat food for sustenance, and pick our clothes for protection and comfort. Various utensils, furniture, and tools are created, used, and appreciated for their respective functional use.

We can and sometimes do adopt a disinterested attitude toward these objects and activities by distancing ourselves from the everyday practical concern. Immanuel Kant would claim that this way of appreciating a utilitarian object for its "free beauty" is more legitimate or "pure" than appreciating it for its "dependent beauty," because the former appreciation is based upon the truly free play of the imagination in pursuit of "purposiveness" and is not regulated by a definite "purpose" for which the object is created and used.[38] However, despite the possibility of appreciating the free beauty of a utilitarian object, such an experience is rather unusual, odd, and artificially induced. In our everyday, normal interaction with a utilitarian object, the aesthetic and the practical are experienced as fully integrated and we lose some dimension of its aesthetic value if we surgically remove its functional value.[39]

---

[38] The section 16 where Kant discusses the difference between free beauty and dependent beauty is entitled: "The Judgment of taste, by which an object is declared to be beautiful under the condition of a definite concept, is not *pure*." *Critique of Judgment*, tr. J. H. Bernard (New York: Hafner Press, 1974), p. 65, emphasis added.

[39] Carolyn Korsmeyer pointed out that rearranging furniture is often for solely aesthetic reasons. Although it may be motivated by a purely aesthetic reason (i.e. wanting a different look), we rearrange furniture *as furniture*, rather than as pieces of sculpture. That is, we attend to things like comfort, convenience, and usefulness, along with aesthetic considerations, by making sure there is enough space for us to walk around and for doors and drawers to open, as well as sufficient lighting near a desk, and arranging the seating in a living room conducive to socialization. If we regard furniture as free beauty, we should be able to arrange them in any way possible, such as stacking a chair on top of

The aesthetic value of a knife consists not only of its visual qualities, but also of its feeling in my hand, determined by its surface texture, weight, and balance, but most importantly by how smoothly and effortlessly I can cut an object *because of* the material, shape, length, texture, and weight of the blade and handle. The appreciation here is not simply directed toward the fact that the knife functions well; it rather concerns *the way in which* all its sensuous aspects converge and work together to facilitate the ease of use. If I appreciate this knife *exclusively* for its cutting performance, I don't think I am appreciating it aesthetically, because as long as I can derive the same degree of cutting capability from any other knife, the specific sensuous qualities do not matter. I suspect that the reason why functionality of an object was generally shunned from the realm of the aesthetic is because exclusive attention to functionality steers us away from attending to the sensuous surface of the object. However, considering an object's functionality does not necessarily lead us away from its surface qualities. I can appreciate *the way in which* the materials, design, size, and craftsmanship are integrated to provide the superb functional quality. So, although it is true that various practical and utilitarian purposes are intimately bound up with our everyday experience, such integration does not necessarily compete with the aesthetic value. In fact, I believe it is a mistake to find aesthetic value in everyday objects and activities only insofar as we momentarily isolate them from their everyday use and contemplate them as if they were art objects created specifically for display. If we divorce them from their practical significance in our lives, we will miss a rich array of aesthetic values integrated with utilitarian contexts.

In this section, I have characterized paradigmatic art as a more or less identifiable and stable object bounded by a frame, spatially or temporally, distinct from its surroundings, typically experienced through sight and sound with a spectator-like, distancing attitude, and in a certain expected and a prescribed mode. I have explored several ways in which paradigmatic art and its (proper) experience are governed by various implicit rules and assumptions derived from conventional agreement and other conceptual considerations. In general, the operative mode underlying our paradigmatic experience of paradigmatic art is "separation," "isolation," "distinction,"

a table, if such an arrangement will maximize the overall aesthetic value of the interior space. So, even when this activity is motivated purely by aesthetic reasons, the practical consideration cannot be separated.

"divorce," or "disengagement" from our ordinary everyday affairs. The following passage by John Dewey best characterizes this aspect of art, even if it was initially intertwined with everyday concerns:

When an art product once attains classic status, it somehow becomes *isolated* from the human conditions under which it was brought into being and from the human consequences it engenders in actual life-experience. When artistic objects are separated from both conditions or origin and operation in experience, a wall is built around them that renders almost opaque their general significance, with which esthetic theory deals. Art is remitted to a *separate* realm, where it is *cut off* from that association with the materials and aims of every other form of human effort, undergoing, and achievement.[40]

In comparison, non-art objects and practices exist and are experienced in their everyday context and usage. As such, they are free from those expectations and conventions governing the institutional artworld, and in turn can be a source of aesthetic appreciation that incorporates qualities not shared by paradigmatic art, such as their functionality and effects on bodily senses. These considerations lead me to a preliminary conclusion that analyzing everyday aesthetic experiences after the model of Western paradigmatic art is misguided as it compromises their rich and diverse content.

iii. *Expanded scope of art-centered aesthetics*

So far I have been characterizing art-centered aesthetics as taking paradigmatic Western art as the model for an aesthetic object. This is because many people versed in Western art would readily recognize such objects as art and, despite various challenges and innovations in the past century, they still seem to form a core concept of the artworld.

However, of course there are a number of newer forms of art which are meant to break out of the confinement posed by all these conventional characteristics. Environmental art, happenings, performance, chance music, installation, conceptual art, and interactive art immediately come to mind. Furthermore, some of today's artists quite specifically create works that simulate or *are* a slice of our everyday life. Finally, from today's global perspective and with the eagerness to overcome the West-centric viewpoint,

---

[40] John Dewey, *Art as Experience* (New York: Capricon Books, 1958), p. 3, all the emphasis added.

today's artworld includes a number of non-Western forms of art that do not share those features characterizing Western paradigmatic art. Inclusion of these kinds of art certainly enlarges the domain of art and questions the assumptions underlying the art-centered aesthetic that I have been discussing. I will take three examples, environmental art, art that simulates or is situated in everyday life, and the traditional Japanese tea ceremony, to illustrate how such changes can take place. However, I will also argue that, in the end, even with a more inclusive view concerning art, art-centered aesthetics still does not provide an adequate account of every aspect of our aesthetic life

a. Environmental art[41]   Environmental art, initiated as "land art" or "earth-works" by Robert Smithson, Robert Morris, and Michael Heizer in the 1960s and 1970s, challenges those characteristics of paradigmatic art explained above. First, environmental art is for the most part frameless, sometimes denying solid object-hood, as in Robert Morris's *Steam* (1974).[42] But the most prominent examples are so-called earthworks. By taking their art projects outdoors and working directly in, on, or with the land, many land artists resisted the spatial determinacy and self-contained identity of the art object. The art objects cannot be confined to what the artists and their crews constructed. For example, Robert Smithson's *Spiral Jetty* (1972) is not just the spiral mound in a lake, nor are Christo's installation pieces simply a giant orange curtain (*Valley Curtain*, 1970–72), white, fence-like fabric (*Running Fence*, 1972–76), pink plastic (*Surrounded Islands,* 1980–81), yellow and blue umbrellas (*The Umbrellas, Japan–USA*, 1984–91), or a series of orange gates (*The Gates*, 2005). The environment surrounding and accentuated by each constructed object is equally part of these artworks. This is pointed out by two commentators on earthworks:

[41] I present a more detailed discussion of this section in "Environmental Directions for Aesthetics and the Arts1" in *Environment and the Arts: Perspectives on Environmental Aesthetics,* ed. Arnold Berleant (Hants: Ashgate Publishing Limited, 2002). Detailed discussion and visual images of many of the examples I cite in this section can be found in Barbara C. Matilsky's *Fragile Ecologies: Contemporary Artists' Interpretations and Solutions* (New York: Rizzoli, 1992), John Beardsley's *Earthworks and Beyond: Contemporary Art in the Landscape* (New York: Abbeville Press, 1989), *Sculpting with the Environment: A Natural Dialogue,* ed. Baile Oakes (New York: Van Nostrand Reinhold, 1995), Sue Spaid's *Ecovention: Current Art to Transform Ecologies* (Cincinnati: The Contemporary Arts Center, 2002), and John K. Grande's *Art Nature Dialogues: Interviews with Environmental Artists* (Albany: SUNY Press, 2004).

[42] Jeffrey Kastner and Brian Wallis, *Land and Environmental Art* (London: Phaidon Press, 1998), p. 102.

As manipulations of three-dimensional materials in physical space, many of the first projects are sculptures. Yet, executed and sited in a specific location on which they depend for their power, they have the ability to melt and spread beyond the limits of their individual materiality, confusing the traditional sculptural scheme in which the experience begins and ends with the object.[43]

In addition to rebelling against the museum and gallery system entrenched in the modern Western artworld, which treats art objects as commodities subject to commerce, these land artists also offered an alternative model for art by inviting us to exercise our sensibility, imagination, and creativity in constructing our own object for aesthetic appreciation.

Furthermore, environmental art quite often requires our literal participation through bodily engagement, as well as the "lower senses" of touch and smell. Typical examples include Meg Webster's works with living plants, such as *Glen* (1985), inviting touch and exuding scent, and Walter de Maria's *New York Earth Room* (1977) with its striking smell of earth and peat in the middle of a gallery space. Some works by Carl Andre and Mary Miss, as well as James Turrell's *Roden Crater*, create space for the viewers to walk along, walk or crawl through, or lie down.

Environmental art also embraces and thrives on impermanence and transience, sometimes pre-programmed, as in the temporary installation works by Christo, but more frequently resulting from the artist's submission to nature's process, primarily decay and deterioration. Such was the notion of "entropy," defined by Smithson as "the process of transformation which works undergo when abandoned to the forces of nature,"[44] and exemplified by such works as *Partially Buried Woodshed* (1970), *Spiral Hill* (1971), and *Spiral Jetty* (1972). Another pioneer earth artist, Michael Heizer, considering as obsolete the notion of the permanence of art, reportedly took "pleasure in publishing photographs of the deterioration of pieces years after they were made."[45]

Nature's processes also include various changes brought about by forces such as wind, light, and temperature, as well as organic growth. Michael Singer and Andy Goldsworthy create intentionally fragile outdoor works sensitive to the effects of nature's force. Singer explains the ephemeral aspect of his works, such as *The Ritual Series* (1970s and 1980s), delicately balanced

---

[43] Jeffrey Kastner and Brian Wallis, *Land and Environmental Art* (London: Phaidon Press, 1998), p. 16.
[44] Ibid. p. 99.   [45] Ibid. p. 29.

tree branches and twigs placed in ponds, that " in order to experience and learn from the natural environment ... I felt the need to yield to it, respect it, to observe, learn, and then work with it."[46] Goldsworthy, commenting on his own works, starting with early stick throws and subsequent arrangements of leaves, petals, and pine needles, culminating in works with snow, remarks that art-making activity is his "way of trying to come to terms with the transience of life and not trying to fight that by making always permanent things: to accept and enjoy it."[47]

Some other artists harness nature's growth and maturing process in their works. David Nash's *Ash Dome* (1997−present) relies on the trees' natural growth for its completion, while Agnes Denes's *Wheatfield—A Confrontation* (1982) includes harvesting of the wheat nurtured by the artist and her assistants. Mel Chin's *Revival Field* (1990−93) also consists of various toxin-absorbing plants' growth.

In all of these works, as one commentator observes, the artists are "more concerned with process than with product."[48] While not proposed as a conscious agenda by these artists, their emphasis on the process implicitly challenges the traditional Western ontology which privileges Being over Becoming and may be seen to share an affinity with Taoism and Buddhism. Furthermore, though the authorship of each artwork is specifiable, the actual work results from the collaboration between the artist's contributions and other factors, such as the environment in which the work is situated and nature's force.[49] In short, the artists willingly relinquish total control over their creation.

Finally, in some environmental art works, the aesthetic and the practical are inseparable. Many of today's environmental artists are committed to improving the state of the world in the most literal sense. Various artistic projects to reclaim devastated land constitute one kind. Pioneered by land artists of the 1960s, land reclamation continues to be practiced by more con-temporary, ecologically-minded artists such as Nancy Holt, Agnes Denes, Mel Chin, Patricia Johanson, and Helen Meyer Harrison and Newton

---

[46] Cited by John Beardsley, p. 165.

[47] Recorded in a film directed by C. Guichard, *Nature and Nature: Andy Goldsworthy* (Peasmarsh: The Roland Collection, 1991).

[48] John Beardsley, p. 192.

[49] One of Goldsworthy's books is entitled *A Collaboration with Nature* (New York: Harry N. Abrams, 1990).

Harrison. Whether dealing with toxic landfills or contaminated wetlands, these artists' projects integrate their artistic design, such as geometrical figures or figurative images, with the actual clean-up of the site, as well as the restoration of native plants, providing a habitat for indigenous creatures. Another group of artists attempts to better the world by serving the needs of non-humans. Dubbed "trans-species art," their art objects range from Lynn Hull's raptor roosts in the desert (*Lightning Raptor Roosts*, 1990) and carvings on desert rocks that serve as water containers for birds (*Desert Hydrograph*, 1986–95) to Betty Beaumont's artificial coral reef placed at the ocean bottom to provide habitat for marine creatures (*Ocean Landmark*, 1978–80).

Another kind of environmental art in which the practical significance is inseparable from its artistic value is the engagement in activism. One of the initiators is Joseph Beuys, whose artworks include the project to plant 7,000 oak trees in Germany (1982). Andy Lipkis's *Martin Luther King, Jr. Blvd. Tree Planting* (1990) involved local residents as volunteers, not only for greening and beautifying an otherwise depressed neighborhood but also for fostering a sense of community pride. Mierle Laderman Ukeles's performance pieces and installation, *Flow City* (1983–90), aimed at raising public awareness of issues regarding garbage. The power of artifacts and activities to change the environment, as well as our daily life, is appropriated in those artworks where the aesthetic values cannot be separated from their effects on real life, blurring the distinction between art and life.[50]

These environmental artworks thus do away with various restrictive characteristics of paradigmatic art; instead, they share more features in common with objects and activities outside the realm of paradigmatic art. This consideration provides a prima facie case for defending an art-centered approach to aesthetics by showing how its restrictive nature can be easily overcome by enlarging the realm of art.

b. Art of the everyday   Another example of contemporary art that challenges conventional artworld framework is those objects and performances that simulate or are situated in our everyday life. One example is Rirkrit Tiravanija's installation/performance/interactive piece at Wexner Center for the Arts in Ohio State University, which consists of a life-scale and fully

---

[50] Aforementioned (note 41) *Ecovention* compiles many good examples of this kind of environmental art.

functioning replica of his East Village apartment where he cooked Thai curry and served it to gallery-goers.[51] He provides not only the literal food for consumption and accompanying aroma but also a space and inviting atmosphere for social interactions among people. Similar to the art of Japanese tea ceremony (which I will take up in the next section), there is no clear boundary for this artwork, audience participation is necessary for the work, it is transient, and it responds to one of our basic needs.

Or, consider sculptor Tyree Guyton's *Heidelberg Project*, four derelict houses in Detroit's run-down section buried in "layers of scavenged materials—tires, hubcaps, broken toys, battered dolls, rusty signs, busted appliances, and automobile parts—all brightened with stripes, polka dots, and random splashes of paint."[52] A giant work of "assemblage art," it was meant as a work of art expressive of his anger toward social, political, and economic injustice. As one can imagine, it created quite a stir among nearby residents as well as art critics, their reactions ranging from outrage over this gigantic "eyesore" to admiration for his artistic courage and defense for his artistic freedom of speech. Unlike the environmental art that I discussed before, which in general is meant to improve the environment, this piece, also situated in an actual, everyday environment, is calling attention to a problem by exacerbating it.

These examples, one an attempt to bring the everyday into a museum setting and the other an attempt to bring a particular brand of art to the everyday context, both aim at blurring the distinction between the sphere of art and everyday life. Having become accustomed to the boundary separating the two, we at first feel disoriented by encountering something in what at first appears to be an inappropriate context. As such, like environmental art, they help enlarge the scope of art.

c. The Japanese tea ceremony   Inclusion of non-Western art also helps expand the domain of art. The example I want to discuss, the Japanese tea ceremony, certainly is not intended to challenge the modern Western artworld practice, unlike the previous two examples from contemporary

---

[51] This and other similar pieces by Tiravanija are discussed in *Supermarket*, ed. Jean-Noël Jetzer (Zürich: Migros Museum für Gegenwartskunst, 1998). I thank my student, Kelsey Harrington, for introducing me to his works and providing the reference.

[52] John Beardsley, "Eyesore or Art? On Tyree Guyton's Heidelberg Project," *Harvard Design Magazine* (Winter/Spring 1999), p. 5.

Western art, having been established as an art form in the sixteenth century. However, like the other two, its various aspects are also characterized by all the features *contrary* to those defining Western paradigmatic art.

First, its boundaries are not definite. Though many of its ingredients are works of art in their own right, such as a tea hut, a tea garden, a tea bowl, a flower arrangement, a scroll, and other implements, the possibility is limitless for including other elements. They include the weather condition, bird's chirping, the sound of rain hitting the thatched roof of the hut, the spontaneous conversation between the host and the guest, the bodily movement of the host making the tea, the smell and taste of the tea and snack, the tactile sensation of the tea bowl and warmth of tea conveyed to the palm, gentle movement of the tea swishing inside the bowl, and the slurping sound when we take our last sip from the bowl. Each participant is free to constitute her own aesthetic object by including some or all of these ingredients. In addition, while there are strict rules governing the minute details for every aspect of the ceremony, the actual ceremony itself is unscripted, subject to the spontaneous convergence of various events and phenomena, and the whole event is made possible with every participant's bodily engagement.

Secondly, this is an art form that specifically celebrates impermanence, as exemplified by its motto: *ichigo ichie* (one time, one meeting). Because of its emphasis on the temporally dependent aspects such as the particular season, the time of the day, the specific assortment of implements to suit the occasion, and the particular make-up of the guests, each tea ceremony is a unique event, never to be repeated. In this sense, it is reflective of the vicissitudes of life itself, illustrating Buddhist insight and heightening our awareness of our own existential predicament.

Finally, it is an art form which consists of the most mundane and practical activity that we all engage in everyday—drinking tea and eating a snack. As the sixteenth-century tea master Rikyū states, the art of tea ceremony resides in "simply boiling water, making tea, and drinking it."[53] In addition, all the objects associated with it are ordinary-looking, sometimes impoverished-looking things, such as *Ido* tea bowls which were originally Korean peasants' rice bowls, and the tea huts which evoke the

---

[53] *Nanbōroku o Yomu (Reading Nanbōroku)*, ed. Kumakura Isao (Kyoto: Tankōsha, 1988), p. 350, my translation. *Nanbōroku* is a collection of Rikyū's teachings, most likely compiled by Nanbō Sokei, a Zen priest and one of Rikyū's disciples.

rusticity of peasants' and fishermen's huts. Many implements also show signs of aging, such as chips, cracks, and missing parts, to which our everyday objects are subject. Finally, the guiding principle that dictates how the host and guests should behave is also derived from our everyday concerns—how to treat others with respect and care, how to be receptive to and grateful for others' considerateness, and how to help create harmony and accord among people. Expressed through aesthetic means, the practical, and in this case, moral and social, concerns are thoroughly integrated into this artistic activity.[54]

Thus, inclusion of the tea ceremony also helps enlarge the scope of art and diversify its content. This appears to suggest further that, if there is something problematic about art-centered aesthetics, it is not the theory itself but the scope of its examples; as such, the problem is easy to fix.

d. Limitation of expanded art-centered aesthetics   Is it then the case that art-centered aesthetics with an expanded and updated scope can adequately account for everyday aesthetics? Does the inclusion of the foregoing examples in the realm of art help blur the distinction between art and life so that whatever aesthetic considerations that apply to the one apply to the other? I shall argue in this section that art-centered aesthetics, even with this updated and revised scope, is inadequate as an account of all the facets of our aesthetic life. As long as art is conceived as something different from our daily affairs, *even if* it is meant to illuminate or emulate some aspects of our everyday life, it has already acquired a special status, not shared by our everyday life itself.

Let's examine more closely newer art forms exemplified by environmental art and those that simulate everyday life. Whether conventional or revolutionary, art, by its very definition, belongs to and is governed by the agreement, expectation, and convention of the artworld. This is the case even with art objects whose *raison d'être* consists of the challenge to, or denial of, the artworld conventions. As such, these works still exist in an art-historical context and cannot but participate in the artworld. Their very subversiveness, novelty, or irony is possible *only if* they are interpreted within the context of the prevailing practice of the artworld. In contrast, although non-art objects can be expressive of various ideas,

---

[54] I will pursue such aesthetic manifestations of moral virtues in Chapter V.

values, and qualities (as I will discuss in the rest of the book), they cannot make an "artistic statement" the way that works of art do. Agnes Denes's *Wheatfield* is entirely different from the equivalent wheatfield cultivated by a Midwestern farmer. Its subtitle, "*Confrontation*," is important as it refers to the self-subsisting activity of supplying food source carried out at the most expensive real estate in the world in the shadow of the then-standing World Trade Center twin towers that symbolized globalization of commerce. Joseph Beuys's tree planting performance/activism also differs from other green projects carried out by cities and towns. Though sharing the same farming or planting practice, the resultant landscape, and the care for the environment, Denes's and Beuys's activities, situated at the forefront of the artworld, also carry the connotation of defiance, subversiveness, and unorthodoxy, features which are absent from the farmers' and city workers' identical activities. The significance of eating Thai curry in a museum gallery is also necessarily different from that of eating the same curry in a Thai restaurant or a museum cafeteria. With the former, we cannot but become self-conscious of the fact that we are engaging in a rather un-museum-like activity, which dominates our experience, making the actual taste of the curry not its focus, which *is* the most important dimension of our experience of eating in a restaurant. We are also compelled to reflect critically upon the importance of the mundane and its place in the artworld, which will not happen in the Thai restaurant unless under a very unusual circumstance. So, even when the artwork shares a number of important aesthetic characteristics with non-art objects or activities, an equally significant distinction keeps them separate.

Secondly, by being created outside the museum walls, many recent artworks do make a conscious effort to encourage participation by those who are generally not familiar with the goings-on in the artworld. For example, Christo's *Running Fence* and *Umbrella Project* mobilized the helping hands of area ranchers and village people. His recent installation of orange curtains in New York City's Central Park, *Gates*, was made possible by a number of volunteers, and experienced by numerous people, both residents of the City and the tourists, in their stroll through the park. Guyton's piece involves the passers-by and nearby residents in the debate about what to do about this "eyesore"—to bulldoze the whole thing or to memorialize and preserve it. However, the *art-hood* of these pieces can best be understood and appreciated by those who are familiar with the artworld, many of who are culturally sophisticated and economically privileged. A farmer may not have knowledge of, access to, or interest in the contemporary artworld. So, he may not be in the position to understand and appreciate fully the artistic meaning behind Denes's *Wheatfield*. But I do not think that there is any denying that he has a rich aesthetic life while working in, on, and with his wheatfield. Though it is rarely articulated, Yi-Fu Tuan points out that "the working farmer does not frame nature into pretty pictures, but he can be profoundly aware of its beauty."[55] The same farmer also encounters numerous opportunities for having an aesthetic experience, making an aesthetic judgment, or acting so as to satisfy his aesthetic inclinations, as he negotiates his daily life by eating, clothing, dwelling, cleaning, working, and dealing with the environment and the fellow community members. Similarly, a Detroit resident not familiar with the history of assemblage art or protest art may condemn Guyton's piece as an embarrassing eyesore disturbing the whole neighborhood. We may be tempted to dismiss such resident's reaction as typical of someone who doesn't understand art, and we may believe that if he were to be educated in the vocabulary of the artworld he may change his mind. However, his negative reaction, which we share in our everyday-life-mode, but not in the artworld-mode, regarding a dilapidated and depressed neighborhood, cannot be dismissed as being uneducated, unsophisticated, and uninformed. No matter how unenlightened, such a reaction *is* still a part, indeed an important part, of our aesthetic life. The Midwestern farmer's and the Detroit resident's experiences are universal, regardless of the existence of an artworld in a particular society and one's participation in it. It seems misleading and unproductive to analyze these kinds of aesthetic experiences deeply rooted and embedded in our workaday existence by applying the model derived from the experience of art, even unconventional ones proximating our daily life.

[55] Yi-Fu Tuan, *Topophilia: A Study of Environmental Perception, Attitudes, and Values* (Englewood Cliffs: Prentice-Hall, 1974), p. 97. Lucy Lippard makes a similar observation about the often unarticulated, yet prevalent, aesthetic experience felt by farmers: "the feeling of farmers and farm workers, who directly experience the land, are rarely articulated from the inside" (*The Lure of the Local: Senses of Place in a Multicultural Society* (New York: The New Press, 1997), p. 141). The same point is also made by a twentieth-century Japanese ethnologist, Yanagita Kunio, who states that "though the farmers clearly experience the beauty of the soybean field, they do not have a need to describe this experience in detail because their whole community shares this feeling in the first place," often expressed in songs to accompany work and folklore. (*Mame no Ha to Taiyō* (*Leaves of Beans and the Sun*) (Tokyo: Sōgensha, 1942), p. 5, my translation.)

As for the tea ceremony, while consisting of the most mundane activities, there is an inherent paradox. A "ceremonious" occasion to savor mundane activities isolates them from the flow of everyday life and environment. First, the tea ceremony literally takes place in a special place, tea hut, surrounded by a tea garden, which functions as a shield from the hustle bustle of daily activities happening right outside. Even when the ceremony takes place in the midst of a metropolis like Kyoto, the process of walking through several gates in the garden and washing one's hands and mouth in the water basin for "purification" contributes to transcending, even for a short while, the worldly activities and concerns.[56] Secondly, the mundane acts involved in the ceremony are highly stylized to express the beauty of economized bodily movement. Thirdly, the extreme care given to the minutest details of the ceremony to achieve the aesthetically appreciable result makes the whole occurrence not our everyday affair in which such fussiness rarely takes place. This ranges from the way in which the host arranges the charcoal in the hearth and the mathematical precision required for the placement of each implement on *tatami* mats (referred to as *kanewari*), to the attention required of the guests to the way in which the wet kettle surface dries with the heat and the scale-like texture toward the bottom of a tea bowl resulting from the insufficient heat when it was fired in the kiln. As a result, during the ceremony, one becomes self-conscious of the mundane quality of the activity and objects, rendering the experience of drinking tea and eating a snack as something special and memorable, standing out from the everyday flow. Although this art form celebrates the mundane, it does so by creating a special setting and occasion for us to contemplate and savor the ordinary.

The same applies to Tiravanija's work. In this case, despite the lack of any special implements or stylized bodily movements as in the case of the tea ceremony, the disconnect from everyday life is paradoxically even more marked, precisely because this mundane activity takes place in the museum gallery, which is heavily invested with conventional agreements (no touching, no eating). Whether or not it is the focus or point of this piece, the initial disorientation we cannot but feel dominates the experience of this piece, and we are made even more aware of the difference between

---

[56] Horst Hammitzsch summarizes the atmosphere of tea gardens as "far from the world!" *Zen in the Art of the Tea Ceremony*, tr. from German by Peter Lemesurier (New York: E. P. Dutton, 1988), p. 85.

our eating experience as a part of a work of art and our everyday eating experience. As Arto Haapala points out, "in the context of art the everyday loses its everydayness: it becomes something extraordinary," and because of that, even with the proliferation of art that uses everyday objects and activities as its theme or content, "all this has contributed to the neglect of the aesthetics of the everyday."[57]

Finally, the ultimate paradox of contemporary art that appropriates, emulates, or aspires to be integrated with the everyday is this. As long as the artists maintain their status as artists and the works' distinction as art, the everyday-ness that they try to capture eludes their works. Their artistic intent of integrating art and life must somehow be communicated to "the audience," the most effective vehicle of which in today's artworld is art criticism, gallery announcement, art books, and documentary film. That is, the existence and survival of such art works *qua art* require publicity using the artworld vocabulary and framework. Otherwise, people will not know that tree-planting projects and derelict houses are works of art. Such is not the case with everyday objects and occurrences. It is true that the economic survival of a Thai restaurant may depend upon a good review by a food critic and the civic participation in tree planting certainly requires advance publicity. However, the food critic's review addresses the quality of food and a local newspaper simply advertises the forthcoming tree-planting project. Neither bestows any special status, other than the fact that the food is good and the tree planting will provide a good opportunity for fulfilling civic duty and environmental responsibility. In the case of art, in addition to such information, the most important message that must be communicated is that eating Thai curry or tree planting constitutes *a work of art*, implying that such artistic status somehow elevates the significance of those activities out of the mundane to something special and privileged. The artist (or the critic) has to announce that it is a work of art, though it is just like, or a slice of, everyday life. This to me poses an inescapable dilemma for the artists trying to capture the everyday in some way.[58]

---

[57] Arto Haapala, "On the Aesthetics of the Everyday: Familiarity, Strangeness, and the Meaning of Place," included in Light and Smith, p. 51.

[58] I thank Larry Shiner for suggesting the point of this paragraph. The same kind of dilemma plagues many environmental art projects that are integrated with various pragmatic concerns, such as environmental, political, and scientific. For example, NEA funding was initially denied to Mel Chin's *Revival Field*, a project to clean up a toxic site with the use of plants, because the committee failed to see how it is art and not simply a science project. Many other projects, such as Betty Beaumont's *Ocean*

When taking place in an everyday setting or illuminating an everyday activity, art may certainly change our attitude toward our everyday life by highlighting the special qualities of the mundane, or in the words of E. H. Gombrich, "the marvels of everyday vision."[59] How could anyone not see the landscape of rolling hills differently after their contour was accentuated by Christo's white curtain? How can we not derive a special joy and wonder when making a snowball after seeing Goldsworthy's works? And how can we not savor the seemingly innocuous cup of tea once we participate in a tea ceremony? Though characteristically overstated, Oscar Wilde's dictum that nature and life imitate art contains truth,[60] and these more recent and non-Western art forms that I have discussed confirm his claim more effectively than Turner's paintings and the realists' novels that Wilde cites. So, there is no denying that various art objects help us attend to our everyday life aesthetically, making our aesthetic life richer.

However, I maintain that the content of our aesthetic life is even more diverse and multifaceted than what can be captured by art-centered aesthetics, even with an expanded scope. The aesthetic dimension of our life which is deeply embedded in our everyday affairs, while it can be influenced by art, operates quite independently from our experience of art. Virginia Postrel cautions us that "while 'art' can certainly be a meaningful category, it can also be deceptive, forcing sensory value into a transcendent ghetto *separated from the rest of life*."[61] The civic act of tree-planting, the appreciation of wetland reclamation, and the pleasure of having tea during my break from work or sharing a Thai curry with good friends at a restaurant are different from Beuys's project, Johanson's creation, the Japanese tea ceremony, and Tiravanija's work, because with the latter we cannot but be conscious of our participation in an art work, and its artistic import within the respective art practice and history. Art, whatever its designation, no matter how inclusive that notion becomes, and even when its intent is to blur the distinction from life, is necessarily characterized as an *exception to* or *commentary on* everyday objects and affairs. As such, accounting for the

---

Landmark, is inaccessible because it exists at the bottom of the ocean, hence requiring documentation by divers.

[59] Cited by Jeremy Coote, in Coote, p. 245.

[60] Oscar Wilde, *The Decay of Lying*, first published in 1889, included in *Critical Theory since Plato*, ed. Hazard Adams (New York: Harcourt Brace Jovanovich, 1971): 672–86.

[61] Postrel, p. xiii, emphasis added.

nature of aesthetic object and experience in general by applying the model of art experience thus remains inadequate and misleading.[62]

e. Obliteration of the concept of art   At this point, we may consider those cultural traditions which do not provide a special place or status for art because every facet of life is conducted with artistic sensibility. In such cultures, everyone is an artist and every activity is an artistic activity in the sense that it is practiced with utmost care, skillful execution, and in pursuit of excellence and beauty. As Arnold Berleant points out, "the custom of selecting an art object and isolating it from its surrounding ... has been ... most pronounced since the eighteenth century, with its aesthetic of disinterestedness. Yet it is at variance with the ubiquity of the aesthetic recognized at other times in the West and commonly in non-Western cultures."[63] For example, Melvin Rader and Bertram Jessup point out that the Balinese have a saying: "We have no art, we do everything the best way we can."[64] Or, according to Gary Witherspoon, "nearly all Navajos are artists and spend a large part of their time in artistic creation," and "Navajo artists integrate their artistic endeavor into their other activities," because "art is a way of living."[65] Similarly, Victor Papanek, a designer himself, praises the Inuit people as the world's best designers because, just like the Balinese and the Navajos, everybody is an artist in the sense that "a man should do all things properly."[66] Finally, the Japanese court culture during Heian period (794–1185) exemplifies aestheticism regarding everyday objects, phenomena, and activities beyond what can be identified as art. Dubbed "the cult of beauty," aesthetic concerns extended to letter

---

[62] By the same token, Carolyn Korsmeyer pointed out that transferring the aesthetic properties of the everyday to art is also misleading. For example, the properties of being fertile and productive applicable to the farmer's wheat field are not straightforwardly transferable to Denes's piece, even if it is indeed productive. Because of the political sub-text of her work, the artistic quality will be something like "low-tech and local productivity defiantly self-assertive in the shadow of hi-tech globalization." Furthermore, as the ensuing debate over Guyton's project indicates, while a derelict house that resulted from total neglect and poverty is aptly characterized as an "eyesore," if it is a work of art, as his piece is, it is questionable whether this characterization (without any qualification) will be appropriate and faithful to its artistic integrity.

[63] Arnold Berleant, *The Aesthetics of Environment* (Philadelphia: Temple University Press, 1992), p. 157.

[64] Melvin Rader and Bertram Jessup, *Art and Human Values* (Englewood Cliffs: Prentice-Hall, 1976), p. 116.

[65] Gary Witherspoon, "Navajo Aesthetics: Beautifying the World through Art," included in Higgins, p. 737.

[66] Papanek, p. 233.

writing, color combination of many layers of kimono and how to show its bottom from behind a screen, and the manner of bidding farewell after a night of love-making.[67]

If we were to enlarge the domain of art to include these cultural practices, it essentially amounts to abandoning the art-centered aesthetics that I have been reviewing. If everyone is an artist and everything is art, then those features which characterize art, whether of paradigmatic Western art or including contemporary Western art and non-Western cultural practices, will lose relevance because there will be no distinction between art and non-art. This will signal the demise of art-centered aesthetics. It may be the case that some of the aforementioned art works that simulate our everyday life indicate the artworld's aspiration to move our society closer to those cultural practices.

Now, I certainly welcome and endorse widening our scope of aesthetics by adopting a multi-cultural and global mode of exploration. Exposing ourselves to cultural practices and values different from what we have been accustomed to and taken for granted helps us realize the parochial nature of the modern Western notion of art and of the institutions of the artworld. However, the problem with examining our (contemporary Western) aesthetic life with the help of anthropologists' and historians' accounts of those aesthetic practices unfamiliar to us is that it gives an impression that the only way to acknowledge our multifaceted aesthetic life is to assimilate or proximate those unfamiliar cultural or historical traditions. It appears to imply that the everyday dimension of aesthetics thoroughly integrated with the flow of workaday activities is either unnoticeable or absent from our life *until* or *unless* we adopt a different cultural perspective. But, our aesthetic life in the everyday context is *already* rich and familiar to us. I do not think that we need to exoticize its content; nor should we have to become experts in Balinese, Navajo, Inuit, or Heian traditions or adopt their worldviews in order to investigate the heretofore neglected aspects of our everyday aesthetic life. Instead, I suggest that we acknowledge the already diverse and rich dimensions of our aesthetic life and the fact that we

---

[67] The term "cult of beauty" is taken from Ivan Morris's discussion in *The World of the Shining Prince: Court Life in Ancient Japan* (New York: Kodansha International, 1994). For the best original source of the Heian aesthetic sensibility, see *The Pillow Book of Sei Shōnagon*, written toward the end of the tenth century, ed. and tr. Ivan Morris (Harmondsworth: Penguin Books, 1982). I shall explore this aesthetic sensibility further in Chapter V.

have not unearthed those treasures because of our persistent adherence to art-centered aesthetics. We need to grant and respect the independence of those wider aesthetic aspects from art-relevant considerations and examine their content on their own terms.

2. Special experience-based aesthetics

i. Aesthetic attitude and aesthetic experience

The limited scope of art-centered aesthetics which takes art works as the model for the aesthetic object may suggest that it is much more promising to start with our attitude and experience in exploring difference facets of our aesthetic life. After all, those who hold the aesthetic attitude theory are also the ones most vocal about the ubiquity of what can be an aesthetic object. Whether proposed as a distinct attitude on our part, such as distancing or disinterestedness, or a special experience referred to as an aesthetic experience, the core of aesthetics, according to this alternative, consists of features of our experience rather than of objects.

I believe that most of us have had an aesthetic experience through adopting a disinterested attitude when attending (properly) to a paradigmatic art, or through some unexpected, dramatic break from our humdrum experience facilitated by what Edward Bullough would describe as "distancing."[68] I have had my share of experiences akin to the boat passenger's experience of the fog at sea Bullough relates, leaving an indelible mark on my memory, and I believe that I am not unique in this regard. Although it happened when I was a young child, I still remember the breathtaking view of Bihoro Pass in the Akan National Park located in Hokkaidō, the northern island of Japan, when its wide vista of green hills dotted with evergreens extending downward suddenly appeared after a long bus ride through a series of mountains. Before the vista opened up, I was tired of the bus ride, perhaps a little car sick or hungry, thinking about when we are going to get to the hotel, but the opening up of this spectacular landscape made me forget all of this. Another unforgettable experience concerns the feeling of being struck by a kind of lightning when I first

---

[68] Edward Bullough, "'Psychical Distance' as a Factor in Art and an Aesthetic Principle," *The British Journal of Psychology* 5 (1912–13): 87–118.

heard a Brahms intermezzo at my piano teacher's studio as a high school student while waiting anxiously for my lesson; it was like falling in love at first (sight) sound. In both cases, I would describe my experience as "out of gear" from the normal consciousness and being transported to another dimension, where nothing but the view or the melody mattered. It stood out, separated from what went before and after.

John Dewey would most likely describe each experience as "having *an* experience," because each formed a sort of self-contained unit, "demarcated ... from other experiences," "complete in itself; standing out because marked out from what went before and what came after."[69] Within this unit of experience, each moment leads to the next without any distraction or dispersion, cohering as a completed whole with "unity ... constituted by a single *quality* that pervades the entire experience in spite of the variation of its constituent parts."[70]

Bullough's notion of distancing and Dewey's notion of "an" experience are normally not regarded together; if anything, Dewey's view can be taken as a challenge to disinterested or distancing attitude theory because he did not believe that the aesthetic and the practical were mutually exclusive. However, I am treating their theories as comparable insofar as they both distinguish an aesthetic experience from non-aesthetic experiences by the features of the experience itself, not by its object. After all, Bullough's model example is fog experienced as a boat passenger and Dewey's examples are dominated by mundane events and activities, such as eating a meal, conducting a job interview, or solving a math problem. In this regard, both views account for a wider range of aesthetics than art-centered aesthetics.

However, I maintain that their views are also still too restrictive. What is common to these theories is that the aesthetic (qua experience) is something which contrasts with the humdrum of everyday experience. For Dewey, such "humdrum" and "slackness of loose ends" are "the enemies of the esthetic."[71] Against such a background, the aesthetic experience is described as a kind of encapsulated unit that is hermetically sealed off from our ordinary engagement with daily life. Bullough characterizes it as "a momentary switching on of some new current," or "the cutting-out of the practical sides of things and of our practical attitude to them."[72] Just as art

---

[69] Dewey, pp. 35 and 36.   [70] Ibid. p. 37.
[71] Ibid. p. 40.   [72] Bullough, both from p. 89.

is necessarily defined as an *exception* to the everyday objects, the aesthetic experience conceived as a special experience is also an *exception* to the everyday experience, according to these views.

ii. Limitation of special experience-based aesthetics

While not denying the existence or importance of aesthetic experiences which stand out from our everyday affairs, I do not believe that they can fully and adequately account for many aspects of our aesthetic life. One reason is that these experiences are distinguished from other kinds of experiences by their infrequency. The following description of a distanced experience by Bullough implies that these experiences are few and far between:

This distanced view of things is *not*, and *cannot be*, our *normal* outlook. *As a rule*, experiences *constantly* turn the same side towards us, namely, that which has the strongest practical force of appeal. We are *not ordinarily* aware of those aspects of things which do not touch us immediately and practically... The *sudden* view of things from their reverse, usually unnoticed side, comes upon us as a *revelation*...[73]

Similarly, Dewey regards "*an* experience" as a rare occurrence. He characterizes the ordinary, non-aesthetic experience as either "the loose succession that does not begin at any particular place and that ends... at no particular place" or "arrest, constriction, proceeding from parts having only a mechanical connection with one another," and claims that "there exists *so much* of one and the other of these two kinds of experience."[74]

The impression we get from both accounts is that we have to be lucky for an aesthetic experience to occur, but neither of them make clear whether we can succeed in having an aesthetic experience if we consciously and methodically set out to do so. Jean-Paul Sartre, speaking as Roquentin in *Nausea*, probably would deny such a possibility, except in subsequent "recounting" of the experience which we can structure according to a narrative form of organic unity. In addition to the existential revelation about the *raison d'être* of his existence in this world, Roquentin also comes to realize that "there are no adventures—there are no perfect moments,"[75] both similar to the Deweyan aesthetic experience. They

---

[73] Ibid. pp. 89–90, all the emphasis added.   [74] Dewey, p. 40, emphasis added.
[75] Jean-Paul Sartre, *Nausea*, tr. Lloyd Alexander (New York: New Directions, 1969), p. 150.

can be experienced only by telling a story about it, but it cannot happen together with "living."[76] Our ordinary living is humdrum, just as Dewey describes it: "Nothing happens while you live. The scenery changes, people come in and go out, that's all. There are no beginnings. Days are tacked on to days without rhyme or reason, an interminable, monotonous addition."[77] An adventure, on the other hand, is organized with a distinct and necessary order, without requiring an extraordinary event. A perfect moment, which Roquentin and his former girlfriend try to create without success, is where "there are certain acts which *have to be* done, certain attitudes to be taken, words which *must* be said—and other attitudes, other words are strictly prohibited."[78] In short, it is like "a work of art," which for Roquentin is an organic unity governed by internal necessity.[79]

We may not want to go so far as Sartre in denying the possibility of having an aesthetic experience while undergoing the actual experience, but the account given by the aesthetic attitude theorists and aesthetic experience theorists certainly indicates that an aesthetic experience is a rarified occasion and occupies only a small, though memorable, portion of our life. Part of the reason may be that, for those aesthetic attitude or experience theorists, a special aesthetic experience results from *successful achievement*, brought about by the object and our interaction with it.

However, what about the cases in which we *fail* to achieve such a special experience due to some facts about the object or our response, or both? Or, more importantly for my purpose, what about those cases in which we form an opinion, make a decision, or engage in an action guided by aesthetic considerations without invoking any special experience? For example, most of us attend to our personal appearance almost daily: choosing what to wear and what sort of haircut to get, cleaning and ironing clothes, and deciding whether or not to dye our hair or try some kind of "aesthetic rejuvenation" treatment or body decoration. These decisions and actions are primarily, if not exclusively, guided by

---

[76] Cf. "for the most banal event to become an adventure, you must (and this is enough) begin to recount it. This is what fools people: a man is always a teller of tales, he lives surrounded by his stories and the stories of others, he sees everything that happens to him through them; and he tries to live his own life as if he were telling a story. But you have to choose: live or tell." (Ibid. p. 39)

[77] Ibid.   [78] Ibid. p. 148, all the emphasis added.

[79] Ibid. Roquentin's model for a work of art with organic unity is an old rag-time with a vocal refrain in which each note and the order among them are governed by necessity and inevitability (see pp. 21–2 for his description of this music).

aesthetic considerations.[80] We also involve aesthetic considerations when dealing with our possessions. In addition to economics and functionality, aesthetics often plays a crucial role in our purchasing decisions. Furthermore, aesthetic judgments guide us when choosing the paint color for the house, planting flowers in the yard, cleaning and tidying rooms, removing rust spots from the car and painting them over, maintaining a weeds-free, velvety-smooth, uniformly mowed lawn, replacing shabby-looking drapes, and reupholstering a threadbare couch.[81] Finally, beyond personal decisions, as citizens, we find ourselves forming opinions on societal debates primarily based upon aesthetic reasoning. Examples range from supporting the rehabilitation of a brownfield, criticizing the design of a proposed building, opposing the construction of a wind farm or a cell phone tower, to condemning graffiti while welcoming a mural and objecting to the appearance and location of a billboard.[82]

I believe these examples are quite familiar to most of us. However, many of us, even aestheticians among us, seldom stop and reflect upon the aesthetic reasons and concerns behind these decision and actions. Besides the fact these experiences have nothing to do with art, another reason for their relative neglect is that they normally do not engender a special,

[80] Besides aesthetic considerations, our decisions regarding these items may be motivated by non-aesthetic reasons, such as health and hygiene. The irony is that sometimes aesthetic interests can jeopardize health issues, as in some cases of "rejuvenation" treatment provided by plastic surgery, and body decoration, such as body piercing, tanning, and tattooing. The ultimate consideration guiding decisions regarding personal appearance may be self-expression or desire to impress or shock others, but that does not make the decisions non-aesthetic because such desire is carried out *through aesthetic means*.

[81] Carolyn Korsmeyer questioned whether the reasons for these decisions may not be extra-aesthetic. It is true that I may maintain a nice-looking lawn to impress my neighbors, ensure the property value of my house, or avoid being fined for violating the town ordinance that dictates the length of the grass. I may also remove rust spots from my car because I am worried that, if left untreated, they may eventually eat away the body of the car or because I want to whip the car into shape before selling it as a used car. So, there can be a number of diverse non-aesthetic immediate motivations that prompt me into certain decisions and actions. However, what is important for my purpose is that these issues all stem from the aesthetic response, whether of a prospective buyer, a neighbor, or a town official, regarding the sensuous appearance of the "messy" yard and "shabby-looking" car.

[82] In a recent report on the town of East Greenwich, RI, town officials successfully combated vulgar graffiti by inviting those "graffiti artists" to paint something artistic instead. To everyone's amazement, the resultant artistic spray-painted "graffiti" were never defaced (Andrew C. Helman, "E. Greenwich is Fighting Graffiti with Art," *Providence Journal*, 3 August 2003). It is true that these debates often involve non-aesthetic issues as well, such as economic development, environmental impact, reduction of crime, and safety issues. My point regarding these examples is not that the debates are exclusively about aesthetic matters but rather aesthetic issues are one of the important ingredients of these debates. A good discussion of these aesthetic issues on the societal level can be found in *Aesthetics, Community Character, and the Law* by Christopher J. Duerksen and R. Matthew Goebel (Chicago: American Planning Association, 1999).

distinct experience disconnected from, and standing out from, our everyday affairs; hence, they generally lack memorable presence or lofty intellectual, emotional, or spiritual enlightenment. As a result, they tend to disappear from the aesthetic radar that has been calibrated to capture those special, standout experiences.

iii. *Everyday life ordinarily experienced*

But, are there good reasons for excluding this aspect of aesthetic life thoroughly integrated with everyday life from serious examination? Does the fact that it does not normally involve special aesthetic experience make it unworthy of investigation?

From a psychological point of view, it is understandable that we attend more readily to those events, occasions, and experiences that stand out from the familiar and ordinary, and neglect the daily humdrum with its commonplace, ordinary, mundane, and routine character. This discrimination against the ordinary and inconspicuous is all-too-familiar. Consider, for example, the two approaches to history. One is more familiar to many of us: the great man theory of history which constructs a narrative out of what is usually regarded as the movers and shakers of history, such as kings, emperors, and generals, and landmark events, such as battles, the birth of a nation, and the promulgation of a law. For many of us, this is the kind of narrative we recognize and are taught as history. This approach of weaving a historical account by concentrating only on the mountain peaks, however, tends to ignore the valleys and foothills that support and give rise to mountain tops.[83] So the alternative approach, often provided to supplement the great man account of history, is to focus instead on things like material culture, vernacular history, and common folks' lives.[84] In fact, Judy Attfield defines "the everyday" as

---

[83] It is interesting to note that Dewey uses the mountain metaphor in describing his task of re-integrating art into our life: "This task is to restore continuity between the refined and intensified forms of experience that are works of art and the everyday events, doings, and sufferings that are universally recognized to constitute experience. *Mountain peaks do not float unsupported.*" (Dewey, p. 3, emphasis added.)

[84] A noted Japanese ethnologist, Yanagita Kunio (1875–1962), championed the notion of *jōmin*, common folks or ordinary people, by calling attention to the often-unrecognized contributions their everyday life makes to the direction of history. What is interesting about his theory for our purpose is that he also emphasizes the importance of common folks' experience and appreciation of their workaday landscape, which is often eclipsed by the mainstream, artistic appreciation of scenic landscapes.

"that which does not get recorded in the history made up of important 'events.' "[85]

Our landscape appreciation also offers an example of the dramatic eclipsing the ordinary and the everyday. We are surrounded by some kind of landscape all the time, ranging from our yard, the streets around us, a shopping mall with a huge parking lot around it, office buildings facing concrete pavement, to the beach we walk on during our evening walk and the salt marsh which buffers the sandy beach from the road. However, more often than not, landscape "evokes images of snow-capped mountains and waves beating on a rock-bound coast," or "amusing-looking rocks and picturesque scenery formed by natural processes such as volcanic and water activities and weather conditions."[86] The quintessential examples of "landscape" are scenic, natural landscapes typified by early national parks in the United States or designated scenic sites in the Japanese tradition.[87] Celebrated by various arts and advertised for promoting tourism, those scenic wonders garner our attention and interest, despite the fact, as Arnold Berleant reminds us, "these temples of nature are rarely a part of the ordinary landscape of daily life … For most people, the lived, the living landscape is the commonplace setting of everyday life."[88]

Thus, whether regarding history, landscape, objects, or experiences, the ordinary and mundane that are often overlooked need to receive equal attention as the dramatic and extraordinary. One strategy to promote such attention is to render "the familiar" strange, to borrow Arto Haapala's terms (although he himself is at best ambivalent about this strategy). According to him, "strangeness creates a basis for sensitive aesthetic appreciation" and "art is presented in contexts that create strangeness, and the tendency in aesthetics has been to maximize strangeness and to minimize familiarity."[89] This is true of art that represents or deals with a slice of everyday life, such

---

[85] Judy Attfield, *Wild Things: The Material Culture of Everyday Life* (Oxford: Berg, 2000), p. 50.

[86] The first passage is from Peirce F. Lewis, "Axioms for Reading the Landscape," in *The Interpretation of Ordinary Landscapes*, ed. D. W. Meinig (New York: Oxford University Press, 1979), p. 12. The second is from Satō Kenji, *Fūkei no Seisan, Fūkei no Kaihō: Media no Arukeorogī* (*Construction of Landscape, Liberation of Landscape: Archaeology of Media*) (Tokyo: Kōdansha, 1994), p. 169, my translation.

[87] I explored the three scenic landscapes of Japan in "Scenic National Landscapes: Common Themes in Japan and the United States," *Essays in Philosophy* 3:1 (January 2002).

[88] Arnold Berleant, *Living in the Landscape: Toward an Aesthetics of Environment* (Lawrence: The University Press of Kansas, 1997), p. 16.

[89] Haapala, p. 50.

as the street photography of Cartier-Bresson, cited by Haapala, and Aaron Siskind's close-up photographs of peeling paint and stained walls.

This strategy of sharpening our aesthetic sensibility by experiencing aspects of the everyday as "strange" or "special" is quite prevalent outside art and aesthetics discourses as well. For example, Yi-Fu Tuan, a cultural geographer, observes "how rarely we attend to the world aesthetically," though "alert individuals do, glancingly, during the pauses and among the interstices of practical life."[90] Such alertness affords us small aesthetic pleasures in the midst of everyday life:

> When I vacuum the carpet and create neat swathes of flattened fibers, when I look at a cleanly typed page, when the plowman strives to produce a straight furrow or the carpenter looks at the joints in his woodwork with a sense of pride, there is necessarily an aesthetic tinge to the satisfaction. All these activities are attempts to maintain or create small fields of order and meaning, temporary stays against fuzziness and chaos, which can be viewed, however fleetingly, *with the pleasure of an artist.*

I do agree that a part of the goal of everyday aesthetics is to illuminate the ordinarily neglected, but gem-like, aesthetic potentials hidden behind the trivial, mundane, and commonplace facade, and I explore some of them in the subsequent chapters. However, by making the ordinary extraordinary and rendering the familiar strange, while we gain aesthetic experiences thus made possible, we also pay the price by compromising the very everyday-ness of the everyday. Haapala acknowledges this paradox by observing that "ordinary everyday objects lack the surprise element or freshness of the strange, nevertheless they give us pleasure through a kind of comforting stability," and that "the aesthetics of everyday familiar surroundings and the aesthetics of the strange have their own roles in human life."[91] However, even with this recognition, Haapala still seems to be wedded to defining the aesthetic as something pleasurable, as he goes on to claim that "we should simply become more aware of the pleasurable aspects of the everyday without making them objects of aesthetic appreciation in the traditional sense."

If nurturing this awareness of the neglected, but familiar, aesthetic gems of everyday life is an important mission of everyday aesthetics, which

---

[90] Yi-Fu Tuan, *Passing Strange and Wonderful: Aesthetics, Nature, and Culture* (Washington, D. C.: Island Press, 1993), p. 101. The next passage is from p. 100, emphasis added.

[91] Haapala, pp. 50 and 51. The next passage is from p. 52.

I believe it is, I also believe that it is equally important to illuminate those dimensions of our everyday aesthetic life that normally do not lead to a memorable, standout, pleasurable aesthetic experience *in their normal experiential context*. Our usual reaction to dilapidated buildings, rusted cars, or dirty linens is to deplore their appearance, prompting us to repair, clean, or discard them, in the absence of some other overriding considerations. Such reactions are primarily, if not exclusively, *aesthetic* reactions. As Judy Attfield argues, everyday aesthetics should not be equated with bringing "low" or "pop" culture into a critical discourse. "Everyday things have nothing to do with the 'low' aesthetic of 'high/low' culture that has allowed the popular to infiltrate the prestigious art gallery in order to affiliate it to art."[92] Instead, "what happens in the commonplace is mainly a matter of common sense. Such activities can be thought of as trivial but they do constitute independent acts and as such represent a significant part of the make-up of the everyday world—the commonplace." In this regard, while I agree with Paul Duncum's "case for an art education of everyday aesthetic experience," I don't think he goes far enough, as his notion of the "characteristic sites of everyday aesthetics include environments such as theme parks, shopping malls, city streetscapes, and tourist attractions, as well as mass media images especially on television and now on computer screens."[93] These sites certainly constitute an important part of our everyday aesthetics, but many are still primarily environments that we "visit" and the images that we behold, rather than those environments and objects with which we work or live every day in the most literal sense. With the emphasis on a special aesthetic experience as a defining feature of our aesthetic life, even including those things from "low" or "popular" culture, I am afraid we still neglect the kind of experience that is all-too-familiar to most of us. In this regard, I agree with the following observation by Tom Leddy:

It would seem that we need to make some sort of distinction between the aesthetics of everyday life ordinarily experienced and the aesthetics of everyday life extraordinarily experienced. However, any attempt to increase the aesthetic intensity of our ordinary everyday life-experiences will tend to push those experiences in the direction of the extraordinary. One can only conclude that there is a tension within the very concept of the aesthetics of everyday life.[94]

---

[92] Attfield, pp. 50–51. The next passage is from p. 89.   [93] Duncum, p. 295.
[94] Leddy, p. 18.

This tension he speaks of, however, can be partly resolved if we pay attention to our typical aesthetic response to everyday objects and phenomena, such as eyesores, which often prompts a certain decision or action. My point is that this kind of experience is as much a part of our aesthetic life as a special standout, extraordinary, "strange" experience.

But why is it so important, if it is indeed important as I believe, to attend to ordinary objects and environments "ordinarily experienced"? Is such an investigation valuable for its own sake? One of the main theses of this book is that such seemingly trivial, innocuous, ordinary, mundane, or even frivolous aspects of our aesthetic life do have surprisingly serious, pragmatic consequences: environmental, moral, social, political, and existential. For example, as I will explore in the next chapter, our relative neglect of workaday environments in favor of remote, dramatic, scenic environments does have dire consequences, because people's attitude and societal policies regarding protection of landscape are significantly affected, sometimes determined, by such aesthetic considerations. Furthermore, everyday environments and objects with which we interact every day cannot but exert substantial impact on our lives. As Berleant reminds us, "how we engage with the prosaic landscapes of home, work, local travel, and recreation is an important measure of the quality of our lives."[95]

I am in no way minimizing the profound effect art and special aesthetic experience can have on our lives. Nor am I denying the value and importance of examining their nature, as traditional aesthetic theories have done. What I do find problematic is to allow the significance of the dramatic aesthetic experience to eclipse the other aspects of our aesthetic engagement with the world and life. By neglecting the other aspects of our aesthetic life which is embedded in our everyday judgments, decisions, and actions, we lose not only the opportunity for enriching the dimension of aesthetic inquiry, but also the potential for improving the quality of life and the world. Hence, I am proposing to steer the aesthetic inquiry away from the art-centered and special, experience-oriented approaches that have dominated the modern Western aesthetic discourse. I am not invalidating those approaches, but rather supplementing them; I want to be faithful to the diverse ways in which we engage with the diverse aspects of the world aesthetically. I believe that we have more to gain by

---

[95] Berleant, *Living in the Landscape*, p. 16

recognizing and appreciating the diversity within our aesthetic life than applying a mono-theory of art-centered aesthetics or special experience-oriented theory to different aspects of our aesthetic life. That is, by analyzing our aesthetic experiences outside art on their own terms rather than as proximate or "wannabe" art experiences, we can unearth a wealth of aesthetic issues that are not shared by, or relevant to, our experience of art. Similarly, by exploring the mundane everyday judgments and actions motivated by seemingly trivial aesthetic preferences, we can come to appreciate the ways in which our lives and the world are profoundly affected by aesthetic concerns, different from the way in which art or memorable aesthetic experiences exert their impact on our lives and the world.

For the rest of the book, I will explore some of the aesthetic judgments that we often make in our daily lives, many of which affect our worldviews, society, and the world. I will illustrate how those seemingly insignificant everyday aesthetic preferences and decisions can have serious environmental, moral, social, political, and existential implications. The format of investigation is decidedly exploratory, rather than argumentative, because my whole point is to address the dimension of our aesthetic life hitherto neglected in the academic discourse. I want to characterize what follows as a kind of adventure into the most familiar (because it deals with facets of our daily lives), yet very unfamiliar (because it has not received adequate academic attention) territory.

II

Significance of Everyday Aesthetics

In the last chapter, I have argued that everyday aesthetic concerns, preferences, and judgments cannot be adequately captured by either art-based or
by special experience-based aesthetics. One may agree with this, but may
still question the point of pursuing everyday aesthetics, believing that it
concerns rather trivial, insignificant, and innocuous matters, not worthy of
philosophical investigation. So what if we care about stains and wrinkles
on our shirt, personal grooming, and the appearance of our properties and
possessions? Does anything significant follow from these aesthetic matters?
These concerns may at best contribute toward defining our self-image and
personal relationships, but isn't that as far as they go? Don't these reactions
indicate our preoccupation with superficial appearance, rather than with
substantial and more important matters, such as political, moral, and social
issues?

Art, on the other hand, deals with something much more serious and
socially important, according to this line of argument. As characterized by
Virginia Postrel in her discussion of style and substance, this view would
hold that "appearances are not just potentially deceiving but frivolous
and unimportant—that aesthetic value is not real except in those rare
instances when it transcends the quotidian to become high art."[1] Art
sometimes challenges us, changes our worldview, mobilizes us toward
a certain action, nurtures valuable sensibilities like sympathy, generosity,
and respect, and, last but not least, helps move a society in a certain
direction. An aesthetic experience of it is also a complicated affair, unlike
our unreflecting response to the sensuous surface of the objects, typical of

---

[1] Virginia Postrel, *Substance of Style: How the Rise of Aesthetic Value Is Remaking Commerce, Culture, and Consciousness* (New York: HarperCollins, 2003), p. x.

our everyday aesthetic life. It also occupies a special, standout place in our life by providing an enlightening, illuminating, sometimes uplifting and sometimes devastating, insight into self, life, and the world, so that our life is never quite the same after that. But such is not the case with our preoccupation with a green lawn or a wrinkle-free shirt. Or so this argument would go.

I have announced in the last chapter that, while perhaps lacking in the capacity to facilitate an existentially profound insight or experience, and despite the absence of established discourses providing the context for our experience, our everyday aesthetic choices are neither uncomplicated nor insignificant. As I will argue in the next three chapters, once we start unearthing what is involved in seemingly straightforward and simple everyday aesthetic judgments, we realize that there is a surprising degree of complication surrounding them. This chapter will challenge the belief that our everyday aesthetic judgments and decisions are inconsequential. It is quite the contrary, and I will illustrate how everyday aesthetic tastes and attitudes often do lead to consequences which go beyond simply being preoccupied with and fussing with the surface, and that they affect not only our daily life but also the state of the society and the world.

The power of the aesthetic to influence, and sometimes determine, our attitudes and actions has actually been recognized and utilized throughout history and among different cultural traditions. Let me give a few examples. In the Western tradition, Plato was the first to acknowledge this power of the aesthetic, without which his advocacy for censoring arts would not make sense. In the non-Western tradition, we see Confucius as someone who also recognized the way in which both human beings and the society at large are molded by the proper observance of rites and rituals, which consist not only of appropriate behavior but also of music, attire, recitation, and the like. Nazi Germany's promotion of certain music, literature, film, and even vegetation also comes to our mind.[2] Contemporary scholarship on the modern Japanese intellectual history explores the connection between Japanese imperialism and the formation of national aesthetic, leading up to

---

[2] For their systematic program of promoting native species while eliminating alien species (with an eerie analogy to their program with respect to human beings), see Gert Groening and Joachim Wolschke-Bulmahn, "Some Notes on the Mania for Native Plants in Germany," *Landscape Journal* 11:2 (Fall 1992): 116–26.

World War II.[3] This nationalistic aesthetic celebrated not only traditional Japanese arts but also its landscape, including the beauty of cherry blossoms that became a surprisingly potent symbol for war-time nationalism.[4] A more recent example can be found in the photograph of three firefighters raising an American flag in the ruins of the World Trade Center, reminiscent of the famous Iwō-jima photograph. Whatever our particular reaction to this photograph may be, there is no denying that it affected all of us deeply, along with other images of this catastrophe we could not help but witness. Its photographer, Thomas E. Franklin, himself states: "I've been surprised, all along, that people could react so strongly to a photograph."[5]

In today's style-conscious consumer society, aesthetic considerations often influence our purchasing decisions. As one recent report on the status of design indicates: "Aesthetics now play a greater part in portraying the perceived status of a particular product as functional differences between models are reduced... The visual aspects of design have come to predominate as a means of attracting the consumer."[6] Hence, "style" becomes the crucial factor determining the commercial success of a product. The concern for "style" extends not only to the goods themselves but also the way in which goods are marketed, ranging from their advertisement to the environment in which they are placed, defined by specific lighting, display strategy, color scheme, overall ambience, and even the appearance of the salespeople. This preoccupation with appearance and style extends to the perception of political candidates, such as their hairdo, attire, and gesture, in addition to their qualifications, leadership ability, political platform, and party affiliation.[7]

---

[3] Recent literature on this subject sheds light on the way in which the so-called typically and exclusively Japanese aesthetic values were partly a product of the concerted effort among the nationalistically bent intellectuals to cast the Japanese traditional culture in a superior light. For example, see Yumiko Iida's *Rethinking Identity in Modern Japan: Nationalism as Aesthetics* (London: Routledge, 2002) and Leslie Pincus' *Authenticating Culture in Imperial Japan: Kuki Shūzō and the Rise of National Aesthetics* (Berkeley: University of California Press, 1996).

[4] The most influential book on Japanese landscape that fueled Japanese nationalism is Shiga Shigetaka's *Nihon Fūkeiron* (*Theory of Japanese Landscape*), first published in 1894. I will refer to its significance in Conclusion. As for the significance of the cherry blossoms, I will discuss it in Chapter IV.

[5] "Photographer Says His Life Has Changed since 9/11," *Providence Journal*, 11 September 2002.

[6] Nigel Whiteley, *Design for Society* (London: Reaktion Books, 1993), p. 27.

[7] During the 2004 U. S. Presidential election, *Time* (19 July 2004) ran a tongue-in-cheek comparison of different presidents' and candidates' hair in "Hair to the Chief!" (p. 20), while *Providence Journal* ran an article entitled "The Winner by a Hair" (15 July 2004), as well as "It's Style over Substance: Appearing Presidential is the Goal" (30 September 2004). In addition, particularly among male political candidates, height is also an issue, to the point a shorter candidate (like Michael Dukakis) resorted to a platform behind a podium in a debate setting. Virginia Postrel also describes at length popular press (hence

Those examples suggest that the ways in which aesthetics serves political, social, or commercial purposes have been more or less recognized and sometimes utilized. In contrast, we are less familiar with the power of the aesthetic to affect and sometimes determine the state of the world and the quality of life in ways that do *not* result from a specific program by the government, society, or commercial enterprise. One such example regards the environmental implications of everyday aesthetics.

Environmental ethics, a relatively new but by now firmly established discipline, today examines a wide range of issues: anthropocentrism, the tragedy of the commons mentality, environmental racism, modern Western scientific attitude, rights of non-humans and future generations, to mention only a few. In discussing these issues, reference to aesthetics is typically made with respect to the aesthetic value of nature as pristine and wild, which is then cited as one of the reasons for its protection. This focus on wilderness aesthetics tends to cast any human intervention and creation in a negative light, as "abuse" of nature, an unfortunate consequence lamented by a number of recent critics.[8] It also confines our environmentally relevant aesthetic life to a special experience with nature, a typical subject matter for noted nature writers, such as Henry David Throreau, John Muir, Barry Lopez, and Annie Dillard. This dominance of wilderness aesthetics in environmental discourse consequently eclipses the equally, or even more, crucial significance of our aesthetic reactions to our backyard as well as to everyday objects and activities, which generally do not provide memorable experiences or occasions for reflection. We thus tend to overlook their unexpectedly significant role in affecting, and sometimes determining, our ecological awareness, attitude, and ultimately actions, thus literally transforming the world. They appear trivial, innocent, and insignificant, when in fact they are not.

In this chapter I want to correct this general neglect of environmentally relevant everyday aesthetics. I will first show that our commonly held everyday aesthetic tastes and judgments regarding (1) natural creatures, (2) landscape, and (3) built environment and artifacts have often worked

---

ultimately people's) preoccupation with Hilary Clinton's hairdo and the make-up worn by Katherine Harris, the former Florida Secretary of State who was responsible for overseeing the electoral process that created the controversial outcome of the 2000 presidential election between George W. Bush and Al Gore.

[8] Perhaps the most noted critic is William Cronon for his "The Trouble with Wilderness; or, Getting Back to the Wrong Nature," included in *Uncommon Ground: Rethinking the Human Place in Nature*, ed. William Cronon (New York: W. W. Norton & Company, 1996).

against, rather than in support of, environmental values. This does not result from any consciously formulated agenda, unlike in the case of political or commercial utilization of the aesthetic that I mentioned before. It is rather derived from the lack of awareness on our part as to the environmental consequences of our everyday aesthetic tastes and judgments. The fact that everyday aesthetics has had generally negative environmental impact, however, also indicates a possibility that the same power of the aesthetic to influence our decisions can be utilized to promote a more positive environmental agenda, and I will delineate the tenets of such green aesthetics in Section 2.

1. The environmental significance of everyday aesthetics

i. Natural creatures

Let me begin with popular aesthetic taste regarding natural creatures. I believe that most people are attracted to creatures which are cute, cuddly, awesome, colorful, or graceful, but not to those that are slimy, nondescript, grotesque, or pesky. Empirical studies confirm this tendency in our aesthetic taste. One cross-cultural study indicates that people's response to various creatures is based upon their "aesthetic appeal, greatly influenced by such considerations as color, shape, movement, and visibility."[9] This accounts for the general liking for large mammals and birds which are considered "aesthetically appealing," but not for invertebrates and reptiles which are regarded as "aesthetically unattractive." Responding to this general preference for cute, awesome, or colorful creatures, one issue of *Time* magazine, which contains both an article on the threatened status of sharks and another on the near extinction of cod off the North Atlantic coast, features a dramatic frontal photograph of a shark, but not of codfish, on its front cover.[10] Similarly, an advertisement for DuPont's double-hulled oil tankers consists of attractive visual images of a dolphin, baby seal, and whale, all presumably representing beneficiaries of those tankers. Even the

---

[9] Stephen R. Kellert, *The Value of Life: Biological Diversity and Human Society* (Washington D.C.: Island Press, 1996), p. 102. The next two phrases are also from p. 102.

[10] *Time*, 11 August 1997.

best nature magazines or publications, one critic points out, invariably feature "those with the most vibrant hues; technicolor flora and fauna in arsenic greens, Titian reds, acid yellows, and shocking pinks."[11]

Popular culture also plays a role in formulating these aesthetic tastes, as pointed out by Marcia Eaton, such as many people's attraction to deer as gentle creatures fostered by the Disney classic, *Bambi*.[12] Furthermore, even among cute and cuddly creatures, another writer observes, we are attracted to "heart-warming pictures of koala, kangaroos, and polar bears teaching their children the wisdom of the wild, roughhousing during leisure moments, rubbing snouts like Eskimos, or fraternizing peacefully with other denizens of the forest primeval, images free of the grotesque business of scavenging for decomposed carrion, disemboweling prey, or mauling the blind, new-born pups of other species."[13]

The size, hence the visibility, of creatures, also matters, confirming Aristotle's insight that an object has to be of a certain size, so that it can be taken in one view, to be aesthetically appreciable.[14] Edward O. Wilson laments that "if human beings were not so impressed by size alone, they would consider an ant more wonderful than a rhinoceros" and points out that "when a valley in Peru or an island in the Pacific is stripped of the last of its native vegetation, ... we are painfully aware (of that tragedy), but what is not *perceived* is that hundreds of invertebrate species also vanish."[15]

These popular aesthetic discriminations may appear to be of no great consequence: so what if we find sharks and rhinos more appealing than cod and ants? Actually a great deal *is* at stake. If we are aesthetically

---

[11] Daniel Harris, *Cute, Quaint, Hungry and Romantic: The Aesthetics of Consumerism* (Cambridge: Da Capo Press, 2000), p. 200.

[12] Marcia Muelder Eaton, *Merit, Aesthetic and Ethical* (Oxford: Oxford University Press, 2001), p. 182.

[13] Harris, pp. 185–6.

[14] Although Aristotle's primary concern is tragedy, as Carolyn Korsmeyer noted, he illustrates the importance of a piece to be of certain length by drawing an analogy to natural creatures: "To be beautiful, a living creature, and every whole made up of parts, must not only present a certain order in its arrangement of parts, but also be of a certain definite magnitude. Beauty is a matter of size and order, and therefore impossible either (1) in a very minute creature, since our perception becomes indistinct as it approaches instantaneity; or (2) in a creature of vast size—one, say, 1,000 miles long—as in that case, instead of the object being seen all at once, the unity and wholeness of it is lost to the beholder." *Poetics* (1451a), included in *Philosophies of Art and Beauty*, eds. Albert Hofstadter and Richard Kuhns (New York: Modern Library, 1964), p. 105.

[15] Edward O. Wilson, "The Little Things That Run the World," included in *Environmental Ethics: Divergence and Convergence*, eds. Susan J. Armstrong and Richard G. Botzler, 2nd edn., (New York: McGraw Hill, 1998), p. 34, emphasis added.

attracted to certain creatures, we tend to care about their fate and are inclined to protect them, while we tend to remain indifferent toward those creatures we do not find aesthetically appealing. Stephen Jay Gould puts it best when he complains of how "environmentalists continually face the political reality that support and funding can be won for soft, cuddly, and 'attractive' animals, but not for slimy, grubby, and ugly creatures (of potentially greater evolutionary interest and practical significance) or for habitats."[16] His observation is confirmed by an empirical study which finds that "most Americans support protecting popular and *aesthetically appealing* species like the bald eagle, mountain lion, trout, and American crocodile, even when this protection might result in significant increases to the cost of an energy development project."[17] We are thus familiar with the call for "save the whale" or "save the dolphin," but not "save the cod."

Indeed, there was a remarkable degree of public support for protecting the palila, a member of the honeycreeper family of birds indigenous to Hawaii, with striking appearance due to "an unusually large bill, a golden yellow head and throat, and gray along its beak."[18] In contrast, there was little public support for protecting snail darter, two- to three-inch member of the minnow family, which was threatened to extinction by the completion of TVA Tellico dam.[19] Observing this contrast, one commentator points out the "differing public perception of an *attractive* bird species as opposed to an unknown fish."[20] Similarly, Eaton observes that "the Bambi syndrome," our tender emotion stirred by the sentimental image of all deer as Bambi, makes it difficult for forest managers "to convince the public that their numbers should be severely decreased in some areas."[21]

[16] Stephen Jay Gould, "The Golden Rule—A Proper Scale for Our Environmental Crisis," included in Armstrong and Botzler, *Environmental Ethics*, 1st edn., (1993), p. 312.

[17] Kellert, p. 170, emphasis added.

[18] Ibid. p. 167. In 1978, the Sierra Club and the Hawaiian Audubon Society entered a suit on behalf of this bird species, with palila as the plaintiff (Palila v. Hawaii Department of Land and Natural Resources) and the bird won. See p. 177 of Roderick Nash's *The Rights of Nature: A History of Environmental Ethics* (Madison: The University of Wisconsin Press, 1989) about this legal case.

[19] The fascinating account of the political and legal maneuvers before and after the 1978 U.S. Supreme Course ruling in favor of the fish is given by Nash in pp. 177–9.

[20] Kellert, p. 170, emphasis added. Kellert, however, also points out the significance of the snail darter case in the history of environmental consciousness: "The snail darter case may one day be viewed as a profound turning point in the evolution of a new consciousness toward the preservation of all life. It forced many to confront for perhaps the first time the scope of the problem of species loss, and it elevates the plight of an obscure species to unprecedented heights in questioning powerful economic and political interests." (p. 166)

[21] Eaton, p. 182.

These aesthetic preferences affect not only the individuals' attitudes and resulting actions (such as supporting a certain environmental cause) but also the content of laws, according to some findings. For example, one study concludes that the *"aesthetic enjoyment* in part accounts for our sense that public discussions of species preservation most often cite large mammals—not rodents, insects, or lichen. This is sometimes reflected in law, as in the Marine Mammal Protection Act, which gives mammals such as whales, dolphins, and seals greater protection than fish, some of which are equally endangered."[22] Qualifying for an endangered species also seems to be, at least partly, affected by the aesthetic considerations. Despite the rather remarkable increase in the number of bald eagles, thanks to the Endangered Species Act of 1973, from 417 nesting pairs in 1963 to more than 6,400 pairs today, it has only been de-listed recently. On the other hand, there are many other creatures that have not been included, such as "the lesser prairie chicken, the Mazama pocket gopher, the Zuni bluehead sucker and the beaver cave beetle," though they "stand in far greater peril than the bald eagle." Part of the reason seems to reflect the popular aesthetic taste which tends to dismiss those "more *humble* species—adorning no coins, atop no flagstaffs."[23]

ii. Landscape

Similar problems exist with respect to landscape. As I mentioned in the last chapter (2.iii), the general public tends to be more attracted to the unfamiliar and the spectacular, typified by the crown jewels of our national parks, such as Yellowstone and Yosemite, with their dramatic elevation, waterfalls, unusual geological formation, and thermal phenomena. The eighteenth-century legacy of the picturesque tradition, particularly in its most literal sense of a "picture-like" aesthetic, still seems to govern our taste. We tend to admire those landscapes which can be made into a nice picture (today often in the form of a photograph), but remain indifferent to other parts of nature which do not lend themselves to a nice pictorial composition due to a lack of sufficient complexity, variety, harmony, or eye-catching features. Even the staunch advocate of the creation of

---

[22] Willett Kempton, James S. Boster, and Jennifer A. Hartley, *Environmental Values in American Culture* (Cambridge: The MIT Press, 1995), p. 106, emphasis added.

[23] "Bald Eagle Numbers Soar, but Endangered Status Remains," *The Providence Sunday Journal,* September 29, 2002, emphasis added.

national parks, Frederick Law Olmsted, recognized this popular taste with growing apprehension. He warned the Yosemite Park Commission that "most Americans considered the grant a mere 'wonder or curiosity,'" without appreciating "the preserve's 'tender' esthetic resources, namely the 'foliage of noble and lovely trees and bushes, tranquil meadows, playful streams,' and the other varieties 'of soft and peaceful pastoral beauty.'"[24] Indeed Olmsted's worry foreshadows John Muir's experience with two artists whom he encountered on Mt. Ritter in the High Sierras. Muir complained that the artists were satisfied only with a few scenic spots affording spectacular, startling views. However, other parts that attracted Muir, such as the autumn colors of the surrounding meadow and bogs, were "sadly disappointing" to the artists because they did not make "effective pictures."[25]

Aldo Leopold reiterates this concern by calling attention to people's tendency to be attracted by dramatic, sublime, or picturesque landscapes while showing no interest in other more "boring" parts of nature: "there are those who are willing to be herded in droves through 'scenic' places; who find mountains grand if they be proper mountains with waterfalls, cliffs, and lakes. To such the Kansas plains are tedious."[26] Desert areas will also appear monotonous and unworthy of aesthetic experience, "because of that under-aged brand of esthetics which limits the definition of 'scenery' to lakes and pine trees." Indeed one empirical study on people's landscape preference confirms Leopold's description of people's taste; according to it, "prairie scenes were invariably rated aesthetically poor."[27]

I shall refer to this landscape aesthetics that favors scenic landscapes "scenic" aesthetics.[28] As with our taste regarding various creatures, this scenic aesthetics has serious consequences. In the words of one critic, scenic aesthetics "blinds us to the subtlety of the browns and grays of our *everyday*

[24] Cited by Alfred Runte in *National Parks: The American Experience* (Lincoln: University of Nebraska Press, 1987, second edn.), p. 30.

[25] John Muir, *The Mountains of California*, originally published in 1894, included in *The American Landscape: A Critical Anthology of Prose and Poetry,* ed. John Conron (New York: Oxford University Press, 1974), p. 255.

[26] Aldo Leopold, *A Sand County Almanac* (New York: Ballantine Books, 1966), pp. 179–80. The next passage is from p. 268.

[27] Neil Evernden, "Beauty and Nothingness: Prairie as Failed Resource," *Landscape* 27 (1983), p. 3.

[28] I explore various ramifications of scenic aesthetics in more detail in "The Aesthetics of Unscenic Nature," *The Journal of Aesthetics and Art Criticism* 56: 2 (Spring 1998): 101–11.

landscapes, which look positively sallow next to the fly-traps and orchids that have become the botanical centerfolds of *Sierra* and *Natural History*."[29] As a result, we care about the fate of the scenic wonders of national parks and oppose any activities that would "disfigure" their appearance. We protest loudly against logging of redwoods or any constructions that might compromise the performance of the Old Faithful. On the other hand, other landscapes which are generally considered aesthetically unattractive, such as wetlands and prairie, have historically been vulnerable to abuse and destruction, because we don't care as much about what happens to them. The research that found people's low aesthetic rating of prairie concludes by stating, "any use of prairie would be acceptable, because no one cares about viewing the prairie."[30] The sorry history of what happened to wetlands, not only in the United States but also globally, indicates that many people believe that wetlands should be made more "productive" by draining, filling, and paving.[31] Their perceived lack of any aesthetic value contributes to the public's eager attitude toward such transformation. Aldo Leopold thus warns: "We console ourselves with the comfortable fallacy that a single museum-piece will do, ignoring the clear dictum of history that a species must be saved *in many places* if it is to be saved at all."[32]

Even with "a museum piece" like national parks, the problematic consequences of scenic aesthetics still linger. The American institution of the national park, first of its kind in the world, was established exclusively motivated by the perceived need for protecting scenic wonders, but not ecological integrity, from cultivation and development. As such, protection of unscenic lands for ecological reasons historically met with resistance and sometimes even with ridicule. For example, the Everglades was not designated as a national park until 1947, despite the nearly twenty-year effort by concerned scientists, politicians, and citizens. It was initially ridiculed as merely a swamp with "mighty little that was of special interest, and absolutely nothing that was picturesque or beautiful," leading even someone considered at the time to be one of America's foremost spokesmen for

---

[29] Harris, p. 200, emphasis added.

[30] Evernden, p. 3. Needless to say, Evernden is simply making a factual statement here rather than endorsing this attitude.

[31] The history of wetlands in the United States is documented by Ann Vileisis in *Discovering the Unknown Landscape: A History of America's Wetlands* (Washington, D.C.: Island Press, 1997).

[32] Leopold, p. 194.

wildlife conservation to declare: "it is yet a *long ways* from being fit to elevate into a national park, to put alongside the magnificent array of scenic won-derlands that the American people have elevated into that glorious class."[33]

Another ramification of scenic aesthetics associated with national parks is their boundary. The boundary of Yellowstone, for example, was initially determined primarily to protect scenic wonders, such as geysers and thermal phenomena, without regard to its ecological integrity. As a result, habitats for native animals and the quality of the groundwater feeding into parkland, for example, have been compromised by development adjacent to the park boundary.

Finally, there is the problem of fire, natural or prescribed, in national parks. Until the resurrection of prescribed burning in 1970, the policy was to suppress it. It is partly because of a misconception that national parkland such as the Yosemite was an untouched wilderness, sometimes requiring the displacement of its native residents. In fact, the redwood forest had been managed by Native Americans for centuries, including periodic burning that helped its growth while controlling the growth of underbrush that will act as fagots for a massive fire.[34] Another reason for prohibition against forest fire was the popularly held scenic aesthetic, represented by the following 1929 statement by a respected conservationist that fire "without a doubt" was "the greatest threat against the perpetual *scenic* wealth of our largest National Parks."[35]

Overall, scenic aesthetics is vulnerable to those projects, like logging, mining, and drilling, which promise not to disturb the scenic beauty of the area by, for example, carrying out the operations away from our field of vision as drivers and hikers.[36] Furthermore, it can be subversively used to support major modifications of the land, such as construction of dams, by showing the dramatic increase in scenic beauty, sometimes even illustrated

---

[33] Cited by Runte, p. 131. The second passage is also from p. 131.

[34] See pp. 37–8, pp. 58–60, and p. 216 of Alfred Runte's *Yosemite: The Embattled Wilderness* (Lincoln: University of Nebraska Press, 1990). Also see Kenneth R. Olwig's "Reinventing Common Nature: Yosemite and Mount Rushmore—A Meandering Tale of a Double Nature," in Cronon.

[35] Runte, *National Parks,* p. 201. An interesting aesthetic discussion of forest landscape manage-ment, including fire, given from a practitioner's point of view, can be found in Paul. H. Gobster, "An Ecological Aesthetic for Forest Landscape Management," *Landscape Journal* 18:1 (Spring 1999): 54–64.

[36] A very controversial discussion regarding federal agencies' "visual resource management" that includes such a "deception" is given by Denis Wood in "Unnatural Illusions: Some Words About Visual Resource Management," *Landscape Journal* 7:2 (Fall 1988): 192–205.

by a touched up photo, as in the case of the Hetch Hetchy in Yosemite.[37] Thus, our prevalent scenic landscape aesthetics has consequences not only regarding the fate of unscenic lands but also regarding our protection and management of scenic lands.[38]

iii. Built environment and consumer goods

Another way in which a commonly held aesthetic value conflicts with ecological values regards the built environment and consumer goods. One prime illustration is the popular obsession with green, velvety-smooth, weeds-free lawns. The quintessential example of this aesthetic ideal is the conventional golf courses which suffer from the so-called "Augusta National Syndrome," named after the Georgia golf course that hosts the Masters tournament each spring. Its televised appearance sets an unattainable standard, consisting of "wall-to-wall green fairways and blooming flowers wherever you look," as well as ponds which are "dyed with aquatic colorant, turning them a deep turquoise."[39] Many homeowners in the United States try their best to emulate a similar look for their property by investing inordinate amount of time, energy, and resources. The environmental cost of this toxin- and energy-intensive, resource-guzzling endeavor is by now well-documented, raising a growing concern among environmentalists as well as landscape designers.

Furthermore, people's aesthetic aspirations and expectations often dictate the particular appearance of various consumer goods, determining the kinds of resources and manufacturing processes needed for the desired results. For example, one reason for the destruction of the rainforest is driven by the consumers' appetite for rare wood, such as mahogany, for furniture. The off-white, "imperfect," and coarse surface of recycled paper is considered inferior to pristine white, perfectly smooth paper with a glossy finish made

---

[37] See Runte, *National Parks*, pp. 78–81, and Nancy Lee Wilkinson's "No Holier Temple: Responses to Hodel's Hetch Hetchy Proposal," *Landscape* 31: 1 (1991): 1–9.

[38] One may question the relevance of such scenic beauty when discussing everyday aesthetics, because I am claiming that such places are for the most part not everyday environment for most people. Furthermore, scenic landscapes typically provide memorable aesthetic experiences, standing out from general flow of experiences. My point in discussing scenic aesthetic is twofold: (1) it exacerbates the general neglect of most people's everyday environment which is not scenic, and (2) various environmentally problematic consequences of scenic aesthetics were generally unforeseen.

[39] Jay Stuller, "Golf Looks beyond the 'Augusta National Syndrome,'" *Smithsonian* 28:1 (April, 1997), p. 60, and Alex Markels, "The Greening of America: Environmental Impact of Golf Courses" *Audubon* 100: 4 (July–August 1998), p. 42.

of virgin wood. Similarly, soy ink or vegetable dye looks dull compared to the vibrant, vivid colors produced by chemically based inks and dyes. Objects made with salvaged materials, reused products, or recycled parts may be amusing and possibly innovative, but they remain curio items not suitable for mass acceptance by consumers at large. Even the production of so-called "natural" fibers, such as cotton and wool, involves extensive finishing processes that utilize large amounts of energy, water, and a number of toxic chemicals, in order to meet the consumers' demand for a particular appearance and feel of the fabric, such as absence of impurity, easy dyeability, smooth luster, and softness to touch.[40] Our care of fabrics is also motivated by aesthetic considerations and is not without environmental ramifications. We want to keep the color of white fabric bright white, and the washing detergent manufacturers meet our demand by putting bleach and "optical brightener," which is essentially a fluorescent dye, in their product. The environmentally conscientious people, on the other hand, have resigned themselves to "the reduction in standards from the 'whiter-than-white' effect we have come to expect from conventional washing powders to the noticeably less-than-white we get from bleach-free, environmentally friendly ones."[41]

Finally, there is still a strong resistance to green architecture not only because of the initial high cost but also due to the assumption that ecological value compromises the aesthetic value of such projects. This assumption is partly justified by the initial stage in the development of green architecture which, many point out, promoted environmental benefits at the cost of the aesthetic, an understandable move because of the previously exclusive concern with aesthetics regardless of environmental impact. The following statement by Ian McHarg in his manifesto on "design with nature" is typical of this attitude: "ecology provides *the single* indispensable basis for landscape architecture and regional planning."[42] According to William McDonough

[40] With respect to fibers, I am indebted for the research done by my student Joann Notkin for Environmental Ethics Seminar (Spring, 2002). We can also find discussion on this point in *Natural Capitalism: Creating the Next Industrial Revolution* by Paul Hawken, Amory Lovins, and L. Hunter Lovins (Boston: Little, Brown and Company, 1999), pp. 171–2, and Juliet B. Schor's "Cleaning the Closet: Toward a New Fashion Ethic," included in *Sustainable Planet: Solutions for the Twenty-first Century*, eds. Juliet B. Schor and Betsy Taylor (Boston: Beacon Press, 2002), p. 49.

[41] Whiteley, p. 92.

[42] Ian McHarg, "An Ecological Method for Landscape Architecture," in *To Heal the Earth: Selected Writings of Ian L. McHarg*, eds. Ian L. McHarg and Fredrick R. Steiner (Washington, D. C.: Island Press, 1998), p. 212

and Michael Braungart, both ecological design practitioners, such exclusive emphasis on the ecological often resulted in built structures that address "environmental 'solutions' in isolation, tacking new technology onto the same old model or coming up with giant solar collectors that overheated in the summer. The resulting buildings were often ugly and obtrusive."[43] A case in point is the recent ordinance in the city of Los Gatos, CA, that cracks down on solar panels placed on top of buildings in ways that "threaten[s] to make their upscale Silicon Valley village an ugly place."[44] Though fully cognizant and supportive of the environmental values of solar panels, not to mention the state tax benefit, the city officials cite the pursuit of "architectural excellence" as the rationale behind their ordinance.

A similar aesthetic objection to what many consider an environmentally desirable structure is the response to wind power facilities. Though the initial problems of noise pollution, bird kills, unreliability, and frequent loss of blades were overcome with improved technology, aesthetic objections still persist, even in a place with special affection for windmills like the Netherlands.[45] The most recent controversy is the Capewind project to construct 130 wind turbines, 260 feet each, in the middle of Nuntucket Sound off the coast of Cape Cod, Massachusetts. Because of their full visibility, they are invariably decried as "marring," "spoiling," "ruining," and "intruding on" the otherwise pristine scenic vista, creating an "eyesore." The extent of this objection can be gauged by the fact that many of the opponents are self-proclaimed environmentalists, like Robert Kennedy, Jr., who fully embrace the environmental value of wind power.[46]

These examples are evidence of what one writer claims is "the perceived incompatibility between aesthetics and wholesomeness" among consumers; "the tension between aesthetics and morality lingers on in the conviction that that which tastes good, that which is delicate to the touch and pleasing

---

[43] William McDonough and Michael Braungart, *Cradle to Cradle: Remaking the Way We Make Things* (New York: North Point Press, 2002), p. 9. I also explored this problem in the last part of "Ecological Design: Promises and Challenges," *Environmental Ethics* 24:3 (Fall, 2002): 243–61. For a specific discussion on landscape architecture, see "The Aesthetics of Ecological Design: Seeing Science as Culture," by Louise A. Mozingo, *Landscape Journal* 16:1 (Spring, 1997): 46–59.

[44] I thank my student, Erica Chung, for calling attention to this case. See "When Solar Clashes with Aesthetics," *San Jose Mercury News* (Aug. 5, 2003) reprinted in *EV World: People & Technology*<http://www.evworld.com>.

[45] Pointed out by Robert W. Righter, *Wind Energy in America: A History* (Norman: University of Oklahoma Press, 1996), p. 286.

[46] This case of windfarm will be discussed in more detail at the end of this chapter (2.v).

to the eye, cannot be good for you."[47] Indeed, one designer's research on his profession found that "only 15% of those interviewed saw any strong connection between aesthetics and environmental issues in design, while 70% saw virtually no connection at all."[48] He concludes from this that "largely ignored until now in discussions about environmental issues and design...is the area of aesthetics." Advertising for green products often downplays their ecological value, for fear that emphasizing it may give an impression of their aesthetic inferiority. For example, a new sustainable floor-covering called Solenium produced by Interface "won't even be marketed as an environmental product," while a vegetarian restaurant is praised for the taste of its food which states: "with food this good, it's easy to forget all the dishes...are strictly vegetarian."[49]

The unfortunate outcome of the popular penchant for vivid colors, smooth texture, and slick appearance in consumer goods is that it discourages designers and manufacturers from producing green objects made with sustainable resources and environmentally benign manufacturing processes, which promote, rather than jeopardize, the health of the environment and ultimately of ourselves. A design critic, Nigel Whiteley, admits that "the actions of manufacturers, marketers, designers and advertisers are ideologically loaded—and overwhelmingly often that ideology runs counter to the interests of the environment and is, therefore, in the longer run also counter to human interests" and part of the reason for this anti-environmental ideology is the green products' perceived lack of aesthetic appeal, a significant factor for commercial success.[50]

The examples enumerated in this section testify to what I call "the power of the aesthetic," the contribution aesthetics makes in shaping the world and ultimately our life. This power of the aesthetic is for the most part unrecognized when it comes to our everyday aesthetic judgments unless they lead to a standout aesthetic experience. Our attraction to cute animals,

---

[47] Harris, pp. 184 and 181.

[48] Stuart Walker, "The Environment, Product Aesthetics and Surfaces," *Design Issues* 11:3 (Autumn, 1995), p. 18. The next passage is from p. 15. The presumed incompatibility between the aesthetic and the environmental is also evidenced in the foreword to a collection of sustainable design that makes a point of stating specifically: "design innovation and environmental concern are not mutually exclusive." (Joseph Duffy, *Eco Design: Environmentally Sound Packaging and Graphic Design* (Rockport, MA: Rockport Publishers, 1995), foreword.)

[49] The reference to Solenium is from p. 140 of Hawken, et al. The praise of a local vegetarian restaurant comes from "Vegetarian by Taste." *Providence Journal*, 23 October 2002.

[50] Whiteley, p. 81. Also see p. 93.

green lawn, and bright white shirt normally do not induce such aesthetic experiences. The collective and cumulative environmental ramifications of such seemingly innocuous aesthetic tastes and preferences, therefore, go unnoticed, or at best underestimated. Thus, this section concludes with some rather bad news. Not only are we unaware of the environmental effects of such everyday aesthetics but also those effects generally seem to work against environmental agendas. However, is the situation then hopeless?

2. Green aesthetics

The bad news of the last section fortunately also seems to suggest the possibility of some good news. That is, if the power of the aesthetic has had environmentally negative consequences, isn't it possible to redirect the power toward a more positive end?

A skeptic may respond that we cannot do anything about our aesthetic taste and preference because nobody can impose that on us. What *could* be imposed upon us, however, is ecological literacy. We should be willing to be made aware of the ecological implications of our actions through scientific, but not aesthetic, persuasion. We can come to appreciate the *ecological* value of swamps and snail darter, although a swamp is still an ugly muck and a snail darter a nondescript fish. By the same token, we can learn the ecological price of maintaining a green lawn and bleaching white shirts, but the aesthetic attraction to them remains the same. This strategy is similar to appreciating the nutritional value of bran or the medicinal value of cod liver oil without liking their taste, or recognizing the harm of high-calorie, high-fat food while loving its (sinful) taste.

In response to this skepticism, I shall first argue why it is not sufficient to develop ecological literacy alone. Then I shall also illustrate how it is possible to change popular aesthetic tastes for serving a certain social agenda.

i. The power of the aesthetic

Nobody would deny the importance of increasing our ecological literacy so that we become more aware of the ramifications of our actions. Indeed one empirical study confirms that the degree of positive attitude toward invertebrate species corresponds to the extent of education and knowledge gained about them.[51] However, such knowledge by itself may not be sufficient to effect changes in our attitudes and actions. Our aesthetic reactions can play a rather important role in this regard.

Aldo Leopold is one of the foremost environmentalists who were keenly aware of the crucial role played by the aesthetic in promoting land ethic. His land ethic and land aesthetic are inseparable. His plea for the cultivation of ecological literacy through studying natural history and ecology did not simply end there; he thought it necessary to transport the bookish knowledge gained by such studies to our actual *perception* and *experience* of nature. His well-known "key-log" of land ethic thus states: "Examine each question in terms of what is ethically *and esthetically* right ... A thing is right when it tends to preserve the integrity, stability, *and beauty* of the biotic community," and he repeatedly emphasizes the importance of promoting the "perception" of the land.[52]

Leopold's reason for emphasizing the aesthetic dimension of his land ethic is a rather contra-Kantian view that the respect and resultant protective response toward an object (such as the land) are not forthcoming without some degree of attraction, attachment, in short, the feeling of love. He claims that "we can be ethical only in relation to something we can see, feel, understand, love" and that it is "inconceivable ... that an ethical relation to land can exist without love, respect, and admiration for land, and a high regard for its value."[53]

Now, I think it is *theoretically* possible to develop an ecologically sensitive and responsible attitude toward land without cultivating our aesthetic attraction and affectionate attachment to it. After all, we *can* and *do* develop a respect for an abstract concept or entity, such as freedom, peace, and a nation, by appealing exclusively to our rational faculty, the only proper faculty for Kantian ethics. However, even with regard to these entities, it is noteworthy that they are often represented by concrete symbols, such as a dove with an olive branch, bald eagle, a flag, a national anthem, or the Statue of Liberty. These symbols are powerful; they make it easy for us to cultivate a respectful, affectionate attitude, inclining us toward certain

---

[51] Kellert, p. 126.

[52] Leopold, p. 262, emphasis added. The importance of cultivating "perception" is discussed in "Conservation Esthetic," pp. 280–95.

[53] Ibid. pp. 251 and 261.

decisions and actions. Similarly, except for a diehard Kantian hero, most of us will be much more predisposed to act responsibly and respectfully regarding nature or an artifact if we find them to be aesthetically positive. Without such an aesthetic attraction and emotional attachment, cultivating a respectful attitude toward the land would be, if not *theoretically* impossible, a hard-sell *psychologically* and *pragmatically*.[54]

If Leopold's emphasis on the importance of the aesthetic is a plea to develop an ecologically minded sensibility when experiencing nature, a parallel reminder is given to the designers and creators of the built environment by Joan Nassauer in her discussion of "cultural sustainability." While promoting ecologically sustainable landscape design, she also calls attention to the importance of people's aesthetic reaction toward it. She points out that if people find a landscape attractive and aesthetically appealing, they tend to cherish, maintain, care for, and protect it, rendering it "culturally sustainable."

Landscapes that attract the admiring attention of human beings may be more likely to survive than landscapes that do not attract care or admiration. Survival that depends on human attention might be called *cultural sustainability*. Landscapes that are ecologically sound, and that also evoke enjoyment and approval, are more likely to be sustained by appropriate human care over the long term. People will be less likely to redevelop, pave, mine, or 'improve' landscapes that they recognize as attractive. In short, the health of the landscape requires that humans enjoy and take care of it.[55]

Speaking of green architecture, Christopher Hawthorne makes the same point. It is not enough for a green building to satisfy sustainability require-ments; it also needs to be aesthetically satisfying, because "if a building is beloved, it will be maintained and preserved—and there is nothing more environmentally friendly than longevity."[56]

---

[54] Larry Shiner pointed out that the same criticism of Kantian morality based solely on rationality is given by Friedrich von Schiller. Schiller's primary concern seems to call attention to the power of art to affect desire, sentiment, and passion, which in turn can inspire people to act according to the principles of reason. I believe his theory regarding the power of art can also be extended to the aesthetic dimensions of nature and artifacts.

[55] Joan Iverson Nassauer, "Cultural Sustainability: Aligning Aesthetics with Ecology," in *Placing Nature: Culture and Landscape Ecology*, ed. Joan Iverson Nassauer (Washington, D. C.: Island Press, 1997), p. 68.

[56] Christopher Hawthorne, "The Case for a Green Aesthetic," *Metropolis* (October 2001), p. 122.

A similar point is made by David Orr who also emphasizes the crucial role that aesthetics should play in promoting a sustainable world. He claims, "we are moved to act more often, more consistently, and more profoundly by *the experience of beauty* in all of its forms than by intellectual arguments, abstract appeals to duty or even by fear."[57] That is, "we must be inspired to act by examples that we can see, touch, and experience," toward which we develop "emotional attachment" and "deep affection."[58] Indeed, in tracing the history of the American land trust movement, Richard Brewer acknowledges that, despite limitations, "the aesthetic argument is probably the one most persuasive argument a land trust can use for most of its land projects."[59]

However, even if we agree with Leopold and others that we must cultivate an everyday aesthetic sensibility which helps promote, rather than thwart, environmental agendas, what is its feasibility? Is it simply wishful thinking and do environmental issues ultimately need to be addressed exclusively by non-aesthetic means? Or is it possible to engage in a kind of social engineering regarding everyday aesthetics? Let me first provide a historical precedent where people's aesthetic sensibility was engineered to serve a particular social goal. The history of American landscape aesthetics, though decidedly not developed to nurture ecological sensibility, does illustrate that our aesthetic taste can be guided to serve a specific social agenda.

ii. Landscape aesthetics in the United States

As many scholars have documented, early American settlers' attitude toward what appeared to them as uncultivated "wilderness" was negative, partly because of the overwhelming obstacles to be overcome for sheer survival.[60] The other factors contributing to this negative attitude toward wilderness came from the European intellectual tradition at the time. Raw nature was regarded as worthless "waste" until it was cultivated and worked on by

---

[57] David Orr, *The Nature of Design: Ecology, Culture, and Human Intention* (Oxford: Oxford University Press, 2002), pp. 178–9, emphasis added.

[58] Ibid. pp. 185, 25, 26.

[59] Richard Brewer, *Conservancy: The Land Trust Movement in America* (Hanover: University Press of New England, 2003), p. 59.

[60] I offer a more detailed account of the American attitude toward its own landscape in "Scenic National Landscapes: Common Themes in Japan and the United States," *Essays in Philosophy* 3:1 (January 2002) <http://www.humboldt.edu/~essays>.

humans, John Locke being one of the most vocal proponents of this view. This utilitarian consideration affected the prevailing European aesthetic taste until the development of the new aesthetic categories of the sublime and the picturesque during the course of the eighteenth century. Geometrical regularity, orderliness, and neatness, all characteristic of cultivated land, such as farms and orchards, were considered more beautiful than disorderly, chaotic, messy wilderness.[61]

When survival in the wilderness was no longer a pressing concern, Americans' attitude toward their land became more positive. However, in an interesting parallel to the earlier attitude toward the (literally) uncultivated land, Americans had to contend with another sense in which their land was uncultivated: lack of associations. Nineteenth-century American landscape appreciation borrowed extensively from the prevailing European aesthetic theory, an outgrowth of an aesthetics of the picturesque and the foundation of romanticism, which located the aesthetic value of an object in the series of associated ideas it triggers. The following claim by Archibald Alison, a late eighteenth-century British aesthetician, best characterizes this associationist aesthetic theory: "when any object, either of sublimity or beauty, is presented to the mind, I believe every man is conscious of a train of thought being immediately awakened in his imagination, analogous to the character or expression of the original object."[62] For example, according to Alison, the valley of Vaucluse (residence of Petrarch), the field of Agincourt, and the Rubicon derive their respective aesthetic value from historical associations, while other places may be "embellished and made sacred by the memory of Theocritus and Virgil, and Milton and Tasso." These associations, whether historical or literary, beautify the landscapes which "themselves may be little beautiful."

European landscapes, on this aesthetic theory, were thus easily appreciable because of the long human history associated with them. American landscapes, on the other hand, according to the nineteenth-century interpretation, were considered devoid of equivalent associations.[63] This comparison created a great deal of anxiety and a sense of inferiority complex

---

[61] For this sensibility, see Keith Thomas's *Man and the Natural World: A History of the Modern Sensibility* (New York: Pantheon Books, 1983), chapter VI.

[62] Archibald Alison, *Essays on the Nature and Principles of Taste* (Dublin, 1790), p. 2. The following quoted passages are from pp. 39–40 and p. 15.

[63] It goes without saying that Native American associations did not count at this time.

among the nineteenth-century American intellectuals. To cite only a few examples, Thomas Cole, a noted nineteenth-century painter particularly known for his landscapes, claims that many people judge American scenery to be inferior to European scenery because of the former's "want of associations, such as arise amid the scenes of the old world."[64] Similarly, Sarah Hale, a writer, laments that American landscape on the whole is dull to our fancy because of "the barrenness, the vacancy, painfully felt by the traveler of taste and sentiment," which "arises from the want of intellectual and poetic associations with the scenery he beholds."[65]

The American landscape appreciation familiar to us today came out of the various strategies proposed as remedies for this alleged lack of associations. One was to provide such associations by creating various stories attributable to specific landscapes. The literary works of Washington Irving and James Fenimore Cooper were especially instrumental in establishing some associations for American scenery in order to make it "the great theater of human events."[66] The second strategy was to refer people's imagination to the potential of future economic development of the site. The scenery may be uncultivated, primitive, uncouth, and rough at the moment. However, looking at such scenery, Thomas Cole claims: "the mind's eye may see far into futurity. Where the wolf roams, the plough shall glisten; on the gray crag shall rise temple and tower—mighty deeds shall be done in the now pathless wilderness; and people yet unborn shall sanctify the soil."[67]

Where the Americans could claim *superiority* of their landscape over European landscape, however, was considered to be in the immensity, both temporal and spatial, of the former. By the expansion of the notion of historical associations to include natural history, American landscape can boast advantage over European human history. For example, Clarence King wrote that the Sierra redwoods "began to grow before the Christian era" and Horace Greely stated that the trees "were of very substantial size when David danced before the ark, when Solomon laid the foundation of

---

[64] Thomas Cole, "Essay on American Scenery," first appeared in *The American Monthly Magazine*, 1 (January 1836), included in Conron, p. 570.

[65] Sarah Hale, "The Romance of Traveling," in *Traits of American Life* (Philadelphia: E. L. Carey & A. Hart, 1835), pp. 189–90.

[66] Cole, p. 571.

[67] Ibid. pp. 577–8. A similar view is expressed by N. P. Willis, *American Scenery; or, Land, Lake and River Illustrations of Transatlantic Nature* (London: George Virtue, 1840).

the Temple, when Theseus ruled in Athens, when Aeneas fled from the burning wreck of vanquished Troy."[68]

This temporal immensity associated with American landscape is matched by spatial enormity. The Niagara Falls are stupendous, unparalleled by any falls worldwide; the summits, gorges, and falls of the Yosemite and the Sierra Nevada supercede those found in Europe, the Alps in particular; various natural curiosities situated in Yellowstone, such as geysers and hot springs, surpass similar phenomena found elsewhere in size and might. In 1867, Albert Richardson declared that "in general natural curiosities and wonders, all other countries combined fall far below it."[69]

The final strategy for establishing the unique and superior feature of American landscapes was rather subversive, but effective: to turn this supposed disadvantage of lacking associations into a virtue: the celebration of American wilderness *precisely because* of their untouched status, both literally and conceptually. Roderick Nash claims that Washington Irving and Charles Fenno Hoffman, the first editor of the *Knickerbocker Magazine*, were instrumental in instilling the idea that "America's wilderness constituted an advantage over other countries," leading one traveler familiar with the Alps to declare that "the Alps … cannot … present a scenery more wild, more rugged, more grand, more romantic, and more enchantingly picturesque and beautiful, than that which surrounds (Lake Tahoe)."[70] In short, in the words of Cole, "the most distinctive, and perhaps the most impressive, characteristic of American scenery is its wildness."[71]

Indeed, landscape paintings, particularly of Western wilderness, by such artists as Albert Bierstadt, Frederick Church, and Thomas Moran, emphasized the wild immensity of untouched land by dramatic composition and lighting, as well as the sheer immensity of their canvases. In addition, though originally intended as documentary photos to record a governmental survey project, works by William Henry Jackson and Carleton Watkins

[68] The first passage is from Clarence King, *Mountaineering in the Sierra Nevada* (Boston: James R. Osgood and Co., 1872), pp. 41–3 and the second Horace Greely, *An Overland Journey from New York to San Francisco in the Summer of 1859* (New York: C. M. Saxton, Barker and Co., 1860), pp. 311–12, both cited by Runte, p. 22.

[69] Albert D. Richardson, *Beyond the Mississippi* (Hartford: American Publishing Company, 1867), p. I, cited by Runte, p. 22. Runte's work gives a detailed account of the American attitude toward Western landscape which led to the establishment of the national park system.

[70] The first passage is by Roderick Nash, p. 74. The second passage is by Edwin Bryant, *What I Saw in California*, first published in 1848, cited by Nash, p. 74.

[71] Cole, p. 571.

captured and popularized the scenic wonders of the West, in particular Yellowstone and Yosemite. The images of these landscapes became even more recognizable as illustrations and covers of widely circulated books and magazines, including *Picturesque America*. Today these landscapes provide "popular images of sparkling streams, fall colors, apple blossoms, and the scenes used as backgrounds in cigarette advertisements and calendars."[72]

All of these modes of appreciating American landscape thus formed a part of a cultural project to define the New World's own identity, in particular by distinguishing itself from the Old World, to which the young nation was indebted in many respects, including aesthetic sensibility. This self-imposed pressure to come up with what is distinctly American about its landscape and what makes it superior to the rest of the world is one factor that contributed to the formation of the national park system. It is no accident that the first areas to be designated as national parks, Yosemite and Yellowstone, are distinguished by the size, age, and might of their geological wonders, as well as their (presumed) wildness.[73]

This development of American landscape aesthetics underscores Simon Schama's observation that "national identity... would lose much of its ferocious enchantment without the mystique of a particular landscape tradition."[74] What is most important for my present purpose, however, is that this case illustrates the way in which people's aesthetic tastes and judgments can be guided by a social/cultural agenda and the way in which their power to affect our attitude and resultant actions has been utilized.

---

[72] Ted Relph, "To See with the Soul of the Eye," *Landscape*, 23 (1979), p. 28. Nigel Whiteley, citing the following 1932 remark by Roy Sheldon and Egmont Arens, co-authors of *Consumer Engineering: A New Technique for Prosperity*, points out that this American wilderness aesthetics spills over to its consumerism, described as "The American Way": "Europe, without our enormous natural resources, whose land has been tilled for centuries and whose forests are hand-planted state parks, is naturally conservative in its philosophy of living. But on this side of the Atlantic the whole set-up is different. Not only are our resources greater; they are unsounded, unmeasured, many of them almost untouched... In America today we believe that our progress and our chances of better living are in positive earning rather than in negative saving." pp. 14–15.

[73] I have already mentioned various consequences of this American national park system (Section 1.ii), such as the issues regarding its boundary, management of fire, and displacement of Native Americans. I should add here another problematic ramification, which resulted from a well-meaning, but culturally insensitive, attempt to apply it globally as the model for nature preservation. The best-known critique is by Ramachandra Guha in his "Radical Environmentalism and Wilderness Preservation: A Third World Critique," included in Armstrong and Botzler.

[74] Simon Schama, *Landscape & Memory* (London: HarperCollins, 1995), p. 15. For the role of landscape in the Japanese formation of its national identity, see my "Scenic National Landscape," (above note 60).

This historical precedent then supports the possibility for promoting a green agenda through aesthetic engineering. In what follows, I would like to make a case for what Marcia Eaton calls an "aesthetic ought"; that is, "creating sustainable environments necessitates asking not just what people do find beautiful but what they should find beautiful."[75]

iii. Green aesthetics—nature

First, then, how do we make unscenic aspects of nature aesthetically attractive in our experience? One strategy is to bring out the picturesque, scenic, or dramatic surface qualities in unscenic parts of nature that are normally inaccessible to human perception. Microscope, varied lighting, and photographs with wide-angle or telescopic lens help make the invisible visible. Time-lapse photographs and films also capture phenomena that take place over a period of time that is too long for us to experience.

We can also learn to see scenic beauty in unscenic creatures and landscapes with the help of artistic means. For example, photographs of wetland, desert, and prairie featured in cards and calendars issued by environmental organizations, such as the Sierra Club, the Audubon Society, and the Nature Conservancy, depict them in an attractive manner through strategic framing, lighting, and enhancement. When we appreciate actual landscapes through such an artistic lens, we are acting similarly to the eighteenth-century European travelers in search of the picturesque beauty, whose landscape appreciation was directed toward "improved" versions of actual sites, either reflected in the Claude glass or depicted in their own sketches and drawings à la Claude Lorraine or Salvator Rosa.

Learning to see scenic beauty in unscenic creatures and landscapes with the help of artistic means, however, may backfire. That is, composition in visual arts is by necessity selective and arranged, never an exact duplicate of the actual object. Hence, if we learn to appreciate unscenic parts of nature through an artistic lens, it is possible that we will be disappointed to discover that the actual unscenic nature fails to meet the expectation created by its artistic presentation. For example, even with respect to scenic landscapes, how many of us had at least one experience of building up an expectation through postcards, guidebooks, and posters, only to feel disillusioned when we finally get to see the actual landscape (although a sense of satisfaction of

---

[75] Eaton, p. 176.

seeing the real thing at last may compensate for the disappointment)? Maybe the weather condition is not optimal, as depicted in the photographs, so the vista is obscured and lighting is not as dramatic. Or, the strategic framing may have avoided the inclusion of distracting items, such as a parking lot, souvenir shops, and a nearby highway that are clearly within the actual view. Indeed, Anne Godfrey, both a landscape architect and a photographer, testifies to this manipulated experience of a landscape offered by commercial photographs. She confirms that "through simple devices such as framing, viewpoint, composition, shutter speed, and the use of lighting and filters, the photographer orchestrates his or her idealized image of a place."[76] Specifically, she states: "I crop out anything poorly managed or worn and any ugly views. To obtain such flattering views, I will put myself in awkward positions: perching on top of tables, benches, and my tailgate, or leaning out windows." The scene captured from such awkward viewpoints may not be possible for the viewers on site to experience. Furthermore, according to her, the presence of people is generally shunned in landscape photography. Even without such a framing strategy, it may be the case that our experience is distracted by non-visual elements, such as the noise of traffic, low-flying sightseeing airplanes, and snowmobiles, in addition to the aroma of barbecue from nearby campground or the unpleasant smell coming from overflowing garbage cans.

Moreover, this strategy contains a missed opportunity for education. That is, if our popular aesthetic taste is perpetuating ecologically unenlightened perception and ultimately actions, a new aesthetic sensibility should be cultivated to educate us about the consequences of our aesthetic preferences. As a number of thinkers advocate, starting with Leopold's land aesthetic, green aesthetics must be scientifically informed, rather than exclusively directed toward the sensuous surface. Green aesthetics has to include conceptually based aesthetic value, variously described as "thick" sense, "expressive 'beauty,'" "life values," or "serious" appreciation, which then informs the appreciation of the object's sensuous surface.[77]

[76] Anne Godfrey, "Commercial Photography and the Understanding of Place," *Landscape Architecture* 96:4 (April 2006), p. 34. The next passage is from p. 36. I thank my student Jennifer Surdyk for this reference.

[77] In arguing for the conceptually based aesthetic appreciation of environment, Allen Carlson distinguishes "thick" and "thin" sense of aesthetic values, terms he adopts from John Hospers. Hospers also characterizes the thick sense as the object's expression of "life values," while the same concept is termed as "expressive beauty" by D. W. Prall. Ronald Hepburn distinguishes "serious" from "trivial"

I take it that the necessity of the conceptual in determining the aesthetic qualities and artistic meanings of works of art has been established and the formalist theory has been largely discredited, except for its value in calling attention to the sensuous. For example, Kendall Walton's notion of the "categories of art" demonstrates the necessity of placing a work of art in its proper category, determined by extra-sensory factors like its historical context and the artist's intention, in attributing "the correct" aesthetic qualities, such as dynamic, elegant, coherent, and serene. Arthur Danto's theory of "the artworld" also invokes such necessity in situating an object in the artworld so that we can then proceed to interpret its meaning and expressive properties. Perceptually indiscernible objects can be distinguished by their membership, or lack thereof, to the artworld, which can be determined only by reference to conceptual considerations.

Similarly, the experience of natural objects necessarily invokes the cognitive, first for experiencing them "as nature" rather than a well-crafted fake, and for determining the "correct" aesthetic properties. Walton makes an analogy between the category of art and that of nature by pointing out that our appreciation of a baby elephant as "charming, cute, delicate, or puny" is dependent upon the regular size of elephants that we are familiar with. "To people who are familiar not with our elephants but with a race of mini-elephants, the same animal may look massive, strong, dominant, threatening, lumbering, if it is large for a mini-elephant."[78] While the involvement of such cognitive factors in the aesthetic appreciation of nature may be accepted by many, what is most hotly contested in the aesthetics of nature is the degree and content of the conceptual that is deemed necessary. The debate usually focuses on whether scientifically guided or informed nature appreciation is *the only* or *the most* appropriate or correct appreciation of nature.[79] In the context of my discussion here,

appreciation of natural environment. See Allen Carlson, "On Aesthetically Appreciating Human Environments," *Philosophy & Geography* 4:1 (2001), p. 18, and Ronald Hepburn, "Trivial and Serious in Aesthetic Appreciation of Nature," included in *Landscape, Natural Beauty, and the Arts,* eds. Salim Kemal and Ivan Gaskell (Cambridge: Cambridge University Press, 1993).

[78] Kendall L. Walton, "Categories of Art," first published in *The Philosophical Review,* LXXIX (1970): 334–67, included in *Philosophy Looks at the Arts: Contemporary Readings in Aesthetics,* ed. Joseph Margolis (Philadelphia: Temple University Press, 1978), p. 99.

[79] The first group (those who advocate scientifically based appreciation) includes Allen Carlson, Holmes Rolston, III, Marcia Eaton (though to a lesser degree). I also argued for this position in my past works. Though I am changing my view somewhat (see note 80), I believe promoting green aesthetics requires scientifically informed appreciation. The other group includes Noël Carroll, Stan Godlovitch,

which is to explore the tenets of green nature aesthetics, I am concerned only with scientific associations, without thereby denying the relevance and importance of other conceptual considerations, such as historical, social, and cultural, depending upon the context.[80] Regardless of whether it is the only appropriate mode of appreciation, scientifically informed nature aesthetics has to form a critical ingredient of green aesthetics, because it provides the possibility of a normative function for aesthetics. While "reluctant to 'rank' various ways of responding to nature," Marcia Eaton states that "if we want to develop a basis for rational evaluation of a landscape's ecological sustainability,... we must stress the cognitive."[81] Insofar as cultivating green aesthetics is a normative endeavor to promote sustainable futures, cognitive considerations regarding the ecological value of a natural object must underlie our aesthetic response to it.

For example, take a salt marsh, a typical example of "unscenic" landscape due to its rather nondescript appearance devoid of stunning features. Despite its seemingly simple look, it is a complex system which negotiates between differing saline content of the water. With this knowledge, we can begin to *see* and make sense of how the plant communities are distinctly demarcated to indicate their adaptation to the particular water content. Furthermore, knowing the intricate mechanism of a salt marsh which acts as an efficient water purifier (as well as many other functions it performs) may amuse us because of the contrast to the seemingly low-key, non-dramatic, monotonous appearance.[82] The appreciation here is different

Cheryl Foster, Stephanie Ross, and Emily Brady. For these authors' works, see Salim Kemal and Ivan Gaskell; *The Journal of Aesthetics and Art Criticism* 56:2 (Spring 1998, Special Issue on Environmental Aesthetics); *The Aesthetics of Natural Environment*, eds. Allen Carlson and Arnold Berleant (Peterborough: Broadview Press, 2004).

[80] In the past, I advocated science-based nature aesthetics as the most appropriate, along with Carlson and others (for example, in "The Aesthetics of Unscenic Nature" and "Appreciating Nature on its Own Terms," *Environmental Ethics* 20:2 (Summer 1998): 135–49). However, I am beginning to think that judging what is appropriate/inappropriate must reference a particular context. For example, some natural objects and environments (such the Plymouth Rock and the Gettysburg battlefield) may have such important historical significance that it may be strange to insist that we appreciate them exclusively with scientific associations. I owe this point to Ned Hettinger.

[81] Eaton, p. 184.

[82] According to one recent count, wetland has about two dozen different functions (cited by Sim Van der Ryn and Stuart Cowan, *Ecological Design* (Washington, D. C.: Island Press, 1996), p. 117). Vileisis describes the beginning of the scientists' recognition concerning the wetlands' ecological values during the 1950s as follows: "Scientists soon realized that the *visually monotonous* marsh landscape was ecologically complex" (Vileisis, p. 217). This appreciation of the contrast between appearance and reality can be compared to the by-now classic fog example related by Edward Bullough in " 'Psychical

from simply knowing and appreciating this kidney-like function of a salt marsh, because it would not require our direct sensuous experience of the site; our conceptual understanding of its complex mechanism would be sufficient. The benefit of nature walks, such as through a salt marsh guided by a naturalist, is that we can transfer the conceptual understanding directly to the perceivable characteristics of the object or landscape, thereby appreciating the specific manner in which various facts are embodied, expressed, or even concealed or contradicted, by the sensuous appearances.

Or, consider the cases where natural objects go through dramatic changes as part of their growth pattern or in response to surroundings or season. Examples include various forms of self-defense mechanism of natural creatures, the most notable of which is camouflage; transformation of a caterpillar or a tadpole into a butterfly or a frog; and the green leaves anticipating the change into brilliant red. We imaginatively juxtapose the anticipated change onto the present state of the object in front of us, thus rendering what otherwise may be a nondescript appearance amusing. Such additional information either helps us notice minute or subtle details that anticipate the forthcoming change or creates a sense of amusement because of the absence of such telltale signs. An unpuffed puffer fish may not appear that interesting until we realize the dramatic change of size, shape, and texture that can take place when it is confronted by a predator.[83] Or, Ken Weber points out in his nature writing that his attraction to a monarch butterfly is not simply by its inherent beauty but the fact that its earlier state is "a gaudy—perhaps ugly—striped caterpillar" and "the fact... that creepy caterpillars can be transformed into beautiful winged creatures," in addition to "their migration flights of a couple of thousand miles."[84]

In these examples of scientifically informed nature aesthetics, imagination plays a key role. Emily Brady stresses the importance of perception and imagination in the aesthetic appreciation of nature, in part as a corrective to the overly cognitive approach advocated by science-based nature

Distance' as a Factor in Art and an Aesthetic Principle," (*The British Journal of Psychology* 5 (1912–13)) in which he describes the appreciation made possible by psychical distancing to be directed toward the contrast between the anxiety-provoking danger and the seemingly calm, peaceful sensuous surface of the fog.

[83] I thank my student, Mie Yoshinaga, for her class presentation on this example.

[84] Ken Weber, "Monarchical Magic," *Providence Journal*, 2 September 2006.

aesthetics.[85] While she objects to the exclusivity of scientific knowledge of such an approach, she does not deny that such knowledge can lead one to "imagine well," instead of "shallow, naïve, and sentimental imaginative responses, which might impoverish rather than enrich appreciation."[86] Though not scientific in the technical or academic sense, her examples of an alpine flower that grows under harsh conditions and a sea pebble that has been made smooth by being worn out by waves are similar to my examples of salt marsh and transformation of creatures. Regarding the sea pebble, she explains:

In contemplating the smoothness of a sea pebble, I visualize the relentless surging of the ocean as it has shaped the pebble into its worn form. I might also imagine how it looked before it became so smooth, this image contributing to my wonder and delight in the object. Merely thinking about the pebble is not sufficient for appreciating the silky smoothness, which is emphasized by contrasting its feel with an image of its pre-worn state.[87]

What is noteworthy about ecologically guided nature aesthetics, as compared with green aesthetics regarding artifacts, is that scientific information always seems to help transform our initially negative aesthetic response (such as toward unscenic objects and landscapes) into a positive response. Insofar as nature's operation is not attributable to human agency, green nature aesthetics in general works toward enlarging the domain of the aesthetically appreciable (perhaps except in the case of invasive species and catastrophic natural phenomena, such as massive hurricanes and earthquakes).[88] This observation underscores the notion of "positive aesthetics" developed by Allen Carlson and the similar position held by wilderness advocates, such as John Muir and Holmes Rolston III, not to mention Leopold himself. According to their view, when we are given relevant scientific information, such as ecological values, every part of nature is aesthetically appreciable,

---

[85] She criticizes Carlson's scientifically based nature aesthetics for lacking "sufficient emphasis on other distinctive features of the aesthetic response: *perception* and *imagination*," and characterizes her approach as making "*perception* and *imagination* central to guiding aesthetic appreciation." Emily Brady, "Imagination and the Aesthetic Appreciation of Nature," included in Berleant and Carlson, eds., pp. 156 and 159, emphasis added.

[86] Ibid. p. 166.   [87] Ibid. p. 163.

[88] By invasive species, I am referring to those species which threaten to destroy the extant ecosystem, but not necessarily all species which are alien to the particular habitat, because some may adapt quite nicely to the new home and coexist harmoniously with the other species. I explored this issue in the third section of "Ecological Design." I explored our aesthetic response to natural disasters and catastrophes in the final section of "The Aesthetics of Unscenic Nature."

even including those aspects which are normally not appreciated, such as an elk carcass infested with maggots and scenically challenged "underdogs" like draba, various "weeds," birch trees, bog, brush, marshes, prairies, plains, and juniper foothills, enumerated by Leopold.[89] Leopold claims that we must develop "a *refined taste* in natural objects" which enables us to appreciate "a plain exterior (which) often conceals hidden riches."[90]

In cultivating this scientifically informed green nature aesthetics, however, we must take care to avoid what I call environmental determinism, whereby ecological value of an object automatically determines its aesthetic value. Following environmental determinism will get us away from our direct experience of the object's sensuous surface and lead us to conclude, without reference to the object's sensory attributes, that it is aesthetically positive because of its positive ecological role. Even with necessary incorporation of various conceptual considerations, the ultimate reference and basis of our aesthetic judgment has to be what is directly perceivable. In this regard, we have to take note of Leopold's insistence on cultivating informed "perception" in his promotion of a land aesthetic. Acquired knowledge from ecology and natural history must be translated into *the way in which* nature looks, sounds, smells, and feels. Though referring specifically to cultural landscape, Arnold Berleant is correct in reminding us that gathering various information pertaining to a landscape is necessary, but not sufficient, in understanding it until we "relate this information to perceptual experience."[91]

Brady points out, and I agree, that aesthetically appreciating nature, particularly its unscenic aspects, such as "mudflats and wastelands" requires "the effort of the percipient," as what one picks out for appreciation "depends to some extent on the effort I make with respect to engaging my perceptual capacities."[92] Art appreciation, too, demands the same kind of effort on our part, but help is available from established discourses: art history, art criticism, music appreciation, literary criticism, theater review,

---

[89] The example of an elk carcass is taken from Holmes Rolston, III in *Environmental Ethics: Duties to and Values in the Natural World* (Philadelphia: Temple University Press, 1988), p. 238. The reference to "underdog" is found in pp. 73 and 76 of Leopold. The specific examples compiled are scattered throughout this work.

[90] Leopold, pp. 194, 180, and 197, emphasis added.

[91] Arnold Berleant, *Living in the Landscape: Toward an Aesthetics of Environment* (Lawrence: The University Press of Kansas, 1997), p. 18.

[92] Brady, p. 161.

and the like. In these disciplines, the connection between art historical and technical knowledge and the sensuous surface of the art object is assumed and becomes their central focus. In comparison, the study of nature is concerned primarily with scientific education, with little emphasis on promoting aesthetic appreciation. I believe ecologically oriented scientific study can gain a great deal from the way in which our understanding and appreciation of art is facilitated by these various forms of educational aids and their methodologies. I find it most unfortunate that our educational system does not provide an equivalent of art, music, and literature courses in studying nature.

iv. Green aesthetics—artifacts

Green aesthetics guided by environmental values should be applicable not only to nature but also to artifacts. If green nature aesthetics is not as fully developed and established as aesthetics regarding art, green aesthetics regarding artifacts is even less developed due to specific challenges. First, in the cases of art and nature, we can normally expect a certain degree of knowledge regarding an object. Many of us go to the museum or concert primarily to gain an aesthetic experience and, if we are not already knowledgeable about the art object, we seek and find many means of enriching that experience, such as through exhibition catalogues, curator's notes on the wall, and program notes, not to mention formal studies in art history and music appreciation. As for nature, though many of us may be relatively ecologically illiterate, there are plenty of opportunities for learning biology, natural history, geology, and ecology, not only academically but, perhaps more importantly, through nature museums, nature walks and bird watching guided by naturalists, films, and nature writings by literary figures.

However, these different means of promoting aesthetic appreciation are lacking when it comes to consumer goods and the built environment. Particularly with respect to consumer goods, are there any guides equivalent to those that are available for art and nature? Consumer guides address functionality, durability, and price of various goods and products, and green consumer guides provide information about their environmental dimensions, but such information is offered without any relationship to their aesthetic dimensions. While the aesthetic considerations are often important in making decisions and engaging in actions, there is no guide linking the aesthetic and the cognitive, which would be equivalent to things like nature writings and art history. Furthermore, being preoccupied with the practical task at hand, such as making a purchasing decision or cleaning things, we rarely seek various avenues for enriching our aesthetic experience when dealing with those everyday objects.

Secondly, particularly in comparison with green nature aesthetics, there is a further complication when dealing with artifacts. While green aesthetics regarding nature can help render seemingly unattractive objects aesthetically appreciable, due to their environmental values, green aesthetics regarding artifacts has an additional mission: to render initially attractive objects not so aesthetically positive if they are environmentally harmful. That is, green aesthetic must make it the case that, in Marcia Eaton's words, "what is ecologically bad begins to be seen as aesthetically bad."[93] However, such perception also has to be cultivated without invoking what I called environmental determinism. That is, the information about environmental harm should modify the initially attractive appearance of an object *without* completely nullifying the first impression or rendering it hideous-looking. Consider the example of a green lawn. It is typically maintained by a life-support system consisting of the concoction of a toxic brew of herbicide, insecticide, pesticide, and fertilizer, accompanied by the use of tremendous amount of water that most of us and communities can ill afford, as well as the inordinate amount of fuel needed for periodical motorized buzz-cut, leaf-blowing, and weed-whacking, all indicating the need for extensive and intensive detox program. Once knowing what is involved in caring for a lawn, it will be irresponsible of us not to incorporate this knowledge into our experience of it. However, green aesthetic sensibility should not require that the green carpet then appear downright ugly, as that is succumbing to environmental determinism. Instead, green aesthetic sensibility should guide us to modify our initial attraction with a sense of "disillusionment" created by the discrepancy between the seemingly beautiful appearance and its harmful content.[94] As a result, the lawn starts looking somewhat garish, sinister, or morbidly beautiful; at the very least, it definitely will not stay innocently and benignly attractive.

These challenges specific to green consumer aesthetics indicate an extra responsibility on consumers. That is, they have to educate themselves about

[93] Eaton, p. 179.
[94] The phenomenon of "aesthetic disillusionment" is discussed by Cheryl Foster in "Aesthetic Disillusionment: Environment, Ethics, Art," *Environmental Values* I (1992): 205–15.

the ecological ramifications of products and activities and find a way to relate the knowledge gathered to the sensuous appearance of the object. Unlike in the case of nature, no such discourse has yet been established. However, also unlike green nature aesthetics, the burden is not placed solely on consumers. Designers' role here is crucial, perhaps more important than the consumers'. Indeed, as Victor Papanek reminds his own colleagues in the design profession, "design has become the most powerful tool with which man shapes his tools and environments (and, by extension, society and himself). This demands high social and moral responsibility from the designer."[95] Designers hold both the power and responsibility literally to shape our world; hence, developing green aesthetics of artifacts and built environment poses a challenge, as well as an opportunity, to them.

What then should be their strategy? One possible strategy is to maintain our popular aesthetic taste as is and work on rendering eco-friendly design so that it conforms to prevalent taste. Some advances have been made in these areas. For example, green architecture has come a long way from a solar panel awkwardly plopped up on the roof. Many contemporary green buildings display rather stunning effects, satisfying traditional aesthetic criteria, such as harmony, integrity, and balance.

However, just as there was a problem with an attempt to align the aesthetic of the unscenic nature with the conventional standard of the scenic, there are some problems with this attempt. One is a technical limitation. While some objects, such as architectural structures, may be improved to meet the popular expectations, this may not be possible with other products. For example, in her attempt to cultivate cottons which are colored in their raw material form (facilitated by selective breeding, thus eliminating the need for dyeing), Sally Fox has succeeded in producing various hues, except black.[96] Similarly, fabrics developed by DesignTex which are dyed with 38 non-toxic substances (a result of eliminating 7,962 other toxic chemicals commonly used) do not boast vivid and vibrant colors.[97] The same limitation seems to exist with soy and water-based ink as well. Furthermore, it is not clear how other desirable qualities, such as

[95] Victor Papanek, *Design for the Real World: Human Ecology and Social Change* (Chicago: Academy Chicago Publishers, 1992), p. ix.

[96] Her project is described in *Eco-Pioneers: Practical Visionaries Solving Today's Environmental Problems*, Steve Lerner (Cambridge: The MIT Press, 1998), pp. 101–3.

[97] This "compostable" fabric collection was produced for DesignTex by William McDonough and Michael Braungart and is described in their *Cradle to Cradle* and in "The Next Industrial Revolution"

luster and smoothness of fabric and paper, can be attained in an ecologically responsible manner.

Theoretically, these technical limitations might be overcome in the future. However, just as in the case of nature aesthetics, the green aesthetic sensibility must incorporate something new and different so that we become educated about the environmental consequences of our commonly held aesthetic preferences. Here I agree with one designer's comment that "the aesthetics of environmentally sensitive product designs should... be markedly different from designs in which these considerations have been omitted or ignored."[98]

At the same time, it is unwise to reject the prevailing aesthetic standard altogether by creating what one critic calls "the cult of 'the natural,'" a kind of "an anti-aesthetic," celebrating "plain brown biodegradable dresses and unbleached 'Eco-Tees' made of stiff, cardboard panels of recycled cotton tinted with environmentally sensitive dyes; lip sticks made of beet juice and face powder of brown oat flour; non-toxic, formaldehyde-free woolen pajamas," and the like.[99]

This anti-aesthetic approach is problematic, because, if its efficacy is predicated upon its disenfranchised aesthetic status, those green products will remain specialty goods for select consumers who are already concerned with the green issues. But the goal of cultivating green aesthetics is to make it mainstream, because ecological problems need to be addressed by a whole society, indeed by the global society, not just by a certain group of people.

Joan Nassauer in her discussion of "culturally sustainable" design, points out that the end-result of green design should not be too alien and unfamiliar to us, no matter how ecologically correct, because most likely we either get confused or turned off by the appearance, rendering the object culturally unsustainable. Instead, she recommends that the design be recognizable to us with some familiar cues and clues. For example, a constructed landscape consisting of indigenous wild flowers, while ecologically superior to the ubiquitous green lawn adorned with exotic flowers, if it is without any recognizable design vocabulary, may appear simply "messy," "disorderly,"

by William McDonough and Michael Braungart in *The Atlantic Monthly* (October 1998), as well as in DesignTex's brochure on William McDonough's Fabric Collection.

[98] Walker, p. 19.   [99] Harris, pp. 181–2.

and "ill-kept." She suggests making use of familiar signs, such as a neat border or orderly trim, to cue us in to the fact that the enclosed landscape *is* an important part of the environment, needing care and protection.

So here is a challenge, but also an opportunity, for the designers: to design products that embody their environmental values which are made aesthetically attractive through some familiar means, without simply making them conform to the popular taste which is for the most part not environmentally informed. How can the environmental value be expressed, embodied, or revealed through the object's sensuous surface in an aesthetically positive manner so that we will be attracted not only by its environmental value but also by its aesthetic manifestation? I believe there are several promising candidates for a green consumer aesthetics. Here I shall simply list them with brief remarks, though in subsequent chapters I shall explore some of them more in depth by placing them in a larger aesthetic context.

a. Minimalism   Perhaps the most easily recognizable and appreciable quality is minimalism regarding the sheer size (such as of packaging), the number of parts, and the number of materials used. Indeed, the most important of the 3R's in ecological education ("reduce," "reuse," and "recycle") is "reduce." Many critics are ambivalent about promoting "reuse" and "recycle" because it creates a mentality that we can over-produce and over-consume, usurping various resources, as long as the end product gets reused or recycled.[100] Source reduction is the most fundamental responsibility both for designers and consumers. Contribution to source reduction can underlie our appreciation for minimum packaging instead of bulky and unnecessary packaging, brown cardboard color and single-colored logo on store bags and boxes, and toys made with untreated, unpainted wood. The minimum size, economy of parts, and simplicity of design become all the more appreciable when perceived as evidence of ecological value.[101]

---

[100] For example, Paul Hawken criticizes our society's emphasis on recycling for being as "woefully inadequate" as "bailing out the *Titanic* with teaspoons," as well as being "collective attempts to assuage guilt" (*The Ecology of Commerce: The Declaration of Sustainability* (New York: HarperBusiness, 1994), pp. 5 and 202). William H. Baarschers points out that recycling itself is an industry which requires a large amount of resources for energy and transportation (Chapter 11 of *Eco-Facts & Eco-Fiction: Understanding the Environmental Debate* (London: Routledge, 1996)).

[101] The ultimate minimalism with respect to packaging is its elimination altogether, as in the form of bulk sale or refillable system. I think our appreciation in such a case, which has no perceivable object

b. Durability and longevity   Another possibility is the presence of features indicative of durability and longevity of the object, not only literally but also as an antidote to planned obsolescence-driven style and fashion. They include the use of appropriate materials, easy disassembly, repairability, upgradability, simplicity of construction, as well as absence of excessive trendiness, superfluous additions, or extravagant features. We can come to appreciate not only the fact that the object is made for longevity and durability but also *the way in which* its design reveals these ecologically important values. In particular, because of the consumers' relative ignorance regarding how and with what the object is made, "visual simplicity and visual comprehension" become crucial, as they "facilitate the ease of disassembly, maintenance and repair."[102]

One interesting point about longevity of an object is that its surface must age well. If the aged surface appears shabby, tired, decrepit, or tattered, even if its functionality remains intact, often our impulse as consumers in this throwaway society is to replace it.[103] Specifically, one designer advises against "delicate, high-gloss surfaces" and "monochrome surfaces and surface coatings" because they are "susceptible to being damaged and, perhaps more importantly, make any damage visually obvious."[104] Instead, he promotes "variation in texture, variation in color, irregularities in contours, diversity in finishes from glossy to matt, and intentional 'imperfections.'" Examples include unpainted wood, and metal, leather, and clay, which "contrast abruptly with the coated and fragile surfaces commonly found in many contemporary products; which chip, scratch and degrade so rapidly," seen in "automobile body panels and interior facias,"

---

to experience, is akin to our aesthetic appreciation of the simplicity and elegance of a mathematical or scientific formula.

[102] Walker, p. 23. Hawken, et al, also states: "great engineering ... is *elegantly simple*. Simplicity and elegant frugality are natural partners. Using less material means there is less to go wrong, less work involved, less cost, and better performance. All are products of the same design mentality" (p. 123, emphasis added).

[103] I shall explore this attitude toward the aged surface and its various ramifications in Chapter IV.

[104] Walker, p. 24. He continues: "during use, the product becomes progressively aesthetically deprived. Once the 'newness' literally has worn off, the product is perceived as less attractive than it once was, even if it still functions perfectly well. This often leads to a sense of dissatisfaction in the user, and the desire to replace the product." Victor Papanek also includes as one of the imperatives for the design in the 21st century that "the style of the future will be based on products that age gracefully, and will be more timeless than the quickly changing fads, trends and fashions of the late 20th century" (*The Green Imperative: Natural Design for the Real World* (New York: Thames & Hudson, 1995), p. 48).

as well as "home appliances incased in painted metals or glossy plastics."[105] Furthermore, taking nature's surface as a model, he urges that "the richness of chance effects … also be explored."[106]

c. *"Fittingness," "appropriateness," or "site-specificity"* While the first two features, minimalism and longevity, may be expected in all green design objects, there is also a requirement of diversity.[107] This is the notion of "fittingness," "appropriateness," or "site-specificity," whether it consists of locally available materials or indigenous plants, consideration of a particular site, climate, culture, or a reference to vernacular vocabulary. Qualities such as fittingness and appropriateness seem to be particularly important when it concerns the built environment in and with which we live. Contrary qualities such as incongruity, contrast, or discordance can be aesthetically positive within a work of art, but seem almost always negative for the environment.[108]

For example, landscaping using indigenous plants, such as prairie grasses in the Midwest, initially decried as appearing unkempt and disorderly, in comparison with the ubiquitous, smooth, green lawn sometimes adorned with exotic flowers, is now gaining more acceptance. On the other hand, a luscious green lawn in the middle of arid Arizona would strike us as being "out-of-place" because of its incongruity with the surrounding landscape.[109]

---

[105] Walker, p. 25. Nigel Whiteley makes the same point regarding paper: "some designers believe that not only does the recycled product offer a superior aesthetic quality but, because there is no bleach in the paper, both paper and illustration *age better*." Whiteley, p. 81, emphasis added.

[106] Some of the qualities characteristic of longevity of an object, discussed here, involve a seeming paradox. Papanek, for example, points out the apparent contradiction in "designing things to come apart efficiently," while Walker argues for the simplicity of the overall design accompanied by the complexity of the surface (Papanek, *Green Imperative*, p. 58, and Walker, p. 24).

[107] Whiteley, while promoting diversity and pluralism for green design, points out that "when it comes to packaging and product design, however, there are some important aspects to consider. Even when recycled materials are used in the packaging of Green products, the guiding principle must be 'less is more,'" implying that this principle must be universally adopted (p. 90).

[108] Marcia Eaton discusses the category-specific nature of "natural" as it applies to environment, and I believe that her view is close to what I am here referring to as the "fittingness" (Eaton, p. 194).

[109] It is noteworthy that one of the cardinal principles of ecological design is: "Solutions Grow from Place," typified in the questions posed by Wes Jackson, the director of the Land Institute, Salina, Kansas: "What was here? What will nature permit us to do here? And what will nature help us to do here?" This site-specificity can be applied not only to landscaping, agriculture, and architecture, but also to production of goods (making use of locally available materials and resources). The "Solutions" quote, which is presented as the first principle of ecological design, is the title of one chapter from Van der Ryn and Cowan, pp. 57–81. Wes Jackson's questions are taken from his "Nature as the Measure for a Sustainable Agriculture," included in *Environmental Ethics: Concepts, Policy, Theory,*

The site-specificity of architecture also lends itself to a similar aesthetic appreciation. For example, consider the projects in Alabama by the Rural Studio undertaken as part of Auburn University's architecture students' education. Many may appear crude, primitive, or unsophisticated. However, even a cursory glance at their surrounding informs us that they are situated in rather impoverished communities. Indeed, these are the poorest in Alabama, the region photographed by Walker Evans during the Depression. Another important dimension of these projects, which is visually manifest, is that they are constructed mostly with salvaged materials from abandoned buildings, railroad tracks, scrap yard, and factory remnants. In addition to the ecological benefit of using very little new material, the construction cost was a fraction of that of conventional, commercial solutions. Furthermore, these projects were undertaken with community involvement. These considerations shed a new light on the appearance of these structures, highlighting qualities such as industriousness, resourcefulness, compassion, and pride, manifested in what may at first appear to be somewhat clumsy surfaces. Describing these buildings, one commentator remarks: "the studio's esthetic vocabulary is modern, but its buildings, with their protective roofs and roomy porches, shed-like forms and quirky improvisations, look *right at home here.*"[110] In fact, a slick, high-tech building here would strike us as being out of place, and even if it is built with the students' ingenuity and residents' involvement, it will fail to express the qualities such as hard work and pride.[111]

---

ed. Joseph DesJardins (Mountain View: Mayfield Publishing Company, 1999), p. 359. Papanek refers to Frank Lloyd Wright as someone who was concerned with designing which is sensitive to the place, by quoting the following passage by Wright praising indigenous, humble buildings: "Although often slight, their virtue is intimately related to the environment, to the heart life of the people. Functions are usually truthfully conceived and rendered invariably with natural feeling. Results are often beautiful and always instructive" (Papanek, *Green Imperative*, p. 249).

[110] Andrea Oppenheimer Dean, *Rural Studio: Samuel Mockbee and an Architecture of Decency* (New York: Princeton Architectural Press, 2002), p. 2, emphasis added. Also see Andrea Oppenheimer Dean and Timothy Hursley, *Proceed and Be Bold: Rural Studio After Samuel Mockbee* (New York: Princeton Architectural Press, 2005). My cursory verbal description of their projects does not do justice to the visual images generously provided in these books. I am indebted to my students in Environmental Ethics Seminar (Spring 2002) Ceylan Balek and Joe James for introducing me to the works of Rural Studio, through their class presentation. Hawken, et al, also describe green buildings to "grow organically in and from their place" (*Natural Capitalism*, p. 110). Roger Scruton offers a general discussion on the notion of "appropriateness," ranging in application from architectural details to table manners, in *The Aesthetics of Architecture* (Princeton: Princeton University Press, 1979), pp. 227–36.

[111] I don't want to overstate the point, particularly when it comes to the "fittingness" or "at-home-ness" of a building in an impoverished surrounding, because aestheticization of poverty is problematic

This emphasis on site-specificity results in respect for diversity, as well as the rejection of uniformity and monoculture. Not only does this attitude make ecological and cultural sense but also aesthetic sense, as pointed out by McDonough and Braungart: "human design solutions that do not respect it [diversity] degrade the ecological and cultural fabric of our lives, and *greatly diminish enjoyment and delight.*"[112] Hence, New Urbanism, proposed as an alternative to suburban sprawl to serve a social and environmental ideal better, one critic warns, should not be imposed as the "one-size-fits-all" solution.[113]

d. Contrast between past and present   The examples from the Rural Studio projects suggest another avenue for green design to embody an aesthetic value, when the object is made with recycled, reused, or reclaimed materials or space: the contrast between the past and present uses. For example, the "as-is" use of automobile windshields for a roof or license plates and tires for the walls not only signals to the viewer the origin of the material but also creates interesting visual effects by the uneven, yet nicely patterned, surface. Furthermore, the comparison between the past and present uses of the material deepens our aesthetic appreciation by providing a kind of amusement and entertainment.[114] The same appreciation of the associated past history is a major factor in experiencing the restoration of an abandoned building or the rehabilitation of a brownfield.

We are familiar with this way of gaining aesthetic richness from associated past history in experiencing some fine arts. The use of ready mades and the genre of "appropriation" immediately come to our mind. But a much

from the moral point of view. I will explore this point in Chapter IV (2.iii and iv). The same comment can be extended to many artifacts created by people from impoverished communities or developing nations who have no choice but to make use of scrap materials or to reuse parts for different purposes. However, as I shall argue in Chapter V, the Rural Studio projects avoid the common mistake of considering only the utilitarian function, not to mention the economic limitation, of built structures for the poor or the displaced. Typically those structures do not address the aesthetic needs of the residents; they are ugly, cheap-looking, and exude the appearance of being hastily and carelessly put together. Instead, the end products of the Rural Studio embody the care taken in designing and constructing, as well as respect and honor paid to the residents' humanity and dignity.

[112] McDonough and Braungart, *Cradle*, p. 143.

[113] Postrel, p. 151. The specific tenets of New Urbanism include a compact community with walkable streets as its public and social spaces, mixed neighborhoods with nodes of shops and services, a variety of residential forms, and preservation of nature such as parks and community gardens.

[114] Another benefit of these reused materials in these structures is that they give "a feeling that they've been rained on; they look durable" (Dean, p. 9).

earlier example can be found in the Japanese tea ceremony, developed during the sixteenth century, which features Korean peasant rice bowls used for tea bowls, votive lights from shrines for lanterns in the garden, and temple foundation stones and mill stones for stepping stones.[115]

In order to facilitate these aesthetic values through reuse, it is crucial that the design retain the original appearance of the reused materials in some way. If the evidence of reuse is obliterated, an opportunity will be lost not only for the aesthetic appreciation based upon the associated past history but also for educating the viewer/user about the environmental contribution made by the object. Green design is aesthetically successful when it makes its ecological significance apparent to the senses.

e. Perceivability of nature's function   If green design is premised upon working "with" nature, instead of working "against" or "irrespective of" it, and if a part of the problem of conventional design is the imperceptibility of environmental processes, one feature of green object and structure should be to make environmental processes perceivable. Sim Van der Ryn and Stuart Cowan, the co-authors of *Ecological Design*, make the following observation with respect to our typical experience with rainwater:

With a conventional storm-drain system, for instance, water quickly disappears into subterranean arteries, picking up various toxins along the way. The water is hidden, and so are the impacts of the system itself—contamination of downstream rivers or wetlands, altered hydrology, and decreased groundwater recharge.[116]

In contrast, with a constructed or restored wetland, such as the sewage treatment facility at Hornsby Bend in Austin, Texas,[117] or an indoor simulation of wetland, such as John Todd's "Living Machine," the nature's process of purifying water is "made visible," "reacquainting us with wider communities of life," as well as informing us "about the ecological consequences of our activities."[118] *And*, as Van der Ryn and Cowan observe, "the *delightful* thing about such a design is that people love to watch it in action, rushing out in the rain to watch the water flow. All

---

[115] The technical term for this act of appropriation is *mitate*.

[116] Van der Ryn and Cowan, p. 164.

[117] I thank Kevin Anderson and Jody Slagle for an in-depth presentation and tour of the facility during the Harrington workshop at the University of Texas-Austin, Nov. 2003.

[118] Van der Ryn and Cowan, pp. 164–5, emphasis added for the subsequent passage.

of this suggests a new kind of *aesthetic* for the built environment, one that explicitly teaches people about the potentially symbiotic relationship between culture, nature, and design."

f. Health   Another possibility of green aesthetic value is the embodiment of health. Sometimes its appreciation is more dependent upon conceptual understanding, as in the case of landscape. The state of health of a constructed landscape, which in turn affects the well-being of humans and non-human creatures, may not always be apparent to the senses. It may require conceptual knowledge, "such as the number of hidden beetles or the presence or absence of microorganisms affecting a species of orchid," as Eaton points out in her writing on "The Beauty That Requires Health."[119] But such knowledge, once gained, cannot but affect one's perceptual experience, so that "as one learns more about the invisible things that make particular ecosystems healthy, landscapes begin to *look* more or less healthy." As discussed earlier, although I don't advocate environmental determinism, such information regarding ecological concerns modifies the sensuous appearance of the landscape without nullifying its initial impression.

Some other times, however, the healthfulness of an environment can be directly experienced. This is particularly the case with architecture. In contrast to "sick" buildings with tightly sealed windows, perpetual artificial lighting, carpets and other interior materials emitting toxic fumes, green buildings promote health, both physical and psychological, through ventilation, lighting, and temperature control systems that make use of sunlight, outdoor air, and sometimes rainwater and indoor plants. The occupants and users of the building will literally "feel" the difference in lighting, air quality, temperature, humidity, and air movement. They may even sometimes hear and touch the water used for cooling and moisture, as well as enjoying plants used for both air and water purification.[120] Indeed,

---

[119] Marcia Muelder Eaton, "The Beauty that Requires Health," included in *Placing Nature*. The following passages are both from p. 94. Also see her *Merit*, p. 185 and Hawken, et al, *Natural Capitalism*, p. 220. One clearly perceptible sign of the ecological problem associated with the chemically dependent landscaping is the decrease, or sometimes the demise, of native birds and butterflies. In her discussion of the history of American wetland, Vileisis documents that this phenomenon regarding birds was often one of the first signs to alert the scientists about the damage to the wetlands (throughout her *Discovering the Unknown Landscape*).

[120] For specific examples, see Hawken, et al, *Natural Capitalism*. To cite one of them, they describe the "Living Machine," an indoor simulation of a wetland ecosystem for water purification, as "odor-free and aesthetically pleasing" (p. 230).

one commentator urges green building to "honor the senses" because they are the "guardians of our health"; consequently, "the pleasant scent of the building and its materials is as important as their visual impact."[121] These bodily oriented sensations can contribute to the aesthetic appreciation of the space, which traditionally has been experienced predominantly, if not exclusively, by vision. The benefit of healthy buildings, therefore, is not only the better health of the occupants from the medical point of view, resulting in less absenteeism, but also their immediate sensory and bodily experiences of the provided space, which promotes productivity.

g. Caring and sensitive attitude   Finally, perhaps the most general and all-embracing aesthetic value expressed by green objects may be the embodiment of the virtue of caring and sensitivity. A caring, sensitive, responsible attitude is admittedly a moral virtue, normally not associated with an aesthetic value. However, what is often overlooked is the fact that moral attributes are frequently experienced through aesthetic manifestations. When we get a clue from its sensuous surface that the object is designed with sensitivity to the well-being of both the environment and people, we appreciate not only the moral virtue but also the way in which it is conveyed through the specific features of its sensuous surface that I have discussed so far. It is similar to the pleasure we derive from handling a carefully, meticulously, and sensitively crafted object, which we interpret as expressing the respect for the materials and users, in contrast to other objects which appear to be put together in haste, carelessly, and wantonly, with no thought to their impact on the users, giving us an impression of indifference, insensitivity, or downright disrespect.

Green design can also be considered as a counterpart to the all-too-common grandstanding among designers and architects toward individual "statement"-making, irrespective of the effects on the people and the environment.[122] Instead, when successful, green design can be appreciated for embodying a humble, respectful stand toward the environment, material,

---

[121] D. Pearson, "Making Sense of Architecture," cited by Simon Guy and Graham Farmer in "Contested Constructions: The Competing Logics of Green Buildings and Ethics," included in *Ethics and the Built Environment*, ed. Warwick Fox (London: Routledge, 2000), p. 82.

[122] In Chapter V, I will give examples of how some green designers and architects criticize their own profession as being preoccupied with stars making their artistic "statements" and how they call for the cultivation of humility and sensitivity regarding materials, environments, and users/occupants.

and the users/occupants. Later in this book, I will give a more sustained discussion of the aesthetic manifestation of the respectful attitude toward materials and environments (Chapter III) and the general point that moral virtues can be expressed aesthetically, as well as some specific examples, including green design, to illustrate this point (Chapter V).

v. Limits of green aesthetics?

I do believe that the above characteristics help make green structures and products aesthetically appreciable, and ultimately make them more acceptable and commercially successful than if they are promoted exclusively by their environmental values. However, is there a limit to the role of aesthetics in promoting sustainable future by aesthetic engineering, just as I believe there is a limit to "positive aesthetics" regarding nature?

I think one limiting factor is our physiological threshold of tolerance particularly regarding unpleasant odor. As I will argue in Chapter III, our reaction to unpleasant smell can to a certain degree be mitigated by experiencing it as a part of "the sense of place." The smell of manure, to borrow a Japanese expression, is "a perfume of farmland," while the odor of a rotten egg can be appreciable in a volcanic sulfur vent. However, no matter how enlightened we become about the ecological benefit of composting, for example, it seems almost impossible to overcome our visceral reaction to its bad smell.[123] The same is true of certain sounds, as indicated by people's objection to the whirling sound of wind turbines at their early stage of development, a problem which subsequently seems to have been overcome with better technology. Part of the difficulties with these modes of sensing is that we cannot escape from these sensations, unless we literally escape, unlike the sensation of vision which, if necessary, we escape by closing our eye or turning our head.

Furthermore, vision, among all the senses, traditionally considered closest to our intellectual faculty, seems most amenable to conceptual transformation (as in the brilliant sunset and luscious lawn beginning to look garish after revelation of the environmental harm involved). When we protest loudly against an eyesore scarring an environment, it is usually directed

---

[123] Our reaction here may also be context-dependent. For example, we may tolerate the putrid smell of a rotten elk carcass in the wild but it is not tolerable in the urban setting. The problem with composting is that generally it must be done in our backyard or in an urban setting in close proximity to our dwelling.

toward that aspect which is actually detrimental to the environment, such as littering, belching black smoke, clear-cutting, and the like. So it would appear that visual impressions can be relatively easily manipulated by a certain agenda, such as greener future. Just as environmental disvalue gives rise to the experience of aesthetic disillusionment, positive environmental value should help "beautify" objects initially experienced as unattractive.

However, the Capewind project illustrates that is it not that simple, though I will ultimately argue for the possibility of another form of aesthetic engineering. This is the case in which the support of its environmental value does not seem to overcome negative aesthetic reactions, evidenced by the fact that many opponents do embrace the project's environmental import. Is there any way in which an *aesthetic* argument can still be given for environmentally sound structures, such as this wind farm?[124]

A number of possibilities can be raised. For example, we can urge Capewind to eliminate clearly aesthetically negative factors which plagued past wind farm projects: juxtaposition of differently designed wind turbines, inconsistent directions of the blade movement, neglect of malfunctioning or broken blades, inconsistent or insufficient spacing between turbines, and turbines' color unsuitable for the setting.[125] Or, we can urge the opponents to compare the seascape with wind turbines with an imaginary seascape with environmentally harmful structures, such as nuclear power plants, oil rigs, or belching smoke stacks. Most likely the wind farm-scape is not going to be considered as aesthetically negative as these imaginary seascapes. Or we can ask them to look at the wind farm as if it were an environmental installation piece, similar to Christo's *Valley Curtain, Running Fence, Surrounded Islands, Umbrella Project*, or Walter de Maria's *Lightning Field*. We can also remind them that landscapes are never static; neither is our reaction. New structures in a familiar landscape are often met with resistance initially, but subsequently accepted and ultimately aesthetically appreciated. Think about people's initial reactions to the Eiffel Tower and the Vietnam Veterans' Memorial. Even the Golden Gate Bridge, when new, was decried as an "eye-sore to those living and a betrayal of future generations."[126]

These strategies may all be helpful, but not wholly effective. The first attempt may reduce or minimize aesthetically negative factors, but it

---

[124] I discussed this issue in "Machines in the Ocean" and "Response to Jon Boone's Critique" in *Contemporary Aesthetics* (<http://www.contempaesthetics.org>2004 and 2005 respectively).

[125] These aesthetic problems are compiled from chapter 11 of Righter.   [126] Postrel, p. 156.

is doubtful whether that attempt renders the overall effect aesthetically positive. The second strategy essentially consists of choosing the "lesser of two evils," hence, again, not arguing positively for the aesthetic value of the wind farm. The third requires the suspension of disbelief and is ultimately not workable, because the wind farm simply is *not* a work of art—it is strictly a utilitarian structure. Finally, "the test of time" argument is at best iffy because, for every new structure which subsequently became praised, there is another example which makes us question in retrospect: "what were we/they thinking?" Examples include "highways constructed that interrupt neighborhoods or parks or views."[127] As Postrel reminds us, "the test of time works both ways."[128]

Perhaps a more promising strategy is to encourage us to experience the specific wind farm in a larger context, both spatial and temporal, and to imagine the overall aesthetic consequences with and without such a facility. David Orr suggests that the definition of beauty required for green aesthetics would have to be elevated to "a higher order of beauty" that "causes no ugliness somewhere else or at some other time."[129] Wind farms then will embody, both literally and symbolically, a cleaner environment, with no air or water pollution, no mining for earth's resources, or no creation of toxic waste. It will be experienced as "appropriate" or "congruent" with its surrounding, because not only does it not pollute the air or water nor harm creatures, but it is also gratefully accepting and deriving maximum benefit out of the site-specific gift nature is providing—wind and open space. And we can witness this nature's gift at work in the movement of the blades.

In promoting this new aesthetic sensibility of sustainability, Robert Thayer, a landscape architect, insists that we make the embodiment of sustainable design fully visible and accessible, contrary to our usual tendency to hide signs of technology. That is, this new aesthetic sensibility should be facilitated and nurtured by our experiencing and living with those mechanisms which are its major players, such as wind turbines, solar panels, constructed wetland, and natural storm drainage.[130] Thayer calls these

---

[127] I owe these examples to Carolyn Korsmeyer.   [128] Postrel, p. 157.

[129] Orr, pp. 185 and 134.

[130] In addition to these, Thayer includes material recycling facilities, minimum tillage and organic farming practices, drip irrigation systems, bicycle transportation networks, and multipurpose wastewater treatment wetlands which double as wildlife reserves or recreation areas. Robert L. Thayer, Jr., *Gray World, Green Heart: Technology, Nature, and the Sustainable Landscape* (New York: John Wiley & Sons, 1994), p. 126.

"conspicuous nonconsumption" and regards them "essential markers along the road to a more sustainable world."[131] When there are enough cases of such aesthetic endorsement, landscapes with wind farms will become integrated into our aesthetic vocabulary through what Thayer calls "an accrual of positive environmental symbolism"[132] and they will add to the cumulative and collective memories of our cultural landscape.

However, Thayer himself is well aware of the impediment to developing this new aesthetic sensibility: our almost knee-jerk reaction to "the machine in the garden." "The ideal image [of pastoralism] ... seems to resist change" because "people prefer 'natural' landscapes over those influenced by humans"; hence, "although arguably a philosophically bankrupt notion, it shows little sign of relinquishing its power over American landscape esthetics."[133] This challenge is particularly pertinent in the Capewind case, because the environmental values and the larger contexts are already recognized and appreciated by many opponents; they are fully educated and enlightened about its environmental benefit and the big picture. That is, cultivating ecologically informed aesthetic sensibility should be the most crucial ingredient of green aesthetics, but, as the case of the wind farm indicates, there seems to be a limit to that approach. So are there any other strategies left for green aesthetics in this case?

Let me offer one more possibility of furthering this mode of aesthetic engineering. I am taking a cue from Yi-Fu Tuan's notion of "topophilia," which states that our attitude toward and resultant appreciation of a place cannot be dissociated from the personal, as well as cultural and societal, relationship we have with it.[134] Very often our direct involvement in altering a landscape seems to generate our affection and attachment toward the resultant landscape, which then leads to a positive aesthetic appreciation. Consider, for example, a well-known anecdote related by William James in one of the few examples outside nature aesthetics where conceptual considerations

---

[131] Taken from *Gray World*, included in *Theory in Landscape Architecture: A Reader*, ed. Simon Swaffield (Philadelphia: University of Pennsylvania Press, 2002), p. 192.

[132] Cited by Robert W. Righter in "Exoskeletal Outer-Space Creations," included in *Wind Power in View: Energy Landscapes in a Crowded World*, eds. Martin J. Pasqualetti, Paul Gipe, and Robert W. Righter (San Diego: Academic Press, 2002), p. 36.

[133] Robert L. Thayer, Jr., "Pragmatism in Paradise: Technology and the American Landscape," *Landscape* 30 (1990), pp. 2, 3, and 2.

[134] Yi-Fu Tuan, *Topophilia: A Study of Environmental Perception, Attitudes, and Values* (Englewood Cliffs: Prentice-Hall, 1974).

render initially negative aesthetic response positive. He describes how "coves" in North Carolina, a recently cleared field left with charred tree stumps and irregularly planted corn, which to him was "unmitigated squalor" and "a mere ugly picture on the retina," turned out to be a landscape redolent with pride and dignity to the residents, because it symbolized "a very paean of duty, struggle, and success," based on their honest sweat and labor.[135] I believe that a similar observation can be made concerning the way in which urban dwellers take pride and find aesthetic appeal in what otherwise may appear as a crude-looking, amateurish community garden.

This personal connection and resultant affection with a built environment should be tapped into, particularly when planning and designing a structure that alters a landscape. When a new structure modifies or transforms a familiar landscape, I wonder how much of people's resistance toward what is regarded as "the machine in the garden" is based upon an underlying feeling of resentment that the project was concocted by outsiders and "imposed" upon them. If the residents do not feel they are a part of the process, they don't have ownership of the project; in short, they feel alienated. What if, hypothetically, they took part in designing the structure, placement, and arrangement of the turbines, if not as professional designers and engineers but as concerned citizens by voicing their ordered preferences among a number of possibilities? What I am exploring is whether their aesthetic judgment that the ocean view is spoiled, destroyed, ruined, marred by wind turbines would remain the same, if they had some say in the process, making them feel that the resultant project was at least partially *their* idea, *their* initiative, and *their* design.[136]

---

[135] William James, "On a Certain Blindness in Human Beings," in *Talks to Teachers* (New York: Henry Holt and Company, 1915), pp. 231–4. I think James goes too far by committing the fallacy of environmental determinism, when he discounts his initial response, declaring that "the spectator's judgment is sure to … possess no worth." I believe that his first impression of "unmitigated squalor" remains important because the subsequent appearance of heart-felt pride is facilitated *precisely because* of its crude, unsophisticated appearance; the effect would have been quite different if the clearing appeared slick and orderly, executed with expert skill and technique.

[136] If we subscribe to the traditional, art-oriented aesthetic theory, our personal relationship to and stake in an object should be irrelevant to its aesthetic value. For example, the fact that my friend composed a particular piece of music is irrelevant to its musical merit; similarly, the fact that a particular landscape photograph depicts my hometown in Japan has nothing to do with whether or not it is a good photographic work. We certainly do not want art critics and art historians to bring in their very personal associations and investment to bear upon their professional aesthetic judgments of a work of art. However, what is appropriate and expected in the field of art is not always readily applicable to our aesthetic life outside the realm of art.

Thus, one effective way of ensuring a positive aesthetic experience of a particular environment is for us to be participants in some way, which generates our affection and attachment. I believe such a personal relationship and affective response is inseparable from its perceived aesthetic value. And this "topophilia" resulting from people's involvement and engagement should be fully attended to and utilized.[137] My thinking here stems from a newly emerging environmental ethic called civic environmentalism, which recognizes and emphasizes that solutions to various challenges facing environment need citizens' commitment to better their environment. That is, no matter how environmentally sound and well-meaning a certain goal, policy, or project may be, if it is perceived as something imposed on citizens from above or outside, such as a government or an outside environmental organization, its success and cultural sustainability is doubtful.[138] Citizens need to be enfranchised and the sense of empowerment will positively affect their aesthetic experience of the object and project.[139]

But, as I mentioned earlier, wind farms in general do have disadvantages compared with other community projects. We can "engage" with them only visually, but not literally.[140] Offshore facilities have further disadvantages compared with inland facilities because there is very little possibility for each resident to interact actively with the structures. It is not impossible, however. For example, the residents *can* be a part of the process of choosing colors, spacing, and arrangement. They can also act as a distant and visual caretaker by reporting damaged or malfunctioning turbines. Or,

[137] The importance of attending to people's attitude toward their landscape is explored by Laurence Short in "Wind Power and English Landscape Identity," included in Pasqualetti, et al. For example, he claims that "the wind industry must respect our cultural connection to the land, an attachment to the landscape that has been reaffirmed in the United Kingdom as a metaphor for national identity." (p. 57).

[138] In advocating civic environmentalism, Andrew Light points out that, while legal, political, and even philosophical and religious persuasion is indispensable, "if all environmental legislation were mandated from above and local populations had no reason to take an interest in environmental protection, then little would motivate citizens to respect laws other than threats of punitive consequences which are often difficult to enforce." ("Urban Ecological Citizenship," *Journal of Social Philosophy* 34:1 (Spring 2003), p. 53).

[139] The importance of empowering citizens in a project like wind farm is stressed by a number of writers in *Wind Power in View* (Short, Brittan, Pasqualetti, Gipe).

[140] Gordon G. Brittan, Jr. points out that wind turbines "preclude engagement. The primary way in which the vast majority of people can engage with them is visually. They cannot climb over and around them. They cannot get inside them. They cannot tinker with them." ("The Wind in One's Sails: A Philosophy" in Pasqualetti, et al, p. 71.)

after the example of Austin, Texas, which made a tourist attraction out of a bat colony, this seascape with a wind farm, the first in the United States and the biggest in the world, can be promoted as a new tourist destination.[141] Thus, in the context of aesthetic engineering for promoting a sustainable world, what may otherwise be dismissed as being irrelevant by art-centered aesthetics or disinterested aesthetic attitude theory, such as our personal relationship with and stake in the object or a commercial interest in promoting tourism, needs to be considered and sometimes taken advantage of.[142]

I started this chapter by arguing that, contrary to our initial impression that they are trivial, insignificant, and innocuous, the aesthetic judgments we make on everyday matters do have serious implications and exert a surprising degree of power over the state of the world and our life. In order to illustrate this phenomenon, what I call the power of the aesthetic, I first presented the ways in which our popularly held aesthetic sensibility seems to work against environmental values. As much as this is a problematic aspect of our everyday aesthetics, the other side of the coin is that this power can be utilized to achieve a more desirable end, in this case sustainable world and living. I remain hopeful that it is possible to formulate and instill in us an ecologically sensitive aesthetic taste regarding both nature and artifacts, although the designers of artifacts and built structures also bear responsibility in realizing green aesthetic values in their products. All of these considerations are meant to underscore the power of the aesthetic in our everyday life, as it can be wielded for a better world and life. Of course any social change needs to be driven by a concerted effort among various sectors: political, social, legal, educational, economic, and technological. I also believe that some aesthetic disagreements cannot be resolved by aesthetics alone. Particularly with respect to environmental aesthetics, the aesthetic judgments are subject to deeper visions and commitments regarding social and political issues, such as economic justice, capitalism, the notion of good life, and the

---

[141] I thank Sheila Lintott for this reference. There are also precedents for marketing wind farms by using them as a backdrop for advertising or a film scene. See Brittan, p. 63, Martin J. Pasqualetti, "Living with Wind Power in a Hostile Landscape," in Pasqualetti, et al, 165, and Robert L. Thayer, Jr., *Gray World,* p. 131.

[142] I found Marcia Eaton's discussion of "aesthetics and ethics in the environment" to be valuable and relevant to my discussion here. Her discussion is particularly helpful because it is illustrated with ample examples. See chapter 12 of her *Merit.*

like.[143] They are also amenable to change with new scientific discovery.[144] However, what I want to point out is that aesthetics *does* have a surprisingly important, if not decisive, role to play and our current neglect needs to be challenged and corrected.

[143] I will explore this issue more in Chapter V (2.ii) by discussing the issue of "eyesore."

[144] For example, while I currently maintain that wind turbines are environmentally valuable and I developed an argument for their positive aesthetic values based upon this belief, I also admit that the positive aesthetic values that I attribute to them are subject to change, if unforeseen environmental harm is discovered in the future. I don't think, however, that this possibility of revision should prevent us from forming an aesthetic judgment based upon the best available information. This possibility of revision is not unique to aesthetic judgments but characterizes any forms of knowledge and moral judgments, all of which should be subject to revision with a new information (see my "Response to Jon Boone's Critique").

III

Aesthetics of Distinctive Characteristics and Ambience

In Chapter I, I called attention to the aesthetic dimensions of our everyday life that do not result in "an aesthetic experience." I discussed some examples of such judgments, decisions, and actions and their serious environmental consequences in Chapter II. However, I am in no way denying that we do sometimes have an aesthetic appreciation of everyday objects or activities that make us pause and take note. Among those instances of aesthetic experience, one particular kind that is quite familiar is the appreciation of something for the way it expresses or articulates its distinguishing characteristics. When we experience a squirrel, a cherry tree, an early winter morning, or a typical suburban neighborhood, we seem to have a rough prototype of what the object is supposed to look, sound, and smell like and we appreciate it if it fulfills the expectation to the maximum. For example, I think most of us appreciate a squirrel for its jerky and sprightly movement when running, or for its busy and incessant movement of its front legs and mouth when perched on a tree branch eating acorns. These actions highlight the quintessential squirrel-like qualities, which is not quite forthcoming if it is just slowly walking across a street. We admire a weeping cherry tree if there are many drooping branches gently swaying in the wind supported by a gnarled, stocky trunk. The more drooping, swaying, and gnarled, the more appreciable. How many of us have been mesmerized by an overnight transformation of the outdoors into a winter wonderland? We run outside to feel not only the snow but also a crisp air biting into our face, the faint glow of the sunrise over the horizon, smell of smoke coming out from nearby houses, and the sound of snow creaking under our feet as we enjoy making a fresh track on the blank canvas. Finally, in my morning walk, I take in the atmosphere of a typical suburb, consisting of well-maintained houses with neatly trimmed hedges, abundant greens, joggers and cyclists doing their morning exercise, and the sound of school busses accompanied by children's laughter.

In all these examples, I have a "stop and smell the coffee (or rose?)" kind of experience, primarily directed toward the way in which each object or a phenomenon expresses its distinctive characteristics. I argued in the last chapter that, although our everyday aesthetic tastes at first glance appear quite trivial, they actually do lead to some serious consequences. The aesthetic experience that I discuss in this chapter is no exception. In what follows, I shall not only analyze what is involved in this kind of aesthetic experience but also pursue some of its important social and environmental ramifications.

1. Aesthetics of distinctive characteristics

i. Eighteenth-century European aesthetics

In the Western aesthetic tradition, the appreciation of the eloquent expression of an object's defining features was initially referred to not so much for itself but as a means of arguing against the legitimacy of some prevailing aesthetic theories. Edmund Burke, for example, discusses how proportion and fitness are not true causes of beauty by enumerating a series of examples taken from nature and the human body. He is concerned with repudiating the view then in vogue that beauty can be defined by a set proportion, lack of defects/deformity, or fitness of form to function. However, in his treatment of various examples given for this purpose, I believe he is referring, perhaps unwittingly, to the kind of aesthetic appreciation of typical characteristics that I have in mind. By comparing the proportion of length, size, and volume of various parts making up a rose and an apple blossom, or a swan, a peacock, a horse, a dog and a cat, and pointing out that there is no one standard of beauty based upon proportion which governs all these species, Burke concludes that each species has its own proportion, common form, which determines the rose-like-ness and swan-like-ness. Comparing a rose and an apple blossom, he claims that "the rose is a large flower, yet it grows upon a small shrub; the flower of the apple is very small, and it grows upon a large tree; yet the rose and the apple blossom are both beautiful, and the plants that bear them are most engagingly attired notwithstanding this disproportion."[1] Or, examining different birds, he questions: "how many birds are there that vary infinitely from each of these standards, and from every other which you can fix, with proportions different, and often directly opposite to each other! and yet many of these birds are extremely beautiful."[2]

In his examples repudiating fitness as the cause of beauty, on the other hand, Burke seems to imply that a swine, a pelican, a hedgehog, a monkey, and an elephant are not beautiful despite the construction of their body parts most fitted for their respective function, such as a swine's "wedge-like snout... with its tough cartilage at the end, the little sunk eyes, and the whole make of the head," which are "so well adapted to its offices of digging, and rooting."[3] Because Burke does have a definite idea of what constitutes beauty, namely small size, gradual variation, and soft colors, he disqualifies these animals from being beautiful. However, it is interesting to speculate what his judgment on their aesthetic value might have been had he considered their respective aesthetic quality, different from beauty, in their own right. Certainly swine are neither graceful nor elegant, but can't a swine be still appreciable if it exhibits maximally those characteristics fitted for digging and rooting, particularly when it is busily engaged in this excavating business? Comical or amusing, perhaps, but nonetheless isn't this creature appreciable for exuding its swine-like-ness to the fullest degree? A swine has *its* own charms, different from those of a swan or a leopard, and if a particular swine exhibits the swine-like appearance and behavior to the fullest, I think it can lead to an aesthetic appreciation.

Immanuel Kant distinguishes perfection of an object or an object's conformity to its "normal idea" or "archetype" from the pure judgment of taste. If we experience an object according to what it is supposed to be or "the standard of our judgment ... as a thing belonging to a particular animal

---

[1] Edmund Burke, *A Philosophical Enquiry into the Origin of Our Ideas of the Sublime and Beautiful* (Oxford: Oxford University Press, 1990), p. 86. Carolyn Korsmeyer pointed out that this kind-specific beauty is also found in Francis Hutcheson's notion of "comparative" beauty. Hutcheson defines comparative beauty as "a conformity, or a kind of unity between the original and the copy," and emphasizes that the original does not itself have to possess what he calls "absolute beauty" that consists of uniformity amidst variety, deriving most of his examples from works of art. I suppose comparative beauty can also be interpreted as conformity of individual members of a natural kind to its prototype, a sort of ideal that is composed of the clear expression of its distinctive features. (Section IV of *An Inquiry into the Original of Our Ideas of Beauty and Virtue* (1725), included in *What is Art?: Aesthetic Theory from Plato to Tolstoy*, ed. Alexander Sesonske (New York: Oxford University Press, 1965), p. 127).

[2] Burke, p. 87.   [3] Ibid. p. 95.

species,"[4] we are subsuming our judgment under a certain concept; hence our judgment is not "purely" (or "merely") aesthetical. If an animal, for example, is free of any defects or idiosyncratic features, "its presentation pleases, not by its beauty, but merely because it contradicts no condition, under which alone a thing of this kind can be beautiful. The presentation is merely correct." This "mere correctness," Kant admits, is "the form constituting the indispensable condition of all beauty," but it does not itself constitute beauty.

Kant may be arguing against a popular view that equates beauty with perfection, such as the one held by Joshua Reynolds. According to Reynolds, natural beauty is "the most general form" toward which all individual objects of its kind aspire, which is free of "accidental blemishes and excrescences."[5] In order to find beauty, therefore, it is necessary to know many members of the same kind; "no man can judge whether any animal be beautiful in its kinds, or deformed, who has seen only one of that species." Furthermore, it is impossible to engage in an inter-species comparison of beauty, according to a standard of beauty such as "a particular gradation of magnitude, undulation of a curve, or direction of a line," because "the great Mother of Nature will not be subjected to such narrow rules." Hence, "the works of nature, if we compare one species with another, are all equally beautiful."[6]

I believe both Kant and Reynolds are partially correct in their respective views. I agree with Reynolds's claim (partly shared by Burke) that each species can be beautiful (or aesthetically appreciable) in many different ways. At the same time, I believe Kant is correct in his claim that just because an object satisfies all the anatomical norms associated with it does not automatically mean that it is beautiful. What Kant fails to distinguish, however, is between the mere satisfaction of the norm and an exquisite expression of the quintessential characteristic of what the object is supposed to be. If the appreciation is directed toward *the fact that* the particular object satisfies its norm, it may be a cognitive judgment dealing more with classification. However, it seems to me that we can have an appreciation of *the way in which* the object's appearance gives rise to the articulation of its particular object-hood and defining character. When I enjoy watching

---

[4] Immanuel Kant, *Critique of Judgment*, tr. J. H. Bernard (New York: Hafner Press, 1974), p. 70. The next two passages are from pp. 72 and 71.

[5] Joshua Reynolds, *Idler* #82 (Nov. 10, 1759).   [6] Ibid.

a squirrel in my yard running around or busily eating nuts on the tree branch, I am not taking an anatomical inventory, but rather attending to the way in which all of the anatomical parts work together to give rise to the quintessential personality of squirrel-like appearance and behavior.

It is in the writing of a late eighteenth-century aesthetician, Archibald Alison, where we find independent descriptions of the kind of aesthetic appreciation I have been referring to. When discussing beauty found in different kinds of natural objects, he points out that:

in the different species of vegetables which possess expression, and which conse-quently admit of Beauty in Composition, it is observable also, that every individual does not possess this Beauty... The Oak, the Myrtle, the Weeping Willow, the Vine, the Ivy, the Rose, &c. are beautiful classes of Plants: but every Oak and Myrtle, &c. does not constitute a beautiful Form. The many physical causes which affect their growth, affect also their Expression; and it is only when they possess *in purity the peculiar Character of the class,* that the individuals are felt as beautiful.[7]

Rather than locating the beauty of various natural objects in things like uniformity amid variety, Alison locates it in "some determinate Expression or Association," which is typically expressed "by epithets significant of this Character."[8]

As soon... as we feel this Expression in any Vegetable Form, we perceive, or demand a relation among the different parts to this peculiar Character. If this relation is maintained, we feel immediately that the Composition of the Form is good. ... If, on the contrary, the different parts do not seem adjusted to *the general character,* if instead of an agreement among these parts in the maintaining or promoting this Expression, there appears only a mixture of similar and dissimilar parts, without any correspondence or alliance, we reject it as a confused and insignificant Form, without meaning or beauty.[9]

ii. Aesthetics of the rare and the uncommon

This kind of appreciation of various objects, as exuding the typical charac-teristics of what it is supposed to be, may appear to lead to formulating and maintaining a stereotypical idea of each kind of object, denying any aes-thetic value to an object which is unusual, defying the norm, and possessing

---

[7] Archibald Alison, *Essays on the Nature and Principles of Taste* (Hartford: George Goodwin & Sons, 1821, 2nd American edition), pp. 225–6, emphasis added.

[8] Ibid. p. 224.   [9] Ibid. p. 225, emphasis added.

abnormal qualities. But are anomalies always aesthetically unappreciable? Can't rarity and novelty be a source of aesthetic experience? Alison's view may indeed be vulnerable to this challenge.

However, my own perspective on the aesthetics of essential characteristics is not committed to a claim that such is *the only* instance of positive aesthetic experience. It is true that novelty or rarity is a relative quality, determined entirely by the context, as the following passage by Thomas Reid succinctly points out:

> Novelty is not properly a quality of the thing to which we attribute it, far less is it a sensation in the mind to which it is new; it is a relation which the thing has to the knowledge of the person ... It is evident, therefore, with regard to novelty, ... that it is not merely a sensation in the mind of him to whom the thing is new; it is a real relationship which the thing has to his knowledge at that time.[10]

Novelty also wears off rather quickly, which is why Burke denies that novelty plays any significant role in our aesthetic life.[11] However, though it is often short-lived and subject to change depending upon the context, I believe that we often do have an aesthetic appreciation of *the way in which* certain objects deviate from their norm. Joseph Addison certainly thought so, as he lists them as one of the three pleasures of the imagination, along with beauty and what would later be termed sublimity. For him, it is the pleasure derived from the uncommon that "bestows charms on a monster and makes even the imperfections of nature to please us."[12] Thus, the fact that we appreciate those objects for eloquently expressing their quintessential characteristic traits does not necessarily preclude the possibility of aesthetically appreciating other objects which deviate from the expected norm.[13]

[10] Thomas Reid, *Essays on the Intellectual Powers of Man* in *Philosophical Works*, originally published in 1785 (Hildesheim: George Olms Verlagsbuchhandlung, 1967), p. 493. It should be pointed out that this context-dependent-ness applies equally to that which maximally expresses its distinctive characteristics, as the above passage from Reynolds indicates (note 6).

[11] Burke must have felt strongly compelled to deny any aesthetic significance to novelty, as his *Philosophical Enquiry* begins with the discussion of this subject.

[12] Joseph Addison, "Pleasures of the Imagination," *Spectator* (June 23, 1712), included in *Essays in Criticism and Literary Theory*, ed. John Loftis (Northbrook: AHM Publishing Corporation, 1975), p. 143. Larry Shiner pointed out that the aesthetics of the novel, the rare, and the strange was quite popular, though not mainstreamed, in the eighteenth century, as discussed by Ronald Paulson in *The Beautiful, Novel, and Strange: Aesthetics and Heterodoxy* (Baltimore: The Johns Hopkins University Press, 1996).

[13] A problematic issue associated with aesthetically appreciating something which defies its norm is the moral dimension of appreciating "deformed" human beings, as they were displayed in a circus,

Historically, there are examples to illustrate the aesthetics of rarity and novelty. Consider, for example, the early American appreciation of "wonders of nature" or "freaks of nature." A British traveler in the mid-eighteenth century, Andrew Burnaby, reports that people in the town of Winchester, Virginia, recommended that he visit "some natural curiosities," such as "a medicinal spring, specific in venereal cases," "a river called Lost river, from its sinking under a mountain, and never appearing again," and "a natural arch, or bridge, joining two high mountains, with a considerable river running underneath."[14]

Commenting on the appreciation of such natural curiosities, Hans Huth observes how it lacks genuine aesthetic appreciation:

> All these sites had a 'curio' value of long standing which had little to do with their aesthetic merits. Every traveler inspected landmarks just as he did any man-made curiosity or freak of nature; therefore in appraising 'rapture' one must distinguish between the visitor's delight in a curiosity and his possibly growing appreciation of the scenic value.[15]

Huth's warning is helpful. However, with respect to these objects of landscape, their "curio" value may not be as clearly distinguishable from their "aesthetic" value. Unlike a four-leaf clover which may have a curio value without much distinctive aesthetic value, these works of nature, with their features and size, exhibit some *striking* characteristics such as the soaring height of the Natural Bridge. Insofar as we get enjoyment out of such *perceivable* characteristics of those works of nature, our appreciation, I think, is an aesthetic one. However, our appreciation toward other kinds of rarity of nature such as "a medicinal spring, specific in venereal cases," unless they exhibit some perceptually striking features, such as color or smell different from what we would normally expect, would be wholly conceptually based. In such cases, it is debatable whether our appreciation is an aesthetic one. In order for a quality of an object to be aesthetically

or even when they themselves choose to exhibit their bodies for commercial gain. Another morally problematic case involves various organisms and creatures created through genetic engineering, such as a glow-in-the-dark bunny or a mouse growing a human ear on its back. Though it is an important as well as fascinating subject in itself, I will not pursue it because it will get me off the subject of this chapter.

[14] Andrew Burnaby, *Travels through the Middle Settlements in North America, in the Years 1759 and 1760* (Originally published in 1775; London, 1798), pp. 46–7.

[15] Hans Huth, *Nature and the American* (Lincoln: University of Nebraska Press, 1972), p. 27.

relevant, I believe it has to be perceivable or have the power to affect the perceivable features.[16]

Another historical example is the Japanese governmental program of protecting *tennen kinenbutsu* (natural monuments), initiated in 1919 and combined with the protection of cultural treasures in 1950.[17] An interesting aspect of this program is that the protection includes both those objects which exquisitely display their native characteristics and those which deviate from the norm in an interesting and dramatic manner. For example, one old wisteria tree under protection features drooping branches, characteristic of this tree, measuring as long as 2.7 m, while another wisteria tree is notable for its unusual feature: a huge twisted trunk split in half with the circumference of 1.8 m. Several wide areas populated by lily of the valley are protected for exhibiting their gregarious manner of spreading, while uncommon species of bamboo, such as those with drooping leaves or stalks with green and yellow colors or smooth and ridged textures alternating according to sections, are also designated for protection. Protected landscapes include some wetlands supporting a variety of indigenous plants and creatures, pristine pine forests, as well as unusually shaped rocks and bizarre-looking volcanic formations, much like the "freaks of nature" celebrated by early Americans.

iii. Examples from the Japanese aesthetic tradition

I have discussed above how Western aesthetic thought is not silent on this kind of aesthetic appreciation of objects' distinctive characteristics. I also provided evidence from Japanese culture that appreciation of things for rarity, due to deviation from the expected norm, takes place, alongside the appreciation of objects exquisitely expressing their expected personality.

However, by far, the Japanese aesthetic tradition is noted for its respect and appreciation for the quintessential characters of objects. Furthermore,

[16] I suppose that an argument could be made to show that the medicinal value of the water does affect its expressive qualities without altering its immediate sensory qualities, such as color and smell. Similar to the example of puffer fish that I cited in Chapter II, knowing the medicinal value may render the water feel "magical" or "mysterious." To the extent the medicinal value does this, I would include this knowledge as aesthetically relevant. However, the specific fact that this spring water is beneficial for rheumatoid arthritis but not for high blood pressure seems too conceptual and removed from the sensory experience to be integrated into our sense experience in some way.

[17] Katō Mutsuo, et al. *Nihon no Tennen Kinenbutsu (Natural Monuments of Japan)* (Tokyo: Kōdansha, 1995). All the examples in this paragraph are taken from this book.

such an appreciation is appropriated and utilized as a guiding principle of design, whether or not it regards giving expression to the native characteristics of the object, the material, or the subject matter. The application of this design principle ranges from art created with natural materials, such as garden and flower arrangement, art dealing with nature as subject matter, such as painting and haiku, to everyday objects, such as food and packaging.

The earliest explicit reference to the notion of respecting and appreciating the character of something can be found in the oldest extant writing on garden making, *Sakuteiki* (*Book on Garden Making*), written by an eleventh-century aristocrat. The author states that the art of garden making consists of creating *the scenic effect* of a landscape. Toward this end, he recommends one principle of design: "obeying (or following) the request" (*kowan ni shitagau*). Referring specifically to rocks here, this principle suggests that the arrangement of rocks be dictated by their individual characteristics. For example, the gardener "should first install one main stone, and then place other stones, in necessary numbers, in such a way as *to satisfy the requesting mood* of the main stone."[18]

In later centuries, the same design strategy extends to include the placement and maintenance of plant materials. Instead of allowing their free growth or inevitable destruction by natural processes, Japanese gardeners meticulously shape and maintain the trees and shrubs by extensive pruning, clipping, shearing, pinching, plucking, or by the use of various gears such as wires, ropes, poles, and weights, and even sometimes stunting the growth of some parts by applying retardants. Unlike topiary in European formal gardens, however, where shapes are designated regardless of the characteristics of the plant materials used, the desired shape of a tree in a Japanese garden is defined by the particular form of the individual tree itself. According to a fifteenth-century manual, for example,

When it comes to horizontal trees, observe the natural growth pattern of the tree, and then prune it *to bring out its inherent scenic qualities* ... Do not prune back the

---

[18] Tachibana-no-Toshitsuna, *Sakuteiki: The Book of Garden-Making, Being a Full Translation of the Japanese Eleventh Century Manuscript: Memoranda on Garden Making Attributed to the Writing of Tachibana-no-Toshitsuna*, tr. S. Shimoyama (Tokyo: Town & City Planners, 1985), p. 20. The other places with reference to the notion of "obeying the request" are pp. 7, 10, and 13. I explore this principle of Japanese garden design in "Japanese Gardens: The Art of Improving Nature," *Chanoyu Quarterly* 83 (1996): 40–61.

longer of those branches inherent to a tree's natural growth pattern ... Prune out only those branches that wander erratically or are long and unkempt, so as to achieve a visually harmonious effect.[19]

The gardener is thus required to discern the defining features of the particular material and give them a clear, forceful articulation by eliminating adventitious, inessential, and irrelevant parts. The whole art-making here requires the creator to work closely *with*, rather than *in spite of* or *irrespective of*, the material's natural endowments.[20]

Similar considerations also govern the art of flower arrangement (*ikebana*), elevated to an artistic status primarily through its contribution to the tea ceremony and given theoretical foundation during the sixteenth century. While this art form begins paradoxically by cutting off a live flower or branch, initiating its death, its primary aim is to "let flower live," literally the translation of *ikebana*, or to "let flower express itself" (*ikasu*).[21] This can be achieved by further cutting of branches, leaves, and blossoms so that only the essential parts defining the particular plant can be clearly delineated. One contemporary commentator summarizes that "the ultimate aim of floral art is to represent nature in its inmost essence."[22]

The same design principle of articulating the distinctive characteristics of an object is found with respect to the art of representation. Take a literary form, haiku, for example. A 5–7–5 syllable verse, established in the seventeenth century by Matsuo Bashō (1644–94), it also aims at presenting the essence of the subject matter. According to Bashō, the *raison d'être* of poetry is to capture the essence of nature by entering into and identifying oneself with it, summarized in his well-known saying: "Of

[19] Zōen, *Illustrations for Designing Mountains, Water, and Hillside Field Landscape*, tr. D. A. Slawson, included in D. A. Slawson, *Secret Teachings in the Art of Japanese Gardens: Design Principles, Aesthetic Values* (Tokyo: Kodansha International, 1991), s. 56, emphasis added. Allen Carlson uses the expression, "a look of inevitability," to refer to this design principle in Japanese garden ("On the Aesthetic Appreciation of Japanese Gardens," *British Journal of Aesthetics* 37:1 (January 1997)). It is interesting to note that the same term was used by William Morris in his instruction regarding how to design a pattern after a plant: "above all, pattern, in whatever medium, should have the inevitability of nature." (William Morris, "Textiles," included in *Arts and Crafts Essays*, originally published in 1893 (Bristol: Thoemmes Press, 1996, reprint), p. 36.

[20] I touched upon the ecological significance of this design principle of working *with* nature in Chapter II. I will explore it further in Section 3 of this chapter.

[21] For the paradox involved in the art of *ikebana*, see Ryōsuke Ōhashi's entry on "Kire and Iki" in *Encyclopedia of Aesthetics*, ed. Michael Kelly (New York: Oxford University Press, 1998), Vol. 2, p. 553.

[22] Makoto Ueda, *Literary and Art Theories in Japan* (Cleveland: The Press of Case Western Reserve University, 1967), p. 86.

the pine-tree learn from the pine-tree. Of the bamboo learn from the bamboo."[23] For this, what he calls "the slenderness of mind" is required, as one has to overcome one's personal feelings and concerns in order to grasp and appreciate the qualities of the object for what they are. Sometimes described as "impersonality," the ideal of haiku-making should be object-centered, rather than subject-governed.[24] When successful, the poet's effort will " 'grow into' (*naru*) a verse," rather than " 'doing' (*suru*) a verse."[25]

Bashō's contemporary, Tosa Mitsukuni (1617–91) develops a similar theory regarding the art of painting. For him, mimesis is the main purpose of a painting and he repudiates factual errors in depiction. However, it is "the spirit of the object" that the painter must grasp and present.[26] Toward this end, the painter can and should omit certain elements, making the overall effect "incomplete" and "suggestive," facilitating more readily the presentation of the essential characteristics of the subject matter, such as bird-ness. Exhaustively faithful, realistic rendition on the paper, such as found in both Chinese painting and the rival Kanō school paintings, according to Mitsukuni, is like prose, which is contrasted with the poetry of Tosa school paintings.[27] Most likely conscious of the teachings by Bashō and Mitsukuni, another painter Tsubaki Chinzan (1800–1854) also claims: "even when painted with black ink, bamboo is bamboo; with red ink, bamboo is also bamboo. If the spirit of bamboo is embodied in the brush, the *ambience* of bamboo will naturally arise. This is the essence of painting."[28]

The Japanese design principle based upon grasping and giving a further articulation to the inherent characteristics of the material or subject matter

---

[23] Recorded by Bashō's disciple, Hattori Dohō, in *The Red Booklet*, first published in 18th century, tr. Toshihiko and Toyo Izutsu, included in Toshihiko and Toyo Izutsu, *The Theory of Beauty in the Classical Aesthetics of Japan* (The Hague: Martinus Nijhoff Publishers, 1981), pp. 162–3.

[24] Makoto Ueda explains this notion of impersonality as follows:

The poet's task is not to express his emotions, but to detach himself from them and to enter into the object of nature. A pine tree has its own life, so a poet composing a verse on it should first learn what sort of life it is by entering into the pine tree: this is the only way by which he can learn about the inner life of the pine. (Ueda, p. 158)

[25] Dohō, p. 134.   [26] Ueda, p. 137.

[27] Ibid. pp. 138–9. Ueda explains Mitsukuni's view by stating that "the painter can give spirit to his painting only by *growing into the object of the painting himself*—that is to say, by *identifying his spirit with the spirit of the object* in his painting." (p. 138, emphasis added.)

[28] Tsubaki Chinzan, *Chinzan Shokan* (*Correspondence of Chinzan*), from the 19th century, my translation, included in *Nihon no Geijutsuron* (*Theories of Art in Japan*), ed. Yasuda Ayao (Tokyo: Sōgensha, 1990), p. 251, emphasis added.

applies not only to these artistic media but also to objects and activities which concern everyday life, a subject more relevant to the theme of this book. From lacquerware to pottery, paper to textile, woodwork to metalwork, Japanese crafts are transmitted generation after generation, firmly rooted in the respect for materials, process, tools used, as well as the tradition itself. One commentator observes: "Craftmakers working within Japan's ancient traditions respond to the generations of passed-on knowledge. This collective memory includes a deep respect for material and process, and respect too for the intended user."[29]

Let me take packaging and food as illustrations of this attitude. Traditional Japanese packaging is well known for its aesthetic and functional use of the materials. A noted Japanese architect, for example, offers the following praise:

I was struck at the abundance of the traditional wrapping materials and methods in Japan ... I know of no other culture that has produced such a rich accumulation of wrapping systems so beautiful and functional, for accommodating the wide variety of contents and shapes of the enclosures.[30]

Various packaging materials are manipulated not only for protecting and hiding the content but also in such a way as to bring out and fully take advantage of the typical characteristics of the materials. With packaging predominantly made of relatively natural materials, such as bamboo, straw, paper, and wood, traditional Japanese package design takes advantage of and fully utilizes the native characteristics of these materials. In a sense, the design is suggested by the qualities of the material itself. For example, Japanese paper lends itself to be folded, twisted, layered, torn, and made into a cord by tight twisting. A bamboo stalk can be sliced into thin strips which are both flexible and strong; they can then be woven. Or it can be cut into section to take advantage of its natural section dividers. Bamboo leaves and bark can be used for wrapping food items because of their thinness and flexibility, as well as their scent. Similarly, some wood material, such as cedar, imparts distinct, pungent scent to its content. Straw

---

[29] Jack Lenor Larsen, "The Inspiration of Japanese Design," included in *Traditional Japanese Design: Five Tastes* (New York: Japan Society, 2001), p. 12.

[30] Fumihiko Maki, "Japanese City Spaces and the Concept of *Oku*," *The Japan Architect* 265 (1979), p. 60. For a more detailed discussion of the aesthetics of Japanese packaging, see my "Japanese Aesthetics of Packaging," *The Journal of Aesthetics and Art Criticism* 57:2 (Spring 1999): pp. 257–65.

can be tied, woven, or bound together. All of these native characteristics of the materials are fully utilized in various Japanese package designs, ranging from a ceremonial envelope made with layers of folded paper tied with paper cord, to a bamboo basket, a cedar box for pound cake and preserved seafood, a bamboo leaf wrapper for *sushi*, and straw strings woven to hang eggs.[31] These designs are not only pragmatic and economical but also express an attitude of quiet respect and humility toward the material.

The highly sophisticated aesthetics involved in Japanese food, engaging all the senses, is also well known. In addition to various forms of purely sensory attraction, such as its picture perfect arrangement on an appropriately chosen container, an important focus of Japanese food is its handling of the ingredients.[32] In general, the manipulation of each ingredient (cutting, choice of cooking method, seasoning, arrangement) is done so as to bring out the best of its native qualities. For example, sometimes fish is presented without any cooking, or grilled whole with a skewer weaving through the length of the body in order to create a wavy shape suggestive of its movement in the water. Various condiments and ornaments, such as herbs, blossoms, leaves, and seaweed, are arranged individually so that their individual characteristics are retained and showcased, as well as giving us the opportunity to create our own seasoning. In *nimono*, a Japanese version of vegetable stew, each vegetable is cooked and seasoned separately to retain the respective color, taste, and texture, and then arranged in a bowl in such a way so that each can be presented in the best light, instead of being dished out as a heaping mound of mixture into the bowl. The outcome of such labor-intensive fussiness is that each ingredient preserves and expresses its own native characteristics, complements each other, and we the consumers enjoy the synthetic orchestral sound created by each instrument playing up its own tonal quality, as it were.

Taking Japanese lunchbox as a microcosmic illustration of this Japanese aesthetic sensibility and worldview, Kenji Ekuan, a noted industrial designer, describes its content as follows: "our lunchbox…gathers together normal, familiar, everyday things from nature, according to season, and

---

[31] The discussion here is best accompanied by the visual images form Hideyuki Oka's *How to Wrap Five Eggs: Japanese Design in Traditional Packaging* (New York: Harper & Row, 1967) and *How to Wrap Five More Eggs: Traditional Japanese Packaging* (New York: Weatherhill, 1975), as well as from *Package Design in Japan*, ed. Shigeru Uchida (Köln: Benedikt Taschen Verlag, 1989)

[32] Another important aspect, seasonableness, will be discussed later in this chapter.

enhances their inherent appeal... [T]he aim of preparation and arrangement revealed in the lunchbox is to include everything and *bring each to full life*." In short, the mission of Japanese "culinary artifice" is "to render fish more fishlike and rice more ricelike."[33]

iv. "Truth to materials"

Partly influenced by this Japanese aesthetic sensibility with respect to materials, the arts and crafts movement that began during late nineteenth century in Britain also upholds the notion called "truth to materials." This concept was initiated by John Ruskin who called for "honesty" in materials:

All art, working with given materials, must propose to itself the objects which, with those materials, are most perfectly attainable; and becomes illegitimate and debased if it propose [sic] to itself any other objects better attainable with other materials... The workman has not done his duty... unless he even so far *honours* the materials with which he is working as to set himself to bring out their beauty, and to recommend and exalt, as far as he can, their peculiar qualities.[34]

The subsequent arts and crafts movement advocated this notion as a foundational attitude toward their design work. Initially applied primarily to organic materials crafted by hand, but not to newly emerging synthetic materials or mechanically produced objects, this ideal refers to respecting and working with "the quality, *the very essence of things*."[35] Referring to textiles, William Morris, for example, states: "Never forget the material

[33] Kenji Ekuan, *The Aesthetics of the Japanese Lunchbox*, tr. Don Kenny (Cambridge: The MIT Press, 2000), the long passage from p. 6 and "fishlike...ricelike" passage from p. 77, emphasis added. Short of actually experiencing Japanese lunchbox, Ekuan's book has abundant photographic images of Japanese lunchbox; so does *Ekiben: The Art of the Japanese Box Lunch* by Junichi Kamekura, et al (San Francisco: Chronicle Books, 1989). This latter book provides not only the food arrangement but also various forms of packaging for box lunch sold on train stations. This Japanese design principle of respecting and taking advantage of the materials' native characteristics is not limited to more traditional, natural materials. Contemporary designers adopt the same stance toward new materials. For example, Tadao Andō's architecture often emphasizes the concrete-ness of concrete, while Issey Miyake, in his apparel design, explores synthetic materials and rubber.

[34] John Ruskin, *The Stones of Venice*, Vol. II (1853), cited by Nigel Whiteley, "Utility, Design Principles and the Ethical Tradition," in *Utility Reassessed: The Role of Ethics in the Practice of Design*, ed. Judy Attfield (Manchester: Manchester University Press, 1999), p. 192.

[35] Cited by Gillian Naylor, in *The Arts and Crafts Movement: A Study of its Sources, Ideals and Influence on Design Theory* (Cambridge: The MIT Press, 1971), p. 106, emphasis added. While Morris generally favors handicraft production over mechanized production, he does advocate the same principle for the latter as well, summarized in his recommendation: "let your design show clearly what it is. Make it mechanical with a vengeance... Don't try, for instance, to make a printed plate look like a hand-painted one" (cited by Naylor, pp. 106–7).

you are working with, and try always to use it for doing what it can do best: if you feel yourself hampered by the material in which you are working, instead of being helped by it, you have so far not learned your business."[36]

This ideal was handed down to subsequent generations of the arts and crafts movement. Romney Green (1872–1943), for one, while giving a hierarchical ordering to materials, namely stone, then wood, then iron, insists that "the character of each need[s] to be respected." His disciple also states: "We like to sense the living bond between the furniture we make and the forest trees that gave it birth; to manifest the *'woodiness'* of our woodwork."[37] Summarizing the attitude among the craftspeople of the inter-war period, one historian remarks that they "developed their own aesthetic codes of practice which to a greater or lesser extent centered on the question of truth to the qualities of specific materials."[38] This attitude, according to another commentator, has been handed down to contemporary craftspeople as well: "These modern designers uphold aesthetico-moral principles such as 'truth to materials', and try to bring out the unique quality of that material."[39]

It is not only among craftspeople where respect for materials is upheld as a principle of design and creation. Some contemporary artists, working primarily with natural materials, also embrace this notion. British artist, David Nash, who works with wood and trees, is described as engaging in "consistent efforts to tap nature's initiative."[40] In light of this commitment,

[36] Morris, "Textiles," pp. 37–8.

[37] Both Green's and his disciple's comments are cited by Tanya Harrod in *The Crafts in Britain in the 20th Century* (New Haven: Yale University Press, 1999), p. 145, emphasis added.

[38] Ibid. p. 146.

[39] Nigel Whiteley, *Design for Society* (London: Reaktion Books, 1993), p. 92. Carolyn Korsmeyer questioned whether Bernini's use of marble in the sculpture of St. Teresa would go against the notion of "truth to materials," as it seems to float. I think that in this case the weight of marble is crucial in appreciating its gravity-defying lightness. This is an example of a fine arts artist expressing his respect for the material by *contradicting*, rather than following, its characteristics. In order to come up with a design that purposely goes against the distinctive characteristic of marble, the sculptural piece calls attention to it, thereby indicating his intimate understanding and respect for the material. A similar example is Howard Ben Trè's massive chunk of glass that comprises a chair at the Rhode Island School of Design Museum. It is utterly contradictory to the typical qualities of glass: delicate, fragile, and elegant. However, because of its exquisite denial of these qualities, we are made to become more aware of the material itself. This way of highlighting the characteristics of the material through denying them is more endemic to fine arts. When it comes to utilitarian objects, for practical and technological reasons, "truth to materials" is observed by taking advantage of and following, rather than contradicting, the native characteristics of the material.

[40] This and Nash's remark about *Ash Dome* come from Ann Wilson Lloyd, "David Nash," *Sculpture* (Sept.–Oct., 1992), p. 22.

Nash himself is critical of his own project, *Ash Dome*, a planting and training of twenty-two ash trees to form a dome-like structure by remarking: "knowing what I know now, I wouldn't have done it. It's actually manipulating the trees more than I feel comfortable with." The same attitude of accepting, respecting, and working with the inherent characteristics of the material also underlies projects by Andy Goldsworthy and Michael Singer, in working with materials available on site, thereby emphasizing the sense of place, and celebrating the ephemerality of their creations, one essential feature of objects located outdoors. Or, Alfio Bonamo, working with felled trees, describes a particular challenge and lively tension when "working... directly with natural materials... not knowing exactly where the process will lead you, *feeling and listening to what they have to say.*"[41] He claims that it has become important that "each component I use maintains *the essence of its identity,* no matter if it's natural or man made," and that "a functional work is created while still respectfully maintaining most of the tree's original identity" so that "the tree... continues to tells [sic] its own story."

2. Aesthetics of ambience

i. Creation of ambience

So far, I have been exploring the aesthetic appreciation of a single object or a material for expressing its own characteristics. However, an equally significant part of our everyday aesthetic life is the appreciation directed toward an ambience, atmosphere, or mood surrounding a certain experience, comprised of many ingredients. Take our experience of eating, for example. First of all, it is always a multi-sensory experience, going beyond taste and smell, to include other sensory qualities like tactile sensation (crunchy, mushy, chewy), visual impression, and sometimes even sound quality. Much of our enjoyment of bubbly beverages, such as soda and champagne, is the tingling sensation on our tongue; without it they taste "flat." Japanese food is well known for its picture-like presentation, as well

---

[41] Alfio Bonanno, et al, "Materials," included in *Ecological Aesthetics Art in Environmental Design: Theory and Practice*, ed. Heike Strelow (Basel: Birkhäuser, 2004), p. 96. The next passages are from pp. 98 and 100, emphases added.

as for mandatory slurping when eating noodle soup or drinking tea in a tea ceremony. Even in cultures where the sound of eating is discouraged, as in Anglo-American societies, the experience of biting into a juicy apple cannot be separated from its crunching sound; the same with potato chips. Diane Ackerman also observes: "there's a gratifying crunch to a fresh carrot stick, a seductive sizzle to a broiling steak, a rumbling frenzy to soup coming to a boil, an arousing bunching and snapping to a bowl of breakfast cereal."[42]

The multi-sensory dimension of our eating is not limited to ingesting food itself; it extends to the entire experience induced by our handling of the container, utensil, and the like. Jun'ichirō Tanizaki describes in the most sensual manner the moment of drinking soup (in the proper Japanese expression, instead of the English expression of "eating") from a lacquer bowl with a lid:

Remove the lid from a ceramic bowl, and there lies the soup, every nuance of its substance and color revealed. With lacquerware there is a beauty in that moment between removing the lid and lifting the bowl to the mouth when one gazes at the still, silent liquid in the dark depths of the bowl, its color hardly differing from that of the bowl itself. What lies within the darkness one cannot distinguish but the palm senses the gentle movements of the liquid, vapor rises from within forming droplets on the rim, and the fragrance carried upon the vapor brings a delicate anticipation. What a world of difference there is between this moment and the moment when soup is served Western style, in a pale, shallow bowl. A moment of mystery, it might almost be called, a moment of trance.[43]

Furthermore, in addition to the multi-sensory experience surrounding the act of eating and drinking, our appreciation of food is inseparable from the whole ambience orchestrated by a number of other ingredients: table setting, the environment in which we are eating, its occasion, time of the day and year, the atmosphere created by the conversation between and among our eating companions, and so on. Sometimes all the parts somehow fit together to give rise to a very satisfying experience, "an" experience as Dewey might say, while other times one mismatched element acts as a dissonance. For example, a background *koto* music will be a welcome

---

[42] Diane Ackerman, *A Natural History of the Senses* (New York: Vintage Books, 1991), p. 142.

[43] Jun'ichirō Tanizaki, *In Praise of Shadows*, tr. Thomas J. Harper and Edward G. Seidensticker (New Haven: Leete's Island Books, 1977), p. 15.

addition to our experience of eating *sushi*, but not when eating an Italian meal. The food itself does not change, but our *experience* regarding the food certainly does.[44]

We again find a number of examples to illustrate this point in Archibald Alison's associationist aesthetic theory. Regarding the quality of a sound, he offers the following series of examples:

> The scream of the eagle is simply disagreeable, when the bird is either tamed or confined: it is sublime only, when it is heard amid rocks and deserts, and when it is expressive to us of liberty and independence, and savage majesty. The neighing of a war-horse in the field of battle, or of a young and untamed horse when at large among mountains, is powerfully sublime. The same sound in a cart-horse, or a horse in the stable, is simply indifferent, if not disagreeable … (T)he call of a goat, … among rocks, is strikingly beautiful, as expressing wildness and independence. In a farm-yard, or in a common inclosure, it is very far from being so.[45]

Sometimes, besides the physical context, temporal context makes a difference in the aesthetic quality of "the same sound."

> The hooting of the Owl at midnight, or amid ruins, is strikingly sublime. The same sound at noon, or during the day, is very far from being so. … The twitter of the Swallow is beautiful in the morning, and seems to be expressive of the cheerfulness of that time: at any other hour it is quite insignificant. Even the song of the Nightingale, so wonderfully charming in the twilight, or at night, is altogether disregarded during the day.[46]

For my purpose, it does not matter whether we agree with the specifics of his judgment. What is important is that, whatever our particular aesthetic taste

---

[44] The foregoing discussion renders one of the questions raised by Kant's theory of beauty a moot point: the aesthetic status of a single sensory quality like the taste of Canary wine, the color violet, the tone of wind or string instruments, and the green of a grass plot. Because beauty proper consists of purposiveness without a purpose for him, which presupposes parts that are arranged in some way, Kant characterizes these sensory qualities as merely "the pleasant" or "charm to the senses," not beautiful in themselves. He reaches this conclusion after considering and rejecting the possibility that such a single sensory quality results from a certain arrangement of parts which we can sense. However, as the example of food shows, we almost never experience a single sensory quality in isolation. Taste is inseparable from smell and texture and the experience of eating is always contextual. Even in a special circumstance like wine tasting where participants are supposed to tune out everything and focus on wine's sensory qualities, the tasting experience cannot be separated from the feel of the wine glass from which we drink. (Kant, *Critique of Judgement*. The wine reference is from p. 46, color violet p. 47, tone of instruments p. 47, and green p. 59. As for the possibility of single sensory qualities consisting of perceivable parts, see p. 60. Also see p. 169.)

[45] Alison, pp. 135 and 140.   [46] Ibid.

may happen to be, we almost never experience animal cries and birdsong in the abstract. We experience the whole complex, including the cause of the sound (warhorse or carthorse), physical environment, time of the day, and the season, which together sometimes give rise to a unified expression, such as cheerfulness or fierceness, or at other times fail to do so due to incongruous elements, preventing the events from coming together into a whole.

Our everyday experience of smell is similar. Even a clearly pleasant smell may not be appreciable in a certain context. For example, the smell of turkey roasting in the oven, the indispensable ingredient of the American celebration of Thanksgiving Day, will not be appreciable if it is wafting through an operating room in a hospital. Curt Ducasse similarly points out that "the odor of roast beef... is a pleasant odor; yet a woman who perfumed herself with it would hardly become more fascinating."[47] The strong smell of coffee that we enjoy in a Starbucks cafe is not going to be positively experienced if it permeates a small Japanese *sushi* stand. On the other hand, an odor that is universally detested can be a part of a positive experience, if it contributes to defining the sense of place. Examples include the smell of manure in a farmland ("perfume of countryside" in the Japanese parlance) and the stench of a rotten egg in a volcanic formation such as hot spring, previously mentioned in Chapter II.[48]

This contextual appropriateness/inappropriateness is most notable with built structures. Marcia Eaton gives an example of a log cabin or an abandoned shack that may be generally experienced positively in a pristine landscape, but not appreciated in an urban setting. Conversely, fast-food restaurants will be accepted as "'natural' landmarks" in a busy urban environment, but are unacceptable in the middle of what otherwise appears to be a pristine landscape.[49]

In Chapter I, I pointed out the relatively "frameless" character of the object of our everyday aesthetic appreciation. Unlike our experience of standard fine art objects, our everyday aesthetic experience is seldom directed toward a clearly demarcated object; hence, it may appear to lack

[47] Curt Ducasse, *Art, the Critics and You* (New York: Oskar Piest, 1944), p. 168.

[48] Yi-Fu Tuan calls attention to the often-neglected importance of smell in city planning and nature preservation in *Passing Strange and Wonderful: Aesthetics, Nature, and Culture* (Washington, D. C.: Island Press, 1993), pp. 62, 64, and 69.

[49] Marcia Muelder Eaton, *Merit, Aesthetic and Ethical* (Oxford: Oxford University Press, 2001), p. 194.

a unifying theme that organizes various ingredients provided by different senses and associated ingredients. However, sometimes our multi-sensory and multi-dimensional experiences come together to provide a unified experience which becomes the source of aesthetic appreciation. When so many disparate, but not incongruous, elements come together under one unifying theme, such as a particular sense of place, season, time of the day, or occasion, we often have a memorable experience even within our humdrum life. We savor the distinctive character of the place, the season, or the atmosphere associated with the particular occasion.

How many of us have experienced going to New York City and absorbed its "sense of place" by walking on the street, which sometimes vibrates under our feet with the subway passage, noisy with honking taxis, surrounded by skyscrapers, with aroma of burned chestnut and pretzels and the saxophone melody by a street musician wafting in the air? These ingredients together give rise to the atmosphere of vibrancy and zaniness. Similarly, "a dog day of summer" experience requires not only its heat and humidity but also very still air with no breeze, the droning sound of a distant lawnmower accompanied by a faint smell of grass, people moving very slowly with perspiration dripping, dark green leaves of trees harboring cicada with their incessant monotonous nasal cry, and only the occasional relief provided by the chime of an ice cream truck. A festive occasion, such as a wedding, is also characterized by many ingredients, ranging from the venue, flowers, dresses, music, to the food served, the table setting with a thematic centerpiece, the order and content of speeches, and the seating arrangement. As a matter of fact, there are professionals who oversee every detail to make sure that a certain ambience is created. Similarly, the United States' celebration of Thanksgiving is defined by a range of pre-determined ingredients: food, color scheme (brown, orange, and yellow), decoration (potted chrysanthemums, orangish leaf decoration pasted on windows), associated events (morning football game in many high schools, then a turkey dinner, followed by an NFL game broadcast on TV), and so on. There would be nothing wrong per se with choosing a pastel color scheme for Thanksgiving dinner, but it does not help bring out the Thanksgiving-ness of the occasion.

What we appreciate in these examples is not any one particular sensation (indeed some of the sensory experiences by themselves may be unpleasant, such as heat and humidity or traffic noise) but the way in which various elements come together to give expression to a unified quality, atmosphere, or ambience. I believe our everyday aesthetic life is full of these experiences; however, they are rarely articulated or reflected upon, unless our experience concerns something unfamiliar, such as when we consciously try to define the sense of place as a tourist in a foreign country.[50]

ii. Japanese aesthetic appreciation of ambience

The Japanese aesthetic tradition, again, provides ample examples for this kind of aesthetic appreciation, in particular regarding seasonableness. The Japanese aesthetic tradition in both its artistic and broader forms is dominated by the celebration of the distinctive character of each season provided by the assembly of disparate ingredients. This is partly due to its temperate climate with four distinct seasons and the diversity of nature that provides rich tapestry to its landscape for each season. More importantly, however, this awareness and celebration of each season was nurtured by Shintoism and Buddhism, together comprising Japan's spiritual and cultural foundations in their encouragement of the sensitivity and acceptance of *what is*, in particular transience, most notably expressed by passing seasons.

Japanese classical literature, whether poetry, essays, or novels, is full of descriptions and celebrations of each season. Notable passages are found in *The Pillow Book* (c. 1002) of Sei Shōnagon, *An Account of My Hut* by Kamo no Chōmei (1153–1216), and *Essays in Idleness* by Yoshida Kenkō (c.1283–c.1350), all constituents of the Japanese Great Books tradition. *The Pillow Book*, for example, opens with memorable descriptions of the best of each season. The best of spring is experienced at dawn, summer at night, autumn in the evening, and winter in the morning, according to Sei Shōnagon. The character of winter, for example, is best expressed by early morning: "beautiful indeed when snow has fallen during the night, but splendid too when the ground is white with frost; or even when there is no snow or frost, but it is simply very cold and the attendants hurry from room to room stirring up the fires and bringing charcoal, *how*

---

[50] This mode of appreciating the unified mood of a season, an occasion, and the like, can be interpreted as providing perhaps the best instantiation of Kantian notion of beauty: purposiveness without a purpose. Although some of the ingredients are predetermined and required, such as a certain food for a specific occasion and a certain activity for a specific time of the year, there is no regulative principle dictating the organization among various parts. Rather, they come together *as if* governed by a rule to give rise to a unified whole, in this case a certain expressive quality, ambience, or atmosphere.

well this fits the season's mood!"[51] Indeed, the colder the better for winter's mood. She reinforces this in later section that "in the First Month when I go to a temple for a retreat I like the weather to be extremely cold; there should be snow on the ground, and everything should be frozen." In similarly describing the essential characteristic and festival and occasion accompanying each month, she concludes that "each month has its own particular charm, and the entire year is a delight."

Clearly conscious of the standard of seasonal appreciation set by Sei Shōnagon, several centuries later, a retired priest Yoshida Kenkō presents a follow-up passage in his *Essays in Idleness,* which begins thus: "the changing of the seasons is deeply moving in its every manifestation."[52] He then describes the essence of early spring to consist in birds singing, gentle sunlight, sprouting bushes, late spring in mists over landscape, cherry, orange, and plum blossoms, rain, and wisteria. The sense of season is comprised not only of seasonal flowers and creatures, but also by festivals, agricultural practices, and human activities. For example, "At the end of the year it is indescribably moving to see everyone hurrying about on errands." Indeed, the classical name for the month of December, *shiwasu,* means "even teachers run." This is followed by the New Year when "as the day thus breaks on the New Year the sky seems no different from what it was the day before, but one feels somehow changed and renewed. The main thoroughfares, decorated their full length with pine boughs, seem cheerful and festive, and this too is profoundly affecting."

Just as many outside Japan cherish fond memories of Christmas, Hunnukah, and Kwanza, I have fond memories of the Japanese New Year celebration. Its special character comprises many elements, such as very specific dishes, the sweetened sake served in special lacquered, tiered bowls, a room decoration consisting of a tier of rice cakes, an orange and a small branch of evergreen at the top, a door decoration of straw, paper, and sometimes seaweed, a classical melody played on *koto* broadcast on TV, and many people dressed in kimono. It is also inseparable from the extreme

[51] Sei Shōnagon, *The Pillow Book of Sei Shōnagon*, tr. Ivan Morris (New York: Columbia University Press, 1967), vol. 1, p. 1. The following passage regarding the First Month is from p. 126 and each month from p. 1, emphasis added.

[52] Yoshida Kenkō, *Essays in Idleness: The Tsurezuregusa of Kenkō*, tr. Donald Keene (New York: Columbia University Press, 1967), p. 18. The following passage regarding the end of the year is from p. 20, the New Year from p. 21.

hustle-bustle of the end-of-the year frenzies of shopping, cleaning, and cooking in preparation for the first three days of January. The scene of crowds descending on the food section of big stores, with the vendors' shouting almost drowned by equally robust customers, is part and parcel of the festive occasion culminating in the midnight of December 31 and morning of January 1.

Japanese food is also an eloquent expression of the similar appreciation of seasonableness. In addition to respect for each ingredient and multi-sensory aesthetic appeal, Japanese cooking is also known for giving expression to the sense of season. Not only does this expression of seasonableness have to do with the use of fresh ingredients of the season, but also it concerns the ornamental garnishes, some eatable and some not, such as tree buds and leaves, and the containers used to serve the food.[53] With respect to food served in a restaurant, the seasonal theme extends to the decorations accompanying plastic food displayed in windows, the design of menus, and even advertisements in print media or TV. For example, a printed menu of the month/season and its window display may sport a flower evocative of the season, such as an iris in late spring/early summer, a morning glory in the summer, and red maple leaves in the autumn. When discussing the aesthetics of the Japanese lunchbox, Kenji Ekuan points out: "To the Japanese, beauty has never existed outside a seasonal context. The scenery of the lunchbox is scarcely other than an expression of such a poetic."[54]

As consumers of such food, we derive pleasure not only from the multi-sensory appeal of the actual food but also savor the spring-like-ness or winter-like-ness ("...*rashii*" in Japanese parlance) resulting from the integration of all the disparate elements enumerated in the last paragraph. We enjoy inhaling the atmosphere, ambience, and mood created by the food and its context.[55]

---

[53] Unlike the Western tradition of using "a set" of dishes that includes a dinner plate, a soup bowl, a salad plate, a cup and saucer, and other serving dishes, Japanese food is served in a variety of containers on a mix-and-match basis. Hence, even a common household usually has several sets of plates, bowls, and serving dishes, from which the cook "chooses" the one appropriate for the food, season, etc. This mix-and-match aesthetics was established as the notion of *yose* (gathering of disparate elements) in the tea ceremony, where the host chooses the tea bowl, kettle, tea container, hanging scroll, flower vase, and the like, at each occasion, depending upon various factors, such as the guest, weather, season, and the time of the day.

[54] Ekuan, p. 28.

[55] This aesthetics of ambience finds a contemporary expression in a rather surprising arena: the art of comic books. According to one comparison between Japanese comic strips and Western ones, one

While the seasonable aesthetics of Japanese food is primarily chef-guided, the Japanese tea ceremony offers an experience of appreciating seasonableness or a sense of time or weather resulting from the cooperation between the host's preparation, the guest's participation, and happenstance of circumstances. The initiator of *wabi* tea, Sen no Rikyū (1522–1591), is known for his attention and sensitivity to the particular season and weather in which the tea ceremony takes place. For example, he would sometimes gather an impromptu tea ceremony at the first snow of the season, giving detailed instructions regarding how to clear the snow off the tea garden path and fallen branches off the path, how to fill the water in the water basin, what sort of flower arrangement to display in the alcove, and what implements to use. But the aesthetic experience must be created by each guest, attending to those aspects which have been intentionally prepared by the host but also to those items such as falling snow and wind felt as they walk through the garden, ice formed in the water basin, the flight of migratory birds passing above, the sound of evening temple bells, and the like. Here, unlike in the case of an eating experience carefully choreographed by the cook to give rise to a sense of season, the unified atmosphere in the tea ceremony is not as definite and the coherence among various elements results from our exercise of imagination as much as the host's preparation.[56]

What is noteworthy of the Japanese aesthetic sensibility toward the ambience is that what otherwise may cause discomfort, dissatisfaction, or dislike often becomes subsumed under an umbrella of aesthetically positive, unified atmosphere. Sei Shōnagon, for example, declares that "summer is best when it is extremely hot, winter is best when it is excruciatingly bitter cold."[57] The poetic spirit behind haiku also prominently features this mode

important difference is the kind of transition between frames "most often used to establish a *mood* or a *sense of place* in which time seems to stand still in these quiet, contemplative combinations." (S. McCloud, *Understanding Comics: The Invisible Art* (New York: Harper Perennial, 1993), p. 79, emphasis added. I thank my student Dallas Robinson for this reference.)

[56] One aspect of us, rather than the chef, choreographing the experience of eating is the order of eating various food items presented at once. As I discussed earlier, Japanese cooking juxtaposes different ingredients treated individually; hence, particularly with chopsticks, we pick each ingredient one by one in the order we choose. This aesthetic effect is explored more in Chapter V.

[57] My translation of section 114 of *Makura no Sōshi* (*The Pillow Book*), ed. Ishida Jōji (Tokyo: Kadokawa Shoten, 1980). The Morris translation has "a very cold winter scene; an unspeakable hot summer scene," along with "Pines. Autumn fields. Mountain villages and paths. Cranes and deer" under the section titled "Things That Gain by Being Painted"(p. 124). But two other Japanese editions,

of appreciation. Summer, for example, is characterized by heat, with all the accompanying discomfort:

> Heat waves shimmer
> on the shoulders of my
> paper robe

> In a cowshed
> Mosquito buzz sounds dusky …
> Lingering summer heat

> Dead grass—
> imperceptibly, heat waves
> one or two inches high.[58]

Winter, on the other hand, is epitomized by the bone-chilling cold of its wind, rain, or snow:

> First winter shower—
> the monkey also seems to want
> a small raincoat.

> A wintry gust—
> cheeks painfully swollen,
> the face of a man.[59]

In all these examples, what is appreciated is not simply some aspects of weather conditions but more importantly the way in which the distinctive character of each season is expressed by a certain weather condition. The object of appreciation is the summer-like ambience created by hot, humid air, or the wintry atmosphere conveyed by the bitingly cold air. These experiences, which may not necessarily be pleasant in and of themselves, can nevertheless be appreciated aesthetically for defining the quintessential character of the respective season. Even in contemporary Japan, Ekuan points out, in comparison with foreigners who would wear short-sleeve

---

one by Iwanami Shoten, the other by Shōgakukan, both have the phrase regarding summer and winter as an independent section, not as a part of things that gain by being painted.

[58] *Bashō and His Interpreters: Selected Hokku with Commentary*, comp. and tr. Makoto Ueda (Stanford: Stanford University Press, 1991), pp. 225, 320, and 180.

[59] Ibid. pp. 275 and 303.

shirts or blouses on a mid-autumn Indian summer day, the Japanese would wear season-appropriate clothing, by "match[ing] our clothing to season than to temperature."[60] This indicates that the aesthetic appreciation of the unified atmosphere expressive of a particular season sometimes supercedes people's concern with comfort.

3. Ramifications of the aesthetics of distinctive characteristics and ambience

i. Expansion of aesthetic horizon

Our aesthetic appreciation of objects (in the broadest sense, including season, time of the day, place) for expressing their distinctive characteristics has important ethical and pragmatic consequences. It nurtures an attitude of open-mindedness by encouraging us to appreciate each kind of object for what it is, rather than imposing a certain predetermined standard of beauty. As a result, our aesthetic life becomes diversified; hence, enriched. Let me refer to this attitude as appreciating something "on its own terms." This kind of appreciation entails that, while a hierarchy may exist among more or less appreciable objects *of the same kind*, there is no inter-kind hierarchy concerning aesthetic values. This is what I think is the insight of those aestheticians I cited previously, that each kind of object has its own characteristics, the expression of which constitutes its own unique aesthetic value. The beauty of a rose is different from the beauty of an apple blossom, as Burke points out. The appreciable mood of summer is diametrically opposed to that of winter, both of which can equally be savored. New York City's sense of place is different from that of a small New England town, yet both can appeal to us. We may personally prefer the peace and quiet of a New England town, but that does not preclude our recognizing and appreciating the zaniness of the city. Recognizing and celebrating these varied qualities both pre-supposes and nurtures our sensibility regarding each kind of object and our willingness to submit ourselves to the guidance of the objects themselves.

Something like this attitude is acknowledged with respect to philosophical theories of art appreciation. Although there is no explicit reference to

---

[60] Ekuan, p. 100. He goes on to point out how some contemporary industrial products in Japan that are season-sensitive, such as cooling or heating systems, bear season-evoking names.

moral dimensions, Kendall Walton's notion of "categories of art," I believe, is supported by an underlying belief that it is important to understand and appreciate a work of art "on its own terms." Walton's thesis regarding categories of art is that "we *must* learn to *perceive* the work in the correct categories, as determined in part by the historical facts, and judge it by what we then perceive in it."[61] Placing an art object in its proper art category, informed by the historical, cultural, and technical contexts of its creation and the artist's intention, would ensure that we identify its appropriate expressive qualities. Otherwise, we may "incorrectly" judge a monochrome film as a faded color film, or an abstract painting as a failed attempt at realism.

This need for interpreting and judging a work of art within the "correct" category may at first appear to be a purely epistemological issue. Akira Kurosawa's early films simply *are not* faded color films. However, I believe that the ultimate reason for insisting on the correct appreciation goes beyond epistemic concerns. That is, the epistemic problem of misidentification can be overridden by the possibility of deriving maximum aesthetic thrill, unless there is a further reason for not doing so. For example, experiencing the object in an incorrect category may render the otherwise "grating, cliché-ridden, pedestrian" object "exciting, ingenious"—hence, a "masterpiece."[62] Or, reading a literary work with "deliberate anachronism and erroneous attribution" may "fill the most placid works with adventure."[63] These deliberate attempts to experience a work of art "incorrectly" sometimes do have an educational merit, as when we view a representational painting as a non-representational painting, which helps us focus on its pure compositional features. However, aside from such educational benefits, it seems that we are doing something wrong if we deliberately misinterpret an art object, and I believe that the ultimate reason for correctly experiencing a work of art resides in *moral* considerations. It has to do with our paying respect to what the object is and experiencing it for what it is, rather than using it merely as a means for

---

[61] Kendall L. Walton, "Categories of Art," originally published in *The Philosophical Review*, LXXIX (1970), included in *Philosophy Looks at the Arts*, ed. Joseph Margolis (Philadelphia: Temple University Press, 1987, third edn.), p. 75, first emphasis added.

[62] Ibid. pp. 71–2.

[63] Jorge Luis Borges, "Pierre Menard, Author of the *Quixote*," in *Labyrinths*, ed. Donald A. Yates and James E. Irby (New York: New Directions Books, 1964), p. 44.

gaining an aesthetic kick. An art object has been created under a particular historical/cultural circumstance by a specific artist with a certain intention, using a particular technique and materials. We have to go out and meet the object on its own terms, rather than demanding that the object come and meet our expectations and satisfy our desires.[64] Art, in particular art from the past or from a different culture, both challenges and entices us to overcome the confines of our own perspective by inviting us to visit an often unfamiliar world created by the artists. John Dewey is most articulate regarding this function of art, which he defines as follows: "to remove prejudice, do away with the scales that keep the eye from seeing, tear away the veils due to wont and custom, [and] perfect the power to perceive."[65] In other words, Dewey continues, "works of art are means by which we enter…into other forms of relationship and participation than our own." Appreciating art on its own terms, within the right category, helps us cultivate this moral capacity of recognizing and understanding the other's reality through sympathetic imagination.

Our aesthetic appreciation of non-art objects as expressing their quint-essential qualities also helps us widen our aesthetic horizon, though at first glance it may not strike us as having any moral relevance. However, if the prerequisites for our moral life include understanding, appreciating, and respecting the reality of the Other, understood as not only other people but also other-than-humans, the capacity to experience and appreciate things on their own terms can contribute to cultivating this fundamental moral attitude and outlook. As Yi-Fu Tuan puts it:

One kind of definition of a good person, or a moral person, is that that person does not impose his or her fantasy on another. That is, he's willing to acknowledge the reality of other individuals, or even of the tree or the rock. So to be able to stand and listen. That to me is a moral capacity, not just an intellectual one.[66]

In Chapter II, I have pointed out that we generally find sharks, panda bears, roses, national park-like landscapes to be aesthetically more appealing than

---

[64] I also believe that the artists have the responsibility to make the communication possible to the viewer/reader/listener, rather than expecting and demanding that the viewer do all the work to come and meet their idiosyncratic or esoteric world. Each party, I think, has to meet halfway.

[65] John Dewey, *Art as Experience* (New York: Capricon Books, 1958), p. 325. The next passage is from p. 333.

[66] Yi-Fu Tuan, "Yi-Fu Tuan's Good Life," *On Wisconsin* 9 (1987). I develop the aesthetico-moral implication of this view as it applies to nature appreciation in "Appreciating Nature on Its Own Terms," *Environmental Ethics* 20 (1998): 135–49.

cod, snail darters, weeds, and wetlands. These seemingly innocuous aesthetic preferences regarding nature, I argued, do have serious environmental ramifications. That is, these aesthetic underdogs become disadvantaged by not being able to garner our attention, care, and protective attitudes in comparison with the poster-children of attractive nature. Because of the serious ecological damage created partly by our indifference, neglect, or sometimes downright repulsion regarding those underdogs of nature, Aldo Leopold and others urge the importance of developing a land aesthetic that renders those parts of nature aesthetically appreciable by incorporating cognitive (scientific in particular) considerations.

The mode of aesthetic appreciation that I have been discussing in this chapter can also contribute to nurturing this land aesthetic-like sensibility. It develops our capacity to appreciate diverse modes of aesthetic values by embracing not only the glamorous and jazzy but also, more importantly, the subdued, the humble, and the quiet that require much thoughtful and patient contemplation.

Furthermore, this ambience-oriented aesthetics helps expand our aesthetic and moral capacities by encouraging us to find positive values in things we normally dislike or detest. I discussed the way in which bodily discomfort, such as summer's heat and humidity, and inconvenience caused by inclement weather become aestheticized in the Japanese aesthetic tradition. While indiscriminately aestheticizing the negative can have problematic consequences (as I shall point out in Section iii), aestheticizing weather conditions, good or bad, particularly today, provides an effective antidote to the kind of hubris created by our increasing ability to control and improve nature. The Baconian vision outlined in *New Atlantis* has been extremely powerful, and its legacy has been guiding scientific and technological endeavors for several centuries in the West, as well as worldwide after modernization changed non-Western cultures' ethos. In light of this "progress," weather remains one of the last frontiers that defy human cultivation, manipulation, and control. We humans still have not figured out a way to control and manipulate, let alone precisely predict, the weather, while we can change the course of a river, cure a disease, or even clone animals. In this hi-tech age of manipulating most aspects of nature at our will, weather serves as a warning that not everything around us is subject to our control. Rather than lamenting or feeling frustrated with our impotence before the force of nature, I think it is particularly important today to appreciate aesthetically those forces that are beyond human power of control. It suggests to us that accepting and submitting ourselves to a natural force that cannot be tamed by humans does not necessarily have to be a disappointing or frustrating experience. Instead, it can be a source of aesthetic pleasure, if we learn to humble ourselves and gratefully receive and celebrate the positive aspects of its gift to us. The Japanese aesthetic tradition provides a model for aesthetically appreciating those aspects of the world which do not please us, particularly if they are things that are and should remain beyond human control.

ii. Humility among designers and artists

The moral significance of this mode of aesthetic appreciation is not limited to our attitude as appreciators of objects and phenomena. Perhaps more prominently, it also applies to designers and creators. This sensitivity and respect for the objects' essential characteristics underlie the attitude toward design and creation shared by traditional Japanese artists and crafts people, as well as contemporary artists committed to "truth to materials" and ecologically minded designers and architects. All of them, though from disparate backgrounds and each with distinct concerns and interests, are guided by the attitude of submitting to the objects' and materials' guide in their work. They willingly relinquish the power to impose their own ideas and wishes on the materials.

Japanese art and design practitioners, for whom their vocation determines their way of life in general, are deeply affected by the worldview of Buddhism. One of the most important factors contributing to Japan's spiritual, cultural, and social foundation, Buddhism emphasizes the importance of transcending one's ego. It is no accident that most master artists and craftsmen, whose teachings have been handed down through generations, have historically been students or practitioners of Zen Buddhism, transmitted to Japan in late twelfth century to early thirteenth century by priests Eisai (1141–1215) and Dōgen (1200–1253). Its thoroughgoing rejection of egocentric and anthropocentric worldviews is summarized by Dōgen as follows: "acting on and witnessing myriad things *with the burden of oneself* is 'delusion.' Acting on and witnessing oneself *in the advent of myriad things* is enlightenment." He continues, "studying the Buddha Way is studying oneself. Studying oneself is *forgetting oneself.* Forgetting oneself is *being enlightened by all things.*"[67] This transcendence of ego is facilitated by our recognizing and overcoming all-too-human schemes of categorizing, classifying, and valuing. Once we succeed, unlike Kant who is skeptical about our possibility of experiencing the thing-in-itself, Zen is optimistic about our ability to experience directly the thus-ness or being-such-ness (*immo*) of the-other-than-me or -humans. At this level of direct unmediated encounter with the Buddha nature of each object and phenomenon, our ordinary valuation and hierarchy disappear, rendering "a horse's mouth," "a donkey's jaw," "the sound of breaking wind," and "the smell of excrement," all expressive of their respective Buddha nature just as other more noble or elegant objects and phenomena.[68] This worldview will then encourage our recognition and appreciation of the diversity of objects, not just those we ordinarily enjoy and cherish. Thus, guided by the Buddhistic transcendence of ego, the Japanese artists' and designers' practice of respectfully listening to the subject matter's or material's voice and directing their creative activity accordingly manifests not simply an aesthetic wisdom but also a moral virtue and the outlook of enlightenment. In observing a common thread running through the Japanese lunchbox and contemporary Japanese industrial design, such as calculators and automobiles, Ekuan points out: "we have an intuition of the true 'essence' of everything here" and "it is owing to this grasp of the value of each entity that nothing is abandoned."[69] As a result, "beauty brought to accomplishment through gathering many different qualities and elements reveals itself in a 'nonviolent' loveliness, radiating tolerance and acceptance."

I suspect that the principle of "truth to materials" advocated by the arts and crafts movement and contemporary artists derives its inspiration from this Japanese design philosophy and its spiritual root in Buddhism. Despite William Morris's disparaging remarks on Japanese art,[70] one commentator

---

[67] Dōgen, *Shōbōgenzō: Zen Essays by Dōgen*, tr. Thomas Cleary (Honolulu: University of Hawaii Press, 1986), p. 32, all the emphases added.

[68] The specific examples of a donkey's jaw and a horse's mouth come from the chapter on Busshō (Buddha Nature), the sound of breaking wind and the smell of excrement from the chapter on Gyōbutsu Iigi (The Dignified Activities of Practicing Buddha) from *Shōbōgenzō: The Eye and Treasury of the True Law* by Dōgen Zenji, tr. Kōsen Nishiyama (Tokyo: Nakayama Shobō, 1986).

[69] Ekuan, p. 25. The next passage is from p. 21.

[70] After praising Japanese draughtsmanship for its deft and skillful naturalism, Morris claims that "with all their brilliant qualities as handicraftsmen, ... the Japanese have no architectural, and therefore no decorative, instinct. Their works of art are isolated and blankly individualistic, and in consequence, unless where they rise, as they sometimes do, to the dignity of a suggestion for a picture (always devoid

on the arts and crafts movement states: "many designers from the 1860s onwards were to see in Japanese work a logic, fitness and control that European design lacked."[71] In addition, the theoretical discussion of Japanese aesthetics, firmly rooted in Buddhism, by Yanagi Sōetsu (1889–1961) and the pottery work of Hamada Shōji (1894–1978) were introduced to the West by Bernard Leach (1887–1979), one of the protean figures of the arts and crafts movement. The pottery workshop in St. Ives he set up with Hamada is described as promoting "a sensitivity to materials that came from the traditional Japanese potter's search for aesthetic purity of form."[72]

As for contemporary artists, David Nash's approach to his work is often characterized as "Zen-like."[73] Furthermore, it is reported that, while working in Japan, Nash quickly developed "a remarkable sense of mutual self-recognition" with his Japanese hosts, and that "Nash's sensitivity to the biomorphically suggestive forms inherent in wood—what might be termed a reverence for the spirit of the material—drew comment from the Japanese for its relationship to Shinto."[74]

Though ecologically minded designers are driven by pragmatic interests—to promote sustainable design—they share this aesthetic-moral attitude of respect for the others (i.e. other-than-humans). In the context of modern design, this mode of listening to the material's voice and working *with* it comes as a welcome shift in attitude. In the West, supported by the ethos of modern philosophy and science, the legacy of Francis Bacon, Rene Descartes, and Isaac Newton among others, the design strategy for the last few hundred years generally conceives of our role to be that of conquerors and controllers of nature. Instead, pioneers of green design stress the importance of working *with*, instead of *against* or *irrespective of*, nature. For example, Sim Van der Ryn and Stuart Cowan, early advocates of sustainable architecture, encourage "listening to *what the land wants to*

---

of human interest), they remain mere wonderful toys, things quite outside the pale of the evolution of art, which ... cannot be carried on without the architectural sense that connects it with the history of mankind." "Textiles," pp. 34–5.

[71] Naylor, p. 117.

[72] Lionel Lambourne, *Utopian Craftsmen: The Arts and Crafts Movement from the Cotswolds to Chicago* (Salt Lake City: Peregrine Smith, 1980), p. 207. Yanagi's Buddhism-based aesthetics was introduced to the Western audience by *The Unknown Craftsman: A Japanese Insight into Beauty*, forwarded by Shōji Hamada, adapted by Bernard Leach (Tokyo: Kodansha International, first published in 1972).

[73] Lloyd, p. 22.

[74] John Beardsley, *Earthworks and Beyond: Contemporary Art in the Landscape* (New York: Abberville Press, 1989), p. 50.

be" and creating a solution or design to take advantage of its own wisdom, rather than imposing a design strategy upon nature irrespective of its own workings and patterns.[75] In emphasizing the importance of this attitude of "humility" in design practice, they point to Taoism for providing a model.[76] In a similar vein, Victor Papanek also makes a plea for designers "to find sorely needed *humility,*" deriving his own inspiration from Buddhism.[77]

Ecological design projects based upon this attitude include perma-culture, an agricultural practice that mimics the working of the native land, such as prairie, and the sewage treatment system that recreates wetland, which I have referred to in Chapter II. Let me discuss another such example: the program of re-meandering de-meandered streams. Many streams and rivers in both the United States and Europe have traditionally been "straightened" with concrete walls to provide an efficient drainage system for area farms, obliterating their earlier meandering flow. In discussing their river restoration projects, eco-artists Marta González del Tánago and Diego Garcia de Jalón claim:

From the historical point of view ... man really knew how to live with rivers until the late 18th century. He conducted a *dialogue* with them in which he acknowledged the superiority of the laws of river dynamics ... It is only a short time ago that man broke off this dialogue with his natural environment and thought he could usurp its superiority by technical means. With the onset of industrialization people tried to *regulate* nature's laws, showing a misplaced understanding of power and the need to control nature. Since then rivers have been forced into *straight courses* and *simplified forms* [canal systems] to reduce their area and make maximum use of flood areas.[78]

They criticize this practice for being "*not honest*" by "simplifying rivers, redesigning them mathematically or forcing them into the monotonous geometrical straitjacket of modern urban development."[79]

Indeed, such a method of regulating river courses backfires, both ecologically and economically. It is economically bankrupt because of "enormously high maintenance costs," such as "pumped water circulation for rivers that

---

[75] Sim Van der Ryn and Stuart Cowan, *Ecological Design* (Washington, D. C.: Island Press, 1996), p. 35.

[76] Ibid. pp. 7 and 136.

[77] Victor Papanek, *The Green Imperative: Natural Design for the Real World* (New York: Thames &. Hudson, 1995), p. 12, emphasis added.

[78] Marta González del Tánago and Deigo Garcia de Jalón, "Ecological Aesthetics of River Ecosystem Restoration," in Strelow, p. 188, emphasis added.

[79] Ibid., emphasis added.

have been cut off from their own catchment area or bank vegetation in completely dried-out and sealed edaphic profiles that has to be sustained by irrigation systems."[80] It also creates ecological disaster because, with the static, regulated, and simplified design, contradicting the innate characteristics of the river, comes the lack of "the diversity and complexity of dynamic rivers" essential to the diversity of complexity of a riparian eco-system.[81] Furthermore, de-meandering streams disrupts the previously existing nutrient cycle that incorporates the agricultural practice of the surrounding areas.[82]

What we need is a restoration of rivers' innate function, with "erosion and sediment formation processes linked to the natural dynamic of the flow volumes, so that the morphology of the riverbed, the diversity of hydraulic conditions, the heterogeneity of the substrate and the wetness of the banks can be restored," which in turn will restore the biodiversity of the area.[83] Such a restorative re-meandering project requires not only scientific knowledge and technological know-how but also an aesthetic and intuitive grasp of "what the river wants to do" so that we can engage in a "dialogue" with it. It is true that what sounds like a poetic musing needs to be both supported by and translated into scientific understanding. However, what these practitioners seem to be getting at is the importance of observing nature's working carefully with an open attitude: to let it speak to us. We need a sensibility toward "the aesthetic canon of ecological processes, with the heterogeneity and transience of the forms and processes revealing *the essential being* of the restored river landscapes."[84] Just like de-damming projects, re-meandering projects are also based upon returning to a close observation and appreciation of the inherent characteristics and workings of the stream and taking advantage of them to the fullest in designing structures that serve both the environment and ourselves.

In one sense, this is a very pragmatic, economical, and labor-*un*intensive approach, because we are having the material/object partly do the job for us. The designer/operator functions more as a facilitator or a choreographer,

[80] Ibid.   [81] Ibid. p. 192.

[82] Kenneth R. Olwig discusses this issue with Denmark as an example in "Reinventing Common Nature: Yosemite and Mount Rushmore—A Meandering Tale of a Double Nature," included in *Uncommon Ground: Rethinking the Human Place in Nature*, ed. William Cronon (New York: W. W. Norton, 1996), pp. 404–7.

[83] González del Tánago, p. 192.   [84] Ibid., emphasis added.

rather than as a designer/creator in the traditional sense who needs to come up with an entire blueprint.

One may challenge this call for an ego-less-ness and a submission to the objects' and materials' dictate as an unachievable feat. Both the Zen training for overcoming one's self and the artists' and designers' listening to and submitting their creative process to the objects and materials are still ultimately guided by our desire to achieve enlightenment or to design good objects. We can never get away from such a desire; neither can we truly listen to the "object's voice," because we cannot but rely on *our* selection, interpretation, and sometimes construction of what *we* take to be the object's essential characteristics, its true voice. How can we figure out that meandering is *what the river wants to do* or that *a stone requests* that it be manipulated in a certain way? Aren't these all *our all-too-human* judgments?

This challenge, I believe, is legitimate, but uninteresting. It is similar to a typical strategy moral egoism invokes in arguing that a seemingly altruistic action is in fact guided by an egoistic motive, such as gaining fame or feeling good about oneself. In a sense, it is a truism that we can never overcome our self and adopt the view from nowhere or a super-human perspective. So, any kind of religious practice or self-discipline is an attempt at bettering one's self and life in some way. Similarly, any effort to understand the other is inevitably reliant on our own perspective, whether as an individual or as human species. Given this general framework from which we cannot escape, I think what is truly interesting and at issue is what kind of attitude gets us closest to transcending oneself and achieving self-discipline, or what sort of attitude toward the other is best suited to respecting them and, in the present case, creating good objects. That is, within the inescapable boundary of self-interest and human perspective, there are varying degrees of attempts at transcending it. So, the notion of overcoming oneself and letting objects speak to us, whether applied to a spiritual training or our creative process, I believe, *is* viable and valuable, despite the fact that it is necessarily governed by a self-interested motivation and an all-too-human scheme.

iii. *Limitations on the aesthetics of ambience*

So far I have discussed the moral and pragmatic benefits of ambience- or distinctive characteristics-directed aesthetics. However, is there a limit to such aesthetic appreciation?

I do believe that there are certain limits to aesthetically appreciating distinctive characteristics and unified mood of things and events. I have discussed that Japanese aesthetic tradition is predominated by this aesthetic sensibility. However, that observation must be qualified. While the Japanese cultural tradition is almost universally praised for its "love of nature" and the aesthetic appreciation of nature permeates every aspect of Japanese life, including keen sensitivity and appreciation of weather, there is a conspicuous absence of the appreciation of the sublime, exemplified by an extreme weather condition like a typhoon. In spite of the frequent occurrences of devastating typhoons, it is noteworthy that the morning *after* a typhoon, not the typhoon itself, is praised for its aesthetic appeal in Japanese classics. For example, in *The Pillow Book*, Sei Shōnagon praises the beauty of the morning after the storm without describing her experience of the storm itself during the previous night. The only reference made to the storm is her amazement at recognizing that the arrangement of leaves "one by one through the chinks of the lattice-window" is the work of "the same wind which yesterday raged so violently."[85] Another famous passage on a typhoon in the novel, *The Tale of Genji* (c.1004) describes the storm itself, but does not express a sense of awe at being wholly overpowered by nature's brutal force. This is partly because the experience during the storm is narrated from a house, looking out onto a small, enclosed garden, rather than onto a vast moor or an open ocean where the effect of the storm would have been felt to the utmost degree.[86]

This conspicuous absence of aesthetically appreciating the typhoon itself seems to be in keeping with the general lack of appreciating the sublime in the Japanese aesthetic tradition. It is also suggestive of the inherent challenge of experiencing the sublime when the phenomenon threatens our safety and very existence, the threat typically posed by extreme weather conditions and other natural disasters, like earthquakes. Our overwhelming concern for our safety tends to interfere with the experience of their sublime power. This is why both Burke and Kant characterize the experience of the sublime to be conditional upon our being, or at least upon our belief

---

[85] Sei Shōnagon, p. 194.

[86] Murasaki Shikibu, *A Wreath of Cloud: Being the Third Part of "The Tale of Genji"*, tr. Arthur Waley (Boston: Houghton Mifflin Company, 1927), chapter on "Typhoon." See also section 19 of Kenkō's *Essays*.

in being, safe from danger. However, being (or believing to be) safe in turn tends to compromise the very nature of the sublime: the imminent and dramatic manner in which those phenomena envelop and threaten our existence. While it is not impossible to experience the sublime dimension of extreme weather or a natural catastrophe while actually being in it and threatened by it, at least we can conclude that such an experience is more an exception than a common response.[87]

In addition to the psychological limitation to appreciating aesthetically all kinds of objects and phenomena for expressing their essential characteristics, there is also a moral limitation. Consider the following cases. During the two years I was preparing this manuscript, the world witnessed several hurricanes, including Katrina and Rita resulting in history-making devastation, as well as the 2004 tsunami catastrophe in the Indian Ocean. The fury, hence the quintessential character, of these hurricanes and the tsunami was vividly conveyed by many signs of destruction: flooded fields, raging rivers, flying roofs and signs, shattered windows, downed trees entangling electric wires, the anguish and fear in the residents' faces, not to mention thousands of deaths. Another devastation still raw in our collective memory, though caused by human act rather than nature, is of course 9/11. The aftermath consisting of sheer wreckage, some walls sticking out from the ground, smoldering smoke, and dusty air all speak of the immensity of the tragedy. These ingredients all work together to express the tragic character of this event of unimaginable magnitude.

Extreme weather and natural disasters are not the only phenomena that are hard to appreciate aesthetically for their ambience or distinctive characteristics. There are similar examples from built environments, artifacts, and man-made phenomena. What better way for a ghetto area to express its defining characteristics than by broken windows, boarded-up windows and doors, weeds- and rats-infested abandoned lots, gang members loitering on street corners harassing passers-by, garbage-strewn streets reeking of urine and rotten food? All of these elements converge to give rise to a sense of desperation and hopelessness, as well as providing the most eloquent illustration of social ills.

---

[87] Carolyn Korsmeyer pointed out that there are those who chase storms. Sometimes the purpose is to gather scientific data, such as of tornado or the eye of a hurricane, but I grant that sometimes it is purely for thrill-seeking. Their sublime experience, contrary to Burke's and Kant's stipulation, would have to be premised upon being in actual danger.

What about the opposite case of the almost obscene expression of excessive affluence, such as the largest private estate under construction in Long Island which, according to one writer's calculation, would accommodate 720 of Thoreau's cabin at Walden Pond?[88] Or, how about the problematic, but ever more popular practice in the United States of "teardown," whereby an older structure, still intact and perfectly fine, is torn down to make way for a massive house, sometimes dubbed McMansion, which is really too big for the property, not to mention the accompanying massive energy consumption?[89] The size of the house in proportion to the property and surrounding neighborhood, gorgeous landscaping, expensive-looking swimming pool, multiple-car garages, brand new facade, and so on, all converge to express the characteristic qualities of such new structures: affluence, independence, self-assertion, and comfort, but also ostentation, obnoxiousness, egoism, and social and environmental irresponsibility. The bigger the structure and the smaller the property, the more exquisite such an expression becomes. Similar arguments can be made with respect to SUVs. The more massive it is, the more eloquently does it express qualities similar to those exhibited by McMansions.

The Exxon Valdez oil spill of 1989 was a quintessential environmental disaster. Its expression of devastation and destruction was eloquently and vividly seen in the massive area of glistening oil clearly demarcated from surrounding water by a black tar-like substance covering everything ashore on the nearby Alaskan coastline, including numerous hapless sea creatures. These ingredients all converged to make a powerful visual narrative. Insofar as its dramatic expression of gloom and doom goes, it was rather remarkable.

How are we to react to these cases of an exquisite expression of the defining character—of a catastrophic hurricane, derelict ghetto, grandiose McMansion, or devastating oil spill? I believe that most of us feel uneasy about aesthetically appreciating such expressions. We feel that our positive aesthetic appreciation somehow implies our endorsement of these objects/phenomena, when in fact we object to their continued existence for moral, social, or environmental reasons. We feel that our aesthetic fascination with the dramatic expression of these objects and phenomena

---

[88] Christopher Hawthorne, "The Case for a Green Aesthetic," *Metropolis* (October 2001), p. 114.

[89] "The 'Teardowns' Threat," *The Providence Journal* editorial (Feb. 8, 2004); William Morgan, "The Bloating of the Beach House," *The Providence Journal* (August 20, 2004); Joan Lowy, "McMansions in the Cross Hairs," *The Providence Journal* (February 13, 2005).

must be held in check for fear we take pleasure, even an aesthetic one, in other people's and creatures' misery or social injustice.

However, I think that the matter is more complicated than it may at first appear. I think we have to distinguish two senses of aesthetic appreciation. One sense implies an endorsement of the object's continued existence. This is the sense according to which it is contradictory to recognize positive aesthetic values in an object and at the same time to support its destruction (in the absence of any extra-aesthetic considerations).[90] We believe positive aesthetic values count toward the worth of the object's existence. In this sense of aesthetic appreciation, it would be problematic for us to appreciate the sense of place exquisitely displayed by a ghetto or the quintessential characteristic of a hurricane illustrated by the destruction of people's properties and lives.

But does that mean that the moral, social, and political significance of the object should have the censoring power over our aesthetic life by determining what we should and should not appreciate aesthetically? As a cultural geographer, D. W. Meinig points out, aesthetic appreciation can mean either "approval," in the sense I discussed above, or "to perceive distinctly" and "to be keenly sensible of or sensitive to."[91] Even in common parlance, we use "appreciation" in this second way, as when we appreciate the gravity of a situation or the difficulty of a problem. As such, the object of our appreciation need not be something whose continued existence we praise or support. Because of the vivid experience facilitated by our aesthetic appreciation in this second sense, we may want to condemn the object's continued existence, as in the case of a ghetto.

Even if our experience of the sense of place results in an unpleasant reaction, such as sadness or anger, due to the perceived human tragedy or social injustice, prompting a call to action for its change or elimination, our experience is nonetheless meaningful, enriching, and, in short, appreciable in the second sense. That is, we attend to and understand the way in which human tragedy or social injustice is dramatically expressed in the sensory

---

[90] Unless one has a rather warped or peculiar obsession with a beautiful object whose continuing existence somehow detracts from its aesthetic value, as believed by the protagonist of Yukio Mishima's *The Temple of the Golden Pavilion* (1956) who proceeds to set fire to the temple. Mishima's novel is loosely based upon a true story of a Buddhist monk who committed this arson.

[91] D. W. Meinig, "Environmental Appreciation: Localities as a Humane Art," *Western Humanities Reviews* XXV (Winter 1971), p. 1.

qualities of the environment. I would even go further and make a case that we *should* engage in this kind of appreciation, because what better ways are there to diagnose what is and is not working in our society, or fully and truly to fathom the severity of environmental disaster or human tragedy? As Arnold Berleant claims, gathering various information pertaining to, for example, a landscape is necessary, but not sufficient, in understanding it until we "relate this information to perceptual experience."[92] It is one thing to understand conceptually the extreme poverty in a community from various statistics and data, but it is quite another to *see* and *feel* it in those perceptual elements typical of an impoverished community. This is the reason why we often feel it crucial that the government officials, politicians, and other people in power have a direct experience of the problem by touring these areas in question, whether their devastation was caused by natural disaster, riot, war, or social and economic injustice. As I will argue in Chapter V, it is not enough for a good society to ensure people's rights, freedom, equality, and opportunity. There has to be a tangible indication that their well-being is taken seriously and attended to in their surroundings as well. Conversely, social problems, such as poverty, are derived not only from lack of wealth, education, political power, and employment opportunity, but also constituted by the deteriorating environment that can be directly sensed. Such perceivable evidence acts as a barometer to gauge the condition of a society and the quality of people's lives.

The importance of the direct perceivability of something unpleasant or undesirable is also shared by a number of environmental artists working to restore brownfields, industrial waste lands. For example, Jörg Dettmar describes his intention to "preserve the special atmosphere" by not obliterating "the mysterious, to an extent dangerous, character of a piece of waste land."[93] Malcolm Mills, commenting on Herman Prigann's restoration project at Marl, states:

The concrete halls of a water purification plant and the rusted steel skeletons of subsidiary building stand against the sky and are reflected in water as gaunt reminders of a history which will take decades to decay, its positive and negative

---

[92] Arnold Berleant, *Living in the Landscape: Toward an Aesthetics of Environment* (Lawrence: The University Press of Kansas, 1997), p. 18.

[93] Jörg Dettmar, "Ecological and Aesthetic Aspects of Succession on Derelict Industrial Sites," in Strelow, p. 129.

aspects in a tension which will relax only in a future beyond the present transition to a post-industrial world. It seems important and helpful ... that the site's adaptation does not abolish those tensions, does not heal them.[94]

Those directly experienceable sensory qualities constitute the tangible testimony to the underlying social or environmental problems, much more powerfully, effectively, and immediately than a set of data. Just as I discussed in the issues surrounding green aesthetics, aesthetics has the power to affect the nature of our decisions regarding what we should do with the object in question. Hence, in the sense of perceiving with keen sensitivity and sensibility, aesthetic appreciation is to be encouraged, whatever the object of appreciation happens to be.

I want to explore one more social consequence of the ambience-directed aesthetic appreciation. The notion of "sense of place" is a very powerful force behind our interest in preserving a historic district, regulating various aspects of what makes up the feel of an area, whether commercial district, suburb, or relatively uncultivated countryside. Many regulations have been enacted throughout the United States and many parts of the world to restrict various aspects of the built environment, ranging from the height of a building, the color of its walls, permissibility of front porch and white picket fence, ornaments on the front lawn, to the appearance, size, placement of an advertising sign, the facade of a store, and appearance and placement of telecommunication facilities. Though some aspects of these regulations are non-aesthetic concerning safety and economics, a large number of these regulations are motivated by aesthetic considerations, most notably for preserving the sense of place.[95] An ultra-modern building is not allowed to be built in a historic district; all new structures in such a place must be in keeping with the historic style; supermarkets, fast food restaurants, gas stations in some communities have to reflect the local flavor with sensitivity, rather than plopping down their cookie-cutter corporate designs indiscriminately. Our desire not to disrupt the sense of place is so

[94] Malcolm Miles, "Aesthetics and Engagement: Interested Interventions," in Strelow, p. 206.

[95] Christopher J. Duerksen and R. Matthew Goebel traces the history of aesthetic regulations in the United States and points out that the purely aesthetic regulations developed relatively recently. In the past, aesthetic regulations had to be justified by non-aesthetic reasons, such as safety. (*Aesthetics, Community Character, and the Law* (Chicago: American Planning Association, 1999), pp. 3–7) Virginia Postrel compiles some recent examples of aesthetic regulations in the United States, which she states are proliferating at an accelerating pace. (*The Substance of Style* (New York: HarperCollins, 2003), pp. 122–63)

strong to the point that we even tolerate downright deception in the form of a cellphone tower disguised as a tree or a cactus, and a satellite dish camouflaged as a giant clam shell.[96]

However, this tendency to protect the sense of place can wreak havoc with another value dear to us, particularly to Americans: the right of the property owner. What if my aesthetic taste leads me to place a bunch of plastic pink flamingo on my front lawn located in a rather conservative, old-fashioned community? It is *my* property, so can't I do with it whatever I please, as long as I am not literally hurting my neighbors or their properties?

This clash of community interests between preserving the unified character of the place and the property owner's individual rights to free (aesthetic) expression creates a newsworthy drama almost daily across the United States. Both sides are guided by aesthetic interests. Virginia Postrel summarizes this conflict as follows:

Does the aesthetic imperative mean letting all of us pursue our individual aesthetic dreams? Or does it demand that we eliminate stylistic oddities to maintain a consistent theme? Both approaches generate meaning and pleasure. Both create aesthetic value.[97]

Her own conclusion to this familiar conflict is "to find the right boundaries—to discover rules that preserve aesthetic discovery and diversity, accommodating plural identities and tastes, while still allowing the pleasures of consistency and coherence."[98] I agree with this strategy of seeking the proper boundary to what she terms "design tyranny" and I believe such boundaries depend upon the specific context, varying from case to case. However, because it is the upholders of the sense of place who demand restrictions on individual aesthetic expressions (because the other party to this conflict would advocate laissez-faire aesthetics), it seems to me that the onus falls on them to negotiate their agenda carefully so that it does not fall into extreme cases of aesthetic tyranny.

Perhaps the most ominous project to provide a certain sense of place, appropriate to a particular view of cultural and historical heritage, is Nazi Germany's concerted effort to eradicate alien species of vegetation in favor of native vegetation. Apart from the biological concern for ridding its soil

[96] Some successful examples of locality-sensitive design of a national chain, such as McDonald's and K-Mart are shown in Duerksen and Goebel.
[97] Postrel, p. 123.   [98] Ibid.

of invasive, foreign species, this program was clearly fueled by the chilling parallel between the political ethnic cleansing and the botanical ethnic cleansing, thereby providing a worthy environment to its residents. It was thought that "the area must be given a structure which corresponds to our type of being... so that the Teutonic German person will feel himself to be at home so that he settles there and is ready to love and defend his new home"; hence, it is necessary "to cleanse the German landscape of unharmonious foreign substance."[99]

Of course none of today's municipal aesthetic regulations under consideration is meant for this kind of chilling agenda. However, even legislated without such an agenda, some aesthetic regulations may end up marginalizing those people whose aesthetic tastes are different from the commonly accepted mainstream tastes, because of their low socio-economic status or different ethnic and racial backgrounds. An expression of their ethnic identity and pride in their house and garden decorations, for example, may be regarded as "eyesore" or "visual pollution" by the community.

"The sense of place" or "the character of town" is generally backward-looking; we want to *maintain* and *preserve*, and not disturb, the ambience created by the cumulative historical effects. As such, a certain amount of conservativism accompanies this notion. I think, however, that the proponents of aesthetic regulations to preserve the sense of place should recognize that it too changes with time and demography. Of course we should protect many aspects of townscape from changing trends; however, at the same time we should also be forward-looking by actively incorporating some positive changes and continuing to "create," not just "preserve," the sense of place. In my earlier discussion of challenges facing the "intrusion" of wind turbines in the ocean, I suggested that we will be better off, both environmentally and aesthetically, by positively embracing such machines in the ocean-garden as an integral part of the vision of our sustainable future. If we regard the windfarm as a step toward greener future, the pristine ocean is not necessarily "ruined" by the addition of these machines.

Similarly, we should think carefully before rejecting as an eyesore an expression of ethnic identity and pride in our new neighbor's garden

---

[99] Gert Groening and Joachim Wolschke-Bulmahn, "Some Notes on the Mania for Native Plants in Germany," *Landscape Journal* 11:2 (Fall 1992), pp. 122 and 123.

ornaments, such as the yard designed by Edward Houston, an African-American, described by Grey Gundaker. Consisting of arrangements of various artifacts, mostly "broken," such as a chair without a seat and broken china and pottery, or "rubbish," such as tires, hubcaps, empty bottles and shoe soles, the yard would simply strike the uninitiated outsiders as a "rubbish heap," suggesting "abandonment, trash ... *junk*."[100] However, Gundaker gives a reading of this yard as presenting a definite view of the relationship between this world and the other world and the human place in it, interpreted by Houston, grounded in "southern European-American gardening conventions" and "traditional African-American cosmology."[101] Granted this is an extreme case and his yard is located in northwest Alabama, where some aspects of the symbolism may be more comprehensible to the residents than, say, to my community, a small New England town. A heretofore unified expression of my town's Waspish ambience would certainly be threatened by such an addition. However, before dismissing it outright for disturbing our sense of place, we should at least consider the possibility of our community making a subtle adjustment to its sense of place by now showcasing the value of celebrating diversity, multi-culturalism, and pluralism, through the inclusion of this seemingly incongruous, unfitting aesthetic statement.

A similar conflict exists regarding cemeteries. On the one hand, we are interested in keeping the whole area peaceful and dignified. On the other hand, each family may have a unique way of expressing their grief, as well as affection and respect for the deceased, by putting a number of artifacts, such as toys and food, around the grave stone. The cluttered appearance created by such objects may initiate a prohibition of those offerings. However, our feelings attached to the loved one's resting place are even more intense and personal than our feelings for our properties. Hence, it seems to me that aesthetic regulations regarding cemeteries should carefully negotiate between the two opposing forces of aesthetic concerns.

By citing these examples, I am not claiming that aesthetic regulations are always excessive and detrimental in a democratic society. On the contrary, precisely because we do enjoy individual freedom, a certain amount of restriction for public good, particularly an aesthetic good, is necessary.

---

[100] Grey Gundaker, "African-American History, Cosmology, and the Moral Universe of Edward Houston's Yard," *Journal of Garden History* 14:3 (July–Sept. 1994), p. 194.
[101] Ibid. p. 179.

Conversely, precisely because our interest in a coherent, unified sense of place is rather high and precisely because aesthetic regulations for that purpose are increasing at a rapid rate, I think we have carefully to consider possibilities other than simply rejecting anything different as an "eyesore" or "intrusion," as we determine the proper boundary of such regulations.

This chapter began with one noteworthy example of our everyday aesthetic experience: the appreciation of an object's distinctive characteristics and unified mood. As in the case of green aesthetics, this familiar aesthetic experience turns out to contain a number of important moral, social, and environmental ramifications, again confirming one of the theses of this book—that everyday aesthetics, despite its appearance of insignificance, does occupy an important place in our life and society at large. The next chapter will develop this point further through an exploration of another common experience from everyday aesthetics.

IV

Everyday Aesthetic Qualities and Transience

A universal fact about material existence is that everything is subject to vicissitude and transience: everything is impermanent. Even materials usually regarded as impervious to aging and decaying, such as steel, are no exception.[1] The only semi-permanent substance on this earth, which we wish were more impermanent, is nuclear waste. The impermanence of everything is a fundamental philosophical and religious insight, both historically and cross-culturally. It is the starting point of Hinduism, Buddhism, and Taoism. It is also the premise of Western philosophy and religious traditions, giving rise to human yearning for some thing or some sphere that is permanent and unchanging, such as the Platonic world of Forms and the Judeo-Christian notion of afterlife.

"Change" or "vicissitude" in itself is value-neutral; it is neither for better nor for worse. However, in our experience of the changes that material objects, including our bodies, go though, we often regard them evaluatively. Sometimes our attitude is positive and we welcome changes, as things "mature," "ripen," "develop," "mellow," or "season." More often, however, we lament the change as things "age," "decay," "decline," "deteriorate," "wane," "decompose," or simply "get old." These two sets of terms that we use to describe changes indicate that we seem to have constructed a life process for each material and object from inception to an optimal state, prime condition, or peak, after which it is in steady decline. Sometimes the peak point comes years after the inception, as in the case of human beings. Referring strictly to the body and judged solely from the contemporary Western perspective, our optimal state is usually considered

---

[1] Midas Dekkers, *The Way of All Flesh: The Romance of Ruins*, tr. Sherry Marx-Macdonald (New York: Farrar, Straus and Giroux, 2000), p. 68.

to be in our 20s and 30s before "middle age" sets in. The process of aging, with its negative connotations, starts after the prime stage has passed. We usually do not refer to a baby's growth into a child, then to a young adult as an "aging" process; we reserve that term to refer to the "declining" process starting with "middle age." At other times, the optimal state is at the beginning when things are brand new or sometime shortly after the beginning in order to allow enough time for them to be "broken in." Yet other times it takes a while longer, though shorter than our maturation period, as in wine and cheese. Regardless of when the objects' optimal state takes place, there is a sense of process applicable to all material existence, and it is generally one-directional. After the optimal state, the objects are considered "past their prime" and we get the feeling that things are "downhill from here," and most of our effort is directed toward "repairing" and "restoring" the deteriorating objects and "turning back the clock." We undergo the plastic surgeon's knife and laser beam to smooth our skin and eliminate age spots; we certainly don't get surgery to hasten our aging process by increasing wrinkles and creating more blemishes. Nor do we dye our hair white, except for a theatrical effect or an extreme fashion statement; we rather try to hide our graying hair.

In addition to these changes that our bodies and physical materials naturally go through due to biological process, chemical interaction, or physical force, there are other forms of change that are induced by foreign agents. Dust gathers on a bookshelf, food crumbs pile up on a kitchen counter, red wine spills on a carpet, soot accumulates around a chimney, and bird droppings encrust an outdoor sculpture. An office desktop becomes disorderly by the end of a workday with papers scattered and books piled up; our garden looks messy after we come back from a vacation because of overgrown grasses and bushes; and toys no longer look organized after children take them out of the toy chest and play with them. Our reactions to these appearances of mess, disorder, and filth prompt us to "clean," "straighten out," or "tidy up" the objects and spaces. It is an endless battle, however; clutter, for example, "is subject only to temporary diminishment" and "banishment is out of the question," as "clutter erupts back into our lives, however ruthless our attempts to control it."[2] We are

---

[2] Jane Graves, "Clutter," *Issues in Architecture Art and Design* 5:2 (1998), p. 63. Graves's ensuing discussion in this article is not a condemnation of clutter but rather its socio-economic significance

so preoccupied with cleaning and organizing that professionals specialize in cleaning houses, carpets, windows, upholstery, outside walls, and of course clothes, as well as organizing closets, busting clutter, and removing junk.[3] We will be hard pressed to find professionals specializing in dirtying and disorganizing, because many of us are already experts in such activities, without any training!

Just as in the case of material aging, we also seem to have a notion of the optimal state of each object, whatever its age, characterized by being clean and organized. With time, and with or without our activities, things become "marred" and "soiled," as well as messy with disorganization. This chronological order is not always the case, as sometimes the organized or clean condition comes after an originally messy, dirty condition. For example, after the moving company delivers our furniture and other belongings to the new house, we unpack them and arrange them in an organized way, thereby *creating* rather than *restoring* order inside the new house. When I finish sewing my skirt, I will get rid of bits and pieces of fabric and thread still attached to it, thereby finally revealing the neatly finished product. Or, wild bushes get cleared and neatly trimmed for the first time in an effort to create a clean border to the community garden. Just as the chronological sequence of the optimal state of the object or material and its "declining" stage varies, so does the pristine, clean, and ideal state of an object.

Regardless of these variations, what is constant is the contrast between our notion of the object's optimal state and its different state brought about by the process of change. Another noteworthy common thread among these phenomena is that, within our everyday aesthetic life, we respond to qualities such as mess, disorder, filth, and agedness by engaging in certain actions. While sometimes these qualities promote reflection and aesthetic experience without prompting us toward any actions, as I shall discuss later in this chapter, in their mundane context, these qualities most often lead us to erase or counteract them. This is most marked in our daily activity

---

for the poor without proper "property": "clutter is the property of the poor, of the outcast, the bag lady on the tube who is armed with a multiplicity of plastic bags... In the twentieth century only the under-dog is allowed to value their clutter as property" (pp. 66 and 67).

[3] Saulo B. Cwerner and Alan Metcalfe compile a list of recent literature on how to de-clutter in their article, "Storage and Clutter: Discourses and Practices of Order in the Domestic World," *Journal of Design History* 16:3 (2003): 229–39.

of cleaning and straightening out, which constitute, along with cooking, the bulk of our house chores. If, as Elizabeth Spelman suggests, humans are *Homo reparans*, we are even more *Homo purgens*, because in a way we are engaged in cleaning and tidying up more constantly than repairing.[4]

I. "Clean," "dirty," "neat," "messy," "organized," "disorganized"

i. Neglect of everyday aesthetic qualities

Despite the fact that these qualities are so deeply entrenched in our everyday life and govern our activities, there has been very little discussion of them in aesthetics. A few exceptions include personal grooming, the preservation and restoration of art, littering and pollution in environmental aesthetics, and specific aesthetic movements in praise of aging appearance, such as the eighteenth-century British picturesque and the classical Japanese notion of *wabi*. I will discuss some of them later in this chapter. In light of the relative dearth of examination of this major aspect of our everyday aesthetic life, I find Thomas Leddy's discussion both unusual and illuminating. Leddy attributes the neglect of what he calls "everyday surface aesthetic qualities," such as clean, dirty, neat, and messy, to their alleged lack of "perceptual complexity," when compared with more lofty aesthetic qualities applicable to art, such as "unified," "elegant," and "balanced." According to him, there is a deeply embedded assumption in modern aesthetics that "aesthetic qualities should have complex features which make them accessible only after much training."[5] He also points to a gender bias based upon "their association with what has been called 'women's work'" that prevents those everyday aesthetic qualities from becoming a full-fledged subject matter for aesthetic enquiry. Traditional "women's work" includes not only the chore of cleaning the house, dishes, and clothes but also, as mothers, a primary responsibility for teaching children

[4] In a very interesting discussion on our urge to "repair" things as well as human relationships, Elizabeth Spelman describes humans as *Homo reparans*. (*Repair: The Impulse to Restore in a Fragile World*, (Boston: Beacon Press, 2002)).

[5] Tom Leddy, "Everyday Surface Aesthetic Qualities: 'Neat,' 'Messy,' 'Clean,' 'Dirty,'" *Journal of Aesthetics and Art Criticism* 53:3 (Summer 1995), p. 267. The following two passages are from p. 261. He discusses another set of neglected everyday aesthetic qualities, "sparkle and shine," in an article of the same title in *British Journal of Aesthetics* 37:3 (July 1997): 259–73.

personal grooming. A similar observation can be made regarding social class, as "men who do have jobs which are primarily concerned with these activities (of cleaning), for example, garbagemen, often have low social status." Even among women, those who clean the houses and do laundry for others, such as housemaids and servants, have low social status. We can add that the commercial laundry business was stereotypically the domain of Chinese immigrants and yard work that of Hispanic migrant workers.

Leddy argues for the importance of inquiry into the everyday surface aesthetic qualities, because "many of our first aesthetic experiences are associated with everyday surface aesthetic qualities," and that "children are taught to be neat, clean, orderly, and not to be messy, sloppy, and unkempt."[6] However, he seems to concede that these qualities are not as complex as more artistically oriented aesthetic qualities. I share his call for such an inquiry, but I would make an even stronger case for its importance for the following reasons. First, although everyday surface aesthetic qualities may not be as complex as artistic qualities from the structural viewpoint, in some other ways they *are* very complex, because they are often context-dependent. It is true that these everyday aesthetic qualities are recognized by all of us, regardless of training or cultural sophistication, but this does not necessarily mean that there are no interesting and complicated issues involved. Secondly, though, as Leddy points out, the activities associated with these everyday surface aesthetic qualities have traditionally been carried out by women and men of low status, many more of us perform such tasks compared with those of us who create works of art or design artifacts professionally. In addition, all of us, male or female, wealthy or poor, educated or uneducated, engage in the act of cleaning ourselves. Therefore, unlike the case of art with which only some of us are familiar and still fewer of us create, everyday aesthetic qualities are of universal aesthetic interest. Finally, because they are thoroughly integrated with our everyday concerns, our response to these qualities, which often translates into actions, has many pragmatic ramifications: moral, social, political, and ecological. If everyday aesthetic qualities lack the structural complexity of artistic qualities, they still possess pragmatic significance and this fact alone makes these qualities worthy of inquiry. This chapter will explore

[6] Ibid. p. 266.

these issues regarding everyday aesthetic qualities including those qualities indicative of aging.

ii. Construction of everyday aesthetic qualities

That things change is a law of nature, independent of our attitude. However, things "decline," "decay," "get dirty," or "become messy" due to our expectation, desire, and evaluation. As I mentioned before, there seems to be a generally accepted notion of the optimal state of each object, when it is at its prime, and it is because of our construction of the object's life process and our attraction and adherence to its "peak" stage that the object declines and deteriorates.

Such is the recognition behind the Buddhist teaching. The first Noble Truth includes different manifestations of suffering, such as "aging" and "not getting what one wants," and the second and third Noble Truths teach the origin of suffering, identified as our "craving," as well as the cessation of suffering, facilitated by "the complete fading-away and extinction of this craving, its forsaking and abandonment, liberation from it, detachment from it."[7] That is, impermanence and transience in themselves are not the problem causing suffering; our all-too-human attitude is. Accordingly, Dōgen, in his thirteenth-century Japanese text on Zen Buddhism, reminds us that "flowers fall when we cling to them, and weeds only grow when we dislike them."[8] Our normal lament over falling flowers and weed-infested garden is relative to our treasuring the flowers in full bloom and weed-free garden, both considered as their optimal condition.

Notions such as "dirty" and "messy" are similarly context-dependent and culturally constructed. Mary Douglas, in her work, *Purity and Danger*, argues that the notion of "dirt" necessarily depends upon some kind of ordered system: "dirt" is something that is "out of place." In many indigenous cultures, the system may be religious in nature, but in our modern society, "dirt avoidance is a matter of hygiene or aesthetics."[9] She

---

[7] *Thus Have I Heard: The Long Discourses of the Buddha: Digha Nikaya*, tr. Maurice Walshe (Boston: Wisdom Publications, 1987), included in *Voices of Wisdom: A Multicultural Philosophy Reader*, ed. Gary E. Kessler, fifth edn. (Belmont: Wadsworth, 2004), p. 28.

[8] Dōgen, *Shōbōgenzō: Zen Essays by Dōgen*, tr. Thomas Cleary (Honolulu: University of Hawaii Press, 1986), p. 32.

[9] Mary Douglas, *Purity and Danger: An Analysis of Concept of Pollution and Taboo* (London: Routledge, 2002), p. 44. She repeats the claim on p. 92: "With us pollution is a matter of aesthetics, hygiene or etiquette." The following passage is from p. 44.

demonstrates that "dirt...is never a unique, isolated event," but rather is "the by-product of a systematic ordering and classification of matter, in so far as ordering involves rejecting inappropriate elements" by citing the following examples that are all familiar to us in our everyday life:

Shoes are not dirty in themselves, but it is dirty to place them on the dining-table; food is not dirty in itself, but it is dirty to leave cooking utensils in the bedroom, or food bespattered on clothing; similarly, bathroom equipment in the drawing room; clothing lying on chairs; outdoors things indoors; upstairs things downstairs; under-clothing appearing where over-clothing should be.[10]

There is nothing dirty about ketchup, unless it is on my shirt. Mud on our kitchen floor is dirty, but not outdoors on a rainy day or in a dwelling with a mud floor. A pile of clothes in the laundry basket or a cleaner's counter does not invoke the notion of mess, but the same thing in the middle of a living room floor would. Sheets of printed page in random sequence in a recycling bin do not cause any reaction from us, but we would be upset if the same thing appeared in our office file cabinet. Wildly growing bushes belong to a forest, but they simply appear messy and unkempt in an otherwise meticulously maintained garden. Graffiti on a highway overpass requires "cleaning," whereas on an abandoned building it may acquire the status of art and preserved.

Though primarily concerned with environmental pollution, Neil Evernden also points out that "in order for there to be perceptible pollution, there must first be an understanding of systemic order, an environmental norm. Only then is it possible to detect something that is 'out of place.' "[11] Besides water and air contamination, he also refers to the notion of "weeds," those noxious plants, such as dandelion and crabgrass, that "pollute" suburban lawns "manicured and purified by the ablution rites of chemical lawn maintenance." We normally do not refer to dandelions blooming in profusion in an open meadow as "weeds." They are considered weeds when they constitute "intrusions into the order of the lawn, and into the

[10] Ibid. pp. 44–5. Arthur Danto makes a similar claim by citing a passage from Charles Darwin: "A smear of soup in a man's beard looks disgusting, though there is of course nothing disgusting in the soup itself." Danto continues that "there is nothing disgusting in the sight of a baby with food all over its face, though, depending on circumstances, we may find it disgusting that a grown man's face should be smeared with *marinara* sauce." (*The Abuse of Beauty: Aesthetics and the Concept of Art* (Chicago: Open Court, 2004), p. 53).

[11] Neil Evernden, *The Social Creation of Nature* (Baltimore: The Johns Hopkins University Press, 1992), pp. 5–6. The following passages are both from p. 119.

domain of human willing." When we examine the examples of what we consider to be dirty, messy, and filthy, we realize that we are not concerned so much with the objects/substances themselves as with their *displacement*. Something is "out of place" or "out of order" only against the background of an agreed-upon order.

I believe that our detection of "orderliness" and "messiness" is also dependent upon *the kind* of object and environment in question. Some objects and environments demand perfect organization primarily for functional purposes: a report, syllabus, library shelving, doctor's office, and the like. We cannot take any aesthetic pleasure in chaos and mess found there. On the other hand, disorder and clutter in some objects or spaces are expected and welcome. They define the sense of place and the distinctive characteristic of the object, as I discussed in Chapter III. I think I would feel somewhat disoriented if Chinatown shops, mid-Eastern bazaar, Japanese fish markets, curio shops, side streets of downtown Tokyo under train passes, and artists' studios were impeccably organized and devoid of any clutter. There is a certain charm in the dusty and cluttered shelves and disorganized arrangement of merchandize in a Chinatown store. Similarly, in a Japanese fish market, I experience aesthetic pleasure not only in all kinds of fish and seafood piled high but also in the loud and vigorous shouting of vendors trying to entice passers-by; different smells of fish, seaweed, and other ocean bounties; and the wetness of water and the coolness of ice as I walk near iced merchandise. I enjoy the vigor and energy of the fish market, with chaotic noise, fishy smell, and all.

However, our positive aesthetic response to the relative disorder and chaos in Chinatown stores and fish markets does not mean that we welcome any signs of disorganization in those environments, either. Total lack of organization, even in these spaces, will not be appreciated. For example, we would expect that similar items be placed in the same shelf or pile, even if they are not neatly arranged, so that jade objects are not mixed with silk garments, and squids are not placed together with tuna and abalone. So, within the category of Chinatown stores and fish markets, there is a different yardstick of organization, though the yardstick itself is very different from the one we use for a business office or a chic, upscale, brand-name store. It may be that we have a kind of object-specific yardstick to gauge the degree of organization, and without knowing what *kind* of space is involved, we may not be able to tell whether or not the objects there are disorganized.

The consideration here is similar to Kendall Walton's notion of "categories of art" which extends to artifacts, such as "one lifted from the dust at an as yet unexcavated archaeological site on Mars," regarding which "we would simply not be in a position to judge it aesthetically."[12]

It is true that our expectation here is formed by and in turn forms a stereotype.[13] Whether accurate or not, such a stereotype contributes to the sense of place and essential characteristics of things, as I discussed in Chapter III. If this sense of place is dependent upon cultural expectations, it is also dependent upon historical sensibility as well. For example, the museum displays that we are familiar with today, devoid of clutter, and giving each object its due space, against a neutral background, usually of white wall, is a relatively new convention. Several years ago, the Rhode Island School of Design Museum displayed selections from their nineteenth-century European art collection in their largest exhibit space in the old fashioned way; that is, filling the wall with paintings closely spaced both horizontally and vertically. Sometimes there were three paintings above one another, so that viewing the top painting caused neck strain. From today's sensibility, the whole exhibit looked too crowded and the impression we got was one of utter clutter. The same sense of clutter is experienced with old-fashioned natural history museum displays, which originated with eighteenth-century nobility's display of curio items gathered from their Grand Tour and other excursions. At one time, the arrangement of objects at the Victoria and Albert Museum in London also exuded the same feel of clutter, as if it were a grandmother's attic lined with knick-knacks, though filled with wonderful objects and exquisite spatial details on a grand scale. In fact, what we take to be

---

[12] Kendall Walton, "Categories of Art," first published in *The Philosophical Review*, LXXIX (1970), included in *Philosophy Looks at the Arts*, ed. Joseph Margolis (Philadelphia: Temple University Press, 1978, rev. edn.), p.109.

[13] One such stereotype, which does not quite match reality, is the Japanese architectural interior. Inge Maria Daniels dispels the myth, or what she calls "a romantic ideal of the Japanese house," that the Japanese interior is sparse, "restrained and orderly." Constructed by nineteenth-century Western visitors' accounts of Japanese houses and its appeal further romanticized by Western architects and designers as well as enhanced by a contemporary Japanese architect, Tadao Andō, this sparse, orderly, and modest Japanese interior has become a stereotype. However, she points out that the sparseness of pre-modern Japanese architecture is due to the fact that "pre-modern Japanese did not possess an excess of consumer goods as in the West" and today's typical house interior is rather cluttered with all kinds of goods and decorative items, exhibiting an "untidy" and disorganized appearance. "The 'Untidy' Japanese House," included in *Home Possessions: Material Culture Behind Closed Doors*, ed. Daniel Miller (Oxford: Berg, 2001), pp. 201, 201, and 203.

clutter seems to have been a norm, "a decorative virtue," during the Victorian age. It is the aesthetics of modernism which changed this virtue into "an outrage," compelling its advocates to "skin... their houses to the bone."[14]

We still seem to be under the spell of modernist aesthetics today when it comes to cluttered interiors, as recent writings on clutter usually "defend" its aesthetics and significance against the prevailing distaste, similar to the way in which the picturesque advocates and *wabi* aficionados try to "justify" an aesthetics that goes counter to more accepted tastes.[15] However, it is also noteworthy that most defense of clutter usually concerns private interior space, one's home, rather than public space, and the reasoning is often based upon the very personal nature of our attachments and memories regarding each object making up the clutter, contributing to the construction of self-identity, what Russell Lynes calls "visual autobiography."[16]

As these examples suggest, the judgment that something is ruined, dirty, messy, or disorganized is not simply directed at the sensuous surface of the object in question but in important ways dependent upon the surrounding context and our expectation and attitude regarding the object's prime condition. These are constructs, although sensuous appearance is not irrelevant. Our seemingly spontaneous reactions to everyday surface aesthetic qualities, therefore, are not really simple, although we do not need any special training or expert knowledge that may be required for recognizing expressive qualities in artworks.

[14] Russell Lynes, "Kudos for Clutter," *Architectural Digest* 41:3 (March 1985), the first two phrases are from p. 34 and the last one from p. 38.

[15] Such as Lynes; Graves; and Cwerner and Metcalfe. At the time of completing the final manuscript, a new book that sounds pertinent to the discussion came out, which unfortunately I did not have time to read. It is entitled *A Perfect Mess: The Hidden Benefits of Disorder (How Crammed Closets, Cluttered Offices, and On-The-Fly Planning Make the World a Better Place)* written by Eric Abrahamson and David H. Freeman (New York: Little Brown and Company, 2007). According to one review, their main contention is that, despite the common assumption that disorder creates inefficiency, at least some degree of disorder rather promotes efficiency because those who are overly concerned with order will spend all their time and energy organizing. ("Neat is Sooo Last Year," *The Providence Sunday Journal* (7 January 2007))

[16] Lynes, p. 38. The power of modernist aesthetics is also felt in landscape design. John Tillman Lyle points out that the modernist design's pursuit of universality of form, prominently displayed by International Style, seeks "*neatness* and sharpness," rejecting fecundity that is characterized to be "*messy* and hard to predict." He takes this as a particular challenge to promoting "regenerative landscape" respectful of the local conditions, as "we need to be aware that regenerative landscape sometimes may be perceived as strange and different within the industrial context that still prevails." "Landscape: Source of Life or Liability," included in *Reshaping the Built Environment*, ed. Charles J. Kibert (Washington, D. C.: Island Press, 1999), p. 166, emphasis added.

iii. Relevance of functionality

What then accounts for our rejection of filthy, disorderly, untidy, shabby, dilapidated appearance and our preference for the opposite qualities that we usually attribute to the object's prime condition? Probably the most readily available explanation has to do with the decreased functionality, whether real or perceived. When things age, cars don't run well, furniture becomes wobbly, houses become drafty and furnaces do not run efficiently, plates are broken, clothes get ripped and buttons go missing, books are worm-eaten and fall apart at the binding, and electric appliances and computers simply quit working. Similarly, we become alarmed when our bodies start falling apart, afflicted with a number of age-related medical conditions. With old objects, we either repair them or throw them away, and, of course, we are painfully aware of the terminal destination of our aging bodies.

Similarly, our generally negative attitude toward qualities such as disorder, mess, and filth is based upon utilitarian reasons. Dirty dishes, bathrooms, and clothes harm us because of their unhygienic conditions. A disorganized room, like my office right now (!), makes finding things and accomplishing various tasks more difficult. Clutter in the shed, garage, or basement creates an obstacle course as we try to retrieve a tool. On a societal level, litter on the roadside or beach damages the environment and garbage strewn in the vacant lot attracts rats, while the clutter of billboards along the highway distracts the drivers, creating traffic hazard.

However, our negative reaction to those qualities is not always motivated by these practical considerations; sometimes it is directed exclusively toward their *appearance* even when their functionality is unaffected. We decry a threadbare couch, dingy wallpaper, peeling paint on our house, rust spots on our car, clothes that are no longer in style, chipped dishes and cups, and cracked driveway, though each retains its full or near-full function. They *look* shabby, dilapidated, deteriorating, sagging, decaying, tattered, tired, ruined: in short, old. Our negative reaction toward their appearance prompts us to engage in the business of rejuvenating, restoring, sprucing up, renewing, renovating, refinishing, rebuilding, refreshing, and breathing a new life into old objects, unless they are too far gone for salvaging in which case we simply discard them.

Likewise, our effort for clean-up is sometimes motivated by aesthetic considerations, without any functional ramifications. A little coffee stain on my clothes, carpet, or sofa does not interfere with its function; neither does dust on a shelf or a table (unless my family member suffers from asthma). I try to clean up stains and dust because they are "unsightly." I also try to pick up and straighten out things in the living room, not because I may trip over them or they interfere with my activities, but because the room looks "disorderly" and "messy." Similarly, many communities react to graffiti and vandalism to their properties not only by preventive measures but also by cleaning the "defaced" surface because they create an "eyesore." Sometimes a property owner gets legally punished for a messy yard strewn with debris, as exemplified by a case in Minneapolis where an 88-year-old man was actually jailed for not cleaning up his property.[17]

iv. Reflection of personal character and moral values

When functionality is not an issue, so that we can negotiate perfectly a messy room or disorganized office space and derive full function from a stained and wrinkled shirt, threadbare couch, or rusted car, more often than not we are concerned with issues beyond aesthetics: the impression we give to others. The way we and our possessions appear plays a significant role in other people's assessment, not only of our aesthetic taste, but perhaps more importantly of our character. Depending upon our personal grooming, attire, and the interior and exterior of the house, we are often judged to be meticulous, neighborly, civic-minded, responsible, diligent, and hard-working, *or* irresponsible, sloppy, uncaring, lazy, and slovenly. At other times, we may be judged rather uptight, inflexible, rigid, and too formal *or* mellow, relaxed, free, and easy-going. These judgments on personal traits and moral virtues/vices are often formed on the basis of the *appearance* of our possessions and ourselves, sometimes even without the knowledge of who we are and how we behave. One cannot help questioning the neighbors' moral character, even if one doesn't know them, if their house looks shabby with peeling paint, broken windows, backyard sheds half falling down, rusted and broken-down cars permanently parked in the driveway, front yard overgrown with weeds and littered with garbage (of course assuming that they are able-bodied people with adequate income).

---

[17] "They Like it Clean in Minneapolis," *Providence Journal*, 24 July 2005. My town paper also recently ran a front page article about the police cracking down on "junk" cars parked on townspeople's properties. The subtitle of the article states: "Junk: *Eyesores* Evicted from Local Properties," *Barrington Times*, 20 July 2005, emphasis added.

According to one interpretation, when Charles Dickens's character Mrs. Jellyby in *Bleak House* is so concerned with working on social problems that she neglects taking care of her own house, "leaving it disheveled, untidy, even dirty," clutter signifies a problem caused by "the woman of the household taking on issues beyond her proper domestic sphere."[18] Similarly, employers cannot but form a judgment of a person's attitude and character, even competence, if he comes to a job interview with a disheveled and unkempt appearance (again assuming that he has access to a shower, a different set of clothes, and so on). Their negative judgment thus formed sometimes weighs more than his qualifications and work experiences.

Personal appearance has gained more attention than the condition of personal possessions as an indication of our attitude, character, and values. David Novitz, for example, points out that our appearance "identifies us as having certain attitudes and values."[19] Specifically,

To think of a woman as demure, well-groomed, slim, fat, dumpy, homely, ugly, petite, or graceful; a man as rugged, handsome, well-dressed, good-looking, or manly; a minister as doleful, insipid, and colorless; a schoolchild as sprightly, gay, shabby, or skinny is of course to judge their appearances. Such judgments, even when couched in aesthetic terms, are never the application of 'pure' or 'disinterested' aesthetic values.

Consider the following two examples pertaining to the way in which a woman's character is assessed through her appearances. Diane Ackerman recalls being criticized for her "teased" hair by her parents, because for them "serious women have serious hairdos that are formal, sprayed, and don't move" so that "professional women aren't taken seriously if they don't have a 'wet set' (rollers, hair dryer, setting lotion, hair spray)." In the case of long hair, it has to be "tightly controlled in a bun, under a hat or scarf, or with hair spray" because "loose ends on one's head signal loose ends in one's life."[20] In a similar vein, a serious, upright woman in the past had to take care that the back seam of her nylon stockings had to be straight because "a straight one demonstrated *control*, and constant

[18] Cwerner and Metcalfe, p 231.
[19] David Novitz, *The Boundaries of Art* (Philadelphia: Temple University Press, 1992), p. 106. The next long passage is from p. 107.
[20] Diane Ackerman, *A Natural History of the Senses* (New York: Vintage Books, 1991), p. 86.

attention even to the back of one's look." Furthermore, "crooked seams were matched in *shameful delinquency* by wrinkles" around the ankles, and of course wearing stockings with "run" indicates carelessness and indifference.[21]

Today women rarely wear stockings with seams and we have become much more informal and relaxed about our appearance. However, we have not rid ourselves of these judgments on women's characters through their appearance. The most notorious example is the common criticism of the appearance of a female rape victim wearing heavy make-up, super-mini skirt, low cut top that tightly clings to the body and stiletto high heels. The public tends to form a judgment about her character from her appearance and ends up with the pronouncement that "she was asking for it," as if to justify the act of rape. Men are not exempt from this relentless scrutiny of appearance as a presumed reflection of their character, competence, and general attitude, as indicated by the increasing focus on presidential candidates' appearance, consisting of attire, hair-do, general personal grooming, voice inflection, and bodily gesture, and even height. I mentioned in Chapter II that sometimes, to our chagrin, the media coverage focuses more on these items than their agenda, political views, and qualifications.[22]

Besides reflections of personal character, we also often form an aesthetic judgment on the societal level based upon our assessment of the values/disvalues expressed by an object. For example, our negative aesthetic judgments on vandalism and graffiti that "deface" the structure and become an "eyesore" for the neighborhood are derived not simply from their appearance; in fact, some graffiti may look no different from the community-sanctioned mural or those graffiti that become christened as works of art. Our negative judgment is largely motivated by what we

---

[21] Margaret Visser, *The Way We Are: Astonishing Anthropology of Everyday Life* (New York: Kodansha International, 1997), p. 244, emphasis added.

[22] For male politicians, the norm seems to be a full set of hair and tall stature. We recall how Ross Perot was ridiculed for his shortness and overly big ears, while Michael Dukakis stood on a small platform behind a podium when he debated George F. W. Bush who is much taller than Dukakis. Female politicians seem to have more challenge regarding their appearance, because we have not really decided on the norm. If appearing too feminine, they are criticized for not being professional and tough-minded, while if appearing too unfeminine, they are criticized for trying to be more like a man. See Virginia Postrel's discussion on this point in *The Substance of Style: How the Rise of Aesthetic Value is Remaking Commerce, Culture, and Consciousness* (New York: HarperCollins, 2003), pp. 24–33. Also see note 7 of Chapter II.

take to be an attitude of indifference or disrespect for other people's or communal property.

Thus, our aesthetic judgments regarding the appearance of objects as aged, clean, messy, and the like, are intricately intertwined with our moral assessment. The reference to moral evaluation is most clear in the case of "clean" and "dirty." Black belching smoke coming out of a factory smokestack or discolored, foamy water coming out of a pipe are dirtying, hence polluting, the air or water. Terrorists' use of "dirty" bombs can also be described as a "dirty" tactic, while we want to have a "clean" government, and a "clean" election campaign, as well as "clean up" our act.[23]

When things are left alone and nature takes its course, they become aged and dirty. Furthermore, as we handle things in our everyday life, they also become soiled and disorganized. Things do not renew, clean, and organize themselves; it is up to us. If we fail to perform these tasks, not only do things show signs of neglect but also we get criticized for our neglect and lack of control. The task of arresting the aging appearance, of renewing, repairing, restoring, cleaning, tidying, organizing, therefore, is a way of combating the natural course of events and it is a way of showing that we are in control, exerting our stamp and power over the way things naturally become. Representative of the modernist movement, Le Corbusier advocates the benefit of white interior with the following rationale:

Every citizen is required to replace his hangings, his damasks, his wall-papers, his stencils, with a plain coat of white ripolin. His home is made *clean*. There are no more dirty, dark corners. Everything is shown as it is. Then comes *inner cleanliness* ... once you have put ripolin on your walls you will be *master of yourself*.[24]

Thus, the clean, orderly, and tidy appearance, whether it be our hairdo or room, both exudes and instills confidence that we are in charge and we are not simply letting nature take its course or allowing things to happen.

---

[23] The term "clean" is used in the Boy Scouts Law for a moral ideal to be upheld by the members. Both the cleanliness ideal and the ideal of "morally straight" specified in the Scout Oath were cited as the justification for the Boy Scouts' right to exclude gays from the scoutmaster position in the 2000 U. S. Supreme Court case, Boy Scouts of America and Monmouth Council, et al. v. James Dale.

[24] Cited by Penny Sparke in *As Long As It's Pink: The Sexual Politics in Taste* (New York: HarperCollins, 1995), p. 117.

v. Positive value of disorder

Is the indication of our power and control manifested in clean, organized surfaces always aesthetically appreciable? Is the manifestation of opposite qualities always aesthetically negative? Though not prevalent, there are examples where qualities such as disorder and messiness are appreciated and celebrated.[25] That they are exceptions rather than the rule is indicated by the fact that the advocates of such an aesthetic taste are rather vocal and passionate about their preference. One notable example of advocating the aesthetic virtue of disorder and aged appearance occurred in eighteenth-century Europe, where a dramatic reaction against the classical notion of beauty took place by expanding the scope of positive aesthetic values to include the sublime and the picturesque. Many seventeenth- and eighteenth-century British thinkers under the spell of classical notion of beauty consisting of harmony, order, and symmetry, took delight in geometrical order exhibited by formal gardens and orchards. Keith Thomas compiles evidence to illustrate this penchant. To list a few of such observations: "Wood plantations... could be square, triangular, rectangular, oval or circular; but they should not be made 'rudely and confusedly'" (Walter Blith, 1653); "it is a great pleasure and delight... to walk among you, so many beautiful fruit trees; seeing ye grow so handsomely and uniform; ye grow in order, in straight lines every way." (Ralph Austen, 1676); "Beauty requires that the hedges should be in straight lines." (John Lawrence, 1726)[26]

Their reasons for delighting in orderly-looking agricultural appearance was partly efficiency, as Lawrence continues to state that "what will be... more pleasing to the eye will be cheapest and more convenient; straight lines are the shortest."[27] It also embodies productivity, as observed by another eighteenth-century writer: "I see the country of England smiling with cultivation: the grounds exhibiting all the perfection of agriculture, parcelled out into beautiful enclosures, corn

---

[25] "Dirty" and "filthy" are the qualities that do not seem to allow for positive appreciation, except in the metaphorical sense (as in "dirty" dancing and "dirty" pictures, although the moral appropriateness of enjoying them is often called into question) or in very specific situations (when we encourage little kids to play outdoors and get dirty, for example).

[26] These passages are cited by Keith Thomas in *Man and the Natural World: A History of the Modern Sensibility* (New York: Pantheon Books, 1983), pp. 256–7.

[27] Cited by Thomas, p. 257.

fields, hay pasture, woodland and commons."[28] Ultimately, the orderly design also expresses human control over nature. As Thomas observes, "the practice of planting corn or vegetables in straight lines was not just an efficient way of using limited space; it was also a pleasing means of imposing human order on the otherwise disorderly natural world."[29] The aesthetic pleasure in the orderly appearance, particularly by arranging natural elements, should be understood from this perspective.

The story of the reaction to this classical European attraction to strict order has often been told. The growing attraction to the disorderly, wild, and rude appearance of raw nature, particularly of mountains with their grottos, deep canyons, and huge overhanging rocks was first tentatively stated, then steadily developed during the eighteenth century. "Mountain gloom" was transformed into "mountain glory," to borrow Marjorie Hope Nicolson's terms.[30] Shaftesbury, for example, announces, speaking as Philocles,

I shall no longer resist the passion growing in me for things of a natural kind, where neither art nor the conceit or caprice of man has spoiled their genuine order by breaking in upon that primitive state. Even the rude rocks, the mossy caverns, the irregular unwrought grottos and broken falls of water, with all the horrid graces of the wilderness itself,... will be the more engaging, and appear with a magnificence beyond the formal mockery of princely gardens.[31]

Joseph Addison continues in the same vein several years later by declaring his preference for "ground covered over with an agreeable mixture of garden and forest... much more charming than that *neatness* and elegance

---

[28] Cited by Roy Porter, *English Society in the Eighteenth Century* (London: Penguin Books, 1990), p. 186. Needless to say, the notion of "productivity" here is Lockean in the sense of commodity value. That this is one (and predominantly modern Western) notion of productivity underlies Vandana Shiva's critique of what she calls the "monocultures of the mind," which can decimate indigenous practice, in her case Indian agricultural practice, which is based upon a different notion of "productivity." *Monocultures of the Mind: Perspectives on Biodiversity and Biotechnology* (London: Zed Books, 1997).

[29] Thomas, p. 256.

[30] Marjorie Hope Nicolson's *Mountain Gloom and Mountain Glory: The Development of the Aesthetics of the Infinite* (New York: W. W. Norton, 1963) gives a detailed account of the dramatic change in people's aesthetic taste during the eighteenth century in Europe, England in particular.

[31] Anthony Ashley Cooper, Third Earl of Shaftesbury, *The Moralists* (1709) included in *Philosophy of Art and Beauty: Selected Readings in Aesthetics from Plato to Heidegger*, eds. Albert Hofstadter and Richard Kuhns (New York: Modern Library, 1964), p. 245.

which we meet with in those of our own country."[32] Finally, in a well-known passage, Immanuel Kant remarks on William Marsden's comparison between a neatly arranged pepper garden and the wild profusion of jungle. Marsden was reportedly attracted to "a pepper garden, where the stakes on which this plant twines itself form parallel rows" particularly if he encountered it in the middle of a jungle. In contrast, Kant claims that "all stiff regularity (such as approximates to mathematical regularity) has something in it repugnant to taste" and instead says he prefers "free beauties of nature."[33]

The picturesque advocates' celebration of the irregular and disorderly was also promoted as an improvement over both the widely accepted classical canon of beauty and Edmund Burke's notion of beauty as softness and smoothness, the latter most vividly embodied in the popular Capability Brown landscapes. William Gilpin, one of the foremost advocates of the picturesque, for example, does recognize the aesthetic appeal of "smooth-ness" and "neatness" by admitting that "the higher the marble is polished, the brighter the silver is rubbed, and the more the mahogany shines, the more each is considered as an object of beauty, as if the eye delighted in gliding smoothly over a surface."[34] Nevertheless, he claims that such smooth and neat objects do not provide an aesthetically interesting and appealing image for representation in pictures, and denigrates "all the formalities of hedgerow trees and square divisions of property" as "disgusting in a high degree."[35] Instead, he calls attention to the opposite kind of aesthetic values: picturesque qualities consisting of irregularity, disorder, complexity, and roughness. Such qualities can be created by inducing the appearance of disorder, aging, and neglect. A Palladian architecture "may be elegant in the last degree" because of "the proportion of its parts, the propriety of its ornaments, and the symmetry of the whole," but, to make it picturesque, "we must use the mallet instead of the chisel, we must beat down one half of it, deface the other, and throw the mutilated members

---

[32] Joseph Addison, "The Pleasures of the Imagination" (1712) included in *Essays in Criticism and Literary Theory,* ed. John Loftis (Northbrook: AHM Publishing, 1975), p. 151, emphasis added.

[33] Immanuel Kant, *Critique of Judgement,* tr. By J. H. Bernard (New York: Hafner Press, 1974), p. 80. Addison makes a similar point when he states: "the beauties of the most stately garden or palace lie in a narrow compass, the imagination immediately runs them over and requires something else to gratify her; but in the wide fields of nature, the sight wanders up and down without confinement and is fed with an infinite variety of images without any certain stint or number" (p. 149).

[34] William Gilpin, *Three Essays,* 1792, p. 4.   [35] Cited by Thomas, p. 262.

around in heaps. In short, from a smooth building we must turn it into a rough ruin."[36] Similarly, to make a Brownian landscape picturesque, "turn the lawn into a piece of broken ground, plant rugged oaks instead of flowering shrubs, break the edges of the walk, give it the rudeness of a road, mark it with wheel tracks, and scatter around a few stones and brushwood."[37]

This picturesque ideal was also shared by William Payne Knight. In his *The Landscape, a Didactic Poem* (1794), Knight criticizes the Brownian landscape for being "dull, vapid, smooth, and tranquil," and "one eternal undulating sweep."[38] Instead he promotes a garden with signs of aging, neglect, and overgrowth. Regarding its ornaments, he says: "hide each formal trace of art with care: Let clust'ring ivy o'er its sides be spread, And moss and weeds grow scatter'd o'er its head"; it can also feature "the quarry long neglected, and o'ergrown | With thorns, that hang o'er mould'ing beds of stone ... " or "the retir'd and antiquated cot;— | Its roof with weeds and mosses cover'd o'er, | And honeysuckles climbing round the door; | While mantling vines along its walls are spread, | And clust'ring ivy decks the chimney's head." Here again, complexity, roughness, and irregularity, suggestive of agedness and neglect, are preferred to simplicity, smoothness, and regularity, indicative of human control and care.

One reason for the embrace of the picturesque and its precursors' penchant for the appearance of disorder and irregularity is that these qualities are more stimulating to the imagination than the opposite qualities. Addison complains that the "neatness and elegancy" of English (formal) gardens are "not so entertaining to the fancy," because "the imagination immediately runs them over and requires something else to gratify her; but in the wide fields of nature, the sight wanders up and down without confinement and is fed with an infinite variety of images without any certain stint or number."[39] The same observation underlies Alexander Pope's criticism of the formal gardens of Timon's Villa

[36] Ibid. p. 5. Christopher Woodward gives an actual example to carry out a similar act (though it was never materialized) in pp. 148–9 of *In Ruins* (New York: Pantheon Books, 2001).

[37] Gilpin, p. 8.

[38] Richard Payne Knight, "The Landscape, A Didactic Poem," included in *The Genius of the Place: The English Landscape Garden 1620–1820*, eds. John Dixon Hunt and Peter Willis (Cambridge: The MIT Press, 1990), p. 344. The following passages are from pp. 347 and 348. The illustration by Hearne and Pouncy is reproduced on p. 343 in this edition.

[39] Addison, pp. 151 and 149.

where "No pleasing Intricacies intervene, | No artful Wilderness to per-plex the Scene: | Grove nods at Grove, each Ally has a Brother, | And the half the Platform just reflects the other."[40] Similarly, William Hoga-rth declares the serpentine line to be the line of beauty because it leads our eye on a "wanton kind of chase."[41] Kant's reason for his prefer-ring the free beauties of nature to a regularized pepper garden is that a thing "with which imagination can play in an unstudied and purpo-sive manner is always new to us, and one does not get tired of looking at it."[42]

Equally important is the contrast between regularity/orderliness and irregularity/disorder. The picturesque ideal was not only a reaction against both the classical and Burkean aesthetic values, but also a response to the rapidly changing shape of the British countryside during the eigh-teenth century. Eighteenth-century England saw an increasing number of Enclosure Acts that hastened privatization of what previously was the commonly shared and used land. This legal process was vividly mani-fested by the now ubiquitous checkerboard hedgerow, prompting one nineteenth-century visitor to remark that the English countryside was "too much chequered with enclosures for picturesqueness."[43] In light of this, it is instructive that the picturesque values were almost always explained as an improvement upon the opposite qualities, rather than independent values in themselves, often accompanied by the illustrations of "before" and "after" the picturesque improvement. Both Gilpin and Knight illustrate the way in which an otherwise boring-looking, smooth landscape can be improved by breaking up the contour and making the entire composition more complex.[44]

[40] Alexander Pope, "An Epistle to Lord Burlington" (1731) included in Hunt and Willis, p. 213.

[41] William Hogarth, *The Analysis of Beauty* (1753), included in *A Documentary History of Art*, ed. Elizabeth G. Holt (New York: Doubleday Anchor Books, 1958), vol. II, p. 271.

[42] Kant, p. 80. Gilpin also claims that the "Regularity and Exactness" of a perfectly formed and well-maintained building "excites no manner of Pleasure in the Imagination." Cited by Malcolm Andrews in *The Search for the Picturesque: Landscape Aesthetics and Tourism in Britain, 1760–1800* (Stanford: Stanford University Press, 1989), p. 46.

[43] Cited by Thomas, p. 262. For the data on the increasing number of enclosure acts, see p. 209 of Porter.

[44] The illustration of "before" and "after" accompanying Knight's poem was already cited. Gilpin's "before" and "after" illustration of a mountain-scape with a lake in the middle, entitled "Non-Picturesque and Picturesque Mountain Landscapes," appears in *Three Essays*, reproduced in Andrews, p. 32. A late eighteenth-century landscape gardener equally popular as Capability Brown, Humphry Repton, also provides "before" and "after" illustrations of the improvement by his garden design in a

Lest we think that this debate between order and disorder is only an eighteenth-century British preoccupation and has no other relevance than an historical curiosity, consider the following discussions from today, one regarding interior space and the other constructed landscape. Imagine first a living room meticulously designed and maintained with geometrical precision. If everything is arranged precisely, it may look like a remarkable showcase, but we do not feel invited even to sit on a couch or put a coffee cup on the table. In such a tense space, the arrangement of objects on the coffee table that is more relaxed and a little askew, for example, may provide a point of respite and ease. In his remark on Philip Johnson's *Glass House*, Kevin Melchionne claims that, while it may be successful as a work of art, it fails as a domestic space, because it "does not recede into the background, never becomes an environment for the practices of everyday life."[45] Given the "sparseness of the furnishings and the extreme orderliness of the house, where even table-top bric-a-brac are discretely marked with indications of their correct location," *Glass House* is "unlivable as a domestic space" because it lacks "comfort, casualness, and a certain degree of dowdy familiarity." Its severe and unforgiving spatial configuration does not tolerate even a slight deviation from it. Domestic space as a lived space certainly should be cleaned, tidied up, and organized, but it should also allow some degree of mess and disorganization. Mondrian's paintings are as they should be, but the same strict geometry does not work for everyday living space.

At the same time, there is a need for some sign of order accompanying an otherwise wild, unruly appearance. Consider Joan Nassauer's discussion of "Messy Ecosystems, Orderly Frames."[46] She is concerned, on the one hand, with promoting indigenous plants and wildflowers for garden materials for ecological reasons, but, on the other hand, with our reaction to what may appear to be a mess, not worthy of our care and protection. Though

number of books featuring pull-out or fold-out pages. His garden design in part was a reaction against the excessive obsession with the picturesque then in vogue. The best illustration of his critique can be found in the pair of townscape sketches entitled *View from my Cottage* in which the "before" version features a one-legged, one-armed, one-eyed beggar in the foreground, a quintessential picturesque figure (*Fragments on the Theory and Practice of Landscape Gardening* (London: J. Taylor, 1816)).

[45] Kevin Melchionne, "Living in Glass Houses: Domesticity, Interior Decoration, and Environmental Aesthetics," *The Journal of Aesthetics and Art Criticism* 56:2 (Spring 1998), p. 191. The following two passages are also from the same page.

[46] Joan Iverson Nassauer, "Messy Ecosystems, Orderly Frames," *Landscape Journal*, 14:2 (Fall 1995): 161–70.

gardens consisting of indigenous wildflowers are gaining acceptance because of their ecological function, their "messy," "disorderly," and "unkempt" appearance often puts people off, sometimes causing their owners to be punished for creating an "eyesore" for the neighborhood. Michael Braungart, who, together with William McDonough, is working to bring about what they call the next Industrial Revolution, where our every product and by-product of industrial production benefits, rather than harms, the environment, relates the following story of his mother's garden in Germany. In 1982, her garden "which was full of vegetables, herbs, wildflowers, and many other strange and wonderful plants, was determined by town legislators to be *too messy, too 'wild,'*" and she was asked to pay a fine. As she continued with her garden while paying the annual fine, ten years later it "won a local award for creating habitat for songbirds."[47]

Despite ecological benefits, nature that is left to its own device often produces a messy appearance, discouraging our appreciation and attachment. In light of this, Nassauer suggests that such a "natural" space, which needs to be protected and nurtured, be placed within an orderly package: "It requires placing unfamiliar and frequently undesirable forms inside familiar, attractive packages. It requires designing *orderly* frames for *messy* ecosystems."[48] This is because, she points out, "in the everyday landscape of North America, the recognizable system of form typically is characterized by *neatness* and *order*" and such a landscape is usually read "as a sign of neighborliness, hard work, and pride." In contrast, a landscape lacking these qualities, particularly in an urban setting, even when carefully produced to induce biodiversity and ecological health, is considered "messy, weedy, and unkempt," and mistaken for a "neglected land or be readily compromised as land awaiting development" due to "a lack of care." She thus concludes that imposition of order on otherwise unruly-looking nature is not necessarily to indicate the domination of humans or human arrogance. It can be a device to signal to us through its attractiveness that what it encloses or demarcates is worthy of our attention, protection, and nurturing.

The necessity of the contrast between orderly and disorderly, and regularity and irregularity also supports the aesthetic category of *wabi* that

---

[47] William McDonough and Michael Braungart, *Cradel to Cradle: Remaking the Way We Make Things* (New York: North Point Press, 2002), p. 86, emphasis added.

[48] Nassauer, p. 161, emphasis added. The following passages are from p. 163, emphasis added, pp. 163, 162, and 163.

I shall discuss at length later in this chapter. There I shall emphasize *wabi* aesthetics' celebration of irregularity, imperfection, incompleteness, and insufficiency, which is most prominently manifested in tea ceremony implements that are defective due to age, missing parts, years of use, and so on. However, the celebration of *wabi* quality needs to be carefully examined, as it is not an indiscriminate celebration of anything imperfect, insufficient, or disorderly.[49] An irregularly shaped and cracked tea bowl, a vase missing one handle, and a crooked tree trunk used for an alcove support of a tea hut are all aesthetically effective *because* they are placed in a space with strict geometric lines of a *tatami* mat border, the regular pattern of the mats' woven straws, and the regular geometric shapes of windows. The *wabi* aesthetic effect will be lost if every implement is irregularly shaped and defective, placed in a space which is devoid of any regularity or order. Consider the following remarks by Marc Treib on traditional Japanese architecture known for "the modular planning" and "the employment of consistent angles in both plan and section," creating "an ordered field in which the position of all elements and their relationship to one another is easily established," in short, "a chessboard in three dimensions."[50]

Within the architectonic order of the dwelling, the exception to the grid has a more pronounced effect than a similar incident within an unstructured visual field.

[49] This point needs special emphasis today when this *wabi* sensibility has been appropriated and popularized in the West, as indicated by a book such as Robyn Griggs Lawrence's *The Wabi-Sabi House: The Japanese Art of Imperfect Beauty* (New York: Clarkson Potter, 2004) and a newspaper article such as Lisa Marshall's "House not Perfect? Maybe It's Just 'Wabi-Sabi,'" *Providence Journal*, 26 June 2005. Of course we can derive whatever useful ideas from these concepts for practical purposes, as long as we distinguish them from the way in which these concepts were applied in their original context. I came to appreciate this point after publishing "The Japanese Aesthetics of Imperfection and Insufficiency" (*The Journal of Aesthetics and Art Criticism* 55:4 (Fall, 1997): 377–85). A number of students in my Traditional Japanese Aesthetics class, after reading this article, questioned the seeming contradiction between the celebration of imperfection that I discuss in this article and the painstakingly meticulous work demanded and expected of a number of Japanese artifacts, such as traditional lacquerware and textile. In this respect, it is interesting to note that the perfectionist attitude toward lacquerware has also been the Korean tradition. One noted master, Kim Bong-ryong, who is described as "such a perfectionist that he did not allow his students to make even the slightest flaw or blemish," is remembered by one of his students, who then went on to become a master himself, about his experience. When Kim noticed a flaw in his student's mother-of-pearl inlay that the student disguised to make it undetectable, Kim "without a word … pulled out a knife and crudely gouged out the mother-of-pearl." (M. Ryu, "Lee Hyung-man: Even More Beautiful with the Passage of Time," *Koreana: Korean Art and Culture* 18:3 (Autumn 2004)), p. 48.

[50] Marc Treib, "The Dichotomies of Dwelling: Edo/Tokyo," included in *Tokyo: Form and Spirit*, ed. Mildred Friedman (Minneapolis: Walker Art Center, 1986), p. 122. The following long passage is also from p. 122. I inserted in parentheses my translation of the Japanese terms.

The ceiling of evenly spaced wooden planks appears as a neutral surface, as does the floor of beige *tatami*. Against the order of the grid, the painted folding screen, the ornate *fusuma* (sliding paper door), or the post of the *tokonoma* (alcove) contrast significantly, and its aesthetic effect is correspondingly increased.

All these examples, both historical and contemporary, suggest that the aesthetic appreciation of order/disorder or neatness/messiness is based upon their complementarity. That is, whether or not we can have a positive appreciation of order or disorder seems to be context-dependent. This differs from our appreciation of paradigmatic art in a paradigmatic setting. A typical museum makes an effort to make the background of an exhibited object as unobtrusive and neutral as possible. Hence, the museum wall is generally painted white, rather than sporting a striking color or a patterned wallpaper. Or, if it has a competing color or pattern because it is an old mansion converted into a museum, for example, we try to bracket the background in our experience.

Our everyday experience *can* assimilate this context-independent appreciation by focusing only on the pepper garden or on the painting in my living room. However, more often than not, our experience of these objects is continuous with their context, either spatially or temporally. I can understand the feeling of appreciation on encountering a regularly patterned pepper garden after walking through a jungle. It is not clear whether I can have the same degree of appreciation if I encounter it in the midst of strictly regulated landscape. After all, Marsden's praise for the pepper garden is preceded by the following claim: "A pepper garden cultivated in England would not, in point of external appearance, be considered as an object of extraordinary beauty; and would be particularly found fault with for its uniformity."[51]

I think that a similar appreciation of the contrast between the orderly and disorderly, organized and disorganized is at work when we consider our everyday environment and activities. Meticulous and impeccable organization is admirable and we aspire to such a state, whether it regards our living space or life. We do appreciate a clockwork precision of activities or mathematical precision of designed space and object. However, such an appreciation presupposes the background of an otherwise chaotic life or a loosely arranged surrounding. There is something almost inhuman and

---

[51] Cited by Thomas, p. 263.

repugnant about the sign of order that controls every inch of space or every moment of our life. The reverse also holds true; that is, an environment or a life that lacks any order or discernible organization is not appreciable. Such a situation prompts us to exert some control by imposing an order. Our appreciation of order and mess thus does not seem to be directed toward those qualities in themselves. It is rather toward the way in which we negotiate between exerting control over these inevitable natural processes and accepting them by submitting ourselves to such processes. What we find appreciable, it seems to me, is neither a total control over natural processes nor a wholesale submission to them, but rather the appropriate *balance* between them.[52]

2. Appearance of aging

i. Sensuous qualities of aged surface

Although the aesthetic appreciation of messy and disorderly appearance does exist and our appreciation of order and neatness is context-dependent, in our common life there is a stronger preference for clear, coherent, organized, orderly appearance. The same thing applies to the qualities illustrative of aging. The general norm seems to be in favor of the youthful appearance of an optimal state without blemishes and signs of decay. Indeed, in his research into different aesthetic reactions to "the look of age," gathered primarily from various historical examples in the West, David Lowenthal, a cultural geographer, points out that "the balance of

---

[52] Robert Maxwell also claims that "order is...something we count on, so long as we can choose it, and not be too subject to it. An excess of order can be just as disagreeable as subjection to disorder. We are rather finely balanced between the two." *Sweet Disorder and the Carefully Careless: Theory and Criticism in Architecture* (New York: Princeton Architectural Press, 1993), pp. 21–2. Furthermore, he points out that the British picturesque advocates' penchant for disorder and freedom from strict regularity corresponds to the growing appreciation of individual liberty: "the English attitude toward the French Revolution revealed the existence of a finely balanced dichotomy between *the desire for order and liberty*" (p. 23, emphasis added). It is also interesting to note the Korean concept of "Ch'angmun," which refers to doors and windows only snugly, not tightly, fit into their frame, leaving cracks. Despite the fact that Korean carpenters do not lack the skills to make them fit precisely, O-Young Lee explains that "the person who can appreciate the labyrinth called life, with all its subtle tones and gray and which cannot be told to the nearest millimeter or two, is one who is capable of living in the same way a Korean fits a window, the way a Korean lives...The beauty of the Korean window and door is the very same beauty found in life's contradictions." "The Ultimate Chic that Accommodates All Sizes and Shapes," *Koreana* 12:3 (Aug. 1998): 5–7 (obtained online from H W Wilson Art Index).

evidence ... shows general dislike of age and decay," and that "we prefer youth, not only in living creatures but in our surroundings, including our own creations." Those instances of the celebration of the look of age, he observes, are "the exception."[53]

It is noteworthy that the two prominent aesthetic movements advocating the positive aesthetic qualities of aging appearance, the eighteenth-century British picturesque and the Japanese *wabi* aesthetics, are both premised upon the commonly accepted and understood appreciation of the opposite qualities. For example, the picturesque movement's celebration of aged appearance is most effectively illustrated by its obsession with ruins. However, Lowenthal points out that in England, ruins, such as castles and abbeys, were not only not appreciated but rather deplored before the eighteenth century: "the mutilated English monasteries were long abhorred, their 'rotten Foundations, ruinous Arches and Pillars, mouldering and tottering Walls' arousing general revulsion."[54] Declaring the picturesque aesthetic as "England's greatest contribution to European visual culture," Christopher Woodward also points out that "before the Picturesque movement, thatched cottages and creaking windmills were not considered worthy of a designed landscape, nor were Gothic ruins, or gnarled oak-trees, or old walls covered in ivy."[55] The picturesque cult of ruins, therefore, has a particular potency, *precisely because* of the generally negative attitude toward half-fallen structures.

Or, consider the Japanese *wabi* sensibility promoted by the tea ceremony, which celebrates those objects and phenomena that are past their prime, such as falling cherry blossoms and chipped tea bowls. Its proponents claim that such a taste is contrary to something that comes naturally; it has to be cultivated. Yoshida Kenkō (1283–1350), a retired Buddhist monk, for example, extols the beauty of cherry blossoms when falling rather than in full bloom, as well as the obscured, rather than unobstructed, view

---

[53] David Lowenthal, *The Past Is a Foreign Country* (Cambridge: Cambridge University Press, 1990), p. 127. He makes the same claim on pp. 129, 143, and 147. The appearance of aging seems predominantly visual. To some extent we appreciate the sound indicative of age, such as an old music recording and the sound of old piano, but not too many sounds are indicative of age. I am not sure whether tactile sensations can indicate the agedness. I suppose we can feel the smoothness of a once rough surface and vice versa, but I am not sure whether tactile sensations alone, unaccompanied by visual clues, can give rise to recognition of the aged surface. When it comes to smell and taste, agedness is always negative, because it literally indicates decay, unfit for human consumption, except of course for cheese and some wine, and musty smell of an old book, family heirloom, and the like.

[54] Lowenthal, p. 144.   [55] Woodward, p. 119.

of the moon, by admitting at the outset that "people *commonly* regret that the cherry blossoms scatter or that the moon sinks in the sky, and this is *natural*."[56] So, if we can assume that our "natural" attitude toward things showing their age is negative, what accounts for our aesthetic reaction? Are we merely reacting to the sensuous appearance of the aging objects?

When we consider the pure sensuous surface of aging materials, there does not seem to be a consensus as to what features are aesthetically appreciable and what are not. The appearance of aging takes different forms. Sometimes the surface becomes smoother and simpler through weathering and repeated use. For example, a rough surface created by indented design on metal or stone becomes worn off by natural elements or frequent rubbing, so the inscription on a gravestone from long ago is no longer legible and coins become smoother. The "Cleopatra's Needle," an obelisk from 1600 B.C., now located in New York City's Central Park near the Metropolitan Museum of Art, has many of its inscribed hieroglyphics completely obliterated, exhibiting a smooth surface. At other times, however, the aged surface becomes more complex, rough, and irregular than the once smooth and uniform appearance through chips, cracks, tears, rust, patina, stain, peeling, growth of vegetation, and missing parts. Uvedale Price, a picturesque advocate, provides a full range of the ways in which a once beautiful architecture is transformed by organic and natural processes:

Observe the process by which time, the great author of such changes, converts a beautiful object into a picturesque one. First, by means of weather stains, partial incrustations, mosses, etc., it at the same time takes off from the uniformity of the surface, and of the colour; that is, gives a degree of roughness and variety of tint. Next, the various accidents of weather loosen the stones themselves; they tumble in irregular masses, upon what was perhaps smooth turf or pavement, or nicely trimmed walks and shrubberies; now mixed and overgrown with wild plants and creepers, that crawl over and shoot among the fallen ruins...birds convey their food into the chinks and yew, elder, and other berried plants project from the sides; while the ivy mantles over other parts and crowns the top.[57]

---

[56] Yoshida Kenkō, *Essays in Idleness: The Tsurezuregusa of Kenkō*, tr. Donald Keene (New York: Columbia University Press, 1967), p. 115, emphasis added.

[57] Cited by Andrews, p. 58.

In short, he characterizes beauty to be dependent "on ideas of youth and freshness," while the picturesque depends on "that of age, and even of decay."[58]

If the aging effects on materials and objects are thus diverse, so are our reactions to the effect of aging. John Ruskin, for example, takes a positive attitude toward the smoothing effect of weathering by praising: "the effect of time is such, that if... overcharged, simplify it; if harsh and violent, soften it."[59] In contrast, Midas Dekkers points out the grotesque result of smoothing effects on outdoor ancient sculptures: "As gentle rain turns into drops of acid, facial expressions on carvings in ancient cities become contorted grimaces—lepers, noses rotting away, ears falling off."[60] Similar concerns recently led to an extreme makeover of the presidential complexions at Mt. Rushmore by cleaning the "decades of dirt, grime, and lichens."[61]

Or, take the darkening of paint colors as they age. Speaking of paintings by old masters, Eugene Delacroix, for example, laments that "the blacks in the picture always go on increasing, and a background which appeared only middling dark when the work was new, turns to complete darkness in the course of time." In particular, he complains of this "insult of time" on those old paintings noted for brilliant colors.[62] Joshua Reynolds similarly remarks that "old pictures deservedly celebrated for their colouring, are often so changed by dirt and varnish, that we ought not to wonder if they do not appear equal to their reputation in the eyes of unexperienced painters, or young students."[63]

In contrast, some welcome the aging effect on artworks. Constable is known for his saying that "time will finish my painting." Joseph Addison tells of a dream in which he was viewing a row of old paintings by great masters, which were being continuously touched up by an old man. This old man

busied himself incessantly, and repeated touch after touch without rest or inter-mission, he wore off insensibly every little disagreeable gloss that hung upon a

---

[58] Uvedale Price, *An Essay on the Picturesque* (1794), included in Hunt and Willis, p. 355.

[59] John Ruskin, *Modern Painters* (London, n.d.). Pt. II, Sec. I, Ch. VI, p. 97.

[60] Dekkers, p. 66.

[61] "Thomas Jefferson Takes Revitalizing Bath," *The Providence Journal* (8 July 2005).

[62] Eugene Delacroix, *The Journal of Eugene Delacroix*, tr. Walter Pach (New York: Penguin Group International, 1972), p. 403.

[63] Joshua Reynolds, *The Discourses of Sir Joshua Reynolds* (London: J. Carpenter, 1842), p. 24.

figure. He also added such a beautiful brown to the shades, and mellowness to the colours, that he made every picture appear more perfect than when it came fresh from the master's pencil.

He then reveals the identity of this old man: Time.[64] Marguerite Yourcenar similarly describes numerous ways in which ancient sculptural pieces show their age and considers some alterations to be "sublime." For her, "to that beauty imposed by the human brain, by an epoch, or by a particular form of society, they add an involuntary beauty, associated with the hazards of history, which is the result of natural causes and of time."[65]

Despite these various ways in which materials and objects age and our diverse reactions to them, we do seem to share some consistent responses concerning which materials "age well" and which do not. We generally seem to have a positive response to wood, stone, brick, and clay when they age, while we respond rather negatively when concrete, plastic, and aluminum show their age. As Lowenthal points out:

Some substances age less well than others. Concrete becomes more ugly every passing year, looking greasy if smooth, squalid if rough; glass-fibre decays more disagreeably than stonework … The aesthetics of metal decay reflects a host of chemical and cultural variables. Much corrosion—rust on iron, tarnish on silver, white crusts on lead and tin—is normally odious; only to copper and bronze does a time-induced oxidized surface add the lustre of a 'noble' patina.[66]

Tanizaki Jun'ichirō, a twentieth-century Japanese writer, when writing on the traditional Japanese aesthetics in contrast with the modern Western aesthetics that was sweeping across Japan during his time, compares the beauty of wood, the traditional material for bathroom fixtures in Japan, with gleaming white of porcelain used in the Western-style bathroom fixture. He complains of the effect of glitteringly sparkling white of the

---

[64] Joseph Addison, *Spectator* 83, 5 June 1711.

[65] Marguerite Yourcenar, "That Mighty Sculptor, Time" in *That Mighty Sculptor, Time,* tr. Walter Kaiser (New York: The Noonday Press, 1992), p. 58.

[66] Lowenthal, p. 163. Dekkers also makes a similar observation: "How surfaces develop depends on the material involved: brick and slate improve with age, so that stones from antiquity are extremely valuable; aluminum and steel become worse for wear, which is why modern buildings become less valuable with time and older ones more" (p. 51). An additional example of this fairly uniform judgment for or against certain materials when they age is our attitude toward trees. Lowenthal points out that "trees are often most appealing in old age: England's gnarled oak, the enduring American redwood, the shade of the old apple tree, the old familiar oak that George Pope Morris sought to save from the woodman's axe, for 'In youth it sheltered me, | And I'll protect it now'" (p. 135).

Western-style fixture. Instead, from the aesthetic point of view, he would much prefer a fixture made of wood, "as it darkens and the grain grown more subtle with the years."[67] Or, Victor Papanek, an industrial designer, observes that "materials that have aged well hold great appeal. One thinks of the honey-brown of old leather or aged oak; the silver-grey of the boards on a weathered barn."[68]

It may be that those surfaces that are smooth and lustrous when new, such as plastic, glass, and porcelain (and concrete to a certain extent), lose their luster and smoothness with age and their loss outweighs any possibly positive signs of aging. Another consideration may be that materials that "age well" or "gracefully" are primarily natural or minimally processed materials and, as such, they tend to respond rather amicably to changes brought about by nature. Pauline von Bonsdorff, for example, points out that "less processed materials, such as stone or wood, show in their very texture, as traces, processes of nature such as growth or sedimentation... Natural materials... react more smoothly to natural processes and are likely to 'cooperate' with these: they are receptive and interactive in relation to the climate."[69]

Contemporary designers, particularly those who are concerned with the longevity of objects as an antidote to planned obsolescence, are mindful of the way in which materials age. For example, Papanek states: "In an age in which fortunes are spent on beauty creams and lotions to stretch out a semblance of youth, it is difficult to explain that material choices should be made so that objects can age gracefully once more."[70] In fact, he cites graceful aging as the first of the five design principles for the twenty-first century, all of which address the "social, ecological and environmental consequences" of design.[71] Dekkers is also critical of modern buildings,

---

[67] Jun'ichirō Tanizaki, *In Praise of Shadows*, tr. Thomas J. Harper and Edward G. Seidensticker (New Haven: Leete's Island Books, 1977), p. 6.

[68] Victor Papanek, *The Green Imperative: Natural Design for the Real World* (New York: Thames & Hudson, 1995), p. 174. It will be interesting to see how new architectural materials fare in the future. One example is titanium that is used in Frank Gehry's Guggenheim Museum in Bilbao, Spain, and Daniel Libeskind's proposed addition to the Denver Art Museum.

[69] Pauline von Bonsdorff, "Building and the Naturally Unplanned," in *The Aesthetics of Everyday Life*, ed. Andrew Light and Jonathan M. Smith (New York: Columbia University Press, 2005), p. 85.

[70] Papanek, p. 142.

[71] Ibid. p. 48. Specifically, he states that "the style of the future will be based on products *that age gracefully*, and will be more timeless than the quickly changing fads, trends and fashions of the late 20th century" (emphasis added).

primarily built with concrete, steel, and aluminum, because they "become worse for wear." In contrast to old builders who "were aware of the effect of time on material; today they no longer build for the future."[72] He is joined by Juhani Pallasmaa, himself an architect, who also laments that "the impact of time, the effects of use and wear, and the processes of aging are rarely considered in contemporary design or criticism."[73]

Finally, even among materials that age well, only certain kinds of aging seem acceptable. Compare, for example, pottery and lacquerware, both prominent in the Japanese aesthetic tradition for being prized when signs of age appear. The aging of lacquerware is appreciated when the inner layer of red lacquer shows through the exterior black lacquer (or vice versa) through being worn and rubbed off from years of use. The result is a complex pattern of red and black, the inner color showing here and there against the background of the outer color, somewhat analogous to scattering clouds against the blue sky. In contrast, to my knowledge, other forms of aging, such as cracks, chips, and gashes, are not celebrated on lacquerware, while they are welcomed on pottery, particularly the ones with rough surface. For example, a well-known water jug used in the tea ceremony in sixteenth-century Japan, named "*yabure bukuro* (broken bag)" and today designated and protected as an important cultural artifact by the Japanese government, features a gaping crack on its bottom half. Similarly, a simple bamboo flower vase attributed to Sen no Rikyū, the sixteenth-century founder of *wabi* tea, is characterized by a straight crack running along its grain. Other prized pieces of pottery, such as tea bowls and plates, sport fine networks of cracks which appeared after repeated use and they are even given a term for their special aesthetic appeal: *kannyū*. However, similar fine cracks on lacquerware caused by excessive dryness are not appreciated.

ii. *Associationist accounts of the aged appearance*

Thus, even purely on the sensuous surface level, our seemingly simple reactions to the aging appearance of objects are rather complex. However,

---

[72] Dekkers, p. 51.

[73] He continues to state that "Alvar Aalto believed that the value of a building is best judged fifty years after completion," which reminds us of Constable's declaration that time will finish his paintings. Juhani Pallasmaa, "Toward an Architecture of Humility," *Harvard Design Magazine* (Winter/Spring 1999), p. 24.

our aesthetic reaction to an aged object is not simply a response to its sensuous surface. It is heavily invested with various associations, which further complicates this aesthetics. Appreciating or depreciating something *for its aged effect* includes the contrast between the present appearance and its original appearance. Whether we actually experienced the original condition of the aged object or we form its image in our imagination, we need to have some idea of the prior condition of the object in order to experience the current condition as resulting from its aging process. In other words, a purely formalist aesthetics does not adequately account for our complex, and sometimes seemingly contradictory, attitude toward the aged appearance; we need to enlist associationist aesthetics, incorporating associated images and conceptual considerations.

I think it is fairly easy to account for our negative response in this regard, because our judgments that certain objects are "past their prime" or "past their glory" generally spill over to our aesthetic judgment as well. They have "fallen from grace" by deteriorating from once well-formed, meticulously crafted, lustrously shiny, vividly colored, perfectly finished surface, free of blemishes, accidents, and wear and tear. What we depreciate is the present condition *in contrast to* its prior condition.

What is more difficult, but also more interesting, to account for is our occasional positive attitude toward aging appearance. Let me turn to the Japanese *wabi* aesthetics and British picturesque taste again for an explanation of this rather uncommon penchant for the appearance of aging. While separated by time and geography, and with no direct link between them, these two aesthetic traditions interestingly offer similar accounts.

One similarity is stimulation to our imagination. When we are confronted by an aged object, our imagination becomes engaged and it takes a flight of fancy pursuing the comparison with its original condition, actual or imaginary, the weight of time that spans the object's life so far, and the factors that contributed to the change of its appearance. In praising the superior beauty of cherry blossoms after they have fallen from branches and scattered in the garden (usually considered to be the aftermath of the cherry blossoms' beauty), Yoshida Kenkō poses a rhetorical question: "are we to look at … the cherry blossoms with our eyes alone?"[74] Or, consider the following statement by Tanizaki, although it is made in the

---

[74] Kenkō, p. 118.

context of contrasting what he calls the "Oriental" aesthetic taste with the Western counterpart, now considered problematic and outdated. He explains the Japanese and Chinese attraction to the aging effects on objects as follows:

This 'sheen of antiquity' of which we hear so much is in fact the glow of grime. In both Chinese and Japanese the words denoting this glow describe a polish that comes of being touched over and over again, a sheen produced by the oils that naturally permeate an object over long years of handling...We do love things that bear the marks of grime, soot, and weather, and we love the colors and the sheen *that call to mind the past that made them.*[75]

The picturesque appreciation is also explained by the same kind of associated ideas formed by the imagination. Richard Payne Knight succinctly declares that "as all the pleasures of intellect arise from the association of ideas, the more the materials of association are multiplied, the more will the sphere of these pleasures be enlarged."[76] Speaking specifically of ruins, Batty Langley claims that, in addition to the sensuous qualities of variety and irregularity, their aesthetic appeal is derived from "the latitude they afford the imagination, to conceive an enlargement of their dimensions, or to recollect any events or circumstances appertaining to their pristine grandeur, so far as concerns grandeur and solemnity."[77]

In short, the aesthetic experience of an aged object is derived from the associated thoughts and images concerning the object's origin, its historical development, its longevity, and events and activities that brought about changes. This kind of aesthetic experience based upon the association of ideas seems essentially the expressionist aspect of Kant's aesthetic theory, which is developed into an exclusive aesthetic account by aestheticians like Archibald Alison. According to Alison,

When any object, either of sublimity or beauty, is presented to the mind, I believe every man is conscious of a train of thought being immediately awakened in his imagination...The simple perception of the object...is insufficient to excite these emotions, unless it is accompanied with this operation of mind—unless...our

---

[75] Tanizaki, pp. 11–12, emphasis added.
[76] Richard Payne Knight, *An Analytical Inquiry into the Principles of Taste,* included in Hunt and Willis, p. 348.
[77] Cited by Andrews, p. 48.

imagination is seized, and our fancy busied in the pursuit of all those trains of thought which are allied to this character or expression.[78]

The source of the aesthetic pleasure is in the activities of our imagination and fancy, rather than in the qualities of the object per se. However, what makes certain associations of ideas specifically and characteristically *aesthetic*? After all, we experience association of ideas all the time without thereby invoking an aesthetic experience. For example, I may recall a meeting with friends by looking at my appointment book, anticipate rough winter weather after hearing the latest forecast, or think about my personal situation after hearing my neighbor's family problems. The difference between these experiences and my aesthetic appreciation of aged objects is that, with the latter, the associated ideas get triggered by the sensuous appearance of the object: a crack in the pot, wear and tear on a fabric, the faded colors of a painting, and the weather-beaten facade of a building. The locus of our experience is the object's appearance, and the mode of association is the "contrast" between the present condition and the earlier condition.

Then how do we explain the aesthetic pleasure specific to the sense of decay experienced by the contrast between the object's earlier state imaginatively conjured up and the current state? One explanation may be this. While we generally want to exert control over nature and our life, including their aging process, we do not necessarily take an aesthetic pleasure in the mark of *total* human control, as in the case of a spatial arrangement regulated too strictly. Instead, we appreciate the contrast between exerting control and power and letting things and natural process be. As Henry David Thoreau recognized, we need to experience "Wildness," that which cannot be tamed by humans either conceptually or physically.[79]

---

[78] Archibald Alison, *Essays on the Nature and Principles of Taste* (1790, 1821), included in *What is Art?: Aesthetic Theory from Plato to Tolstoy*, ed. Alexander Sesonske (New York: Oxford University Press, 1965), pp. 184–5. The appreciation of clutter, particularly in private sphere, is also dependent upon its associational content. Most of the time we have a specific memory attached to each item (gift from somebody, travel souvenir, family memento, etc.) and we fear that getting rid of them amounts to erasing precious memories from our life. Personal clutter also is a way of manifesting one's self-identity. See Lynes; Graves; Cwerner and Metcalfe, regarding this point.

[79] However, we have to understand his plea for Wildness against the background of the rapidly progressing cultivation of the American continent and the development of tightly controlled and organized life. His preference for the "impervious and quaking swamps" and "impermeable and unfathomable bog" over "lawns and cultivated fields ... towns and cities" and " the most beautiful garden that ever human art contrived" is premised upon living in civilization. It is not clear whether he would have made the same choice if he were living in the midst of true wilderness completely

Aged objects such as old relics, ruins, musty books, and tattered and frayed fabrics exemplify the effects of the march of time, without succumbing completely to its dictate. If they wholly disintegrate, they are no longer fit for positive aesthetic appreciation. Those objects we do appreciate are the ones which are in the process of decay, before losing their identity and integrity altogether. What they present to us can be characterized variously as tension, balance, dialogue, or dialectic, but in short it is the fragile and delicate relationship between two opposing forces: nature's own process and our attempt (via what we create) at defying and counteracting it. Woodward claims in his discussion of ruins that "no ruin can be suggestive to the visitor's imagination... unless its dialogue with the forces of Nature is visibly alive and dynamic."[80]

Our effort to overcome nature's process is ultimately futile, as even our best effort to maintain the object in its current state is never complete. Our positive aesthetic appreciation of aged objects can give us a counterpoint to an otherwise disappointing human experience by providing a possibility that "accepting" and "submitting" ourselves to nature's relentless work does not have to be always discouraging and disappointing. In her discussion of architecture, Pauline von Bonsdorff argues for the importance of accepting and appreciating what she calls "the naturally unplanned," the weathering effect on the materials. Particularly in our technological society which encourages us to believe that we can control practically anything and everything, she points out that "the ability of a building to integrate natural processes in its appearance is an additional quality, compared to buildings on which the climate only produces clashes or cracks."[81] In her view, there is "aesthetic and existential significance" in the aging appearance of the "materials that show the interaction of nature and culture, with humans as mediators, belonging to both sides, erecting and wearing down." This significance is particularly important "in a culture forced to seek sustainable patterns of interaction with the natural environment but infested with a technology that often becomes an end in itself." Wooden structures, with their ability to age well, "can present us with a reconciliation of humans

---

cut off from civilization. Henry David Thoreau, "Walking" (1863) included in *Environmental Ethics: Divergence and Convergence*, ed. Susan J. Armstrong and Richard G. Botzler (New York: McGraw-Hill, 1993), pp. 111–12.

[80] Woodward, p. 73.   [81] Von Bonsdorff, p. 86. All the following passages are from p. 85.

and nature, creation and finitude, in a silent and, for that reason, more powerful way than words."

Other potent associations that are triggered by our experience of aged objects are historical. Historical associations may themselves be pleasant or unpleasant. They are unpleasant particularly when the cause of aging appearance is human violence or natural catastrophe. However, regardless of the nature of conjured images, such an associational experience provides an occasion for much reflection on serious existential issues. Ruins in particular incite various thoughts, as an eighteenth-century essayist declares: "a thousand ideas croud upon his mind, and fill him with awful astonishment."[82] Those reflections range from "some dreadful hidden crime," "a haunting sense of temporal remoteness," "the greatness of the original structures," "the melancholy lesson that all men's works moulder to insignificance," to "tyranny overcome."[83]

By far the most potent and poignant of historical associations, however, is the aged objects' reminder of the impermanence of everything, including our own existence, what Woodward calls "exemplary frailty."[84] In the European tradition, this reminder of human transience via aged objects such as ruins, although occasioning melancholy, has also provided satisfaction that Time is a great equalizer. Whether we are rich or poor, powerful or powerless, Time works relentlessly but democratically on all of us and all of our creations and possessions. That is, "the rich man's mansion is equal to the poor thatched cottage in the divine justice which comes with Time," and "when the Last Trump sounded the end of Time all human edifices would collapse, from the peasant's thatched cottage to the emperor's shining dome."

iii. Aestheticization of transience

In the Japanese aesthetic tradition, aesthetic pleasure in aged objects is also derived from the analogy between our transience and the notion of impermanence triggered by the aging. A major theme of Japanese aesthetics originating in the ancient court poetry, lamentation over aristocrats' passing youth, beauty, love affairs, power, and wealth was invariably expressed

---

[82] Cited by Lowenthal, p. 173.
[83] The first four phrases are from p. 173 and the fifth p. 175 of Lowenthal.
[84] Woodward, p. 89. The next two passages are from pp. 100 and 94.

by reference to the evanescent phenomena of nature: passing of season, rain, mist, snow, changing color of leaves, and falling cherry blossoms. A quintessential example is the following poem by Ono no Komachi, a ninth-century poetess renowned for her beauty:

> The flowers withered,
> Their color faded away,
> While meaninglessly
> I spent my days in the world
> And the long rains were
> falling.[85]

"The flowers" refer to cherry blossoms in court poetry, so here in this poem she is drawing a parallel between her passing beauty and youth, falling rain, and the fading color of cherry blossoms. Although the ancient court culture that flourished during the Heian period (794–1185) was subsequently replaced by the warrior culture, the preoccupation with how to cope with transience continued, even with more urgency because of the warriors' uncertainty of life and fortune, further encouraging the strategy of analogizing human impermanence and transient phenomena. Writing at the beginning of the warrior period, a retired monk, Kamo no Chōmei (1153–1216), begins his famed essay, *An Account of My Hut*, with the following:

The flow of the river is ceaseless and its water is never the same. The bubbles that float in the pools, now vanishing, now forming, are not of long duration: so in the world are man and his dwellings. It might be imagined that the houses, great and small, which vie roof against proud roof in the capital remain unchanged from one generation to the next, but when we examine whether this is true, how few are the houses that were there of old. Some were burnt last year and only since rebuilt; great houses have crumbled into hovels and those who dwell in them have fallen no less.[86]

---

[85] Tr. Donald Keene, included in *Anthology of Japanese Literature*, ed. Donald Keene (New York: Grove Press, 1960), p. 81.

[86] Tr. Donald Keene, included in Keene, p. 196. A similar sentiment is expressed by another well-known opening passage from *The Tale of the Heike*, assembled by mid-thirteenth century: "The sound of the Gion Shōja bells echoes the impermanence of all things; The color of the *sāla* flowers reveals the truth that the prosperous must decline. The proud do not endure; they are like a dream on a spring night; the mighty fall at last, they are as dust before the wind..." *Genji & Heike: Selections from The Tale of Genji and The Tale of the Heike*, tr. Helen Craig McCullough (Stanford: Stanford University Press, 1994), p. 265.

In one sense, to be reminded of our own decay or past glory is not pleasant, except for the morbid satisfaction in wallowing in our misery. However, in the Japanese aesthetic tradition, by drawing an analogy between our own transience and the ephemeral aspects of the world, we console ourselves with the realization that nothing whatever is exempt from this law of nature, accompanied by the feeling of camaraderie that "we are all in it together." That is, if there were some things that stay the same, our own transience will be harder to bear, because we wonder why we cannot be more like them. However, by admitting the common fate that binds everybody and everything in this world, we feel in a way reassured that we are not singled out as exceptions.

Furthermore, the aesthetic pleasure in aged objects is not simply a matter of parallels between the transience of our lives and the world; *aestheticizing* their evanescence will help us adopt a more positive attitude toward our own process of aging and eventual demise. Falling cherry blossoms are elegant and delicate, because each small petal, gently carried by the wind, dances gracefully before reaching the ground. Their movement contrasts with the rather abrupt and awkward way in which some other flowers fall to the ground. For example, Natsume Sōseki (1867–1916), one of the foremost novelists in modern Japan, describes the camellia flowers' life as "flaring into bloom and falling to earth with equal suddenness." When they fall, they "never drift down petal by petal but drop from the branch intact. Although this in itself is not particularly unpleasant since it merely suggests an indifference to parting, the way in which they remain whole even when they have landed is both gross and offensive to the eye."[87]

Besides transience, the Japanese aesthetic tradition aestheticizes life's other challenging conditions, such as insufficiency, imperfection, and accidents beyond our control. I take it as given that we generally desire defect-free objects and conditions that sufficiently satisfy our needs. In addition, we prefer to have control over them so that we won't get caught off-guard or derailed by unexpected happenstance. However, we all know that such wishes and expectations are wishful thinking. Life is full of disappointments

---

[87] Natsume Sōseki, *Kusamakura* (1906), tr. by Alan Turney as *The Three Cornered World* (Chicago: Henry Regnery Co., 1967), p. 136. I should point out that Natsume's writing itself captures the abruptness of this phenomenon of camellia flowers' fall, as he inserts a short sentence, "Another fell," throughout the paragraph, intermingling with his thoughts.

and frustrations because things do not always meet our expectations, our love affairs do not quite work out the way we planned or wanted, and surprises meet us around every corner. Just as transience is something that is inescapable for all of us, these facts about life are also applicable to everyone, causing hardships and challenges. Western existentialism would characterize this human condition as despair, nausea, or angst.

The Japanese aesthetic tradition, heavily indebted to the Buddhist world-view, provides a means of coping with this otherwise painful condition of our existence. Keeping with the general Buddhist foundation, which starts with the recognition of our impermanence and problems derived from it, the Japanese aesthetic tradition works at changing *our* attitude and outlook by aestheticizing these challenging existential conditions, rendering them more appealing. This strategy underlies the medieval poets' aspiration to produce a beauty akin to the moon obscured by clouds and other objects, rather than an unobstructed view of the full moon.[88] However, by far the best-known and most influential writing was a series of essays by Yoshida Kenkō. His aesthetic taste is decidedly in pursuit of difficult, challenging beauty, exemplified by a silk scroll wrapper that "has frayed at top and bottom," a scroll whose "mother-of-pearl has fallen from the roller," a set of books with a missing volume, "gardens strewn with faded flowers," the moon almost disappearing behind the mountains or obscured by tree branches, and the aftermath of a festival with desolate streets.[89] They all exemplify the conditions of decay, imperfection, and insufficiency. Kenkō, however, urges us to derive a positive aesthetic experience from them, because it is precisely the uncertainty and instability of life that give a precious quality to every aspect of life and the world. Otherwise, if things "lingered on forever in the world, how things would lose their power to move us," because "the most precious thing in life is its uncertainty."[90] Furthermore, wishing for permanence, particularly in terms of possessions and life, is inane because nothing and nobody can escape the universal fate. Only foolish people act as though "there is no ending to their greed for

---

[88] For specific examples, see Haga Kōshirō's "The *Wabi* Aesthetic Through the Ages," included in *Tea in Japan: Essays on the History of* Chanoyu, eds. Paul Varley and Kumakura Isao (Honolulu: University of Hawaii Press, 1989).

[89] Kenkō. The reference to a scroll and a set of books comes from p. 70; garden and festival from pp. 115–21.

[90] Ibid. p. 7.

long life, their grasping for profit." But "all that awaits them in the end is old age and death, whose coming is swift and does not falter for one instant." Such a person "grieves because he desires everlasting life and is ignorant of the law of universal change."[91] Kenkō's aesthetics of difficult beauty, therefore, challenges us not only to recognize and accept, but also to celebrate, the reminder of difficulties in life.

While Kenkō's aesthetics is concerned with *appreciating* such difficult beauty, this sensibility paves a way toward *creating* such difficult aesthetic qualities in the form of the *wabi* tea ceremony. The tea ceremony provides a kind of microcosm in which many ingredients express a sense of impoverishment. This ranges from a rustic-looking, extremely small-size tea hut to utensils and implements used in the ceremony that are simple, ordinary- and at times crude-looking, sometimes downright defective with a crack or a broken part; from minimal decor consisting of a single branch in a vase to restrained actions and conversations that take place during the ceremony, as well as the meager amount of food, insufficient to quell hunger. It is the antithesis of profusion, opulence, and exuberance that can be brought about by ornately decorated, gorgeous objects and architecture, both interior and exterior, packed with theatrical extravaganza. In fact, *wabi* tea was founded by master Sen no Rikyū (1522–1591) as a reaction against the preceding tea practice referred to as *daisu* tea, featuring gorgeous, perfectly formed tea wares from China, called *tenmoku* bowls, presented in lacquered stands. Though highly stylized and guided by almost excruciatingly detailed instructions, the overall purpose of the *wabi* tea is to celebrate and appreciate the aesthetic experience brought about by the chance meeting of many elements beyond human control. The occasion thus created by meticulous preparation *and* chance is for one time only, referred to as *ichigo ichie* (one chance, one meeting).

In a sense, this aesthetic activity represents our entire world and life where the ruling principles are transience, insufficiency, imperfection, and accidents. Compared with opulent architecture and perfectly shaped and gorgeously decorated objects, the things constituting the tea ceremony are more challenging for our ordinary aesthetic taste. According to tea masters

---

[91] Kenkō. p. 66. The next two passages are also from the same page. I thank Carolyn Korsmeyer for pointing out the similarity between Kenkō's view here and Stoicism.

and aficionados, this aesthetic sensibility is higher and more sophisticated than our ordinary taste, and its cultivation is important not only from an aesthetic but also from an existential point of view. For example, Rikyū argues for the desolate, monochrome landscape depicted in the poem by Fujiwara no Teika (1162–1241), a far cry from a quintessentially gorgeous landscape, which is adorned with flowers in full bloom or colorful foliage:

> All around, no flowers in bloom
> Nor maple leaves in glare,
> A solitary fisherman's hut alone
> On the twilight shore
> In this autumn eve.[92]

Rikyū's explanation for the superiority of such a landscape is as follows:

people in the world, in search of a sight of cherry-blossoms, pass their days and nights in anxiety, roaming around, and wondering if the time has come for cherry trees to be in full bloom in this mountain or that forest. Alas, they do not know that the 'flowers and tinted leaves' exist right there, in their own minds. They are merely capable of taking pleasure in the colorful sights which appear to their physical eyes alone.

Another tea master, Sōtaku Jakuan, the author of *Zencharoku* (*Record of Zen Tea*, 1828), is even more explicit about this existential dimension of *wabi* sensibility. He claims almost blatantly that "*wabi* means lacking things, having things run entirely contrary to our desires, being frustrated in our wishes." He continues:

Always bear in mind that *wabi* involves not regarding incapacities as incapacitating, not feeling that lacking something is deprivation, not thinking that what is not provided is deficiency. To regard incapacity as incapacitating, to feel that lack is deprivation, or to believe that not being provided for is poverty is not *wabi* but rather the spirit of a pauper.[93]

This passage clearly indicates that the *wabi* aesthetics in support of the appearance of aging, decay, imperfection, insufficiency, accidents, in short

---

[92] Tr. Toshihiko and Toyo Izutsu in "Record of Nanbō" written by Nanbō Sōkei, Rikyū's disciple during the master's life and after his death. Included in *The Theory of Beauty in the Classical Aesthetics of Japan*, Toshihiko and Toyo Izutsu (The Hague: Martinus Nijhoff Publishers, 1981), p. 155. The next long passage is from pp. 156–7.

[93] Cited by Haga, pp. 195–6.

those qualities that make our life challenging, was not simply an aesthetic preoccupation, but more importantly an existential coping strategy.

iv. Limitations on aestheticizing transience

Those qualities that are difficult to accept in life, such as imperfection, decay, and insufficiency, often result from inevitable conditions of nature and life. We have no choice but to accept them. Aestheticizing them, I have argued in the previous section, is sometimes meant to serve as an existential means of dealing with these human predicaments. If we can sweeten the bitter pill through aesthetic celebration, it can go down much more smoothly.

Some other times, however, those difficult challenges are caused by socio-economic and political conditions. In such cases, the strategy of aestheticizing transience and imperfection is utilized to maintain the status quo of a societal condition or to promote a certain political agenda. In this section, I will first illustrate the ways in which this strategy has been utilized for social and political ends, often with problematic consequences.

One example is aestheticization of poverty, invoked by both the picturesque and the *wabi* aesthetics. The picturesque advocates were primarily well-to-do landed gentry and a circle of educated intellectuals. Not being beggars living in hovels themselves, these members of the polite society were able to have an aesthetic appreciation of both, prime examples of the picturesque according to Uvedale Price.[94] This fact led to a number of criticisms of the picturesque sensibility. Mary Wollstonecraft, for example, was critical of the picturesque estate where "every thing … is cherished but man," and what she saw on a trip to Portugal where "the eye … had wandered indignant from the stately palace to the pestiferous hovel."[95] Commenting on her criticism, Larry Shiner points out hers was "precisely the kind of trip on which Gilpin and other theorists of the picturesque encouraged people to view—from a suitable distance—a landscape embellished with ruined castles, crumbling huts, and ragged peasants picturesquely loitering." John Ruskin was also critical of "the heartless

---

[94] Price's other examples of the picturesque that are associated with poverty and social ills include dilapidated mills, gypsies, bandits, and worn-out carthorse. Cited by Andrews, p. 59.

[95] I thank Larry Shiner for this reference to Mary Wollstonecraft's critique of the picturesque. The passages from her work are quoted by Shiner in his *The Invention of Art: A Cultural History* (Chicago: The University of Chicago Press, 2001), pp. 166 and 167. Shiner's passage is from p. 166.

'lower picturesque' delight in 'the look that an old laborer has, not knowing that there is anything pathetic in his grey hair, and withered arms, and sunburnt breast.' "[96] We are also familiar with the populace's uproar against Marie Antoinette's "playing at" being a milkmaid. Indeed, as Woodward points out, after the 1789 Revolution, folly-ruins and the picturesque imitation farm created for her came to symbolize "the decadence of the rulers."[97]

The same problematic attitude underlies today's popular aesthetic variously described as "shabby chic," "grunge," or "distressed look."[98] In order to sport "shabby chic," I may keep and wear an old pair of jeans with faded colors and holes or create the look of "shabby chic" on a new pair by cutting, slicing, washing with bleach, splashing bleach, and rubbing a pumice stone (to make the holes and edges fray). Or, more typically for today's yuppies, I may pay a lot of money to buy such a pair of jeans.[99] Ironically, Dekkers points out regarding jeans that they were "originally cherished for their indestructibility," but for today's yuppies "the only thing that matters now is their destructibility."[100]

This grunge aesthetic is premised upon the fact that I have a *choice* in sporting shabby appearance; I can *afford* to look impoverished. If I am indeed destitute and can only afford tattered clothes from the Salvation Army, I most certainly will not be able to take a positive aesthetic stance toward them. Though perhaps not morally wrong per se, there is something disturbing about aestheticizing the appearance of poverty. It may be because, other things being equal, positive aesthetic value implies endorsement of its existence. That is, *in the absence of any other considerations*, it sounds contradictory to praise an object's aesthetic value while advocating its destruction.[101] We would normally say: "it is

[96] Cited by Lowenthal, p. 166. We can also cite the current scholarship on the "elitist" nature and "the dark side" of the picturesque movement. To name only a couple: John Barrell, *The Dark Side of the Landscape: The Rural Poor in English Painting 1730–1840* (Cambridge: Cambridge University Press, 1989); Ann Bermingham, *Landscape and Ideology: The English Rustic Tradition, 1740–1860* (Berkeley: University of California Press, 1989).

[97] Woodward, p. 150.

[98] I thank Carolyn Korsmeyer for the term, "distressed" in this context.

[99] *Cosmopolitan* (July 2005) gives an instruction on how to create the shabby look that I summarized in the previous sentence, so that we don't have to pay $242 for a pair that has already been "destroyed" ("Do Some Damage to Your Denim," p. 82).

[100] Dekkers, p. 52.

[101] Except for the main character of Mishima Yukio's *The Temple of the Golden Pavilion* that I referred to in Chapter III.

beautiful, *but* we must destroy it for economic, health, safety, moral, or political reason." Most likely, those who advocate the positive aesthetics of aging, imperfect, insufficient qualities are not intentionally endorsing the condition of human misery. However, their aesthetic appreciation and/or creation of shabby chic will inevitably be regarded at best as indifference toward the actual existence of social ills. As I discussed in Chapter III, there is a sense in which we should develop an aesthetic appreciation, understood as a keen perception, of the sensible manifestation of social problems, such as poverty. Aesthetic appreciation in this sense is a necessary step toward addressing these problems. However, insofar as aestheticization of poverty, such as shabby chic, remains a contemplative experience or extends to its intentional creation, it is subject to moral criticisms.

This socio-economic dimension of aesthetically appreciating aged, defective objects is also raised within the Japanese tradition. Consider the following remark by Dazai Shundai (1680–1747), a Confucian scholar, referring to the rigid class system of feudal society in which the tea ceremony was widely practiced:

Whatever tea dilettantes do is a copy of the poor and humble. It may be that the rich and noble have a reason to find pleasure in copying the poor and humble. But why should those who are, from the outset, poor and humble find pleasure in further copying the poor and humble? ... All that tea dilettante does is to copy everything which looks poor and shabby.[102]

A sense of social injustice expressed in this criticism is justified, particularly in light of the very intentional and specific way in which *wabi* aesthetic sensibility was utilized for political purpose. Utilizing the spirit of *wabi* tea articulated by aforementioned *Zencharoku* for political purposes, Ii Naosuke, a powerful nineteenth-century statesman, writes in his *An Essay on the Tea Cult as an Aid to Government*:

If pleasure is not gratification accompanied by a sense of contentment, it is not real pleasure ... if each individual is satisfied with his lot and is not envious, he

---

[102] Cited by Hiroshi Minami in his *Psychology of the Japanese People*, tr. Albert R. Ikoma (Toronto: University of Toronto Press, 1971), p. 90. I changed Ikoma's translation to be more faithful to the original Japanese. The translation reads: "The rich and noble, however, must have a reason to find pleasure in copying the poor and humble. Why should those who are, from the outset, poor and humble further copy the poor and humble and make fun of them?"

will enjoy life because he knows contentment and will be contented because of enjoying his lot … if the art of drinking tea were widely practiced throughout the country … both high and low would be content with their lots, would enjoy but not grieve, and would do no wrong … The country would become peaceful and tranquil spontaneously.[103]

Even more recent writing on tea also invokes the same lesson of being content with one's lot, not asking for more. A twentieth-century, post-war writer on tea instructions claims:

The tea cult stresses 'accordance with one's lot' and 'knowing contentment and resting upon complacency': it eliminates extravagance and warns against excessiveness … When this state of mind shifts to a positive state of loving privation and taking delight in poverty, *wabicha* (*wabi* tea) arises … . In the state of finding beauty in imperfect things, modesty begins to function and a love of privation and simplicity develops.[104]

Here aesthetics is used unapologetically to justify societal status quo with built-in socio-economic injustice.

In Japanese history, there is an even more ominous implication of this aesthetic justification of decay, imperfection, and insufficiency. It has to do with the way in which this attitude toward aestheticizing these qualities was promoted and utilized by the military government during World War II to justify its war effort and mobilize citizens toward nationalistic goals. In an essay written after the war promoting what he terms "decadence," Sakaguchi Ango criticizes the Japanese attitude of enduring poverty and insufficiency practiced as *bitoku* (beauty and virtue), often attributed to farmers and promoted among soldiers. According to him,

What is true human nature? It is simply desiring what one desires and disliking what one dislikes. One should like what one likes, love the woman one loves, and get out of the false cloak of what is said to be a just cause and social obligation, and return to the naked heart. Finding this naked human heart is the first step toward restoring humanity.[105]

---

[103] Cited by Minami, p. 88.

[104] Sakaki Sanmi, *Sadō Kyōshitsu* (*Tea Cult Classroom*) (Tokyo: Kōbunsha, 1950), cited by Minami, pp. 88–9.

[105] Sakaguchi Ango, "Zoku Darakuron" (Additional Theory of Decadence), (1946), included in *Shōwa Bungaku Zenshū* (*Collection of Shōwa Period Literature*) (Tokyo: Shōgakukan, 1987), Vol. 12, p. 247, my translation.

He is specifically referring to the ethos imposed by the wartime military in the name of the Emperor which instilled perseverance in hardship, inconvenience, insufficiency, and poverty, despite people's natural inclination to complain and rebel against them.[106]

Demanding sacrifice and perseverance during the time of war is of course not unique to Japan. However, what makes the Japanese case relevant for our purpose is that the power of aesthetic persuasion, in particular regarding everyday life, was effectively utilized for this purpose, providing a potent catalyst for directing people's attitude and resultant actions. Note that Sakaguchi's critique is directed not simply toward the virtue (*toku*) of perseverance but rather toward its *beauty* (*bi*) and virtue. By far the most striking example of the mobilization of the aesthetics of impermanence in promoting a nationalistic sentiment and resultant actions regards the beauty of falling cherry blossoms, the subject matter of a recent work by an anthropologist, Emiko Ohnuki-Tierney.[107] Her discussion is particularly interesting and relevant to my present purpose not only because of the focus on cherry blossoms for symbolizing transience but also for her observation that the particular power of this symbol in Japanese culture is derived from their function as "*quotidian* or *everyday* aesthetics."[108]

The cult of celebrating the ephemeral beauty of falling cherry blossoms was, as I discussed earlier, established by the court poets after the ninth century and has since then formed an important aspect of its cultural ethos. Furthermore, cherry blossoms were cherished and celebrated for being quintessentially Japanese in contrast to, or as an alternative to, plum blossoms that characterize Chinese culture, and the connection between cherry blossoms and Japanese-ness has been deeply etched in the Japanese psyche throughout history.

This historical connection of cherry blossoms to Japan's national identity and the aesthetic appreciation of transience were utilized by the military and politicians of the late nineteenth century and early twentieth century to promote nationalism. It was a part of a larger project to distinguish Japan from the West, the seat of both imperialism and modernism, as well as from

---

[106] Sakaguchi Ango, "Zoku Darakuron", Vol. 12, p. 247, my translation.
[107] Emiko Ohnuki-Tierney, *Kamikaze, Cherry Blossoms, and Nationalisms: The Militarization of Aesthetics in Japanese History* (Chicago: The University of Chicago Press, 2002).
[108] Ibid. p. 285, emphasis added.

the rest of Asia, over which Japan was compelled to claim alleged superiority in order to protect them from Western imperialism. For example, Nishi Amane, said to the be the major architect of the Japanese military of late nineteenth century, emphasized in his lectures the "virtue" of cherry blossoms for "not clinging to their blooming."[109] Other intellectuals and scholars, after Japan's Westernization began in the late nineteenth century, were also responsible for this connection, though the later militarization of the symbol was not intended by them. For example, Nitobe Inazō, himself a devout Christian and antimilitary, begins his well-known and influential book on *Bushidō,* the way of the warriors, originally written in English and published in the United States in 1899, by stating: "chivalry [*Bushidō*] is a flower no less indigenous to the soil of Japan than its emblem, the cherry blossom."[110] Furthermore, in 1900, a Japanese language textbook for high schools written by a leading literary figure at the time, Tsubouchi Shōyō, commissioned and sanctioned by the government, includes passages such as: "one should fall like cherry petals without clinging if one realizes one's misbehavior" and "one's soul should be as pure and transparent as the petals of cherry blossoms."[111] Believing that cherry trees truly represent the Japanese spirit and soul, the military government went so far as to plant cherry trees on those Asian soils that Japan colonized as well as on the ground of Yasukuni Shrine that houses the souls of the war dead, somewhat similar to Nazi Germany's comprehensive program of ridding its soil of any "alien" species and replacing them with those "indigenous" species worthy of their Aryan race.[112] Ultimately, this aestheticization of falling cherry blossoms served as a potent and poignant symbol for falling Kamikaze pilots, whose death was praised and celebrated by the wartime nation.[113]

---

[109] Cited by Ohnuki-Tierney, p. 107.   [110] ibid, p. 13.   [111] ibid, p. 127.

[112] Yasukuni Shrine is the focus of much friction between Japan and China (and to a lesser degree Korea) today, as the former Japanese prime minister, Koizumi Jun'ichirō, insisted on an official annual visit there to pay respect to the war dead, including war criminals. Nazi Germany's program for replacing "alien" species of plants with the native plants is detailed in Gert Groening and Joachim Wolschke-Bulmahn's "Some Notes on the Mania for Native Plants in Germany," *Landscape Journal* 11:2 (Fall 1992): 116–26.

[113] Belonging as I do to a post-war generation in Japan, my understanding of the potency of this symbol for the pre-war generation is purely conceptual. However, its emotive power was somewhat brought home to me with the recent discovery of a Japanese soldier, Ishinosuke Uwano, 83, who has been living in Ukraine since the end of war. When interviewed, he expressed his desire to come back to Japan for a visit specifically to see two things: his parents' graves and Japan's cherry blossoms. ("Japanese WWII Soldier Found in Ukraine," *Providence Journal,* 19 April 2006)

We can draw at least two lessons from this historical and anthropological analysis of cherry blossoms in Japan. First, the point most pertinent to the present chapter is that aestheticizing transience and impermanence, while a lofty and worthwhile goal from spiritual and existential point of view, can have a dire consequence when utilized for a certain social and political purpose, in particular the promotion of political nationalism requiring citizens' sacrifice of their own lives. Secondly, a more general lesson relevant to the theme of this whole book is that this is another instance that testifies to the power of everyday aesthetics in shaping our worldview, attitude, and most importantly our actions. Cultural nationalism which often, though not always, develops into political nationalism is nurtured by many factors. Art is one important factor, as the music of Wagner and the film, "Triumph of the Will," for the Third Reich vividly exemplify. Japanese nationalism of the twentieth century is also indebted to various arts, in particular so-called "uniquely" or "quintessentially" Japanese arts that are usually Zen-based. Traditional arts were considered to be the only area of Japanese culture that could hold its own and compete against the West, because the latter was perceived to be superior in every other aspect, ranging from technology to philosophy, political system to military power.[114]

An equally important, but often overlooked, factor helping to promote cultural nationalism is people's aesthetic response to everyday objects, such as landscape and nature.[115] Although the Japanese reaction to cherry blossoms is supported by the time-honored tradition constructed throughout its long history by literature and representational images, it was ingrained in the psyche of its people, not just the cultural elite but also common folks, and that is precisely the reason why it was used as a potent symbol uniting people for nationalistic fervor and wartime effort. Nurturing cultural identity and pride through aesthetic means in itself may be a worthwhile endeavor. It is when cultural nationalism thus fostered aesthetically becomes political nationalism, particularly in the context of asserting its power militarily, as in the Japanese historical precedent, the power of the aesthetic becomes dangerous.

---

[114] I will discuss this historical context a little more in Conclusion.
[115] I will discuss this landscape appreciation more in Conclusion.

This is why it is crucial fully to recognize this power of the aesthetic and to question how and for what purpose this power is to be utilized. With respect to green aesthetics, aesthetics of ambience, and aesthetic appreciation of naturally induced imperfection and transience, I made a normative claim that we should expand the scope of positive aesthetic values by recognizing their diversity. It is because we gain environmental or existential benefits by developing a positive aesthetic attitude toward those objects and qualities normally not appreciated. However, I believe that the task of everyday aesthetics is also to shed light on the opposite directions: to question positive aesthetic tastes and judgments that prevail in everyday life. The foregoing example of aestheticizing insufficiency and transience brought about by a questionable social agenda constitutes a prime example for such examination.

There is another sense in which we have to be cautious with expanding the scope of positive aesthetic values through everyday aesthetics. I argued that such aestheticization is often an existential strategy to encourage positive acceptance of human predicament over which we have no control. To what extent, however, is this strategy effective? Does the sensibility cultivated by appreciating impoverished-looking tea wares and the rustic, desolate tone of poems really guide us to accept and appreciate difficult conditions of our life, such as transience, insufficiency, and accidents? Some critics of this kind of aesthetics question the genuineness of forcing oneself to appreciate that which is otherwise normally unappreciable. Within the Japanese intellectual tradition, perhaps the most noted in this regard is Motoori Norinaga (1730–1801), a philologist and literary critic who established the school of thought called Nativism by pursuing what he characterizes as the pure Japanese tradition "unpolluted" by foreign thoughts, Chinese in particular. He is squarely opposed to the aesthetics of imperfection and insufficiency promoted by Kenkō, claiming that such a tendency is a distortion of our "natural" inclination, hence undesirable:

Who else in his poem would have expressed a wish for wind on the flowers and a cloud over the moon? What that monk said *does not accord with human feelings* but is a *fabricated* aesthetic taste formed in the impertinent mind of a man of a later age, and it is not a truly aesthetic taste. What that monk said can be described ... as *contrived* only to make what does not accord with human wishes a refined taste ... It is a true feeling of the people that there has never been a time when they are really satisfied, yet many talk knowingly as if they knew how to be contented and take pride in it. It must be a *fabrication* customary with the Chinese.[116]

Cherishing those feelings which are considered to be "natural" or "pure" and identifying the Japanese indigenous culture with accepting and nurturing those "natural" feelings and reactions, Norinaga and other Nativist scholars condemn the more challenging aesthetic taste for being pretentious.

Even some Confucian scholars share Norinaga's criticism. Dazai Shundai admits that musical instruments sound better when broken in and mellowed, but he criticizes the indiscriminate use and celebration of old bowls in tea ceremony, because, "as for vessels for eating and drinking, people are uniform in taking pleasure in those which are new."[117] However, "today's Way of Tea, an amusement for dilettantes, is utterly incomprehensible ... as they seek dirty, old tea bowls with unknown age that feature chips and cracks and, sometimes, evidence of repair with lacquer."

The advocates of *wabi* aesthetics would agree with the claim that *wabi* sensibility is not "natural," but they would also claim that this sensibility is on a higher level than our natural attraction to that which is new, perfect, gorgeous, and plentiful, precisely because it has to be acquired, and cultivated with increased sophistication and existential awareness. However, apart from whether such an aesthetic taste is "natural" or "fabricated," what I think is more interesting and important to ask is whether or not this difficult aesthetic taste really serves the existential function that it is meant to serve.

I am somewhat skeptical about the *wabi* aesthetic mentality's efficacy in facilitating the acceptance and celebration of human predicament. The reason is this. I believe that cultivation of this aesthetic sensibility is certainly possible and has been accomplished by a number of people who derive aesthetic pleasure from the tea ceremony implements, tea huts, meager food served there, poems with desolate tone, and the like. However, these items are all experienced within the sphere of artistic activities, not as part of our everyday life. Kenkō certainly takes as examples for this aesthetic taste things from everyday life, such as a set of books with a missing

---

[116] Cited by Minami, p. 91, emphasis added.

[117] Dazai Shundai, *Hitorigoto (Soliloquy)*, (1816), included in *Nihon Zuihitsu Taisei (Collection of Japanese Essays)* (Tokyo: Yoshikawa Kōbunkan, 1975), Vol. 17, p. 269. The next passage is from p. 266. My translation.

volume, falling cherry blossoms, and frayed silk wrapper. However, the subsequent development and the establishment of *wabi* aesthetics take place primarily in the activities and environments which are meant to *emulate* the everyday but are still separated from it. As I discussed in Chapter I, this is the ultimate paradox of the tea ceremony. The same paradox prevails in contemporary art works that embody this *wabi* sensibility. For example, Tanaka Chiyoko, a contemporary Japanese textile artist, produces woven textile pieces which are then placed outdoors. She not only accepts natural weathering process as a part of the work but also induces transformation by rubbing and pounding the cloth with application of mud, clay, or sea water.[118] Or, items exhibited in "Transforming Trash" at Redding Art Museum are described as sporting "the *patinas* and nuances of textures and surfaces created by time, weather and neglect," and "the marks of 'events' one usually tries to avoid—rust, dirt, oxidation and stains—become the *aesthetic* qualities celebrated here."[119] Finally, Catherine Murphy's painting, *The Windsor* (1999), depicts the aftermath of a dinner on a white, luxurious damask tablecloth, on which only "traces, detritus, crumbs, and stains" remain.[120] Despite our negative reaction to what it depicts, one critic praises this painting for its "sheer gorgeousness" and "the accuracy and lushness with which these souvenirs and relics of a meal and the underlying cloth have been rendered."

However, after experiencing the positive aesthetic values of challenging qualities in these art works, such as aging effect, chance, mess, imperfection, and insufficiency, are we going to be able to use the sharpened *wabi* sensibility to appreciate the heretofore unappreciated aesthetic values of aging phenomena and imperfect objects in our everyday life? Or is such a sensibility going to get in the way by making the contrast more prominent between artistically orchestrated transience and imperfection and unorchestrated real life conditions? If there is a difference in our aesthetic response to transience, one positive and the other negative, it is not because of the difference in the sensuous surface. Tanaka's fabric and my blanket that was neglected and soiled by various elements in my wet basement may

---

[118] I thank my student Laura Shirreff for introducing me to Tanaka's works.

[119] Jo Ann Stabb, "Transformations: Trash to Art," *Surface Design Journal* 26:2 (Winter 2002): 14–19 (obtained online from H W Wilson Art Index).

[120] Francine Prose, "A Dirty Tablecloth, Deconstructed," *ARTnews* 98:9 (October 1999), p. 126. The next passage is from p. 128.

appear similar; so are Rikyū's tea bowl and my coffee mug with chips and broken handle. Murphy's tablecloth could have been mine after my dinner party. The difference rather has to do with the status of the object and our accompanying attitude toward it. It is no accident that most aged and imperfect objects toward which we have a positive aesthetic appreciation are things that do not involve everyday use and are not things in which we have a personal stake. Oftentimes they are not our possessions, such as historic buildings and art objects. The beauty of the aged appearance of ancient sculptural pieces, Yourcenar points out, is easy to accept because it is "remote from us and *lodged in museums rather than in our homes.*"[121] We are "distanced" from those objects similarly to the way in which some temporal distance is required before a structure devastated by human violence or natural catastrophe becomes an aesthetically charged ruin.

In this regard, Gay Leonhardt's account of having an "eye for peeling paint" is typical. Such sensibility helps her notice "common materials rarely noticed before," and enables her to be struck by "the sudden prominence of beauty" and to "become a connoisseur of screens and broken glass."[122] However, her appreciation is directed toward an abandoned building, not toward her own house. Most of us don't want our house to be a dilapidated shack. The only exception is if such a structure is not used for any practical purpose. If it is located within a large estate more as a decoration than as a functional structure, it is possible that we find some charm and appreciate a touch of rusticity and character to the property. It certainly becomes an object of positive aesthetic appreciation if we, as tourists, encounter it on our walk through a picturesque garden. Similarly, we appreciate Japanese "*boro,*" tattered fabrics, nineteenth-century and twentieth-century folk "rag textiles" and quilts made with used cloths and coarse stitches when they are exhibit items at various art museums, including Whitney.[123]

When we derive an aesthetic pleasure from the aged, imperfect condition of some of our possessions, they are mostly special objects not "in use" in our everyday context and function more like works of art, such as a family heirloom, antique furniture, a quilt, or prized tea ceremony implements. In contrast, when it comes to those objects of everyday use, such as our

---

[121] Yourcenar, pp. 60–1, emphasis added.
[122] Gay Leonhardt, "An Eye for Peeling Paint," *Landscape* 28:2 (1985), p. 25.
[123] For an account of these exhibits, see Lois Martin, "*Patina* of Cloth," *Surface Design Journal* 28:4 (Summer 2004): 16–21.

house, car, household items, and clothes, we seldom derive an aesthetic pleasure from their decayed, imperfect conditions. Our relationship to these objects is too immersed in everyday, practical concerns to allow for a more detached, spectator-like stance from which to contemplate. So, our immediate aesthetic reaction toward a soiled tablecloth, a five-year-old coffee table with nicks and scratches, a moth-eaten jacket, dingy and stained wallpaper, and a chipped soup bowl, is negative, accompanied by our impulse to clean, repair, or discard if deemed beyond repair.

Uvedale Price points out the limitation of picturesque appreciation when it regards something with which we are intimately engaged in our everyday life, in this case, a wife. Price describes a woman who grew picturesque, "when her cheeks were a little furrowed and weather-stained, and her teeth had got a slight incrustation." However, another picturesque advocate, Richard Payne Knight, points out that consistency requires that she also develop "the same happy mixture of the irregular and picturesque ... throughout her limbs" and "consequently she must have hobbled as well as squinted; and had hips and shoulder as irregular as her teeth, cheeks, and eyebrows." Responding to this comment, Price had to admit that " 'you will hardly find any man fond enough of the picturesque' ... to marry a girl so thoroughly deformed."[124] Commenting on our attraction to the picturesque in human appearance, most typical of old people, Dekkers makes a similar point:

We think it picturesque when they linger a little towards the end, but mostly we're glad we're not them ... It's all wonderful, as long as it's not us who's the hunchback, one-legged or orphaned. At school we couldn't hear enough stories about lepers, whose fingers would fall off if you shook their hands, or who had fewer toes every day ... how wonderful misery can be—as long as it doesn't affect us.[125]

While we have only limited control over our own aging process, when it comes to our material possessions, we are expected to take good care of them by keeping them in good condition. Just as in the case of our appearance or belongings that are dirty and disorganized, the decayed, imperfect condition of our everyday objects symbolizes "neglect" and that in turn reflects on our character. Whether or not it is accurate, we are inevitably judged as being lazy, slothful, slovenly, uncaring, irresponsible,

---

[124] This exchange between Knight and Price is cited by Lowenthal, p. 166.
[125] Dekkers, p. 53.

and not civic-minded or neighborly. In extreme cases, we may even be judged either morally suspect or mentally ill. So, unless we are wholly indifferent to others' opinion or eccentric in our aesthetic taste, most of us have a vested interest in projecting the image of ourselves for being responsible, fastidious and industrious, and in control of ourselves, through the appearance of our possessions. Even if we don't have the economic means of renewing or replacing those decayed, defective things, we will try our best to hide the defects, repair them, or refurbish them the best we can.

Of course, as advocates of aesthetic attitude theory would remind us, we *can* decide to experience all these expressions of aged appearance, picturesque beauty, and *wabi* qualities in our everyday objects *as if* they were an encapsulated aesthetic unit. I probably *can*, with training and practice, acquire a sharper *wabi* sensibility and aesthetically appreciate my threadbare and stained couch, frayed wallpaper, rusty car, and chipped plates, as if I were a photographer creating a work of art depicting them. Developing such a sensibility toward generally unnoticed aesthetic treasures of everyday life is certainly one important mission of everyday aesthetics. The discovery of hidden gems, such as the cracks on the floorboards, the way in which mold and mildew grow, and the oil stains on the driveway surface, indeed enriches our aesthetic life, and *that* I see is one of the values of exploring everyday aesthetics.[126] In this regard, a work of art like Murphy's *The Windsor* contributes toward questioning our ordinary aesthetic response and, in the words of one critic, "we are obliged to question our own definitions of beauty and ugliness, preservation and defilement, the precious and the worthless."[127]

However, as I discussed in Chapter I, doing so will deprive the object of its everyday-ness; its ordinariness becomes extraordinarily experienced. While we gain perhaps a more satisfying aesthetic experience, we also lose the dimension of personal engagement that characterizes our dealing with everyday environment and objects.[128] Our everyday aesthetic life is not

---

[126] I have witnessed many of my students' fascination and artistic treatment of these and similar phenomena.

[127] Prose, p. 128.

[128] Characterizing it as a "kind of trap," Crispen Sartwell points out the inherent irony of aesthetic appreciation of the ordinary exemplified in *wabi* aesthetics: "As soon as the tea masters began to venerate

exhausted by those aesthetically positive experiences facilitated by rendering the ordinary extraordinary. If I have a negative response toward objects because they *look* shabby, neglected, and old, that is *also* part of my aesthetic life. Perhaps it may be that the positive reaction toward them is more sophisticated and cultured, requiring more refined sensibility and training, or that it enlarges the horizon of our aesthetic life. But the possibility of this more refined and enlightened aesthetic life does not nullify or negate the existence and the role played by the other, more commonplace, dimension of our aesthetic life.

Nor does such a possibility mean that we *should* always work at realizing it. I questioned whether things like signs of poverty, vandalism, environmental harm should be aesthetically appreciated in the sense of being grateful for their existence.[129] I also criticized the ways in which aestheticization of transience, imperfection, and insufficiency has been used for dubious, and sometimes dangerous, political ends. In light of these examples, I regard another normative task of everyday aesthetics is to examine whether there is a compelling reason for finding positive aesthetic values in those objects and qualities that are normally not appreciated.

Exploring everyday aesthetics on the one hand encourages us to be more aware of and cherish what Hermann Hesse called "little joys" that celebrate the beauty of things "so inconspicuous and scattered so liberally throughout our daily lives that the dull minds of countless workers hardly notice them."[130] With some effort and practice, we will indeed be able to find positive aesthetic values in things and qualities that are usually regarded as aesthetically negative. At the same time, however, the inquiry into everyday aesthetics should also challenge an attitude of *indiscriminate* aestheticizing. While acknowledging the possible existential reward of aestheticizing transience, imperfection, and insufficiency, we should also pay due regard to our all-too-common negative response to

---

ordinary-looking wares, master potters began to use wabi-sabi as a set of guidelines for their own work, which eventuated in raku ware and also in the sheer imitation of 'the ordinary' by extraordinary artists. The ordinary became something simulated by intense application of self-consciousness, like artistically weathered blue jeans or distressed furniture." *Six Names of Beauty* (New York: Routledge, 2004), p. 117.

[129] But not in the sense of perceiving clearly, which I distinguished from the sense of being grateful and endorsing the existence of the object.

[130] Hermann Hesse, "On Little Joys," (1905) in *My Belief: Essays on Life and Art*, tr. Denver Lindley (New York: Farrar, Straus and Girouux, 1974), p. 9.

those qualities, particularly when such familiar responses do not lead to problematic consequences. Finally, given the power of the aesthetic to influence people's attitudes and determine their actions, and in light of the past precedents of using it for socially and politically problematic agenda, everyday aesthetics should also highlight the importance of being vigilant about the way in which aesthetics is utilized.

V

Moral–Aesthetic Judgments of Artifacts

For most of us, our everyday life is dominated by living in a built environment surrounded with artifacts. This modern condition makes the experience of nature all the more precious and urgent. However, given that most of us "spend around 90 per cent of our time in cities, buildings and vehicles,"[1] artifacts and built environments cannot but exert an inordinate amount of influence on our lives. By creating them and interacting with them, we are all participating in the project of world-making on a daily basis. In the words of David Orr, designed objects and environments "structure what we see, how we move, what we eat, our sense of time and space, how we relate to each other, our sense of security, and how we experience the particular places in which we live" and, as such, "by their scale and power they structure how we think."[2] In the most extreme case, the design of an artifact can literally change the course of history by determining our action, as we witnessed in the case of the now-infamous butterfly ballot used for the 2000 U. S. Presidential election in Florida.[3]

Though most of the time without invoking a memorable, standout experience traditionally associated with the "aesthetic," we constantly respond and react to the sensuous appearance and design of artifacts on a

---

[1] David Pearson, "Making Sense of Architecture," *Architectural Review* 1136 (1991), p. 68.

[2] David Orr, *The Nature of Design: Ecology, Culture, and Human Intention* (Oxford: Oxford University Press, 2002), p. 31.

[3] Carolyn Korsmeyer questioned whether the flaw in the ballot was more practical than aesthetic. I do agree that it is not aesthetic in the sense of being inelegant, ugly, or unsightly. However, insofar as its design, that is, the specific configuration of the list of names, failed in accomplishing its task, I believe that the matter belongs to the aesthetic arena. As I will argue in this chapter, whether or not a particular design is thoughtful and considerate by taking into account the users' experience is an aesthetic issue, because the evidence of these moral virtues (or lack thereof) is reflected in the specific design features.

daily basis. Our aesthetic response is one crucial way in which we gauge the effects artifacts exert over our lives. One such example is the way in which we experience, appreciate, or criticize artifacts by attributing moral qualities to them, such as "respect," "considerateness," "sensitivity," "caring," "humility," and "responsiveness," or their opposites. We normally apply these terms to describe the moral character of a person or an action. People may praise me for such things as my considerateness when I schedule a meeting not at my convenience but for everyone else's convenience, for my sensitivity and responsiveness when I try to meet a conscientious but struggling student's needs, for a caring attitude when I assist my friend who is crying for help, or humility for not boasting my accomplishment even when I deserve to do so. On the other hand, I may be blamed for being disrespectful by not thanking for a gift, inconsiderate for blasting music late into the night and disturbing my neighbors, insensitive to my students' collective complaint regarding my unreasonable expectations, and arrogant for tooting my own horn all the time.

However, we do make various moral judgments not only about persons and actions but also regarding artifacts. We may condemn or praise the existence of an artifact depending upon the purpose for which it was designed and made, distinguishing, for example, a built structure such as a Nazi gas chamber from a temporary shelter to house displaced refugees. Or, the evaluation may be directed toward the political agenda specifically intended to be served by the object's design. This underlies the disagreement between Frederick Law Olmsted's democratic ideal and Richard Morris Hunt's aristocratic ideal over the design of entrance gates to Central Park in New York City.[4] Another example is Robert Moses' design of overpasses over Long Island Parkway that was intentionally low to prevent the passage of busses, the only means of transportation for poor and black people to get to the beach.[5] Moral judgments regarding artifacts may also involve various moral implications in their production process, usage, disposal, and the like. For example, we may take a negative attitude toward a certain brand of sneakers because of its manufacturing company's poor record regarding

---

[4] See pp. 12–13 of Albert Fein's *Frederick Law Olmsted and the American Environmental Tradition* (New York: George Braziller, 1973) for this debate. Fein is right in pointing out that "Olmsted's conception of physical form as a function of social planning was perhaps his most important contribution" (p. 14).

[5] See p. 23 of Langdon Winner's *The Whale and the Reactor: A Search for Limits in an Age of High Technology* (Chicago: The University of Chicago Press, 1989) about this example.

child labor and the working conditions in its overseas factories. We may also condemn or praise a product because of its ecological implications regarding its raw materials, manufacturing process, transporting process, packaging, and its afterlife (throw away, recycle, or reuse?).

While these are moral judgments *regarding* artifacts, they are not directly judging the artifacts themselves. We object to a gas chamber and Nike sneakers, regardless of their design and sensuous appearance.[6] It may appear that our moral judgments regarding artifacts are exhausted by these types of cases. As we negotiate the interior space of a building, eat lunch, use a tool, open a package, and draft/read a report, it is difficult to imagine that there is any issue of moral relevance, unless we consider the purpose of the object (that the tool is for torturing people, like the one described in Franz Kafka's *In the Penal Colony*, or the report is an Enron secret document), or the implications of the object (its negative environmental effect or its contribution to a meat industry that does not respect animal rights). Attribution of any moral qualities to artifacts themselves seems like a prime example of a category mistake.

1. Moral-aesthetic judgments

However, although seldom articulated or pondered, there is a familiar way in which moral values, such as respect, considerateness, sensitivity, and care (or their opposites) are used in evaluating artifacts. Here are some examples. "Good design," Donald Norman declares, "takes *care*, planning, thought" and "*concern* for others."[7] Praising traditional Japanese crafts, Jack Lenor Larsen also calls attention to their "deep respect for material and process, and *respect too for the intended user*."[8] This sentiment is echoed in Mariel

---

[6] The examples of the park entrance and the overpasses are different in this respect, as the political agenda is fulfilled by a specific design. Even between these two examples, there is a difference because there is nothing inherent in the height of an overpass that is racist; the racist agenda is achieved by the height of the busses, as well as the fact that busses happened to be the only mode of transportation for poor blacks at this time. The open, inviting nature of Olmsted's design of the entrance, in contrast to the imposing, auspicious nature of Hunt's design, does not seem to be context-dependent in the same manner.

[7] Donald A. Norman, *The Design of Everyday Things* (New York: Doubleday, 1990), pp. 25 and 27, emphasis added.

[8] Jack Lenor Larsen, "The Inspiration of Japanese Design," included in *Traditional Japanese Design: Five Tastes*, ed. Michael Dunn (New York: Japan Society, 2001), p. 12, emphasis added.

Semal's comment on Japanese packaging, especially of gifts: "packaging must be appropriate to the content and the purpose of giving. It is a craft requiring always thinking of other people … The art of wrapping teaches us that we can show *kind consideration* even towards casual objects. Thoughtfulness is beautiful."[9] In contrast, the lack of such attention and consideration incites the following criticism:

[A]ny lack of care given to the design of a building is also, in effect, a lack of care shown to the public who have to live with it. In these circumstances, … our aesthetic criticism is not solely aesthetic, but also, at the same time, moral. It is an ethical criticism of the aesthetic content of the building.[10]

Let me call these judgments "moral-aesthetic" judgments for want of a better term. I hold that these judgments are *aesthetic* judgments insofar as they are derived from our sensuous (often bodily) experience of the objects, different from the other moral judgments regarding artifacts described above that concern their purposes and implications that are independent of or outside of our perceptual experience.

This phenomenon of moral-aesthetic judgments has not received sufficient attention in the moral discourse. There are some areas of aesthetics where attention is paid to moral-aesthetic judgments, but it certainly is not one of its prominent subject matters. In Western ethical thinking, the ethic of care, feminist ethics, and virtue ethics have been gaining prominence as correctives to overly rule- and principle-governed mainstream ethical theories that emphasize justice, rightness, fairness, and duty. Qualities such as sympathy, compassion, a caring attitude, sensitivity, and humility have traditionally been largely neglected or considered morally irrelevant. These more recent, alternative ethical theories challenge this neglect and illuminate the indispensability of these sensibilities to our moral life. However, even with this welcome and much needed outlook, those moral qualities are usually regarded as attributes of a person or an action and the role played by artifacts in this regard is seldom recognized. I shall argue later that such evaluations of artifacts are crucial in promoting a humane and civilized society as well as a good life for all of us.

---

[9] Mariel Semal, "Tsutsumu: Nihon no Hōsō Geijutsu (Wrapping: The Japanese Art of Packaging)," included in *Tsutsumu: Nihon no Dentō Pakkēji (Wrapping: Traditional Japanese Packaging)*, eds. Oka Hideyuki and Fujita Takashi (Kyoto: Tankōsha, 1995), p. 116, my translation.

[10] Nigel Taylor, "Ethical Arguments about the Aesthetics of Architecture," included in *Ethics and the Built Environment*, ed. Warwick Fox (London: Routledge, 2000), p. 202.

One may object that attributing moral qualities to artifacts commits a category mistake, because, strictly speaking, only moral agents are capable of being respectful, humble, sensitive, responsive, considerate, or their opposites. My response is that this seemingly anthropomorphic characterization of an object's aesthetic quality is a familiar phenomenon often discussed in traditional aesthetics. Primarily, though not exclusively, concerning works of art; one of the perennial questions raised in aesthetics is what it means for a piece of music to be sad and a painting to be joyful. We examine whether a piece of music is "sad" because of some facts about the composer (his state of mind during composition, or his intention), the emotive state induced in us (sad music making us feel sad), or rather as a shorthand way of describing a particular set of features of musical sounds. It is not my interest here to engage in this debate. I only mention this debate because I want to point out that the attribution of human qualities to designed artifacts is not unique to moral-aesthetic judgments.

Furthermore, moral-aesthetic judgments are less complicated than the process of ascribing emotive qualities to works of art. First, except for some built structures by well-known architects and one-of-a-kind designed objects by famous designers/makers, most of the time we don't know who the designer of the object is, let alone her state of mind at the time of designing, her intention, or her *oeuvre*. Nor do we feel, unless under an exceptional circumstance, compelled to track down such information. At the same time, I think we can safely assume that, unless under very strange circumstances, the designer/maker did not specifically intend to embody disrespect, insensitivity, inconsiderateness, and irresponsibility in her creation, although she may not have had a specific intention to embody the opposite qualities, either. Or, it may be the case that she aimed at designing an object to respond sensitively to our needs and experiences, but owing to her lack of skill and talent she failed miserably, resulting in an inconsiderate, insensitive design. As a result, whatever judgment we make on most designed objects has to be made on the basis of the object itself, in the absence of information concerning the designer/maker; the object has to stand on its own and be judged solely by its design features.[11]

---

[11] This does not mean that we as consumers are exempt from any responsibility for finding out something about the object we are purchasing, using, etc. Particularly today, we should educate ourselves to be an enlightened consumer by knowing something about the object's environmental impact, the company's records on human rights and trade issues, and the like. However, since it is

In this particular respect, the design profession faces more challenges than the art profession.[12] That is, with respect to art, the onus is partly on the viewers/listeners/audience to try to meet the object on its own terms. This requires that they gain some knowledge regarding the object, including the artist's *oeuvre*, cultural/historical context, allusion and symbolism, technique used in creation, and the like. As I mentioned in Chapter III, John Dewey maintains that the moral function of art is to help widen our horizon by cultivating our willingness to experience a created world that is sometimes quite unfamiliar to us. As I shall argue later, experiencing designed objects can and should make some demand on us as users, but not in the sense of having to widen our horizon to meet the object on its own terms.

These comparisons between art and non-art objects lead me to conclude that, when we make a judgment that a designed object embodies moral qualities (positive or negative), we are referring strictly to the sensuous features of the objects, without reference to the designer's/maker's or the user's/experiencing agent's mental state. As the saying goes, the proof is in the pudding, the tasting of which requires our direct experience. This fact reinforces my claim that such moral attribution is an *aesthetic* matter because our judgment is based upon the sensuous appearance of the object, unlike moral judgments of a person or an action that normally do not refer to the sensuous appearance of my body movement, the tone of my voice, and the like (except in such cases when I say something to a person in a very sarcastic tone of voice or I lend a helping hand to a person but do so in a very rough, spiteful manner).[13]

not easy for us to engage individually in such a research, something like a certification standard or eco-labeling offered by the government, such as the Blue Angel labeling in Germany, is helpful.

[12] On the other hand, what may appear to be a special challenge to designing objects that is not shared by creating works of art is actually not so. I am referring to a number of constraints designers face, such as physical limitations, various regulations, and functional demands. For example, at the very minimum, a chair has to be of a certain size, and has to be stable and strong enough to hold our weight, has to be made with fire-resistant material, not to mention working within a certain budget. These may at first appear as an extra burden fine artists usually do not face, but in a way it makes the designer's job easier in the sense that certain decisions do not have to be made—they are already made for them, unlike artists who have complete freedom over their creation, which means they are faced with numerous decisions. Furthermore, a case can be made that it is easier to exercise one's imagination, creativity, and originality when one is restricted in some way, rather than where there is no restriction and "anything goes."

[13] It may be the case, however, when we judge the moral worth of an action, we cannot separate what the action accomplishes (helping a friend in need) from the manner in which we act (gently, roughly, sarcastically, sincerely, grudgingly, through the body movement, facial expression, and tone of voice). In such a case, the problem for moral theories, such as when formulating the Kantian maxim

One may also question whether a moral-aesthetic judgment of an artifact is an aesthetic judgment because, most often, the considerateness, sensitivity, and responsiveness that we attribute to its design features have to do with how well it functions. If an object is poorly designed and cannot function properly or is very difficult to use, it may be considered an instance of insensitive design or inconsiderate design. But isn't this a judgment based upon the functionality of the object and, as such, not an aesthetic judgment?

The presumed separation of an object's function and its aesthetic value goes back to the eighteenth-century proposal of disinterestedness as the distinguishing mark of the aesthetic. In one sense, the development of modern Western aesthetics can be characterized as a declaration of independence for the aesthetic, emancipating it from the grip of the moral, the conceptual, and the practical. With some exceptions along the way, I believe that aesthetic discourse is still generally guided by this project to secure independence of the aesthetic. The impetus for separating our interested concern with the object's functioning from our aesthetic concern is understandable within the context of this ongoing project. However, I don't think the independent sphere of the aesthetic is compromised by including and integrating the "interested" consideration of functionality, *as long as* we are able to *experience* the way in which the functionality is served/not served by the design of the object.

In this respect, I would liken a computer engineer's appreciation of the way in which the inside mechanism of a computer operates and the car mechanic's appreciation of engine designs to the conceptual appreciation of a mathematician or a scientist regarding a formula or a theory. For most of us, such mechanisms and workings are invisible, hence un-experienceable, and though we appreciate the outcome of its excellent functioning, I don't consider such an appreciation to be an *aesthetic* one.

However, if we judge that something functions well (or poorly) from our firsthand experience through our senses and bodily sensations, I maintain that it qualifies as an aesthetic judgment. So, the way in which various buttons, gauges, and knobs are made, arranged and displayed on my car's dashboard calls for an aesthetic appraisal in terms of how easy, difficult, confusing, or cumbersome it is to use them. Easy readability of a well-organized

for an action, is how to describe "the action." Is it "helping a friend in need," or rather "acting spiteful and hateful when helping a friend in need"?

report, a clear order in which merchandise is arranged, an easy-to-follow and -decipher signage system at an airport, and ergonomically shaped utensils that are comfortable to use, are all appreciated for their excellent serving of their particular function. We depreciate the contrary examples for their poor functionality. In all these examples, our positive or negative experiences are derived from our direct experience of visual, tactile, and bodily sensations. As such, there is no denying that we are engaging in an aesthetic judgment, although, typical of our everyday aesthetic life, it does not generally engender a memorable, standout experience, nor does it involve noble, lofty, sophisticated ideas often expressed by works of art.

Jerome Stolnitz, an advocate of defining the aesthetic as disinterested and sympathetic attention, would object to this line of argument by claiming that our "interested" regard for utilitarian objects would not produce an aesthetic experience, because we are preoccupied only with whether or not they serve the function. "When our attitude is 'practical,'" according to him, "we perceive things only as means to some goal which lies beyond the experience of perceiving them."[14] Hence, when we approach a pen with a practical interest, "it is only the pen's usefulness-for-writing-with, not its distinctive color or shape, that I care about." He is right in claiming that we normally do not pay attention to an everyday utilitarian object's sensuous surface and design in our everyday use—we are too busy to dwell on its aesthetic dimension. If one pen does not work well, I simply grab a different one. However, we are *also* familiar with our experience where we do ponder the reason why an object does or does not function well, and this requires our paying close attention to the details of its design. I may enjoy the excellent functionality of a particular pen and notice how its shape, size, texture, and weight all contribute to easy grip, even dispensing of the ink, and smooth, gliding movement when writing. Even the color of its body may matter, as some of my black ballpoint pens have reddish or greenish tips and caps, always confusing me as to the color of their ink. I deplore some pens for their clumsiness, discomfort, uneven writing and trace these negative qualities to their design features. My analysis regarding the excellent/poor working of a pen, provided it is grounded in my experience of its design features, I contend, does belong to our aesthetic

---

[14] Jerome Stolnitz, "The Aesthetic Attitude," included in *Introductory Readings in Aesthetics*, ed. John Hospers (New York: Free Press, 1969), p. 18. The next passage is also from p. 18.

life. In what follows, I shall provide some other examples of moral-aesthetic dimensions of our everyday life and illustrate how our aesthetic evaluation is sometimes inseparable from moral considerations.

2. Examples from contemporary aesthetic and design discourses

I shall explore five moral-aesthetic concerns in our life, though there are surely many others: (1) appropriateness of a person's appearance; (2) environmental eyesore; (3) design for "special needs"; (4) design responsive to our bodily experience; and (5) design sensitive to the temporal nature of our experience. I will give more extended discussion of the last two of these examples, as their moral-aesthetic dimension may not be readily obvious.

i. Propriety of personal appearance

First, let me explore the issues regarding our appearance. I touched upon this issue in Chapter IV by showing how we can be judged to be civic-minded, responsible, hard-working, and competent or their opposites, purely based upon the appearance of ourselves and possessions. Let me add one more consideration to this phenomenon: the notion of propriety. "Inappropriate" clothing is often taken as a sign of disrespect, whether or not such is intended. A case in point is the recent faux pas made by the female lacrosse team from Northwestern University which was invited to the White House to meet with the President. They all wore flip-flops, thinking that those sandals reflect the casual nature of their sports. Of course the media had a field day, criticizing their attire as a "flip-flops flap" and a show of disrespect.[15] The team insisted that they meant no disrespect and neither understood nor appreciated all the fuss.

When we judge someone's moral character from her appearance, we are pulled in two different directions, as described by David Novitz:

Appearances, our parents warned us, are not everything. Beauty, they said, is skin deep; and we were further warned … that there is more to a person than a pretty

---

[15] Many newspapers, such as *USA Today*, ran the article entitled: "Northwestern lax team sparks White House flip-flops flap" (19 July 2005).

face. ... But they also told us to brush our hair, to use make-up sparingly, and to clean our fingernails. Appearances might not be everything, but in our own lives we soon learned that they were far from trivial and needed to be treated with respect. Most of us are encouraged to attend to and to cultivate our own appearances, but, at the same time, to be mildly skeptical of the appearances of others.[16]

Whether or not it is wise to criticize the lacrosse team for their presumed show of "disrespect," one thing to notice in this kind of moral-aesthetic judgment is that it seems dependent upon social convention. It seems to me that there is nothing inherently disrespectful about flip-flops worn at an auspicious occasion. The social convention regarding proper attire *could* have been the other way around. In Samuel Butler's fictional society of *Erewhon* (1872) where everything is reversed, flip-flops could be the height of formality and dress-up while tuxedo and long dress could signify utmost informality and casualness.[17]

ii. Environmental eyesore

It is in environmental aesthetics where we find examples of moral-aesthetic judgments that do not seem to be dependent upon social convention. Consider, for example, littering, vandalism, and graffiti, that "deface," "defile," or "destroy" the environment. Our generally negative attitude toward these "eyesores" is largely due to the implied attitude of disrespect, irresponsibility, and downright assault and violence.[18] Our condemnation of these phenomena usually concerns property other than the perpetrator's own, such as the neighbors' property or communal space and buildings. Debris and garbage strewn around a person's own yard and the spray-painted marks on his house may still be considered "eyesores" and even shows of disrespect or visual assault on his neighbors and passers-by, but we may tolerate such an eyesore at least to some degree if we have reason to believe that he is consciously exercising his freedom of expression. However, if these activities take place outside his own property, we perceive the act to be literally committing violence to others by defacing,

[16] David Novitz, *The Boundaries of Art* (Philadelphia: Temple University Press, 1992), p. 105.

[17] Except it could be argued that there is something inherently formal about tuxedo and long dress, because they are restrictive, forcing us to move in a stiff manner.

[18] I will not explore here a different take on graffiti that addresses its origin in social and economic deprivation so that walls, bridges, and subways provide the only venue for expression for the powerless and disenfranchised.

defiling, and destroying the possessions and spaces belonging to others. Our moral judgment against such an act seems to play a significant role in our aesthetic judgment on "eyesores," because, from a purely formal point of view, the sensuous appearance of litter or vandalism may not necessarily be aesthetically negative. According to Allen Carlson, eyesore is "unsightly primarily because of ... expressive qualities," and the life values expressed by roadside clutter are "waste, disregard, carelessness, and exploitation."[19] If we adopt the view recommended by aesthetic attitude theorists and concentrate exclusively on the visual and textural aspects of so-called eyesores, they may indeed look interesting, amusing, or captivating. However, in our normal outlook, our reaction toward their appearance is negative; nor do we seem to have any compelling reason to turn them into something aesthetically positive, unless we are training ourselves to be an artist, a photographer in particular, working on cultivating an unbiased aesthetic sensibility. So, it seems to me that we are justified in making a negative aesthetic judgment based upon our negative moral judgment on the act that produced it.

There are subtler cases in which our moral evaluation affects or sometimes determines our aesthetic evaluation of an artifact. Consider another example of Carlson's, "an exclusive, upper-middle class suburban neighborhood."[20] If it is a natural outgrowth of "racist" social forces, "exploitive" economic systems, and "corrupt" political institution, its seemingly beautiful, peaceful, and elegant appearance may begin to be regarded as "expressive" of those morally unacceptable qualities. Similar to his view on the litter, Carlson claims that our appreciation of human environment is "the appreciation of the life values," involving "not simply how it looks, but also why it looks as it does and what it thereby expresses." If this suburban community is "indeed the result of racist, exploitive, and corrupt forces, then it may well express these life values," and as such it will be "difficult if not impossible to aesthetically appreciate and value." Thus, in short, the aesthetic status of a built environment is dependent upon the moral status of its cause and/or effect, as he explicitly states that "in so far as the moral and the aesthetic appear to come into conflict, the former trumps the latter."

---

[19] Allen Carlson, *Aesthetics and the Environment: The Appreciation of Nature, Art and Architecture* (London: Routledge, 2000), pp. 144 and 145.
[20] Allen Carlson, "On Aesthetically Appreciating Human Environments," *Philosophy & Geography* 4:1 (2001), p. 16. The citation in the next sentence is also from p. 16. The citation for the rest of this paragraph is from p. 19.

I find Carlson's view a bit too close to what I called environmental determinism in Chapter II. While Carlson's account may accurately capture some aspects of our common experiences, it seems to me that his analysis does not adequately attend to "the aesthetic" aspect of the issue. That is, if we follow Carlson's view, once we form a moral judgment for or against a certain environment, we don't need to experience it firsthand to formulate our aesthetic appraisal; we know beforehand that a roadside litter and a gated community resulting from and contributing to social ills are aesthetically negative. What makes a moral-aesthetic judgment against littering and gated community an "aesthetic" judgment is that the morally problematic qualities, such as disrespect and exploitation, are evidenced by the sensuous aspects of the object.

In this regard, Arnold Berleant's notion of "aesthetic offense" better highlights the aesthetic dimension of a similar moral-aesthetic judgment. While die-hard capitalists and entrepreneurs may find positive values in a commercial strip development, Berleant characterizes it as an "aesthetic affront" for its "*insensitivity* to place ... the vulgarization of its attractive features or the imposition of contrived or false ones."[21] In a similar vein, "summer cottages whose presence pollutes the scenery of a shoreline are offensive" because "the builders place personal indulgence over the commonly acknowledged attractiveness of an uncluttered and natural landscape, despoiling the very qualities that originally made the area attractive."[22] In these judgments, our negative reaction is not simply directed toward the life values or expressive qualities but also toward the sensuous appearance of the objects. It is undeniable, however, that our judgments on the built environment are often inseparable from our judgments on the moral, social, political values of its cause and/or effect.

One contentious point regarding these moral-aesthetic judgments is that people disagree about what life values are expressed by a certain object or phenomenon. Even a seemingly obvious example is not immune

---

[21] Arnold Berleant, *Living in the Landscape: Toward an Aesthetics of Environment* (Lawrence: University Press of Kansas, 1997), p. 67, emphasis added. The next reference to summer cottages comes from p. 68.

[22] Carolyn Korsmeyer asked whether Berleant meant "condos" instead of "cottages." Berleant's text has "cottages." However, in keeping with the point of this paragraph, slick-looking condos will be more aesthetically offensive than log cabin-type cottages exactly for the reason Berleant gives. Even if the degree of intrusion and indulgence may be equivalent in the literal sense, the *appearance* of these qualities seems to differ depending upon the structural style.

from this difficulty. Smokestacks belching black smoke may repulse the environmentalists among us, not to mention William Blake, but historically they were also welcomed and celebrated as a symbol of progress by many and there is no telling how many of today's industrialists continue to appreciate their appearance. As Neil Evernden points out in his discussion on "the social creation of nature," even the notion of "pollution" (which incidentally has an aesthetic connotation) is socially constructed to serve a particular social and political agenda.[23] The problem is even more acute regarding subtler cases such as gated community or a commercial strip. Those of us committed to social justice may see them as a symbol of injustice, of crass commercialism, or unbridled capitalism. In contrast, those of us who embrace libertarianism and capitalism as the best social and economic set-up would see them as expressing hard work, freedom, prosperity, and the like. In fact, Yi-Fu Tuan offers a different reading of a commercial strip. According to Tuan, if we look at it through "traditional and high-cultural eyes," it is "a visual blight" and "an eyesore," because of "its inhuman scale, ... the makeshift facade, the lurid neon lights, the unsubtle commands (EAT! GAS!)" and "the jungle of competing posters and sculptures."[24] However, having emerged "in the relatively affluent post-World War II period and catered especially to a young clientele" who "found a new way to spend their leisure, cruising up and down the road," the strip also "extends a loud welcome to strangers" and Tuan concludes that "a passerby has to be a pinched puritan not to respond occasionally to the sheer verve of a commercialism that, at its witty best, can wink at itself."[25]

[23] Neil Evernden, *The Social Creation of Nature* (Baltimore: The Johns Hopkins University Press, 1992), ch. 1. I thank Carolyn Korsmeyer for pointing out that "in the 1970's Chinese artists adapted traditional scenic painting to render new factories belching pollutants, and the results were considered beautiful (the traditional elegant style used to present wispy smoke against mountains) and uplifting and progressive (the advance of industry)."

[24] Yi-Fu Tuan, *Passing Strange and Wonderful: Aesthetics, Nature, and Culture* (Washington, D. C.: Island Press, 1993), pp. 159, 160, 159, and 160. The reference in the next sentence comes from pp. 159 and 160.

[25] Larry Shiner called attention to the similarity between Tuan's interpretation here and Robert Venturi's *Learning from Las Vegas* (1972), which created a stir with its interpretation of the so-called crass, commercially oriented structures. Another example of conflicting interpretations is modern architecture of International Style, with its ubiquitous concrete and glass box appearance. While David Orr reads disrespect for locality, "mindlessness," and "disconnectedness," McDonough and Braungart point out that such a design at the outset was meant to convey hope in the "brotherhood" of mankind by providing affordable, sanitary, and clean structure. See p. 129 of Orr, and pp. 28–9 of McDonough and Braungart.

A similar disagreement can occur with respect to the notion of "functionality" of an object/environment. Melvin Rader and Bertram Jessup give an example of a factory building or a machine that may nicely satisfy the function of efficient production, while providing a poor working condition for its workers, thus failing to satisfy another function: health and physical comfort. The tension within the functional-aesthetic judgment created thereby is rooted in the fundamental disagreement over the relative importance of "economic good" vs. "human good."[26]

Carlson acknowledges such conflict of life values attributed to the same object. Instead of expressing "waste, disregard, carelessness, exploitation," Carlson admits that an objector may claim that junkyards and discarded beer cans embody "hard work, determination, vision."[27] Carlson's reply to this conflict is twofold: first, "the expression of acceptable life values does not cancel out the expression of objectionable ones"; secondly, the decision regarding what life values these objects express is "in the last analysis … up to us as a community of individuals."

My reply for my present purpose is threefold. First, such a conflict is certainly not unique to the aesthetic; it is simply reflective of our deep disagreement over moral, political, and existential vision of what constitutes a good society and good life. So, if we were to hope for a resolution of the aesthetic disagreement here, we have to hope first for a resolution among different political ideologies and philosophies of life. Whether black belching smoke coming out of factories constitutes an eyesore and pollution or a proud symbol of economic prosperity cannot be settled by analyzing its color, movement, and volume. Secondly, the existence of these conflicts does not pose a problem for my present purpose because I am here simply illustrating the way in which moral-aesthetic judgments take place regarding artifacts in our everyday life. With or without disagreements, these judgments on the built environment certainly show that we do make such judgments rather frequently.

---

[26] Melvin Rader and Bertram Jessup, *Art and Human Values* (Englewood Cliffs, Prentice-Hall, 1976), pp. 109–10. Of course this conflict can be resolved by showing how "efficient production" can only be maximized by providing a healthy, safe, and comfortable working environment, as shown by recent green factory and office buildings.

[27] Carlson, *Aesthetics and the Environment*, p. 148. The citation in the next sentence is also from the same page.

Thirdly, though I cannot hope for a complete resolution of these disagreements, I wonder whether their severity and/or frequency may be somewhat mitigated if we make these moral-aesthetic judgments based upon a more holistic, and not just visual, experience. Moral-aesthetic judgments of our built environment typically seem to be made from the standpoint of a "viewer," focusing primarily on its visual aspect. As my subsequent discussion will indicate, the judgments made from users' and dwellers' perspectives are going to be somewhat different, focusing more on the visceral reaction and bodily sensations, thereby examining its level of comfort, safety, user-friendliness, responsiveness to our holistic experience (qua user/dwellers). I will return to this point later with a set of examples.

iii. Designing for special needs

One more area in which the moral qualities become relevant in aesthetic consideration is design specifically aimed at serving the needs of a particular group of people, such as the physically challenged, children, senior citizens, sick patients, and displaced refugees. In designing objects and spaces for people with "special needs," we cannot but become sensitive and responsive to their specific interests and capacities. Hence, we attend carefully not only to the size, shape, texture, color, and safety of the objects but also to less tangible factors, ranging from comfort and well-being to the potential for discrimination, marginalization, cultural displacement, social stigma, and the like. Whether it be a built environment, vehicle, tools, utensils, or temporary shelters, the object must be designed with the constituents' specific needs and capacities in mind. Otherwise, the result will be clearly "*inconsiderate* design," such as "the ... spaces interconnect[ed] by means of stairs" which "disregard the needs of a mother with a pram, or disabled users."[28] Speaking of housing for people with "special needs," Barbara Knecht states:

Traditional multiunit housing design has been standardized around construction conventions and an idealized nuclear family, without specifically considering how human beings interact, how they age, how they carry out daily activities, how they suffer infirmity, and how they celebrate. In recent years, what is often designated

---

[28] Nigel Whiteley, *Design for Society* (London: Reaktion Books, 1993), p. 155, emphasis added.

'special needs' housing, by contrast, has been designed to meet diverse human needs—including the desire for a sense of community—with *thoughtful* design.[29]

A case in point is the signage system developed for an obstetric hospital by a Japanese designer, Hara Kenya. Cognizant of the fact that patients here are not "ill" needing treatment, he decided that providing comfortable, homey, and welcoming atmosphere is the priority and created a signage system that is essentially a white roundish cotton cover with letters and symbols printed, sometimes in the shape of a sock that is hung on a rope with clothes pins. The soft texture and roundish shape give out a gentle feeling, appropriate for newborns, compared with standard rectangle-shaped metal or plastic signage system. Furthermore, white cloth is vulnerable to becoming soiled and dirty, perhaps from being touched and played with by the babies' young siblings. But it was intended to be touched and soiled so that the white covering gets washed periodically, exuding cleanliness, another association important for newborns.[30]

Although designing for special groups of people poses its own challenges and obstacles, requiring imagination, creativity, and ingenuity, in another sense it is easier because the need to be sensitive to and considerate of their capacities, needs, interests, and expectations is assumed from the beginning. On the other hand, designing objects and structures for the general public poses more challenges because we hold diverse interests, values, and lifestyles. Rader and Jessup discuss the difficulty of domestic architecture. On the one hand, an "open plan ... gives primacy to ease of access and requirements of sociability" with "picture windows, flexible and common living spaces, and extension visually and otherwise of indoor area into the garden and beyond." On the other hand, such a design disregards an equally valid and important value held by others who put premium on "privacy," hence, prefer "confined rooms and fixed walls."[31]

---

[29] Barbara Knecht, "'Special Needs' and Housing Design: Myths/Realities/Opportunities," included in *Design and Feminism: Re-Visioning Spaces, Places, and Everyday Things*, ed. Joan Rothschild (New Brunswick: Rutgers University Press, 1999), p. 99, emphasis added.

[30] Hara's own description of this project can be found in Hara Kenya, *Dezain no Dezain* (*Design of Design*) (Tokyo: Iwanami Shoten, 2003), pp. 71–7.

[31] Rader and Jessup, p. 111. Knecht points out that accommodating special needs in housing design sometimes does sacrifice attending to the diverse interests and life styles among those people with the same "special needs," reminding us of the complex problems the designers and architects have to deal with (Knecht, pp. 104–7).

3. Design responsive to bodily experience

Now I would like to consider some other examples of the moral–aesthetic judgments of artifacts that are less obvious than the aforementioned three examples. The first example has to do with built structures that are responsive to the users' and dwellers' bodily experience. According to those designers and architects engaged in self-criticism, this design strategy has generally been ignored. For example, Juhani Pallasmaa, himself an architect, criticizes contemporary architectural profession for producing "a climate of arrogance," "narcissism," and an emphasis on the "individual genius" as superstar.[32] The kind of architecture celebrated thereby, according to him, "alienate[s]" us, as it embodies "power and domination," "a formal authority," "self-satisfaction and omnipotence," resulting in something "impudent and arrogant." The kind of architecture that Pallasmaa praises for resisting this tendency, exemplified by works by Alvar Aalto, Renzo Piano, and Lawrence Halprin, among others, de-emphasizes the excessive preoccupation with a singular, memorable visual image and instead is designed to provide a gradually unfolding, multi-sensory, bodily-oriented experiences. The resulting structure is "an architecture of *courtesy* and attention" as well as of "restraint and *modesty*" that is "contextual, multi-sensory, and *responsive*," and we will be rewarded by its "nearness and *affection*." In short, as the title of his article suggests, he calls for "an architecture of *humility*."

Victor Papanek, an industrial designer, is also critical of his own profession which, he claims, encourages designers and architects to think of themselves as artists. This ethos appeals to them "since it makes it possible to see themselves as heroic and romantic figures, heirs to a tradition that beckons with promises of fame and a niche in history."[33] As a result, "a good deal of design and architecture seems to be created for the personal glory of its creator." In contrast, he praises vernacular designs because they are "by definition unselfconscious," and they "don't loudly or aggressively proclaim themselves. Many of the simplest houses were built to

[32] Juhani Pallasmaa, "Toward an Architecture of Humility," *Harvard Design Magazine* (Winter/Spring 1999), p. 22. All the citations in the next sentence are from p. 25. The rest of the citations in the rest of this paragraph are from p. 25, emphasis added.

[33] Victor Papanek, *The Green Imperative: Natural Design for the Real World* (New York: Thames & Hudson, 1995), p. 135. The citations in the next two sentences are from pp. 203 and 135.

display family skills and status, and sometimes individual interpretations of traditional designs, but most vernacular buildings don't make architectural 'statements.'" As in Pallasmaa's view, the virtue of "humility" looms large in Papanek's discussion.

"Humility" is also featured by Sim van der Ryn and Stuart Cowan, both architects, in their writing on ecological design. They characterize sustainable design as requiring "patience and humility," as it attends carefully to "scale, community self-reliance, traditional knowledge, and the wisdom of nature's own designs."[34] It contrasts with the traditional vision of architecture which consists of the accomplishment of a lone architect superstar:

[C]onventional educational practices still largely follow the myth put forward by Ayn Rand in her novel *The Fountainhead*, in which a lone idiosyncratic architect fights against a hostile and philistine world. Architectural design is generally not taught as a collaborative process that clients or users have any stake in. Rather, it is often taught as a 'pure' process that should not be 'contaminated' by any real-world constraints or needs: social, environmental, or economic.

David Orr, in his work on the nature of design, also criticizes the ethos behind modern Western design practice and contrasts it with the design wisdom of "settled culture." Again, his critique uses moral terms:

Settled cultures tend to limit excess in a variety of ways. Showiness, ego trips, great wealth, huge homes, hurry, and excessive consumption are mostly discouraged, while cooperation, neighborliness, competence, thrift, responsibility, and self-reliance are encouraged.[35]

The modern Western design practice is based upon the Enlightenment agenda with its emphasis on human rationality over nature. While it led to many problems, Orr claims that "the design implication is not less rationality, but a more complete, *humble*, and ecologically solvent rationality that works over the long term."

Similarly, Nigel Taylor discusses the importance of "care" in our appreciation of a built structure. If we experience a building that appears to be put together thoughtlessly and carelessly, without regard to our

---

[34] Sim Van der Ryn and Stuart Cowan, *Ecological Design* (Washington, D. C.: Island Press, 1996), p. 7. The notion of humility is also mentioned on p. 136. The next long passage is from p. 147.

[35] Orr, pp. 8–9. The next citation is from pp. 26–7, emphasis added.

experience as users or its relationship to the surroundings, it "would offend us aesthetically, but, more than that, part of our offense might be ethical. Thus we might reasonably be angered or outraged, not just by the look of the thing, but also by the visible evidence that the person who designed it didn't show sufficient *care* about the aesthetic impact of his building"[36] He cites Roger Scruton's comparison between two wall constructions: one made in "brutalist" fashion which appears "hostile, alien, indicative of a world at variance with individual fulfillment" and another constructed thoughtfully, carefully, and sensitively which, according to Scruton, "has an accumulation of moral character, wears a sympathetic expression, and ... inhabits the same world as the man who passes it." Commenting on Scruton's praise of the latter, Taylor points out that "the anonymous designers of this wall *cared* about the wall they designed" and " 'caring' is a moral concept." He concludes by stating that "to care like this for how something looks, and thereby for the people who will look at it, is to exhibit not just an aesthetic but also a moral concern. Or rather, it is to exhibit an aesthetic attentiveness which is itself moral."

These critiques of mainstream design, and architecture in particular, take issue with its status as producing an independent fine art object designed by an artist making his artistic statement that appeals predominantly to the visual sense. Instead, they call attention to the multi-sensory experience and bodily engagement that inevitably accompany our experiencing and appreciating designed objects and spaces. In the Western tradition, vision has been given a special privileged position among the senses because of its likeness to the intellect, particularly in terms of the necessary distance required between the subject and the object of experience and investigation. In addition, ours is a culture dominated by "visual information" which tends "to make sight dominant over the other sensory inputs to ears and nose," rendering "modern architecture ... a reflection of this limited palette of senses."[37] This over-reliance on visual experience tends to make us detached from the constructed space, alienating us from the space with which we should be fully engaged. Pallasmaa complains that "our detachment from experiential and sensory reality maroons us in theoretical, intellectual, and conceptual

---

[36] Taylor, pp. 201–2. The citations in the next three sentences are from pp. 230, 232, 205, and 205.

[37] Pearson, p. 68.

realms."[38] Papanek, quoting a Zen adept's teaching to "think with the whole body," also reminds us that our understanding of the world is facilitated by five senses, kinesthesia, thermal receptors, haptic muscular sensitivity, and intuition: "It is in the interaction of all our senses that we can begin to really see—to experience."[39] Hence, he claims that "seeing helps us to enjoy architecture, but only seeing can hinder us. We need to come to our senses again."

With built environment, this multi-sensory experience and bodily engagement are particularly crucial because only through such an experience can we sense its effect on our well-being, not only physical but also psychological. We need to take seriously the discomfort of sitting in an office without fresh air, natural lighting, or friendly sound, surrounded by sterile-looking walls and toxin-treated carpet, air-conditioning freezing us in the summer while heating system roasts us in the winter, isolated from co-workers. One might say that the feeling of discomfort or comfort is outside the realm of aesthetics, more like the purely bodily sensation of stomach ache after ingesting spoiled food or the feeling of pleasure when waking up from a good night's sleep. However, I contend that the feeling of comfort or discomfort does belong to the aesthetic realm insofar as it is a response to the sensuous qualities of the objects and environments. Granted the feeling is body-centered, generally with no intellectual deliberation and certainly not on the sophisticated and lofty level where we interact with works of art. This does not mean, however, that the bodily-oriented aesthetic experience is insignificant or unimportant. Instead, these experiences *are* extremely important as they are a barometer for our health and safety, ultimately determining the quality of life. David Pearson, for example, declares "the senses as guardians of our health," so that "the pleasant scent of the building and its materials is as important as their visual impact. Paints that smell unappetising cannot be good for you."[40] He therefore calls for "an architecture that 'honours the senses,'" which will be "comfortable, humanising and supportive," "healthy and healing," "caring for the environment," "nourishing to the human being"; in short, it is where we feel "at home."

---

[38] Pallasmaa, p. 24.

[39] By haptic muscular sensitivity Papanek means "visible and involuntary micro-muscular responses that psychologists have recorded when we watch sport or look at paintings," p. 76. The next citation is from p. 104.

[40] Pearson, p. 70. The rest of the citations in this paragraph are all from p. 70.

In addition to this practical significance of providing a healthy, comfortable environment, this wake-up call to a multi-sensory experience is also important for inducing sheer delight—smelling the fresh air and feeling breeze on our skin, hearing the sound of water rushing, splashing water and feeling its coolness. The NMB Bank building in Amsterdam is often praised as a model of green building that is sensitive not only to the environment but also to the workers' experience. Among many of its unique features constituting such sensitivity is the running water that flows in the groove of its stairway rail. It not only provides humidity and a soothing white sound for the workers but also is a source of fun and delight as workers play with it as they go up and down the stairs.[41] Such an architecture that respects and responds to environment and its users and dwellers, according to William McDonough and Michael Braungart, "celebrates a range of cultural and natural *pleasures*—sun, light, air, nature, even food—in order to enhance the lives of the people who work there."[42] In contrast, those structures which "degrade the ecological and cultural fabric of our lives, … *greatly diminish enjoyment and delight*." A delight facilitated by a particular design is not simply an icing on the cake; it makes us feel grateful for the gift of such an environment and entices us to take time and savor such an experience. There is a sense of fundamental civility and reciprocity at work when we take delight in those environments, and, I believe, such an exchange is one indispensable dimension of our moral life.

So, one insight of moral-aesthetic judgments of designed objects and environments has to do with the fact that our experience is always multi-sensory with bodily engagement, attention to which is neglected in our visually dominated tradition and culture. Excessive and exclusive reliance on disembodied visual experience alienates us from who we are: *body and mind*.[43] Those artifacts that restore our sensibility and are faithful to who we are, therefore, are objects of aesthetic appreciation because such a restoration

---

[41] See Pearson, p. 69 and Dorothy Mackenzie's *Green Design: Design for the Environment* (London: Lawrence King, 1997), pp. 56–9 for visual images and descriptions.

[42] William McDonough and Michael Braungart, *Cradle to Cradle: Rethinking the Way We Make Things* (New York: North Point Press, 2002), p. 9, emphasis added. The next passage is from p. 143, emphasis added.

[43] It is interesting to note that in the Western tradition this pair usually takes the form of "mind and body" as in the Cartesian "mind/body problem." In the Japanese Zen Buddhist term, it is always the other way around: "body and mind." This may indicate the contrasting emphasis between the two traditions.

is accomplished by their design features: materials used, color, shape, and size of the parts, the way in which the parts are arranged, and the way in which the object is designed to engage us on many levels and interact with our body movements, as well as with surrounding environment. They "honor," "respect," and are "sensitive" and "responsive" to our experiences.

In this regard, I find Galen Cranz's vision of "ideal workplace" fascinating.[44] Herself an architect but also a certified instructor of the Alexander Technique, she stresses the importance of attending to our "body" in designing. Hence, her ideal office not only addresses green concerns (natural lighting, toxin-free carpet, etc.) but is also responsive to bodily comfort (door lever rather than doorknob, built-in shelves and alcoves and different kinds of furniture that accommodate a lot of postural options, soft clothes worn by all workers that allow them different body positions with ease and comfort), as well as music of Mozart playing in the background which was found to be most conducive to reasoning and higher-order problem solving. By "honoring" the body, such an office design makes one "experience a sense of *being invited* to work here." Commenting on her own ideal workplace, Cranz considers it "promising that body-conscious design and ecologically sensitive design interlock so beautifully."[45]

4. Design sensitivity to the temporal dimension of experience

There is another way in which our experience is honored by designed spaces and objects: the consideration of its temporal nature. Experience of any object and environment "takes time," even though all artifacts are spatial entities. The temporal sequence in which our experience unfolds is particularly accentuated in our dealing with objects with which we interact in the most mundane and literal manner in everyday context, though we

[44] Galen Cranz, *The Chair: Rethinking Culture, Body, and Design* (New York: W. W. Norton, 1998), pp. 217–21. The citations at the end of this paragraph are from pp. 219 and 218. I thank Lefteris Pavlides for introducing me to Cranz's work.

[45] In a way, they are inseparable, because the ecologically sensitive design is not only good for the environment but also for humans and it is through our body that we can experience how healthy the environment is.

seldom pay attention to this dimension. We open a package by using scissors to cut one part and then pull the content out, we read a report starting from the top of page one in the right sequence, we push a sequence of buttons to do calculation on the calculator, we enter a building through an entrance and follow the direction through hallways and stairways to get to the doctor's office. In these all-too-familiar experiences, the spatial arrangements of parts affect, or sometimes dictate, the sequential order in which our experience proceeds. We sometimes appreciate spatial designs for being "thoughtful" and "considerate" if the temporal order of our experience facilitated by them makes sense or helps us accomplish the task with ease, comfort, and efficiency. Some other times, we appreciate those sequences in which experiences unfold that are accentuated by anticipation, surprise, or fulfillment of expectation, in comparison with other sequences characterized, for example, by repetition and monotony. Designing a spatial composition that is experientially satisfying requires not only a sophisticated aesthetic sensitivity and skills but also the ability to imagine how the experience unfolds for its user, recipient, or viewer. In other words, such a design process also engages the moral capacity of care and respect for other people. Let me illustrate this sensitivity to the temporal sequence of our experience by aspects of Japanese garden design, food serving, and packaging.

i. Japanese spatial design

The Japanese aesthetic tradition features many practices and phenomena that respond sensitively to the temporal sequence of experience, though it may not be apparent at first.[46] Consider first the stepping stones in a typical Japanese garden.[47] They are normally made up of rocks of varying

---

[46] By parading various practices from the Japanese tradition to illustrate this sensitivity, I am by no means claiming that this kind of sensitive design is unique to Japanese culture. It just so happens that the Japanese tradition is quite rich with objects and activities illustrative of this sensitivity.

[47] I want to point out that it is also indicative of Japanese sensibility that, when objects that do not usually receive aesthetic attention do receive it, it is often through bodily sensations. Stepping stones, for example, are experienced not only visually but through tactile sensations against our feet. Similarly, the aesthetic appreciation of *tatami* mats, the straw mats for the floor of traditional Japanese dwelling, cannot be separated from the tactile sensation against our feet (as we take our shoes off to enter into a Japanese house) or the *tatami*'s somewhat pungent smell. Also often overlooked is the sound emitted by what we step on. This ranges from practically no sound at all when we glide across *tatami* mats or thick carpet, to the squeaking sound of the so-called nightingale corridor in some old Japanese castles that originally meant to deter enemies' stealth invasion. Outside Japan, Papanek mentions, we are also

sizes, shapes, textures, and colors, arranged in an irregular manner, making our strolling at times awkward and inconvenient but most of the time providing fun similar to playing hopscotch. In addition to forcing us to slow down and savor each stone's texture, color, shape, and size, which we sense not only through our eyes but also with our soles, the irregular positioning of each stone controls both the direction and the speed with which we stroll through the garden.[48] By directing our feet "to changing vistas and fragrances," the stones "will send us on a meandering voyage across a reflecting pool forcing our aesthetic experience to be more astringent through our muscular control."[49] In addition, "our foot movements can be slowed down, speeded up, halted or turned in various directions. And with our legs, our eyes are manipulated, and our visual input from spatial phenomena is structured over time." Irregularly placed, meandering stepping stones provide different angles and distances from which to experience different parts of the garden, rendering our experience constantly varied, hence interesting.

The same consideration exists behind the design of bridges in Japanese gardens. Faithfully observing one of the two cardinal principles of Japanese garden-making, *suji kaete* (changing the axis), specified in the eleventh-century *Sakuteiki*,[50] bridges are often made with two planks or slates placed in a staggered manner so that we are made to pause in the middle, and turn slightly before continuing our crossing. These spatial configurations manipulate our experience as it unfolds in time, making it more sensuously stimulating than if we were to walk straight through without pausing or turning.

Another design strategy often used in Japanese gardens to accentuate the temporal order of our experience is the technique of *miegakure*, literally

familiar with "finished wooden flooring giv[ing] a different springiness to our steps," as it "reverberates quite differently from brick or concrete, and from carpeting, cobblestones, slate, quarry tile or bamboo matting." Papanek also points out that in indigenous homes in West Java and Thailand "walking on bamboo steps gives off sounds similar to those heard made by … a bamboo instrument, and this is not by accident but by design; the bamboo for the steps has been tuned carefully before being installed" (Papanek, p. 82).

[48] It is important to keep in mind that this spatial design that I am praising is specific to gardens. The same spatial design may be inappropriate, indeed inconsiderate and insensitive, for sidewalks or other purely utilitarian passageways because it makes our task inconvenient or sometimes dangerous or impossible, for example for people in wheelchairs or visually impaired people.

[49] Papanek, p. 83. The next passage is from p. 84.

[50] I discussed in Chapter III the other design principle specified there: "*kowan ni shitagau* (obeying the request)."

meaning "now you see it, now you don't," and sometimes referred to as "Zen view" by Western designers.[51] Japanese gardens are often constructed by intentionally blocking or partially obscuring a scenic view or a tea hut by dense planting, giving us only its hint and glimpse. Anticipation of being able to take in a full view excites us and invites us to proceed, and the final, usually sudden, encounter with the full vista is quite dramatic.

The aesthetic appreciation of sequentially unfolding experience in a Japanese garden is also achieved by a series of gates. Gates serve as markers between different spaces and they make us quite conscious of leaving one space and entering into the next space. The unfolding layer of spaces we go through marked by a series of gates is also ubiquitous in Japanese shrines and temples. It highlights and accentuates the procedural passageway into *oku*, translated as the innermost, the remote depth, or deep recess, invoking a sense of "unwrapping."[52] I can report from my firsthand experience of a number of Japanese gardens, shrines, and temples, that the choreography for our sequential experience made possible by spatial design is quite effective, sometimes even stunning.

ii. Japanese food serving

In the Japanese tradition, sensitivity to the temporal nature of our experience expressed by spatial arrangement is not limited to the built environment. It is a feature of food serving as well as packaging. I have already discussed both of them in Chapter III as embodying the moral attitude of respecting and submitting oneself to the dictate of the materials. This other-regarding attitude, in this case regarding other-than-human entities, such as wood, paper, and food ingredients, I pointed out, has a wider significance particularly as we pursue sustainable design practice. It also has a moral dimension of respecting the reality of the other than humans and not imposing one's agenda and design on them irrespective

---

[51] Donald A. Norman, *Emotional Design: Why We Love (or Hate) Everyday Things* (New York: Basic Books, 2004), pp. 109–10. He derives his discussion of "Zen view" from Christopher Alexander, et al, *A Pattern Language: Towns, Buildings, Construction* (New York: Oxford University Press, 1977), pp. 642–3.

[52] See Fumihiko Maki's "Japanese City Spaces and the Concept of *Oku*," *The Japan Architect* 265 (1979): 51–62 on the discussion of this concept. A good, general discussion and various examples for reaching *oku* can be found in Joy Hendry's *Wrapping Culture: Politeness, Presentation, and Power in Japan and Other Societies* (Oxford: Clarendon Press, 1993).

of their characteristics. Although the description by necessity becomes anthropomorphic, such as "obeying the request" of the rock or "listening to" pine trees, learning from the native characteristics of the materials and creating a design by accommodating, taking advantage of, and highlighting them, amounts to respecting the other, in this case, non-human entities.

Here, my concern is the respect for the other humans, that is, the experiencing agents of the designed objects and environments. Again, what we appreciate in Japanese cooking and packaging is the way in which the temporal dimension of our experience of eating or opening the package is fully considered and respected by the specific spatial configuration and arrangement. Japanese food serving is well known for its meticulous arrangement of various ingredients on a plate. From my personal experience of growing up in Japan, I can testify that such attention given to the arrangement is not only evident in restaurants but also in everyday meals at home. Food is never slopped onto a plate indiscriminately but often each ingredient is arranged one by one for maximum visual effect, as well as for complementary texture and taste. For example, in serving *nimono*, a Japanese version of vegetable stew, light brown bamboo shoots and gray taro roots, the black top of *shiitake* mushrooms, sometimes with ornamental star-shaped cuts exhibiting the white color inside, orange carrots, and green pea pods are carefully arranged to appeal to visual, tactile, and taste sensations. In addition to accentuating the innate characteristic of each material, such an arrangement invites us to dismantle it by chopsticks one ingredient at a time in the sequence determined by us. The order of eating has to be orchestrated not only with respect to one dish. A typical Japanese meal consists of several dishes, including a rice bowl, a soup bowl, a pickle plate, two or three other plates of vegetables, fish, and meat, all served at once. Hence, it is up to us to decide the order in which we eat food from various containers: one bite of rice followed by a slice of pickle, a bite of a carrot, then a sip of soup, back to rice, then to a bite of fish, and so on. Sometimes in a resort hotel or an upscale Japanese restaurant, dinner is served on one, sometimes two, individual tray table(s), holding so many dishes that we stare at them for a moment before deciding with which plate of food we begin our feast. Even when there is one container holding everything, as in a lunchbox, the Japanese version of fast food, so many ingredients are packed in with thoughtful arrangement that we also take time to survey the entire box and decide on the order of eating.[53]

The overall effect of such spatial arrangement is that it accentuates the temporal sequence of eating in our experience. An integral and important part of such an experience is the way in which we ourselves orchestrate the sequence by picking up one piece of food at a time with chopsticks. The activity of eating here is not just a matter of consumption, but also of making aesthetic choices concerning the best order for elucidating each ingredient's taste and texture. In this case, the sensibility of the cook is reflected in the careful spatial arrangement on the plate, which sets the stage for us to compose our own gustatory symphony. Such an experience would not be possible if the food were haphazardly mixed or heaped onto a plate. Graham Parkes aptly describes this aesthetic effect:

[M]ost of the meal is served at one time, rather than course by course as in the West. The advantage of this 'nonlinear' way of eating is a remarkably wide range of tastes, as one gradually works one's way through the various combinations of flavors afforded by a large number of small dishes laid out at the same time.[54]

"Drinking"[55] of Japanese soup intermittently during a meal, according to him, also has the following effect:

[T]hey are able not only to savor the progression of different tastes as it cools but also to orchestrate the combinations of these changing tastes with the flavors of the other dishes. The meal can then be appreciated as a multilayered process rather than a single linear event.

[53] The aesthetics of Japanese lunchbox and its implication for design in general are fully explored, accompanied by exquisite visual images, by Kenji Ekuan in *The Aesthetics of the Japanese Lunchbox* (Cambridge: The MIT Press, 2000). Equally informative in the visual sense is *Ekiben: The Art of the Japanese Box Lunch*, Junichi Kamekura, et al. (San Francisco: Chronicle Books, 1989), though in this book equal attention is given to the packaging.

[54] Graham Parkes, "Ways of Japanese Thinking," included in *Japanese Aesthetics and Culture: A Reader,* ed. Nancy G. Hume (Albany: SUNY Press, 1995), p. 80. The next passage is also from p. 80.

[55] Japanese soup is in general liquid with ingredients floating, served in a lacquer bowl, which we lift with our hand and "drink" the liquid portion directly from the bowl while using chopsticks to fish out the ingredients. This act lends itself to us feeling the warmth and liquid movement inside the bowl, as well as the sound of slurping that is not considered impolite but sometimes expected, as we eat noodle soup directly from a big bowl.

iii. Japanese package design

Japanese gift packaging is another example of sensitive design that is attuned to the bodily engagement and the temporal sequence of the recipient's experience.[56] Sometimes the maneuver needed for opening consists of one step: untying the cord made of straw for stringing together a row of fish, opening a bag of bamboo sheath wrapping sweets, peeling off bamboo wrapping from candies, or removing the lid of a can or a box for crackers.[57] However, quite often more than one step is needed for us to get to the content. When we receive a gift, sometimes it is wrapped in *furoshiki*, the traditional square-shaped carrying cloth, so the first thing is to untie its corners which will reveal a gift inside which itself is also housed in a box. To get at some candies, we first open a box and then untwist the thin paper that wraps individual candies. A nice piece of pottery is usually first wrapped in a cloth, then placed in a wooden box with the potter's signature in calligraphy on the lid, which is then tied by a cloth cord, requiring at least three steps for opening. Finally, when opening a ceremonial envelope containing money, we first have to remove the ornamental paper cord and then carefully open the envelope made with a particular fold, only to find another piece of paper that needs to be unfolded.

Of course there are other kinds of packages that we are familiar with, both here in the United States and in Japan today, such as plastic blister packaging covering everything from pens, scissors, and toothbrushes to batteries, phones, and CDs, that requires some time (and sometimes skill or sheer might!) for us to open, engaging our bodily movement.[58]

---

[56] I explored the aesthetics of Japanese packaging in "Japanese Aesthetics of Packaging," *The Journal of Aesthetics and Art Criticism*, 57:2 (Spring 1999), pp. 257–65. The examples discussed in this section are primarily, though not exclusively, gift packaging, not packaging for everyday items that we buy for ourselves, such as pens, toothpaste, noodles, coffees, and the like. However, Japan is a gift-giving culture. In addition to two annual gift-giving seasons, we give gifts for every conceivable occasion; hence, gift packaging does not occupy a special place in people's lives. Its frequency and prevalence make it almost an everyday occurrence for everyone alike.

[57] The discussion here is best accompanied by the visual images from Hideyuki Oka's *How to Wrap Five Eggs: Japanese Design in Traditional Packaging* (New York: Harper & Row, 1967) and *How to Wrap Five More Eggs: Traditional Japanese Packaging* (New York: Weatherhill, 1975), as well as *Package Design in Japan*, ed. Shigeru Uchida (Köln: Benedikt Taschen Verlag, 1989).

[58] I am not claiming that all the packaging for all kinds of objects should adopt the aesthetic sensibility expressed in Japanese gift packaging. For example, with gift packaging, we don't have to consider protection of content as much as if we were shipping many products long-distance, the primary concern for packaging most of the consumer goods. Furthermore, a downside of exquisite gift packaging in Japan is that it creates excess garbage. My parents, a typical middle-class family in Japan, for example,

However, most of the time we don't derive an aesthetic satisfaction from the experience of opening these packages; instead, it is usually an exercise in frustration. One difference between this experience and the experience of opening those Japanese gift packages is that the task required for the former can be rather taxing, as sometimes we wonder whether the thick plastic protecting its content is meant not only to be child-proof but also adult-proof as well. Furthermore, opening these packages sometimes requires tools, such as scissors and staple remover, whereas opening those Japanese gift packages does not require any tools: we untie, unfold, or peel off the packaging materials, requiring only gentle movements of our hands and inviting us to *take care* in opening. Finally, because force is often necessary for opening those blister packages, its aftermath is messy: packaging materials are torn and ripped apart. The end product of opening Japanese gift packages, in contrast, is itself aesthetically pleasing, because nothing is destroyed: a piece of paper or cloth now unfolded, a box with lid open, a cord untied, prompting us to save and savor them either for their own sake or for some other use. Though it is possible to destroy gift packaging materials just as we destroy the plastic bubble packaging, we spontaneously feel we should refrain from doing so. We are led to feel that the respectful sensitivity embodied in the beautiful packaging requires reciprocal respect and sensitivity on our part when opening.

The care and sensitivity evident in the design of Japanese packaging, aesthetically manifested, carries over to an unlikely dimension of everyday life: disposal of garbage. The Japanese manual for non-Japanese business people, for example, when discussing "aesthetics and perfectionism," notes that "when eating a mandarin orange, many Japanese will remove the peel in one, unbroken piece, and place segment membranes inside the outer peel, so that the leftover materials end up in a neatly wrapped little package."[59] I find the same sensibility and attitude behind this quite familiar practice in the way my parents stuff their garbage bags for pick-up. Because their municipality mandates that garbage bags be transparent, they

---

after receiving so many gifts and saving and reusing as many packaging materials as possible, run out of space to keep them and have no choice but to throw them away. Each time I go back, I ship them to the United States to use them as teaching tools, sometimes for discussing Japanese aesthetics and some other times for showing the unfortunate waste that is created, exacerbating the already-serious Japanese environmental problems.

[59] Yasutaka Sai, *The Eight Core Values of the Japanese Businessman: Toward an Understanding of Japanese Management* (New York: International Business Press, 1995), p. 56.

try to hide the unappetizing-looking content, such as food debris, by using innocuous-looking garbage, such as unrecyclable plastics and papers, as a buffer between the bag and the food debris. (In Japan, unlike in the United States, the garbage bags are placed in a designated community spot with no garbage cans.) In a sense, it is a wasted effort because garbage bags will soon be picked up, thrown into garbage trucks, and become out of (our) sight, but my parents' act is motivated by avoiding giving an unpleasant visual experience to the neighbors and passers-by even for a short period of time.[60]

5. Aesthetic expression of moral virtues

This Japanese practice of expressing one's sensitive, caring, and considerate attitude via the *sensuous appearance* of the artifacts and actions has a long tradition. It became a culturally established practice during the Heian court period (794–1185). Dubbed "cult of beauty" by Ivan Morris,[61] Heian aristocrats' lives revolved around communicating their moral worth *aesthetically*, through the sensitivity expressed in the composing and writing of poems, one's attire, and the *manner* surrounding love-making. It is not only the content of the poem that indicates a person's moral-aesthetic sensibility; it extends to the style of writing, choice of paper, and accompanying fragrance and attachment, such as a branch or a flower. Sei Shōnagon, a court lady writing in the tenth century, for example, describes a letter to a court lady from her suitor that "is attached to a spray of bush-clover, still damp with dew, and the paper gives off a delicious aroma of incense."[62] She

[60] This other-regarding sensitivity expressed in design is not free of criticism. In comparing Japanese and Western automobile designs, Hara admits that the former does invite a criticism that it lacks strong self-expression and manufacturers' passion because it is made to accommodate Japanese consumers' desires, rendering it warm, kind, and obedient. However, ultimately he is more critical of European and American design for being "egotistical" and "selfish" (Hara, pp. 133 and 134).

[61] Ivan Morris, *The World of the Shining Prince: Court Life in Ancient Japan* (New York: Kodansha International, 1994), ch. VII. Also see Donald Keene's "Feminine Sensibility in the Heian Era," included in Hume, pp. 109–23.

[62] Sei Shōnagon, *The Pillow Book of Sei Shōnagon*, tr. Ivan Morris (Harmondsworth: Penguin Books, 1981), p.62. The next two passages are both from p. 49. We appreciate the extent to which these aesthetic concerns permeated the aristocrats' daily life by the description of a fictional princess who rebelled against them. This "lady who admired vermin" in *Tsutsumi Chūnagon Monogatari* (*The Riverside Counselor's Stories*), written between the end of the Heian period and the beginning of the Kamakura period that marks the age of warriors, is depicted as breaking all the codes of proper behavior primarily

also contrasts a lover's elegant leave-taking with a clumsy one, criticizing the latter as "hateful." An "elegant" behavior has him taking time and lingering as he prepares to leave the lady, with wistful longing. "Once up, he does not instantly pull on his trousers. Instead he comes close to the lady and whispers whatever was left unsaid during the night. Even when he is dressed, he still lingers, vaguely pretending to be fastening his sash." In contrast, "charmless" and "hateful" behavior describes a man who makes a big commotion as he looks for things when getting dressed and hurriedly gets ready for the day; in short, concerned exclusively with what he has to do (get up, get dressed, and leave) with no regard to the lady's feelings. Sei Shōnagon thus declares that "one's attachment to a man depends largely on the elegance of his leave-taking."[63]

It is true that this predominantly aesthetic concern sometimes seems to have bordered on frivolous triviality, such as the color and fabric combination of a lady's many-layered kimono.[64] Morris also points out the class discrimination inherent in this cult of beauty, as "the ability to understand this type of aesthetic emotional experience … was … limited to the 'good people'," meaning those of noble birth, something that "no member of the provincial or working classes could hope to acquire."[65] Even with these problems in mind, however, I don't want to dismiss this moral-aesthetic sensibility as a mere historical curiosity, because the foundation of this moral-aesthetic sensibility is the other-regarding nature of aesthetic choices. Though many of these aesthetic choices have to do with courtship

based upon aesthetics. She uses "very stiff and coarse" paper on which she writes poems filled with imagery of "vermin and caterpillar fur" with *katakana* script that is more angular and reserved for male courtiers and monks rather than "the beautifully flowing *hiragana*," in addition to her attire and appearance that are opposite of what was considered to constitute feminine beauty at this time. See pp. 63–4 of Michele Marra's *The Aesthetics of Discontent: Politics and Reclusion in Medieval Japanese Literature* (Honolulu: University of Hawaii Press, 1991).

[63] During Heian period, female aristocrats are supposed to remain hidden inside their residence or inside a carriage allowing only a glimpse to the male suitors. This required the male suitor to gain entry into the lady's residence as well as her heart, through showing his aesthetic sensibility entrusted in poems. Even after the relationship began, they never lived together and the man had to commute to her place for the night of love-making. This makes the time of morning leave-taking another test of his moral-aesthetic sensibility. In a way, when it comes to love affairs and setting the aesthetic standard, women at this time had an upper hand.

[64] For this point, see p. 222 of Liza Crihfield Dalby's *Kimono: Fashioning Culture* (New Haven: Yale University Press, 1993), and pp. 194–5 of Morris. It is possible, however, that what may appear to us as frivolous concern could have been important the way in which we frown upon wearing flip-flops to the White House as a show of disrespect, as I discussed earlier.

[65] Morris, p. 197.

ritual which is guided by one's desire to win the prospective partner's heart, this ultimately self-regarding goal is achievable only through acting and making aesthetic choices with other-regarding attitude. This requires going outside one's ego-oriented world and putting oneself in the other's shoe by *imagining* what it would feel like to receive a letter written in a certain style infused with a certain incense or to see the lover leave with a certain manner after love-making. Such a capacity is an indispensable dimension of moral life. While we can dismiss the specifics of conventions (regarding which color combination of layers of kimono or writing style is in good taste) as historical curiosities, we cannot easily dismiss the underlying moral sensibility as a frivolous preoccupation of nobility with too much leisure time on their hands.

The communication of one's caring attitude through aesthetic means also underlies the art of tea ceremony, usually credited for setting the model for civilized behavior and rules of etiquette that are still alive and well in Japan today. The almost excessive fussiness involved in the host's preparation for the ceremony is not for its own sake, but is guided by the host's desire/obligation to please the guests. This fussy preparation includes not only the obvious, like preparing the snack and choosing the tea bowl, but also the less obvious. They include: the timing of refilling water in the stone basin and sprinkling water on plants in the garden, choosing implements and decorations to provide a cool feeling in the summer and warmth in winter, sometimes brushing off and some other times leaving snow accumulated on trees, rocks, and basins, depending upon the most amusing effect, and not wiping water drops off the kettle's surface to allow the appreciation of the way in which it gradually dries over the hearth.[66]

Decisions regarding these minute details are guided by imaginatively considering what would most please the guests and make them feel comfortable as well as entertained. Interpreting *Nanbōroku*, Sen no Rikyū's teaching recorded by his disciple, Nanbō Soseki, a contemporary commentator, Kumakura Isao, points out the frequent use of the term "*hataraki*," literally meaning function, and explains that this term refers to the function of the way in which the host's heart and intention get translated into some kind of

---

[66] These items were culled from remarks scattered throughout *Nanbōroku* in *Nanbōroku o Yomu (Reading Nanbōroku)*, ed. Kumakura Isao (Kyoto: Tankōsha, 1989).

sensuous manifestation in the form of his body movement, the manner of tea making, and objects' appearance.[67] Similarly, another Japanese philosopher, Hisamatsu Shin'ichi, comments on the original moral dimension of tea etiquette as follows:

Inherent in the way of tea is the morality that goes beyond everyday life. Thoughtfulness toward the guest is the foundation of tea manners, which realize this attitude in the formal manner. This heartfelt consideration is both profound and elevated in its moral dimension.[68]

As in Heian court sensibility, it is not important for us to consider here whether leaving accumulated snow on a lantern is or is not in good taste, capable of entertaining and amusing the guest. What *is* relevant for my purpose is the fact that the host's considerateness and caring attitude toward the guests is expressed through aesthetic means.

Furthermore, we should note that these moral-aesthetic dimensions in Japanese culture, whether historical or contemporary, require moral-aesthetic sensibility not only on the part of those who provide objects of appreciation but also for those who experience, receive, and appreciate them. The aesthetic experience of a tea ceremony is facilitated not only by the host's effort but also by the guest's grateful recognition and appreciation of the sensitivity and considerateness embodied in the object and act.

Similarly, as I remarked before, a beautifully and thoughtfully wrapped gift induces a respectful and careful manner of opening it. As the afore-mentioned manual for non-Japanese business people correctly points out, "if the situation makes it desirable for the receiver to unwrap the gift, he or she will do so carefully, keeping the wrapping paper in a hypothetically reusable condition before admiring the gift. This derives from a concern for appearance as well as *an expression of gratitude to the giver*."[69] In the same vein, a recent writing on the manner of eating a Japanese meal establishes the cardinal principle of etiquette: "the most important rule is to be grateful

---

[67] Kumakura, p. 242.

[68] Hisamatsu Shin'ichi, *Sadō no Tetsugaku* (*The Philosophy of the Way of Tea*) (Tokyo: Kōdansha, 1991), my translation, pp. 53–4, emphasis added. He means by "formal" sensuous, rather than the contrary of "informal" or "casual." Hisamatsu discusses how this original spirit of tea ceremony has become lost in recent years as practitioners busy themselves with observing the rules and forget the moral implications on everyday life that gave rise to the rules in the first place.

[69] Sai, p. 57, emphasis added.

to the cook's thoughtfulness and considerateness ... and to humbly receive the cook's sincere heart and savor the food," because "failure to do so would not only diminish the taste itself but also waste the thoughtfulness of the host."[70] Although the attitude of "thanks-giving" regarding food is hardly unique to the Japanese culture, in Japan this "thanks-giving" is not simply directed toward the nourishment provided by the prepared food, but also toward the sensuous dimension of our experience.

A person who rips apart a beautifully wrapped gift or gobbles up a Japanese lunch-box meal without savoring each ingredient is often judged not only deficient in aesthetic sense and manner but also lacking in moral sensibility. In this sense, thoughtful design, such as Japanese gift package and food presentation, functions as a vehicle of communication. Communication here, however, is not that of a certain idea, ideology, religious feeling, or the like, as maintained by the so-called expression or communication theory of art in Western aesthetics. It is rather moral virtues, such as thoughtfulness and considerateness, which are conveyed and acknowledged through specific design features. Communication is not possible if it is a one-way street. What is communicated must be appropriately received and appreciated by the users, guests, inhabitants, and recipients, and this requires them to be endowed with not only an aesthetic keenness but also a moral sensibility to gratefully acknowledge, and reciprocate, the considerateness and respect.

6. The significance of moral-aesthetic judgments in everyday life

In all these examples, the distinction between the aesthetic and the moral is blurred. Or, to put it in another way, the supposed distinction between the two realms can be seen as an artificial boundary imposed upon those concerns that are thoroughly integrated. A person's aesthetic sensibility, whether for providing or receiving an aesthetic experience, can be an important measure of his moral capacity. This illustrates again how the

---

[70] Shiotsuki Yaeko, *Washoku no Itadaki kata: Oishiku, Tanoshiku, Utsukushiku* (*How to Eat Japanese Meals: Deliciously, Enjoyably, and Beautifully*) (Tokyo: Shinchōsha, 1989), pp. 12 and 9. Though it is awkward in English, I provided the literal translation of the title.

aesthetic considerations in our lives are neither mere dispensable luxuries nor, to borrow the phrase from Yrjö Sepänmaa, "high cultural icing."[71] Neither are they confined to works of fine arts that tend to encourage or facilitate our disengagement from everyday life. Rather, they are often thoroughly entrenched in and integral to our profound, yet everyday, concerns, such as moral virtues.

Sensitive, responsible, and aesthetically pleasing design of the built environment and artifacts is thus not a matter of window-dressing. Promotion of and support for sensitively designed objects and environments is an indispensable ingredient of what Sepänmaa calls "aesthetic welfare."[72] He points out that true welfare states should guarantee not only "health care, education, and housing," but also "an experiential aspect of welfare. An aesthetic welfare state should offer a beautiful living environment and a rich cultural and art life," because they provide "the basic conditions of life." Such environments and artifacts provide an experientially verifiable indication that people's needs and experiences are taken seriously and responded to with care.

Consider a revised version of G. E. Moore's thought experiment and imagine two societies with identical political systems, economies, educational systems, and other social amenities.[73] They share equal degrees of individual rights, freedom, and social welfare. However, one society is full of thoughtfully, carefully, and sensitively designed environments and objects, facilitating easy living and fostering community spirit. The other one is full of the opposite kind of artifacts: thoughtlessly, carelessly, and insensitively designed environments and objects. Things fall apart easily and are difficult to use, with no thought given to the environment regarding their materials, manufacturing process, and their afterlife. The buildings are uncomfortable for work and living and there is no rhyme or reason for the relationship among them though they may individually look spectacular as gigantic pieces of sculpture. The

---

[71] Yrjö Sepänmaa, "Aesthetics in Practice: Prolegomenon," included in *Practical Aesthetics in Practice and in Theory*, ed. Martti Honkanen (Helsinki: University of Helsinki, 1995), p. 15.

[72] Ibid. The following passages are also all from p. 15.

[73] G. E. Moore's thought experiment is for us to imagine the most beautiful world and the ugliest world, neither of which will be experienced by any human beings. We are then asked: "is it irrational to hold that it is better that the beautiful world should exist, than the one which is ugly?" *Principia Ethica* (first published in 1903) (Cambridge: Cambridge University Press, 1993), p. 135. I thank Don Keefer for tracking down this example.

built environment in this society is not conducive to interaction among citizens.

We could add to this thought experiment John Rawls's idea of a "veil of ignorance," in the way in which Elaine Scarry does with her thought experiment regarding beauty.[74] My thought experiment asks one to situate oneself behind this "veil of ignorance" and decide which of the two societies we would prefer to inhabit. Since we are ignorant of our profession (architect, politician, housewife, capitalist entrepreneur?), our orientation (artistically inclined, pragmatically oriented, economically conservative, politically liberal?), and how the artifacts and environments affect our life, including financial situation, our choice of the society is assured to be objective and neutral.

I think most everyone would prefer the first society to the second, unless she is a person characterized by Marcia Eaton as someone who "leads a moral/unaesthetic life," so that she "may litter streets or deface buildings" and "destroy beautiful buildings only after taking care that there are no people in them."[75] Such a person "fails to see that a world with fewer beautiful buildings is less worth inhabiting"; hence, she may not have a strong reason to prefer the first society to the second. But I believe the majority of us do, and the reason for our preference for the first world is not simply a desire for prettier surroundings and better functioning artifacts. It goes farther than these immediate concerns; I think it goes to the core of what a good life and an ideal society should be like. It is one thing to be secured of our rights, freedom, equality, and welfare in the legal sense. However, in a good society we should also be able to *experience* the basis of such moral values reflected in the built environment and designed objects. Care, respect, sensitivity, considerateness regarding the other, whether human or non-human, have to be the moral foundation of a good society, as well as a good life. Surrounded by and being able to enjoy the ease, comfort, and aesthetic pleasure provided by artifacts induces a sense of belonging; such an environment tells us that our needs, interests, and experiences are considered important and worthy of attention. In turn, it encourages us to adopt the same attitude toward others not only in our direct interaction with them but also in our dealing with objects

---

[74] Elaine Scarry, *On Beauty and Being Just* (Princeton: Princeton University Press, 1999), pp. 118–24.
[75] Marcia Muelder Eaton, *Aesthetics and the Good Life* (Rutherford: Fairleigh Dickinson University Press, 1989), p. 179. The next passage is also from p. 179.

and surroundings. We are more inclined to take *care* in maintaining the public space in good condition, cleaning our house and yard, planting flowers, composing a reader-friendly document, and serving a meal that is not only nutritious and tasty but also reflective of thoughtfulness and mindfulness.

If surrounded by poorly and wantonly designed artifacts, in contrast, I may react in the following two different ways. First, I may be led to form an attitude that nobody pays attention to or cares about my experiences. I will be demoralized and feel that it does not make any difference if I remain indifferent and insensitive to others' experiences; I would say to myself: "Why bother? Nobody else seems to care."[76] This attitude is not conducive for developing moral sensitivity and civility. Or, alternatively, I may be spurred to become an activist for cleaning up the environment and promoting more humane environment and better artifacts. But if I react in this second way, it is because I feel that the creation of an aesthetically sound environment and artifacts is an important social agenda. What this means is that this moral-aesthetic demand is not only directed to the designers and makers of the world. We as users and dwellers of this world are not exempt from such a responsibility. Everyone's engagement in this on-going project of literal world-making, I believe, is as important as every citizen's political participation in a democratic society.

Aesthetic interests and concerns in our everyday life, therefore, are neither frivolous nor trivial. As Roger Scruton points out, "in so far as there is ... an aesthetics of everyday life, all men must to some extent engage in it, or, if they fail to do so, have a defective understanding of the world."[77] Marcia Eaton also makes a connection between the aesthetic and the moral by claiming that "it is one thing to fail to take the time to view sunsets, quite another to take the time and fail to respond. Surely there is something missing in the character and experience of a person who never delights in such things."[78] Ultimately, there is a "connection between being a person who has aesthetic experience and being a person who has *sympathies and insights of a kind required for successful social interaction*."

---

[76] This may happen if I live in a run-down neighborhood with no attempt at clean-up or beautification either by the residents themselves or by the municipality.

[77] Roger Scruton, *The Aesthetics of Architecture* (Princeton: Princeton University Press, 1979), pp. 239–40.

[78] Eaton, p. 165. The next passage is from p. 175, emphasis added.

Our everyday experience, which consists of our interacting not only with other people and natural elements but also with numerous artifacts, therefore, cannot but be affected by their quality. If I am right that there is a moral dimension to our experience with the sensuous surface of built environments and artifacts, our aesthetic life regarding everyday objects and phenomena has an important moral significance. While our aesthetic life has an independent sphere all on its own, it does not, nor should it, exist in complete isolation from other aspects of our life, the moral dimension in particular. As Eaton points out, "when aesthetic and moral values are both seen as part of a more general value, construed as the overall meaning of life, then we begin to see how complicated the linkages of the network are."[79] I believe that it goes to the core of what constitutes a good life. Aldo Leopold's criterion of what he calls "a special nobility inherent in the human race" is "a society decently respectful of its own and all other life, capable of inhabiting the earth without defiling it."[80] Leopold, of course, was primarily concerned with the issues of our dealings with nature, but his vision can and should be extended to apply to the issues of what we design, as it can enhance or thwart our collective effort to achieve this vision. Aesthetics, as Eaton declares, "is a matter of basics, not of frills," but the justification of aesthetics' crucial role in our life and society needs to be given by "its connection to our humanity."[81] In this chapter, I have tried to show how the way in which we design the world we inhabit determines the quality of life, both in the literal, physical sense and more importantly the moral sense.

[79] Eaton, p. 169.

[80] Aldo Leopold, "Some Fundamentals of Conservation in the Southwest,"(1923) included in *The Essential Aldo Leopold: Quotations and Commentaries*, eds. Curt Meine and Richard L. Knight (Madison: The University of Wisconsin Press, 1999), pp. 318–9.

[81] Eaton, p. 179.

Conclusion

It is not easy to come up with a conclusion to the preceding five chapters, as they constitute only a modest beginning of the investigation into everyday aesthetics. I did develop discussion on some specific issues, such as the aesthetics of the distinctive characteristics of an object, everyday aesthetic qualities such as clean and messy, the aesthetics of transience, and the aesthetic expression of moral virtues. However, these issues constitute only a small fraction of the rich treasure trove of everyday aesthetics. Furthermore, I expect that there will be disputes over my particular views on these issues. Thus, I characterize my preceding discussion as an initiation for further exploration rather than a definite theory of everyday aesthetics. One thing I do hope I have established, however, is the *importance* of embarking on a journey into the most mundane aspect of our aesthetic life which had been hidden in plain sight.

I argued that everyday aesthetics needs to be pursued for the following reasons. First, exploring everyday aesthetics remedies a deficiency in the mainstream art-based philosophical aesthetics by being truthful to the diverse dimensions of our aesthetic life, which is not confined to the artworld and other art-like objects and activities. Secondly, by analyzing various ways in which we interact with everyday objects and phenomena aesthetically, we can enrich the content of aesthetic discourse. Finally, even the seemingly trivial, insignificant everyday aesthetic attitudes and judgments often wield surprising power that can determine the quality of life, the state of the world, or social and cultural ethos in the most literal manner. For most of us, engagement with everyday objects and environments far exceeds interactions with art, both in frequency and in regularity, rendering the former's effect on every aspect of life immeasurable. As such, there is a pressing need to cultivate aesthetic literacy, so to speak, with respect to everyday objects and environments. By doing so, we can become more aware of how the power of the everyday aesthetic is instrumental in steering our actions and societies' policies in a certain direction, sometimes toward problematic ends such as environmental irresponsibility or dubious political agenda while other times toward positive goals such as the creation of humane and environmentally sound world for everyone. Everyday aesthetics, I firmly believe, has to be a part of the strategies for the project of world-making, to which all of us in some way participate, both personally and professionally, sometimes quite consciously and some other times unwittingly.

In my preceding discussion of some specific issues in everyday aesthetics, I detect a recurrent theme. What emerged from my brief exploration of them can be characterized as a kind of tension between two different directions toward which everyday aesthetics is pulled, giving rise to a series of further issues to be developed rather than a set of definite conclusions. One could say that it is a tension between the descriptive function of everyday aesthetics and its normative function. In what follows I will give four examples of such tension between the descriptive and the prescriptive in everyday aesthetics discourse.

First, a part of the mission of everyday aesthetics is to follow the guide suggested by the traditional aesthetic theory regarding aesthetic attitude and disinterestedness. Since our everyday mode of experiencing things with which we interact daily is primarily practical, there is an impetus in everyday aesthetics to free us from that perspective and adopt an aesthetic (qua non-practical) perspective. We are encouraged to suspend our usual reaction in the everyday mode, such as appreciating a utensil purely for its functionality or deploring a dirty linen that prompts us to clean it. By bracketing those objects from typical everyday concerns and by closely attending to their sensuous surfaces, we can discover hidden gems: the way in which the stain on the linen appears, an interesting shadow cast by a broken window, or a pattern created by mold growing on a piece of bread. There are many aesthetic gems hidden in our everyday life, but we do not notice, let alone appreciate, most of them because we usually do not engage with them as aesthetic objects. Here we appreciate the help provided by photographs, literature, and other visual arts for revealing, highlighting, and illuminating those aesthetic treasures. Such is one way everyday aesthetics functions normatively.

However, as I argued in Chapters I and IV, everyday aesthetics also pulls us in the opposite direction, away from this recommended aesthetic mode back to the ordinary mode. The above way of experiencing the aesthetic gems hidden in everyday life is to render the ordinary extraordinary. While there is no denying that we gain aesthetic enrichment by adopting such an approach, we also lose something of the everyday life's everyday-ness or ordinary-ness. Since the first recommended approach is fairly familiar to those of us versed in aesthetic attitude theories, I put a particular emphasis on this second approach that is more descriptive. Everyday aesthetics, I argued, should not be exclusively concerned with discounting ordinary and seemingly pragmatically directed reactions that often result in various actions, such as cleaning, throwing away, purchasing, and preserving, while promoting positive aesthetic experiences from unlikely objects and phenomena from our daily life. I hope to have shown in the preceding discussion that this first kind of reactions are actually not that simple; nor are they insignificant because of possible consequences that affect the quality of life and the state of the world.

Certainly there are some normative claims that I have made with respect to our familiar, mundane aesthetic reactions, such as those that have environmental ramifications, existential values regarding the signs of aging, and designed objects reflective of moral virtues. However, perhaps the most challenging aspect of everyday aesthetics is to negotiate between the direction toward the normative mode of aestheticization facilitated by de-contextualizing the experience and the direction toward grounding our aesthetic reaction in the everyday practical concerns. That is, I believe that one of the projects of everyday aesthetics is to discern when we should render the ordinary extraordinary so that we can derive the maximum aesthetic value and when we should rather preserve and focus on the ordinary, seemingly non-aesthetic, reaction. Indiscriminate aestheticization can lead us far from our aesthetic life in its very everyday life context, making it more art-like experience, when extricating everyday aesthetics from art-like experience is one of its *raisons d'être* in the first place.

Another way in which this tension is played out is the judgments on a person's character, personality, and competence based upon her outward appearance and the appearance of her possessions. Here, on the one hand, one can make a case that it is wrong to judge a book by its cover; hence, the aesthetic judgment on a person's and her possessions' appearances should be kept separate from other assessments we make of her, such as her personality and moral character. For example, her sloppy appearance and her house in disarray may not necessarily indicate that she is incompetent as an office worker or that she is irresponsible. We resist falling prey to a stereotype based upon appearance. On the other hand, many of us try our utmost to present ourselves as being responsible, morally upright, considerate, neighborly, competent, and so on, not only by our actions but also by tending to our personal grooming, choosing appropriate attire, and taking care of our property and possessions. If not for the purpose of aestheticizing, then for the purpose of keeping an open mind and avoiding preconceived ideas and downright prejudice, there is a pull toward suspending aesthetic concerns as they tend to influence our non-aesthetic judgments of a person. However, pushing too far into this direction will lead one to a rather awkward, and ultimately equally problematic, position that would prohibit us from ever forming a judgment of a prospective employee or a neighbor based upon the way in which he and his possessions appear. Although not judging a person by his cover is a wise cautionary reminder, it would be strange for everyday aesthetics to discredit this all-too-familiar "judgment by cover" experience. This common experience should be taken as is and should be subjected to *its* own analysis, including the cautionary warning.

Another issue that illustrates a possible tension within everyday aesthetics regards what I called the power of the aesthetic. I hope to have demonstrated how people's aesthetic reaction to something importantly affects their attitude and action toward it. If the reaction is positive, there is an effort toward protection, preservation, and promotion; if negative, the movement is toward indifference, neglect, change, abandonment, or rejection. Sometimes there is a conscious appropriation of this power of the aesthetic to serve a specific social, political agenda. I myself recommended such a strategy by arguing for developing green aesthetics. However, particularly in light of various historical precedents, this strategy needs to negotiate between two poles: aestheticizing certain objects and phenomena and at the same time being mindful of the agenda it is meant to serve.

In this regard, I was fascinated with the way in which landscape and nature contribute to the formation of cultural and national identity, as illustrated by the nineteenth-century American landscape aesthetics and the appropriation of the aesthetics of falling cherry blossoms in pre-war Japan. I also mentioned Nazi Germany's project of creating an environment that is worthy of the Aryan race by promoting native plants and eradicating non-native species. Built environments and cultural artifacts, while providing equally potent symbols of national and cultural identity, can be more easily destroyed than landscape, as the famous line from a well-known poem by the eighth-century Chinese poet, Tu Fu, states: "The empire is shattered but rivers and peaks remain. Spring drowns the city in wild grass and trees."[1] People's attachment to, affection for, and pride in their native landscape and its vegetation and non-human inhabitants are inseparable from their aesthetic appeal, and such an attitude provides a powerful motivation for protecting them, particularly when national identity is at stake. That is, such sentiment may have been always present but a threat from outside or a self-imposed pressure forces its articulation and promotion.

Let me illustrate this by the post-Westernization and pre-war Japanese landscape aesthetics, which parallels the aesthetics of cherry blossoms from the same period that I discussed in Chapter IV. When the sudden and rapid process of Westernization began during the latter part of the nineteenth century, Japan had to overcome a sense of inferiority complex caused by perceiving almost everything Western to be superior. In its own assessment, Japan could not compete against the West in terms of technology, political ideology, legal system, military might, and academic accomplishments. This negative self-assessment led Japan to an intense project to define and celebrate its own culture unadulterated by anything foreign, and it was found in nature and art, thought to be the only truly native endowments in which Japan could take pride. The turn of the century produced now classic works on Japanese arts and aesthetics primarily for the benefit of English-speaking audience, such as *Bushidō* (1899), *The Ideals of the East* (1904), and *The Book of Tea* (1907), all first published in English. However, within Japan, one of the most popular and influential works was *Nihon Fūkeiron* (*Theory of Japanese Landscape*), written by Shiga Shigetaka and published in 1894, the year of the Sino-Japanese war. It enjoyed tremendous popularity, going through fourteen printings within eight years, and, in the estimate of one historian, was " 'one of the most widely read books among students' in the latter half of the Meiji period."[2] In addition to being a dedicated mountaineer and a scholarly geologist, Shiga was also a member of an ultra-nationalist group, and this popular book

---

[1] *The Anchor Book of Chinese Poetry*, eds. Tony Barnstone and Chou Ping (New York: Anchor Books, 2005), p.133.

[2] Kenneth B. Pyle, *The New Generation in Meiji Japan: Problems of Cultural Identity, 1885–1895* (Stanford: Stanford University Press, 1969), p. 161.

served not only as a guide for landscape aesthetics, but also as a part of the "campaign to promote national pride and unity."[3] A curious mixture of Western aesthetic categories of beauty, sublimity, and picturesqueness as well as comparison with Western landscapes, Shiga's essay argues for the presumed uniqueness and aesthetic superiority of Japanese landscapes, which include both memorable scenic sights worthy of tourist destinations and everyday environments. The latter consists of mundane environments, such as "a nightscape of a fishing village where fishermen are pulling in a net with captured salmon, their movement accentuated by a tune sung with a tinge of a dialect" and "a group of girls picking mountain azalea flowers to adorn their hair outside of a temple."[4] With the claim that these landscapes are something unique to Japan and aesthetically superior to the rest of the world, Shiga's landscape aesthetics provided a fuel for subsequent nationalism, contributing to the people's resolve to protect them from foreign power.

It is widely acknowledged that arts, such as music, film, and literature, have played an indispensable role in promoting not only cultural but also political nationalism, in Japan and elsewhere. Here the power of the aesthetic is recognized and, hence, utilized. This power of the arts and the strategy to take advantage of it through promotion or suppression was first articulated by Plato. What is often overlooked is the role landscape and nature play in this regard. To be sure, some landscapes that fuel nationalistic sentiment may not be from everyday environment but rather from remote tourist attractions. However, they also include the quotidian, including the aforementioned landscapes Shiga cites and ubiquitous cherry blossoms in the case of Japan. Or, for Germany it may be forests, in particular oak trees.[5]

---

[3] Kenneth B. Pyle, p. 160. It is noteworthy that other noted works on Japanese landscape came out during wartime, *Nihon Sansui ron* (*Theory of Japanese Mountains and Waters*) by Kojima Usui, who was heavily influenced by Shiga's work, was published in 1904 during the Russo-Japanese War. Uehara Keiji's *Nihon Fūkeibi ron* (*Theory of Japanese Scenic Beauty*) was published in 1943 during World War II. Corollary to the praise for Japanese landscape to promote nationalistic fervor was the concerted effort to determine the Japanese people's national characteristics. Among various traits, the aesthetic sensibility, in particular their "love of nature," was considered to be the most distinguishing and praiseworthy national characteristic. For a critical analysis of this aspect of the nationalistic agenda, see Karatani Kōjin's "Uses of Aesthetics: After Orientalism," included in *Edward Said and the Work of the Critic: Speaking Truth to Power*, ed. Paul A. Bove (Durham: Duke University Press, 2000) and "Japan as Museum: Okakura Tenshin and Ernest Fenollosa," tr. Sabu Kosho, included in *Japanese Art after 1945: Scream against the Sky*, ed. Alexandra Munroe (New York: Harry N. Abram, Inc., 1994).

[4] Shiga Shigetaka, *Nihon Fūkeiron* (Tokyo: Iwanami Shoten, 1976), pp. 29 and 31. My translation.

[5] I thank my student Kate Copeland for her research paper on this subject.

Thus, it behooves everyday aesthetics to analyze the perceived aesthetic value of those landscapes and people's attachment to them.

Nationalistic political agenda today may appear too remote from our daily experience of close-to-home environment. For example, contemporary Japan is vastly different from the pre-war Japan of the early 1900s. So, a Japanese resident's experience of cherry blossoms in a nearby park in the twenty-first century may not have any association with the nationalistic pride once associated. Or the nineteenth-century America's need to define the distinctive and superior feature of American landscapes, resulting in the notion of wilderness, may no longer be a relevant issue today. If anything, people are becoming more aware of the problematic consequences of the notion of wilderness thus developed, as I sketched in Chapter II. However, this seemingly dated nature of this issue does not mean that similar issues do not exist today, if not on a national level, then on more local scale. I discussed briefly how the aesthetics surrounding the distinctive features of an object can raise issues regarding "the sense of place." Just as the affection for national landscapes fuels people's protective attitude toward them, local communities' attachment to certain features of their environment, both natural and cultural, leads to protective actions, policies, and the like. However, various issues emerge. Can there be one uniform "sense of place" particularly in today's multicultural societies? Is one kind of sense of place formulated by the racially/economically/ethnically dominant class to be favored over different senses of place held by minority groups? To what extent should the unified sense of place, if there is one, be protected and preserved and to what extent should it be allowed or encouraged to evolve? What is the threshold of integrating changes and evolution into the sense of place before completely destroying it? What is the role that people's topophilia should play in the planning practice? From my recent conversation with a long-time planner, human factors such as a sense of place and affections regarding place are largely ignored or neglected in the planning practice, with some negative consequences. If so, how can everyday aesthetics regarding a familiar environment contribute to improving the process? If these questions are important, they underscore one of my theses that the aesthetic in our lives do have power over other aspects of our lives and, as such, deserve attention and careful analysis.

The final example of the tension existing within everyday aesthetics is the relationship between everyday aesthetics and works of art that aim to emulate, appropriate, or incorporate everyday life. In Chapter I, by reviewing environmental art, the Japanese tea ceremony, and recent art works that either reproduce a slice of everyday life in an art museum or are situated in everyday environment, I pointed out the inherent difficulty of art to transcend the framework of art. In Chapter IV, by examining visual art objects, such as photography and painting that capture a slice of everyday aesthetic phenomena such as peeling paint and stain on a tablecloth, I also argued how our experience of such representation of everyday objects and phenomena inevitably differ from the way in which we experience them in their everyday context. However, is overcoming the boundary between art and non-art impossible? Is it possible to resolve the tension between recent art's aspiration to emulate life and art's inescapable placement within the artworld?

At the time of my completing this manuscript, a student of mine informed me of an interesting installation art piece by a performance artist, Mark McGowan, entitled "The Running Tap" (2005).[6] Over a sink already in existence in a gallery in London, he had a running faucet with two handwritten signs, one indicating the title and the artist and the other stating: "If you find this tap off, please would you turn it on and leave it on. Thanks." Its aim was to raise people's consciousness about wasting water; however, ironically it was shut down a month later following the threat of a legal action by Thames Water for the literal waste of water. Apart from a controversy regarding whether it is justified to call attention to water waste by literally wasting water, this piece also pushes the boundary between art and real life. What if the piece had an opposite content with a faucet turned off with a sign reading: "If you find this tap on, please would you turn it off and leave it off"? One can easily imagine this scenario taking place at a number of real (hence, non-art) bathrooms and kitchens. As in the case of Rirkrit Tiravanija's reproduction of cooking and eating within a museum space, McGowan's piece challenges the viewers as to whether the art object also resides in real life so that the viewers have to engage in real life concerns regarding water waste and what they should do to help (in his piece, exacerbate it). It may be that the viewers' feeling of disorientation (by trying to

---

[6] I thank Roger Wei for this example and the following reference. The description and critique of this piece can be found in "Running on empty," *The Guardian*, 7 July 2005.

figure out the boundary between art and life) ends up overwhelming the environmental consciousness-raising message that the artist is trying to convey. Whether or not this is a successful piece, it reiterates the inherent tension within this kind of genre. On the one hand, the desired effect is premised upon the disorienting appropriation of real life situation. On the other hand, the desired effect also demands that it be made distinct from mere slice of life that is all-too-common and familiar. Without some kind of fanfare that it is a work of art rather than a janitor's note, the message remains an isolated, singular plea with respect to the particular faucet, and it does not carry a general environmental message, nor does it stand out in the viewers' experience. But by framing this particular faucet as a part of a work of art, its status gets divorced from the ordinary and mundane, and it then becomes questionable whether our reaction to this special art-faucet can be transferred automatically to not-so-special ordinary faucets.

Is art then forever stuck within the inescapable boundary set by the artworld? I think this is going to be a serious challenge to those artists who are working to break down this barrier. One possible direction such art can take may be to renounce its art-hood in the traditional sense and simply present the message, idea, and the like in the best design possible, so that it fulfills the aesthetic, educational, and practical mission within people's everyday life. For example, if McGowan's piece is supposed to raise awareness of water waste and to motivate people to conserve water, such an aim could be accomplished without creating "a work of art" by "an artist" in the conventional sense. For example, it could take the form of a well-designed signage system to urge people to think of water waste and turn off the faucet, conveying the message not simply through the text (as most ordinary notices and signs do) but also from its design (possibly accompanied by some visual images or even sounds and tactile surfaces) and placement. Such a signage system can be made flexible to suit any contexts. If McGowan's piece and Tiravanija's piece are partly motivated by urging people to be mindful of their everyday activities, like turning off the faucet and eating food, it can be accomplished, I believe, by considerate and sensitive design of the objects, environments, and activities that I discussed in Chapter V. By framing it as a work of art, thus inevitably displacing it from the everyday context *even if* it incorporates or is situated in the everyday, while it may succeed in illuminating the slice of everyday, it may also detract from its everydayness. Attributing art status on an object and activity puts too much focus on this fact and compromises the message relevant to everyday life that the artist aims to convey through the work. Presenting good design to accomplish the same task may be the demise of the role of an artist in the traditional sense. However, it seems to me that the artist in the conventional sense announcing himself/herself *as an artist* and presenting a slice of everyday life *as a work of art* does seem to pose an unbridgeable gap between art and life.

By presenting these examples of tension that I detected in discussing everyday aesthetics, it is my intention to reinforce the complex nature of everyday aesthetics, as well as its status as a wellspring of further exploration. It is my hope that what I have provided in this book opens a door to a further adventure into the most ordinary, mundane part of our life while warning against prematurely closing a book on this familiar, but unexplored, territory.

Bibliography

Abrahamson, Eric, and David H. Freeman. *A Perfect Mess: The Hidden Benefits of Disorder (How Crammed Closets, Cluttered Offices, and On-The Fly Planning Make the World a Better Place)*. New York: Little Brown and Company, 2007.

Ackerman, Diane. *A Natural History of the Senses*. New York: Vintage Books, 1991.

Addison, Joseph. "Pleasures of the Imagination." In *Essays in Criticism and Literary Theory*, ed. John Loftis, 138–82. Northbrook: AHM Publishing, 1975.

Alexander, Christopher, et al. *A Pattern Language: Towns, Buildings, Construction*. New York: Oxford University Press, 1977.

Alison, Archibald. *Essays on the Nature and Principles of Taste*. Dublin, 1790.

——— *Essays on the Nature and Principles of Taste*. 2nd edn. Hartford: George Goodwin & Sons, 1821.

——— *Essays on the Nature and Principles of Taste*. In *What is Art?: Aesthetic Theory from Plato to Tolstoy*, ed. Alexander Sesonske, 182–95. New York: Oxford University Press, 1965.

Andre, Judith, and David James. *Rethinking College Athletics*. Philadelphia: Temple University Press, 1991.

Andrews, Malcolm. *The Search for the Picturesque: Landscape Aesthetics and Tourism in Britain, 1760–1800*. Stanford: Stanford University Press, 1989.

Aristotle. *Poetics*. In *Philosophies of Art and Beauty*, eds. Albert Hofstadter and Richard Kuhns. New York: The Modern Library, 1964.

Ashihara, Yoshinobu. *Zoku Machinami no Bigaku*. Tokyo: Iwanami Shoten, 1995.

Attfield, Judy. *Wild Things: The Material Culture of Everyday Life*. Oxford: Berg, 2000.

Baarschers, William H. *Eco-Facts & Eco-Fiction: Understanding the Environmental Debate*. London: Routledge, 1996.

Barnstone, Tony, and Chou Ping, eds. *The Anchor Book of Chinese Poetry*. New York: Anchor Books, 2005.

Barrell, John. *The Dark Side of the Landscape: The Rural Poor in English Painting 1730–1840*. Cambridge: Cambridge University Press, 1989.

Beardsley, John. *Earthworks and Beyond: Contemporary Art in the Landscape*. New York: Abbeville Press, 1989.

——— "Eyesore or Art? On Tyree Guyton's Heidelberg Project." *Harvard Design Magazine* (Winter/Spring, 1999): 5–9.

Beardsley, Monroe. *Aesthetics: Problems in the Philosophy of Criticism*. Indianapolis: Hackett Publishing Company, 1981.

Berleant, Arnold. *The Aesthetics of Environment*. Philadelphia: Temple University Press, 1992.

——— *Living in the Landscape: Toward an Aesthetics of Environment*. Lawrence: The University Press of Kansas, 1997.

Bermingham, Ann. *Landscape and Ideology: The English Rustic Tradition, 1740–1860*. Berkeley: University of California Press, 1989.

Best, David. "The Aesthetic in Sport." In *Philosophic Inquiry in Sport*, eds. William J. Morgan and Klaus V. Meier, 477–93. Champaign: Human Kinetics Publishers, 1988.

Borges, Jorge Luis. "Pierre Menard, Author of the *Quixote*." In *Labyrinths*, eds. Donald A. Yates and James E. Irby. New York: New Directions Books, 1964.

Brady, Emily. "Imagination and the Aesthetic Appreciation of Nature." In *The Aesthetics of Natural Environments*, eds. Allen Carlson and Arnold Berleant, 156–69. Peterborough: Broadview Press, 2004.

Brewer, Richard. *Conservancy: The Land Trust Movement in America*. Hanover: University Press of New England, 2003.

Brittan, Gordon, Jr. "The Wind in One's Sails: A Philosophy." In *Wind Power in View: Energy Landscapes in a Crowded World*, eds. Martin J. Pasqualetti, Paul Gipe, and Robert W. Righter, 59–79. San Diego: Academic Press, 2002.

Bullough, Edward. " 'Psychical Distance' as a Factor in Art and an Aesthetic Principle." *The British Journal of Psychology* 5 (1912–13): 87–118.

Burke, Edmund. *A Philosophical Enquiry into the Origin of Our Ideas of the Sublime and Beautiful*. Oxford: Oxford University Press, 1990.

Burnaby, Andrew. *Travels through the Middle Settlements in North America, in the Years 1759 and 1760*. London, 1798.

Carlson, Allen. *Aesthetics and the Environment: The Appreciation of Nature, Art and Architecture*. London: Routledge, 2000.

——— "On Aesthetically Appreciating Human Environments." *Philosophy & Geography* 4.1 (2001): 9–24.

——— "On the Aesthetic Appreciation of Japanese Gardens." *British Journal of Aesthetics* 37.1 (1997): 47–56.

——— and Arnold Berleant, eds. *The Aesthetics of Natural Environments*. Peterborough: Broadview Press, 2004.

Carroll, Noël. "Aesthetic Experience: A Question of Content." In *Contemporary Debates in Aesthetics and the Philosophy of Art*, ed. Matthew Kieran, 69–97. Malden: Blackwell Publishing, 2006.

———*Beyond Aesthetics: Philosophical Essays.* Cambridge: Cambridge University Press, 2001.

Cole, Thomas. "Essays on American Scenery." In *The American Landscape: A Critical Anthology of Prose and Poetry*, ed. John Conron, 568–78. New York: Oxford University Press, 1974.

Coote, Jeremy. " 'Marvels of Everyday Vision': The Anthropology of Aesthetics and the Cattle-Keeping Nilotes." In *Anthropology, Art, and Aesthetics*, eds. Jeremy Coote and Anthony Shelton, 245–74. Oxford: Clarendon Press, 1992.

Cranz, Galen. *The Chair: Rethinking Culture, Body, and Design.* New York: W. W. Norton, 1998.

Cronon, William. "The Trouble with Wilderness; or, Getting Back to the Wrong Nature." In *Uncommon Ground: Rethinking the Human Place in Nature*, ed. William Cronon, 69–90. New York: W. W. Norton, 1996.

Cwerner, Saulo B., and Alan Metcalfe. "Storage and Clutter: Discourses and Practices of Order in the Domestic World." *Journal of Design History* 16.3 (2003): 229–39.

Dalby, Liza Crihfield. *Kimono: Fashioning Culture.* New Haven: Yale University Press, 1993.

Daniels, Inge Maria. "The 'Untidy' Japanese House." In *Home Possessions: Material Culture Behind Closed Doors*, ed. Daniel Miller, 201–30. Oxford: Berg, 2001.

Danto, Arthur. *The Abuse of Beauty: Aesthetics and the Concept of Art.* Chicago: Open Court, 2004.

Dazai, Shundai. *Hitorigoto.* In *Nihon Zuihitsu Taisei*, Vol. 17, 259–88. Tokyo: Yoshikawa Kōbunkan, 1975.

Dean, Andrea Oppenheimer. *Rural Studio: Samuel Mockbee and an Architecture of Decency.* New York: Princeton Architectural Press, 2002.

——— and Timothy Hursley. *Proceed and Be Bold: Rural Studio After Samuel Mockbee.* New York: Princeton Architectural Press, 2005.

Dekkers, Midas. *The Way of All Flesh: The Romance of Ruins.* Translated by Sherry Marx-Macdonald. New York: Farrar, Straus, and Giroux, 2000.

Delacroix, Eugene. *The Journal of Eugene Delacroix.* Translated by Walter Pach. New York: Penguin Group Incorporated, 1972.

Dewey, John. *Art as Experience.* New York: Capricon Press, 1958.

Digha Nikaya. *Thus Have I Heard: The Long Discourses of the Buddha: Digha Nikaya.* Translated by Maurice Walshe. In *Voices of Wisdom: A Multicultural Philosophy Reader*, ed. Gary E. Kessler. Belmont: Wadsworth, 2004.

"Do Some Damage to Your Denim." *Cosmopolitan*, July 2005.

Dōgen. *Shōbōgenzō: The Eye and Treasury of the True Law.* Translated by Kōsen Nishiyama. Tokyo: Nakayama Shobō, 1986.

Dōgen. *Shōbōgenzō: Zen Essays by Dōgen.* Translated by Thomas Cleary. Honolulu: University of Hawaii Press, 1986.

Douglas, Mary. *Purity and Danger: An Analysis of Concept of Pollution and Taboo.* London: Routledge, 2002.

Ducasse, Curt. *Art, the Critics and You.* New York: Oskar Piest, 1944.

Duerksen, Christopher J., and R. Matthew Goebel. *Aesthetics, Community Character, and the Law.* Chicago: American Planning Association, 1999.

Duffy, Joseph. *Eco Design: Environmentally Sound Packaging and Graphic Design.* Rockport, MA: Rockport Publishers, 1995.

Duncum, Paul. "A Case for an Art Education of Everyday Aesthetic Experiences." *Studies in Art Education* 40.4 (1999): 295–311.

Eaton, Marcia Muelder. *Aesthetics and the Good Life.* Rutherford: Farleigh Dickinson University Press, 1989.

—— "The Beauty that Requires Health." In *Placing Nature: Culture and Landscape Ecology*, ed. Joan Iverson Nassauer, 87–106. Washington, D. C.: Island Press, 1997.

—— *Merit, Aesthetic and Ethical.* Oxford: Oxford University Press, 2001.

Ekuan, Kenji. *The Aesthetics of the Japanese Lunchbox.* Translated by Don Kenny. Cambridge: The MIT Press, 2000.

Evernden, Neil. "Beauty and Nothingness: Prairie as Failed Resources." *Landscape* 27.3 (1983): 1–8.

—— *The Social Creation of Nature.* Baltimore: The Johns Hopkins University Press, 1992.

Fein, Albert. *Frederick Law Olmsted and the American Environmental Tradition.* New York: George Braziller, 1973.

Foster, Cheryl. "Aesthetic Disillusionment: Environment, Ethics, Art." *Environmental Values* 1 (1992): 205–15.

Gilpin, William. *Three Essays.* London, 1792.

Gobster, Paul H. "An Ecological Aesthetic for Forest Landscape Management." *Landscape Journal* 18.1 (1999): 54–64.

Godfrey, Anne. "Commercial Photography and the Understanding of Place." *Landscape Architecture* 96.4 (2006): 34–44.

Goldsworthy, Andy. *A Collaboration with Nature.* New York: Harry N. Abrams, 1990.

Gould, Stephen Jay. "The Golden Rule—A Proper Scale for Our Environmental Crisis." In *Environmental Ethics: Divergence and Convergence*, eds. Susan J. Armstrong and Richard G. Botzler, 310–15. New York: McGraw Hill, 1993.

Grande, John. *Art Nature Dialogues: Interviews with Environmental Artists.* Albany: SUNY Press, 2004.

Graves, Jane. "Clutter." *Issues in Architecture Art and Design* 5.2 (1998): 63–9.

Groening, Gert, and Joachim Wolschke-Bulmahn. "Some Notes on the Mania for Native Plants in Germany." *Landscape Journal* 11.2 (1992): 116–26.

Guha, Ramachandra. "Radical Environmentalism and Wilderness Preservation: A Third World Critique." In *Environmental Ethics: Divergence and Convergence*, eds. Susan J. Armstrong and Richard G. Botzler, 552–61. New York: McGraw Hill, 1993.

Gundaker, Grey. "African-American History, Cosmology, and the Moral University of Edward Houston's Yard." *Journal of Garden History* 14.3 (1994): 179–205.

Guy, Simon, and Graham Farmer. "Contested Construction: The Competing Logics of Green Buildings and Ethics." In *Ethics and the Built Environment*, ed. Warwick Fox, 73–87. London: Routledge, 2000.

Haapala, Arto. "On the Aesthetics of the Everyday: Familiarity, Strangeness, and the Meaning of Place." In *The Aesthetics of Everyday Life*, eds. Andrew Light and Jonathan M. Smith, 39–55. New York: Columbia University Press, 2005.

Haga, Kōshirō. "The *Wabi* Aesthetic Through the Ages." Translated by Martin Collcutt. In *Tea in Japan: Essays on the History of* Chanoyu, eds. Paul Varley and Kumakura Isao, 195–230. Honolulu: University of Hawaii Press, 1989.

"Hair to the Chief!" *Time*, 19 July 2004, 20.

Hale, Sarah. *Traits of American Life*. Philadelphia: E. L. Carey & A. Hart, 1835.

Hammitzsch, Horst. *Zen in the Art of the Tea Ceremony*. Translated by Peter Lemesurier. New York: E. P. Dutton, 1988.

Hara, Kenya. *Dezain no Dezain*. Tokyo: Iwanami Shoten, 2003.

Harris, Daniel. *Cute, Quaint, Hungry and Romantic: The Aesthetics of Consumerism*. Cambridge: Da Capo Press, 2000.

Harrod, Tanya. *The Crafts in Britain in the 20th Century*. New Haven: Yale University Press, 1999.

Hawken, Paul. *The Ecology of Commerce: The Declaration of Sustainability*. New York: HarperBusiness, 1994.

——, Amory Lovins, and L. Hunter Lovins. *Natural Capitalism: Creating the Next Industrial Revolution*. Boston: Little, Brown and Company, 1999.

Hawthorne, Christopher. "The Case for a Green Aesthetic." *Metropolis* (October 2001): 112–25.

Helman, Andrew C. "E. Greenwich is Fighting Graffiti with Art." *Providence Journal*, 3 August 2003.

Hendry, Joy. *Wrapping Culture: Politeness, Presentation, and Power in Japan and Other Societies*. Oxford: Clarendon Press, 1993.

Hepburn, Ronald. "Contemporary Aesthetics and the Neglect of Natural Beauty." In *Wonder and Other Essays: Eight Studies in Aesthetics and Neighboring Fields*, 9–35. Edinburgh: The University Press at Edinburgh, 1984.

—— "Trivial and Serious in Aesthetic Appreciation of Nature." In *Landscape, Natural Beauty, and the Arts*, eds. Salim Kemal and Ivan Gaskell, 65–80. Cambridge: Cambridge University Press, 1993.

Hesse, Hermann. "On Little Joys." Translated by Denver Lindley. In *My Belief: Essays on Life and Art*. New York: Farrar, Straus, and Giroux, 1974.

Higgins, Kathleen M., ed. *Aesthetics in Perspective*. Fort Worth: Harcourt Brace & Company, 1996.

Hisamatsu, Shin'ichi. *Sadō no Tetsugaku*. Tokyo: Kōdansha, 1991.

Hogarth, William. *The Analysis of Beauty*. In *A Documentary History of Art*, ed. Elizabeth G. Holt, 261–72. New York: Doubleday Anchor Books, 1958.

Humble, P. N. "Chess as an Art Form." *The British Journal of Aesthetics* 33.1 (1993): 59–66.

Huth, Hans. *Nature and the American*. Lincoln: University of Nebraska Press, 1972.

Iida, Yumiko. *Rethinking Identity in Modern Japan: Nationalism as Aesthetics*. London: Routledge, 2002.

Italie, Hillel. "When Authors Rewrite Themselves, It Sparks Debate." *Providence Journal*, 31 July 2003.

"It's Style over Substance: Appearing Presidential is the Goal." *Providence Journal*, 15 July 2004.

Izutsu, Toshihiko, and Toyo Izutsu. *The Theory of Beauty in the Classical Aesthetics of Japan*. The Hague: Martinus Nijhoff Publishers, 1981.

Jackson, Wes. "Nature as the Measure for a Sustainable Agriculture." In *Environmental Ethics: Concepts, Policy, Theory*, ed. Joseph DesJardins, 354–61. Mountain View: Mayfield Publishing Company, 1999.

James, William. *Talks to Teachers*. New York: Henry Holt and Company, 1915.

"Japanese WWII Soldier Found in Ukraine." *Providence Journal*, 19 April 2006.

Jetzer, Jean-Noël, ed. *Supermarket*. Zürich: Migros Museum für Gegenwartskunst, 1998.

"Junk: Eyesores Evicted from Local Properties." *Barrington Times*, 20 July 2005.

Kamekura, Junichi, et al. *Ekiben: The Art of Japanese Box Lunch*. San Francisco: Chronicle Books, 1989.

Kant, Immanuel. *Critique of Judgement*. Translated by J. H. Bernard. New York: Hafner Press, 1974.

Karatani, Kōjin. "Japan as Museum: Okakura Tenshin and Ernest Fenollosa." Translated by Sabu Kosho. In *Japanese Art after 1945: Scream against the Sky*, ed. Alexandra Munroe, 33–40. New York: Harry N. Abrams, 1994.

―――― "Uses of Aesthetics: After Orientalism." In *Edward Said and the Work of the Critic: Speaking Truth to Power*, ed. Paul A. Bove, 139–51. Durham: Duke University Press, 2000.

Kastner, Jeffrey, and Brian Wallis. *Land and Environmental Art*. London: Phaidon Press, 1998.

Katō, Mutsuo, et al. *Nihon no Tennen Kinenbutsu*. Tokyo: Kōdansha, 1995.

Keene, Donald, ed. *Anthology of Japanese Literature*. New York: Grove Press, 1960.

Kellert, Stephen R. *The Value of Life: Biological Diversity and Human Society*. Washington, D. C.: Island Press, 1996.

Kempton, Willet, James S. Boster, and Jennifer A. Hartley. *Environmental Values in American Culture*. Cambridge: The MIT Press, 1995.

Knecht, Barbara. " 'Special Needs' and Housing Design: Myths/Realities/ Opportunities." In *Design and Feminism: Re-Visioning Spaces, Places, and Everyday Things*, ed. Joan Rothschild, 99–108. New Brunswick: Rutgers University Press, 1999.

Knight, Richard Payne. *An Analytical Inquiry into the Principles of Taste*. In *The Genius of the Place: The English Landscape Garden 1620–1820*, eds. John Dixon Hunt and Peter Willis, 348–50. Cambridge: The MIT Press, 1990.

―――― "The Landscape, A Didactic Poem." In *The Genius of the Place: The English Landscape Garden 1620–1820*, eds. John Dixon Hunt and Peter Willis, 342–8. Cambridge: The MIT Press, 1990.

Korsmeyer, Carolyn. *Making Sense of Taste: Food and Philosophy*. Ithaca: Cornell University Press, 1999.

Kuehn, Glenn. "How Can Food Be Art?" In *The Aesthetics of Everyday Life*, eds. Andrew Light and Jonathan M. Smith, 194–212. New York: Columbia University Press, 2005.

Kumakura, Isao. *Nanbōroku o Yomu*. Kyoto: Tankōsha, 1989.

Kupfer, Joseph H. "Sport—The Body Electric." In *The Philosophic Inquiry in Sport*, eds. William J. Morgan and Klaus V. Meier, 455–75. Champaign: Human Kinetics Publishers, 1988.

Lambourne, Lionel. *Utopian Craftsmen: The Arts and Crafts Movement from the Cotswolds to Chicago*. Salt Lake City: Peregrine Smith, 1980.

Larsen, Jack Lenor. "The Inspiration of Japanese Design." In *Traditional Japanese Design: Five Tastes*, ed. Michael Dunn. New York: Japan Society, 2001.

Lawrence, Robyn Griggs. *The Wabi-Sabi House: The Japanese Art of Imperfect Beauty*. New York: Clarkson Potter, 2004.

Leddy, Thomas. "Everyday Surface Aesthetic Qualities: 'Neat,' 'Messy,' 'Clean,' 'Dirty'." *The Journal of Aesthetics and Art Criticism* 53.3 (1995): 259–68.

―――― "Sparkle and Shine." *British Journal of Aesthetics* 37.3 (1997): 259–73.

Lee, O-Young. "The Ultimate Chic that Accommodates All Sizes and Shapes."
    Koreana 12.3 (1998): 5–7.

Leonhardt, Gay. "An Eye for Peeling Paint." *Landscape* 28.2 (1985): 23–5.

Leopold, Aldo. *A Sand County Almanac.* New York: Ballantine Books, 1966.

——— "Some Fundamentals of Conservation in the Southwest." In *the Essential Aldo
    Leopold: Quotations and Commentaries*, eds. Curt Meine and Richard L. Knight,
    318–19. Madison: The University of Wisconsin Press, 1999.

Lerner, Steve. *Eco-Pioneers: Practical Visionaries Solving Today's Environmental Prob-
    lems.* Cambridge: The MIT Press, 1998.

Lewis, Peirce F. "Axioms for Reading the Landscape." In *The Interpretation of
    Ordinary Landscapes*, ed. D. W. Meinig, 11–32. New York: Oxford University
    Press, 1979.

Light, Andrew. "Urban Ecological Citizenship." *Journal of Social Philosophy* 34.1
    (2003): 44–63.

Lippard, Lucy. *The Lure of the Local: Senses of Place in a Multicultural Society.* New
    York: The New Press, 1997.

Lloyd, Ann Wilson. "David Nash." *Sculpture* (Sept.–Oct., 1992): 22–3.

Lowenthal, David. *The Past Is a Foreign Country.* Cambridge: Cambridge University
    Press, 1990.

Lyle, John Tillman. "Landscape: Source of Life or Liability." In *Reshaping the
    Built Environment*, ed. Charles J. Kibert, 151–75. Washington, D. C.: Island
    Press, 1999.

Lynes, Russell. "Kudos for Clutter." *Architectural Digest* 41.3 (1985): 34–8.

McCloud, S. *Understanding Comics: The Invisible Art.* New York: Harper Perenni-
    al, 1993.

McCullough, Helen Craig, tr. *Genji & Heike: Selections from The Tale of Genji and
    The Tale of Heike.* Stanford: Stanford University Press, 1994.

McDonough, William, and Michael Braungart. *Cradle to Cradle: Remaking the Way
    We Make Things.* New York: North Point Press, 2002.

——— "The Next Industrial Revolution." *The Atlantic Monthly* 282.4 (1998): 82–6.

McHarg, Ian. "An Ecological Method for Landscape Architecture." In *To Heal
    the Earth: Selected Writings of Ian L. McHarg*, eds. Ian L. McHarg and Fredrick
    R. Steiner, 212–18. Washington, D. C.: Island Press, 1998.

Mackenzie, Dorothy. *Green Design: Design for the Environment.* London: Lawrence
    King, 1997.

Maki, Fumihiko. "Japanese City Spaces and the Concept of *Oku*." *The Japan
    Architect* 265 (1979): 51–62.

Markels, Alex. "The Greening of America: Environmental Impact of Golf Cours-
    es." *Audubon* 100.4 (1998): 42–9.

Marra, Michele. *The Aesthetics of Discontent: Politics and Reclusion in Medieval Japanese Literature*. Honolulu: University of Hawaii Press, 1991.

Marshall, Lisa. "House not Perfect? Maybe It's Just Wabi-Sabi." *Providence Journal*, 26 June 2005.

Martin, Lois. "*Patina* of Cloth." *Surface Design Journal* 28.4 (2004): 16–21.

Matilsky, Barbara C. *Fragile Ecologies: Contemporary Artists' Interpretations and Solutions*. New York: Rizzoli, 1992.

Maxwell, Robert. *Sweet Disorder and the Carefully Careless: Theory and Criticism in Architecture*. New York: Princeton Architectural Press, 1993.

Meinig, D. W. "Environmental Appreciation: Localities as a Humane Art." *Western Humanities Reviews* 25.1 (1971): 1–11.

Melchionne, Kevin. "Living in Glass Houses: Domesticity, Interior Decoration, and Environmental Aesthetics." *The Journal of Aesthetics and Art Criticism* 56.2 (1998): 191–200.

Minami, Hiroshi. *Psychology of the Japanese People*. Translated by Albert R. Ikoma. Toronto: University of Toronto Press, 1971.

Mishima, Yukio. *The Temple of the Golden Pavilion*. Translated by Ivan Morris. New York: Knopf, 1959.

Moore, G. E. *Principia Ethica*. Cambridge: Cambridge University Press, 1993.

Morgan, William J., and Klaus V. Meier, eds. *The Philosophic Inquiry in Sport*. Champaign: Human Kinetics Publishers, 1988.

Morris, Ivan. *The World of the Shining Prince: Court Life in Ancient Japan*. New York: Kodansha International, 1994.

Morris, William. "Textiles." In *Arts and Crafts Essays*. Bristol: Thoemmes Press, 1996.

Mozingo, Louise A. "The Aesthetics of Ecological Design: Seeing Science as Culture." *Landscape Journal* 16.1 (1997): 46–59.

Muir, John. "A Wind-storm in the Forests." In *The American Landscape: A Critical Anthology of Prose and Poetry*, ed. John Conron, 264–70. New York: Oxford University Press, 1974.

Murasaki, Shikibu. *A Wreath of Cloud: Being the Third Part of 'The Tale of Genji.'* Translated by Arthur Waley. Boston: Houghton Mifflin Company, 1927.

Nash, Roderick. *The Rights of Nature: A History of Environmental Ethics*. Madison: The University of Wisconsin Press, 1989.

Nassauer, Joan Iverson. "Messy Ecosystems, Orderly Frames." *Landscape Journal* 14.2 (1995): 161–70.

—— "Cultural Sustainability: Aligning Aesthetics with Ecology." In *Placing Nature: Culture and Landscape Ecology*, ed. Joan Iverson Nassauer, 67–83. Washington D.C.: Island Press, 1997.

Natsume, Sōseki. *The Three Cornered World*. Translated by Alan Turney. Chicago: Henry Regnery Co., 1967.

Nature and Nature: Andy Goldsworthy. Dir. C. Guichard. Vidocassette. Peasmarsh: The Roland Collection, 1991.

Naylor, Gillian. *The Arts and Crafts Movement: A Study of its Sources, Ideals and Influence on Design Theory*. Cambridge: The MIT Press, 1971.

Nicolson, Marjorie Hope. *Mountain Gloom, and Mountain Glory: The Development of the Aesthetics of the Infinite*. New York: W. W. Norton, 1963.

Norman, Donald A. *The Design of Everyday Things*. New York: Doubleday, 1990.

———— *Emotional Design: Why We Love (or Hate) Everyday Things*. New York: Basic Books, 2004.

Novitz, David. *The Boundaries of Art*. Philadelphia: Temple University Press, 1992.

Oakes, Baile, ed. *Sculpting with the Environment: A Natural Dialogue*. New York: Van Nostrand Reinhold, 1995.

Ōhashi, Ryōsuke. "Kire and Iki." Translated by Graham Parkes. In *Encyclopedia of Aesthetics*, ed. Michael Kelly, Vol. 2: 553–5. New York: Oxford University Press, 1998.

Ohnuki-Tierney, Emiko. *Kamikaze, Cherry Blossoms, and Nationalisms: The Militarization of Aesthetics in Japanese History*. Chicago: The University of Chicago Press, 2002.

Oka, Hideyuki. *How to Wrap Five Eggs: Japanese Design in Traditional Packaging*. New York: Harper & Row, 1967.

———— *How to Wrap Five More Eggs: Traditional Japanese Packaging*. New York: Weatherhill, 1975.

Olwig, Kenneth. "Reinventing Common Nature: Yosemite and Mount Rushmore—A Meandering Tale of a Double Nature." In *Uncommon Ground: Rethinking the Human Place in Nature,* ed. William Cronon, 379–408. New York: W. W. Norton & Company, 1996.

Orr, David. *The Nature of Design: Ecology, Culture, and Human Intention*. Oxford: Oxford University Press, 2002.

Pallasmaa, Juhani. "Toward an Architecture of Humility." *Harvard Design Magazine* (Winter/Spring, 1999): 22–5.

Papanek, Victor. *Design for the Real World: Human Ecology and Social Change*. Chicago: Academy Chicago Publishers, 1992.

———— *The Green Imperative: Natural Design for the Real World*. New York: Thames & Hudson, 1995.

Parkes, Graham. "Ways of Japanese Thinking." In *Japanese Aesthetics and Culture: A Reader*, ed. Nancy G. Hume, 77–108. Albany, SUNY Press, 1995.

Pasqualetti, Martin J. "Living with Wind Power in a Hostile Landscape." In *Wind Power in View: Energy Landscapes in a Crowded World*, eds. Martin J. Pasqualetti, Paul Gipe, and Robert W. Righter, 153–72. San Diego: Academic Press, 2002.

Paulson, Ronald. *The Beautiful, Novel, and Strange: Aesthetics and Heterodoxy.* Baltimore: The Johns Hopkins University Press, 1996.

Pearson, David. "Making Sense of Architecture." *Architectural Review* 1136 (1991): 68–70.

"Photographer Says His Life Has Changed since 9/11." *Providence Journal.* 11 September 2002.

Pincus, Leslie. *Authenticating Culture in Imperial Japan: Kuki Shūzō and the Rise of National Aesthetics.* Berkeley: University of California Press, 1996.

Pope, Alexander. "An Epistle to Lord Burlington." In *The Genius of the Place: The English Landscape Garden 1620–1820*, eds. John Dixon Hunt and Peter Willis, 211–14. Cambridge: The MIT Press, 1990.

Porter, Roy. *English Society in the Eighteenth Century.* London: Penguin Books, 1990.

Postrel, Virginia. *The Substance of Style: How the Rise of Aesthetic Value is Remaking Commerce, Culture, and Consciousness.* New York: HarperCollins Publishers, 2003.

Price, Uvedale. *An Essay on the Picturesque.* In *The Genius of the Place: The English Landscape Garden 1620–1820*, eds. John Dixon Hunt and Peter Willis, 351–7. Cambridge: The MIT Press, 1990.

Prose, Francine. "A Dirty Tablecloth, Deconstructed." *ARTnews* 98.9 (1999): 126–7.

Pyle, Kenneth B. *The New Generation in Meiji Japan: Problems of Cultural Identity, 1885–1895.* Stanford: Stanford University Press, 1969.

Quinet, Marienne L. "Food as Art: The Problem of Function." *The British Journal of Aesthetics* 21.2 (1981): 159–71.

Rader, Melvin, and Bertram Jessup. *Art and Human Values.* Englewood Cliffs: Prentice-Hall, 1976.

Reid, Thomas. *Essays on the Intellectual Power of Man.* In *Philosophical Works.* Hildesheim: George Olms Verlagsbuchhandlung, 1967.

Relph, Ted. "To See with the Soul of the Eye." *Landscape* 23.1 (1979): 28–34.

Repton, Humphry. *Fragments on the Theory and Practice of Landscape Gardening.* London: J. Taylor, 1816.

Reynolds, Joshua. *Idler* 82 (10 Nov. 1759).

―――― *The Discourses of Sir Joshua Reynolds.* London: J. Carpenter, 1842.

Righter, Robert W. "Exoskeletal Outer-Space Creations." In *Wind Power in View: Energy Landscapes in a Crowded World*, eds. Martin J. Pasqualetti, Paul Gipe, and Robert W. Righter, 19–41. San Diego: Academic Press, 2002.

Righter, Robert W. *Wind Energy in America: A History.* Norman: University of Oklahoma Press, 1996.

Rolston, Holmes, III. *Environmental Ethics: Duties to and Values in the Natural World.* Philadelphia: Temple University Press, 1988.

"Running on Empty." *The Guardian,* 7 July 2005.

Runte, Alfred. *National Parks: The American Experience.* Lincoln: University of Nebraska Press, 1987.

—— *Yosemite: The Embattled Wilderness.* Lincoln: University of Nebraska Press, 1990.

Ruskin, John. *Modern Painters.* London, n.d.

Ryu, M. "Lee Hyung-man: Even More Beautiful with the Passage of Time." *Koreana: Korean Art and Culture* 18.3 (2004): 44–9.

Sai, Yasutaka. *The Eight Core Values of the Japanese Businessman: Toward an Understanding of Japanese Management.* New York: International Business Press, 1995.

Saito, Yuriko. "The Aesthetics of Unscenic Nature." *The Journal of Aesthetics and Art Criticism* 56.2 (1998): 101–11.

—— "Appreciating Nature on Its Own Terms." *Environmental Ethics* 20.2 (1998): 135–49.

—— "Ecological Design: Promises and Challenges." *Environmental Ethics* 24.3 (2002): 243–61.

—— "Environmental Directions for Aesthetics and the Arts." In *Environment and the Arts: Perspectives on Environmental Aesthetics,* ed. Arnold Berleant, 171–85. Hants: Ashgate, 2002.

—— "The Japanese Aesthetics of Imperfection and Insufficiency." *The Journal of Aesthetics and Art Criticism* 55.4 (1997): 377–85.

—— "Japanese Aesthetics of Packaging." *The Journal of Aesthetics and Art Criticism* 57.2 (1999): 257–65.

—— "Japanese Gardens: The Art of Improving Nature." *Chanoyu Quarterly* 83 (1996): 40–61.

—— "Machines in the Ocean." *Contemporary Aesthetics* 2 (2004): <http://www.contempaesthetics.org>.

—— "Response to Jon Boone's Critique." *Contemporary Aesthetics* 3 (2005): <http://www.contempaesthetics.org>.

—— "Scenic National Landscapes: Common Themes in Japan and the United States." *Essays in Philosophy* 3.1 (2002): <http://www.humboldt.edu/~essays>.

Sakaguchi, Ango. "Zoku Darakuron." In *Shōwa Bungaku Zenshū,* Vol. 12, 245–50. Tokyo: Shōgakukan, 1987.

Sartre, Jean-Paul. *Nausea.* Translated by Lloyd Alexander. New York: New Directions, 1969.

Sartwell, Crispen. *Six Names of Beauty*. New York: Routledge, 2004.

Satō, Kenji. *Fūkei no Seisan, Fūkei no Kaihō: Media no Arukeorogī*. Tokyo: Kōdansha, 1994.

Scarry, Elaine. *On Beauty and Being Just*. Princeton: Princeton University Press, 1999.

Schama, Simon. *Landscape and Memory*. London: HarperCollins, 1995.

Schor, Juliet B. "Cleaning the Closet: Toward a New Fashion Ethic." In *Sustainable Planet: Solutions for the Twenty-first Century*, eds. Juliet B. Schor and Betsy Taylor, 45–60. Boston: Beacon Press, 2002.

Scruton, Roger. *The Aesthetics of Architecture*. Princeton: Princeton University Press, 1979.

Sei Shōnagon. *Makura no Sōshi*. Tokyo: Kadokawa Shoten, 1980.

_____ *The Pillow Book of Sei Shōnagon*. Translated and edited by Ivan Morris. New York: Columbia University Press, 1967.

Semal, Mariel. "Tsutsumu: Nihon no Hōsō Geijutsu." In *Tsutsumu: Nihon no Dentō Pakkēji*, ed. Oka Hideyuki and Fujita Takashi. Kyoto: Tankōsha, 1995.

Sepänmaa, Yrjö. "Aesthetics in Practice: Prolegomenon." In *Practical Aesthetics in Practice and in Theory*, ed. Marti Honkanen, 13–17. Helsinki: University of Helsinki, 1995.

_____ "The Two Aesthetic Cultures: The Great Analogy of an Art and the Environment." In *Environment and the Arts: Perspectives on Environmental Aesthetics*, ed. Arnold Berleant, 39–46. Hants: Ashgate, 2002.

_____ "The Utilization of Environmental Aesthetics." In *Real World Design: The Foundation and Practice of Environmental Aesthetics*, ed. Yrjö Sepänmaa, 7–10. Helsinki: University of Helsinki, 1995.

Shaftesbury, Anthony Ashley Cooper, Third Earl of. *Characteristics: The Moralists*. In *Philosophies of Art and Beauty*, eds. Albert Hofstadter and Richard Kuhns, 241–66. New York: The Modern Library, 1964.

Shiga, Shigetaka. *Niohn Fūkeiron*. Tokyo: Iwanami Shoten, 1976.

Shiner, Larry. *The Invention of Art: A Cultural History*. Chicago: The University of Chicago Press, 2001.

Shiotsuki, Yaeko. *Washoku no Itadaki kata: Oishiku, Tanoshiku, Utsukushiku*. Tokyo: Shinchōsha, 1989.

Shiva, Vandana. *Monocultures of the Mind: Perspectives on Biodiversity and Biotechnology*. London: Zed Books, 1997.

Spaid, Sue. *Ecovention: Current Art to Transform Ecologies*. Cincinnati: The Contemporary Arts Center, 2002.

Sparke, Penny. *As Long as It's Pink: The Sexual Politics in Taste*. New York: HarperCollins, 1995.

Spelman, Elizabeth. *Repair: The Impulse to Restore in a Fragile World*. Boston: Beacon Press, 2002.

Stabb, Jo Ann. "Transformations: Trash to Art." *Surface Design Journal* 26.2 (2002): 14–19.

Stolnitz, Jerome. "The Aesthetic Attitude." In *Introductory Readings in Aesthetics*, ed. John Hospers, 17–27. New York: The Free Press, 1969.

―――"On the Origins of 'Aesthetic Disinterestedness'." In *Aesthetics: A Critical Anthology*, eds. George Dickie and R. J. Sclafani, 607–25. New York: St. Martin's Press, 1977.

Strelow, Heike, ed. *Ecological Aesthetics Art in Environmental Design: Theory and Practice*. Basel: Birkhäuser, 2004.

Stuller, Jay. "Golf Looks beyond the 'Augusta National Syndrome'." *Smithonian* 28.1 (1997): 56–67.

Swaffield, Simon, ed. *Theory in Landscape Architecture: A Reader*. Philadelphia: University of Pennsylvania Press, 2002.

Tachibana-no-Toshitsuna. *Sakuteiki: The Book of Garden-Making, Being a Full Translation of the Japanese Eleventh Century Manuscript: Memoranda on Garden Making Attributed to the Writing of Tachibana-no-Toshitsuna*. Translated by S. Shimoyama. Tokyo: Town & City Planners, 1985.

Tanizaki, Jun'ichirō. *In Praise of Shadows*. Translated by Thomas J. Harper and Edward G. Seidensticker. New Haven: Leete's Island Books, 1977.

Taylor, Nigel. "Ethical Arguments about the Aesthetics of Architecture." In *Ethics and the Built Environment*, ed. Warwick Fox, 193–206. London: Routledge, 2000.

Thayer, Robert L., Jr. *Gray World, Green Heart: Technology, Nature, and the Sustainable Landscape*. New York: John Wiley & Sons, 1994.

―――"Pragmatism in Paradise: Technology and the American Landscape." *Landscape* 30. 3 (1990): 1–11.

"They Like it Clean in Minneapolis." *Providence Journal*, 24 July 2005.

Thomas, Keith. *Man and the Natural World: A History of the Modern Sensibility*. New York: Pantheon Books, 1983.

Thoreau, Henry David. "Walking." In *Environmental Ethics: Divergence and Convergence*, eds. Susan J. Armstrong and Richard G. Botzler, 108–18. New York: McGraw-Hill, 1993.

Time, 11 August 1997.

Treib, Marc. "The Dichotomies of Dwelling: Edo/Tokyo." In *Tokyo: Form and Spirit*, ed. Mildred Friedman, 107–25. Minneapolis: Walker Art Center, 1986.

Tsubaki, Chinzan. *Chinzan Shokan*. In *Nihon no Geijutsuron*, ed. Yasuda Ayao, 251. Tokyo: Sōgensha, 1990.

Tuan, Yi-Fu. *Passing Strange and Wonderful: Aesthetics, Nature, and Culture.* Washington, D. C.: Island Press, 1993.

—— *Topophilia: A Study of Environmental Perception, Attitudes, and Values.* Englewood Cliffs: Prentice-Hall, 1974.

—— "Yi-Fu Tuan's Good Life." *On Wisconsin* 9 (1987).

Uchida, Shigeru, ed. *Package Design in Japan.* Köln: Benedikt Taschen Verlag, 1989.

Ueda, Makoto. *Literary and Art Theories in Japan.* Cleveland: The Press of Case Western Reserve University, 1967.

——, tr. and comp. *Bashō and His Interpreters: Selected Hokku with Commentary.* Stanford: Stanford University Press, 1991.

Van der Ryn, Sim, and Stuart Cowan. *Ecological Design.* Washington, D. C.: Island Press, 1996.

"Vegetarian by Taste." *Providence Journal,* 23 October 2002.

Vileisis, Ann. *Discovering the Unknown Landscape: A History of America's Wetlands.* Washington, D. C.: Island Press, 1997.

Visser, Margaret. *The Way We Are: Astonishing Anthropology of Everyday Life.* New York: Kodansha International, 1997.

Von Bonsdorff, Pauline. "Building and the Naturally Unplanned." In *The Aesthetics of Everyday Life,* eds. Andrew Light and Jonathan M. Smith, 73–91. New York: Columbia University Press, 2005.

Walker, Stuart. "The Environment, Product Aesthetics and Surfaces." *Design Issues* 11.3 (1995): 15–27.

Walton, Kendall L. "Categories of Art." In *Philosophy Looks at the Arts: Contemporary Readings in Aesthetics,* ed. Joseph Margolis, 88–114. Philadelphia: Temple University Press, 1978.

Weber, Ken. "Monarchical Magic." *Providence Journal,* 2 September 2006.

Welsch, Wolfgang. "Sport Viewed Aesthetically, and Even as Art?" In *The Aesthetics of Everyday Life,* eds. Andrew Light and Jonathan M. Smith, 135–55. New York: Columbia University Press, 2005.

"When Solar Clashes with Aesthetics." *San Jose Mercury News,* 5 August 2003 <http://www.evworld.com>.

Whiteley, Nigel. *Design for Society.* London: Reaktion Books, 1993.

—— "Utility, Design Principles and the Ethical Tradition." In *Utility Reassessed: The Role of Ethics in the Practice of Design,* ed. Judy Attfield, 190–202. Manchester: Manchester University Press, 1999.

Wilde, Oscar. *The Decay of Lying.* In *Critical Theory since Plato.* Ed. Hazard Adams. New York: Harcourt Brace Jovanovich, Inc., 1971.

Wilkinson, Nancy Lee. "No Holier Temple: Responses to Hodel's Hetch Hetchy Proposal." *Landscape* 31.1 (1991): 1–9.

Willis, N. P. *American Scenery; or, Land, Lake and River Illustrations of Transatlantic Nature*. London: George Virtue, 1840.

Wilson, Edoward O. "The Little Things That Run the World." In *Environmental Ethics: Divergence and Convergence*, eds. Susan J. Armstrong and Richard G. Botzler, 32–4. New York: McGraw Hill, 1998.

Winner, Langdon. *The Whale and the Reactor: A Search for Limits in an Age of High Technology*. Chicago: The University of Chicago Press, 1989.

"The Winner by a Hair." *Providence Journal*, 15 July 2004.

Witherspoon, Gary. "Navajo Aesthetics: Beautifying the World through Art." In *Aesthetics in Perspective*, ed. Kathleen M. Higgins, 736–42. Fort Worth: Harcourt Brace College Publishers, 1996.

Wood, Denis. "Unnatural Illusions: Some Words about Visual Resource Management." *Landscape Journal* 7.2 (1988): 192–205.

Woodward, Christopher. *In Ruins*. New York: Pantheon Books, 2001.

Yanagi, Sōetsu. *The Unknown Craftsman: A Japanese Insight into Beauty*. Adapted by Bernard Leach. Tokyo: Kodansha International, 1972.

Yanagita, Kunio. *Mame no Ha to Taiyō*. Tokyo: Sōgensha, 1942.

Yoshida, Kenkō. *Essays in Idleness: The Tsurezuregusa of Kenkō*. Translated by Donald Keene. New York: Columbia University Press, 1967.

Yourcenar, Marguerite. *That Mighty Sculptor, Time*. Translated by Walter Kaiser. New York: The Noonday Press, 1992.

Ziff, Paul. "Anything Viewed." In *Oxford Readers: Aesthetics*, eds. Susan L. Feagin and Patrick Maynard, 23–30. Oxford: Oxford University Press, 1997.

Zōen. *Illustrations for Designing Mountains, Water, and Hillside Field Landscape*. Translated by D. A. Slawson. In *Secret Teachings in the Art of Japanese Gardens: Design Principles, Aesthetic Values*. Tokyo: Kodansha International, 1991.

Index